G000089141

Raising Citizens in the "Century of the Child"

Studies in German History
Published in Association with the German Historical Institute, Washington, D.C.

General Editors:
Hartmut Berghoff, Director of the German Historical Institute, Washington, D.C.
Uwe Spiekermann, Deputy Director of the German Historical Institute, Washington, D.C.

RAISING CITIZENS IN THE "CENTURY OF THE CHILD"

The United States and German Central Europe
in Comparative Perspective

Edited by

Dirk Schumann

berghahn
NEW YORK · OXFORD
www.berghahnbooks.com

Published in 2010 by
Berghahn Books

www.berghahnbooks.com

© 2010, 2014 Dirk Schumann
First paperback edition published in 2014

All rights reserved.
Except for the quotation of short passages
for the purposes of criticism and review, no part of this book
may be reproduced in any form or by any means, electronic or
mechanical, including photocopying, recording, or any information
storage and retrieval system now known or to be invented,
without written permission of the publisher.

Library of Congress Cataloging-in-Publication Data

Raising citizens in the "century of the child" : the United States and German Central
 Europe in comparative perspective / edited by Dirk Schumann.
  p. cm. — (Studies in German history ; v. 12)
 Includes bibliographical references and index.
 ISBN 978-1-84545-696-2 (hardback) -- ISBN 978-1-84545-999-4 (institutional
ebook) -- ISBN 978-1-78238-109-9 (paperback) -- ISBN 978-1-78238-110-5 (retail
ebook)
 1. Children—United States—Social conditions—20th century. 2. Children—
Germany—Social conditions—20th century. 3. Children—Government policy—
United States—History—20th century. 4. Children—Government policy—
Germany—History—20th century. 5. Citizenship—United States. 6. Citizenship—
Germany I. Schumann, Dirk.
 HQ792.U5R343 2010
 306.8740943—dc22

                                                                  2010013220

British Library Cataloguing in Publication Data

A catalogue record for this book is available from the British Library.

Printed on acid-free paper

ISBN: 978-1-78238-109-9 paperback
ISBN: 978-1-78238-110-5 retail ebook

Contents

LIST OF ILLUSTRATIONS

*Every effort has been made to trace the copyright holder and to obtain permission for use of these images.

Introduction

CHILD-REARING AND CITIZENSHIP IN THE TWENTIETH CENTURY

Dirk Schumann

When West German chancellor Willy Brandt proclaimed in his inaugural address in 1969 that "the school of the nation was the school," he confirmed for the Federal Republic what progressives in the US had already emphasized at the beginning of the twentieth century: school education was not just about imparting knowledge; it was also the chief instrument to instill in young people those very values that would enable them to be proper citizens of their nations in the future.[1] Preconditions for this to happen were better than ever before, as mandatory school attendance was widely enforced and young people spent an increasing number of years in this institution.

School, however, was not the only public agency dealing with children that increased its influence over the course of the century. As advanced industrialized states became welfare states, they supported—and controlled—education in and outside the family to an unprecedented degree. Starting around 1900 and picking up speed in the wake of the First World War, a host of reformed and novel institutions disseminated knowledge about child-rearing and hygiene, provided health services and material benefits, and took care of young people considered deviant. Experts from a growing range of disciplines staffed these institutions and also offered advice on child-rearing to an increasingly receptive readership. Thus, the private and the public spheres came to be intertwined in a novel way in the twentieth century. Extended schooling and new services expanded citizenship rights for the young (and their parents) and provided the basis for a more active participation in society. However, they also left out certain groups, served the purpose of control as well as that of agency, and incurred the unintended consequences of bureaucratization. Hence, their overall effect turned out to be limited and ambiguous.

Notes from this chapter begin on page 20.

In 1900, Swedish feminist reformer Ellen Key had hoped for a "century of the child" in which children would be brought up in a sheltered environment by devoted mothers and fathers. This did not become the norm, and states went far beyond the supporting role Key had envisaged.[2] It is the purpose of this volume to explore the complex relationship between attempts to improve child-rearing, child welfare, and education and their results in German Central Europe and the United States in the twentieth century. Raising children now meant raising (future) citizens in a much more systematic and comprehensive way than before. Three aspects are of key interest in the contributions to this volume: the guiding principles, norms, and values of citizenship over the course of the century; the expansion and limits of citizenship rights; and the political, social, and cultural practices employed to implement ideals and fight for rights.

The Concept of "Citizenship"

As it places persons and their agency center stage, the concept of "citizenship" offers a productive framework for linking the formation of the subject through child-rearing and education to the development of political systems and state institutions. "Citizenship," as it is now commonly understood, means not only possessing key rights (and obligations) in a given community but also being actively involved to obtain, use, and possibly expand them. "Citizenship" is therefore not a static category but refers to practices. In this vein, Bryan S. Turner has defined citizenship as "that set of practices (juridical, political, economic, and cultural) which define a person as a competent member of society, and which as a consequence shape the flow of resources to persons and social groups."[3] Hence, "citizenship" refers to various fields of action and a variety of strategies, such as collective action in politics as well as individual strategies of learning in educational institutions. It is this broad spectrum of practices that matters and defines citizenship as referring to much more than the relationship between voters and office-holders. The contributions of this volume substantiate this point. Political campaigns to keep religious instruction in the schools, social work to help lower-class and immigrant parents with child-rearing, and therapeutic counseling for children and their parents can be conceptualized as ways to provide resources[4] to enable children to become fully involved in their local and national communities as adults—to become citizens in the full sense of the term.

Citizenship must also be understood as a historical category denoting the transformation and long-term expansion of citizenship rights. In a seminal essay of 1950, sociologist Thomas H. Marshall described the evolution of modern citizenship rights in three steps, based upon the example of England. Civil rights, such as personal freedom and individual control of property, emerged in the eighteenth century; key political rights such as the gradually expanding right to vote characterized the nineteenth century. Social rights, including widespread access to public schooling and health care as well as social insurance against prevalent life risks to mitigate the class divisions of modern industrial society were the hall-mark of the twentieth century.[5]

While this basic pattern has been accepted, Marshall's model has come under criticism for a number of reasons. Two are relevant in the context of this volume. First, as an explanatory model of historical development, it neatly separates stages that actually remained intertwined and thus also overlooks, as Margaret Somers has pointed out, the variations between sociopolitically and regionally defined milieus that determined the agency of local actors and created huge differences in the emergence of full-fledged citizenship rights.[6] The American South certainly is an example of such a specific milieu, as Charles Israel's contribution to this volume points out. The persecution of German (and Austrian) Jews (or, more precisely, those Germans and Austrians whom the regime defined as Jews) under Nazi rule shows how the loss of civil and political citizenship rights entailed the loss of all social rights and ended in the elimination from society by forced emi-gration and, eventually, mass murder.

Secondly, the model does not take into account those groups that were excluded from the gradual expansion of citizenship until the twentieth century, primarily women and ethnic minorities. In addition to class, which is of central concern in Marshall's argument, gender and race/ethnicity therefore have to be integrated as categories into his model. As Linda Kerber has emphasized, women as well as African Americans, Native Americans, and other groups such as "noncitizen nationals" (e.g., Puerto Ricans) and voluntary migrants from Asia who were not eligible for citizenship for a long period experienced US citizen-ship differently from male white Americans born in the country and immigrants from Europe. The social legislation of the New Deal, for instance, was carefully crafted to exclude blacks and women and thus in effect defined large categories of workers as nonworkers not deserving the protection others were now receiving. Women as wives also remained subordinated to their husbands in many family matters far into the second half of the twentieth century. For large numbers of Americans, therefore, as Kerber stresses, "the dream of an unranked citizenship" throughout the twentieth century was still "in tension with the waking knowl-edge of a citizenship to which people came by different routes, bounded by gen-der, race, and class identities."[7] A very similar argument can be made for women and immigrants in Germany.[8]

Strategies based on the concept of "maternalism," as Seth Koven and Sonya Michel have convincingly argued, helped women in the United States and in the major European countries, including Germany, to acquire citizenship rights by promoting the establishment of a welfare state. Emphasizing women's peculiar abilities as mothers, and by extension as caregivers and nurturers, was not a conservative rear-guard action that blocked emancipation but a way to provide women with political leverage at a time when states began to see the young as an important resource in need of tending through novel welfare institutions and applied life sciences. As Koven and Michel point out, the "maternalist" discourse was particularly powerful because it cut across the lines of political camps. Hence, from the 1880s to the 1920s all major nation-states, including the US and Germany, saw efforts to build up institutions of social work and health care that enlisted large numbers of women.

Meanwhile, these successes came at the price of a growing bureaucratization of welfare work and its subordination to paternalist models of society. The US Children's Bureau, the world's first state agency headed by women, was a case in point, as it became ghettoized in the federal administration and was not given access to funds for redistributive spending.[9] As Katharine Bullard's contribution to this volume shows, other limitations resulting from ethnic stereotyping hampered the work of the bureau as well. Still, the existence of the bureau and women's strong presence in other welfare institutions is evidence that women in the US and elsewhere succeeded in claiming citizenship in matters of child-rearing and child welfare prior to obtaining the right to vote in the wake of the First World War. Another case in point is the considerable influence that women as teachers wielded in the public school system, starting in the early twentieth century.[10] Women's role in raising future citizens was no longer confined to the home alone.

Public education also provides evidence of the ambiguities of the expansion of citizenship rights. While the emergence of social citizenship removed basic inequalities between social classes, it did not put an end to class differences themselves. But, as Marshall argued, it created expectations that this should be the long-term outcome. Welfare policies, however, always operated under financial constraints (and those that resulted from ethnic and racial stereotypes, as already indicated). Moreover, although a comprehensive education of high quality for all was desirable, education continued to be linked to the labor market, resulting in the categorization of students according to measured abilities and their subsequent separation into vocational and university-bound tracks in the school system. Old inequalities were thus to some extent replicated under a new guise. The conflicts created by the novel expectations could therefore only be resolved by agreement on the legitimacy of existing inequalities, not by their abolition.[11] Dirk Schumann's and Tara Zahra's essays in this volume investigate cases of parental involvement that were driven by such expectations and by conflicting ethnic and racial definitions of citizenship. Public education thus harbored an explosive potential for conflict that connected larger political debates directly with the family sphere.

Child-Rearing, Education, and Child Welfare Reforms at the Beginning of the Twentieth Century

At the beginning of the twentieth century, reform movements reshaped policies and practices of child-rearing, education, and child welfare on both sides of the Atlantic. As urbanization and industrialization became the dominant features of societies in the US and the major European nations, middle-class reformers of various political stripes worried that the young in particular might succumb to the dangers of the big cities. In America, the "new" immigration from Southern and Eastern Europe exacerbated these worries. In addition, global competition between the major powers increased the pressure to use a nation's resources most efficiently. As the concept of "adolescence," developed by the American psychologist Stanley Hall, suggested a further prolongation of youth as a developmental phase requiring treatment different from that of adults, reformers and governments launched a wide range of efforts by state agencies and private actors to support, guide, and control the upbringing of children and youth. These measures were part of a "search for order" (Robert Wiebe) through comprehensive social policy and municipal reform. They were devised by intellectuals and experts with a keen interest in what was happening on the other side of the Atlantic.[12] As Sonya Michel points out in her essay, state involvement in this field had already become a fixture throughout the nineteenth century. The range of new activities, however, was unprecedented, and so was the growth of new groups of academically trained experts and professional caregivers that now set in.

In the US, the cornerstone of the new initiatives was the invention of the juvenile court. First introduced in Illinois in 1899 and then spreading rapidly to other states, this new institution was intended to provide young delinquents with various forms of guidance instead of harsh punishments to reintegrate them into society. "Hearings" were held instead of trials; "respondents," not defendants, stood before the judge, who issued "findings" instead of verdicts. Probation officers were then to oversee the delinquents' return to a life in keeping with the law. Carefully examining the family situation of the young boy or girl was a key part of this task. More difficult cases were sent to a reformatory. While these features of the new system clearly showed a recognition of youth as a distinct developmental phase that deserved a benign and understanding treatment in contrast to adults, other features were more problematic. Young offenders were brought before the juvenile courts not only for ordinary criminal acts but also for status offenses that no adult could commit, such as underage drinking and curfew violations. More importantly, they did not have the right to be represented by a lawyer and could be confined to a reformatory for an indefinite period. Girls were more often placed there than boys, as bringing their sexual behavior in line with middle-class mores seemed of paramount importance to reformers.[13] In Germany, too, juvenile courts that operated under the same basic conditions were introduced in 1908, in the wake of a Prussian law that had considerably broadened the function of correctional education in foster care and reformatories. Corporal punishment became a common instrument of control in the reformatory and came to symbolize its problems, after a scandal broke about the brutal treatment of inmates of such an institution in the town of Mieltschin in 1911. Staff shortages and lack of qualified personnel prevented the full implementation of the reformers' plans in both countries.[14]

It is therefore no surprise that the reform movement of the turn of the century has drawn criticism as an essentially conservative attempt to extend middle-class control over the lower classes. As Anthony Platt has argued, a wide range of youthful activities now came under the surveillance of the government and private welfare agencies. Deviance was defined as a problem of "personal maladjustment" that subjected the boys and girls in question to a regime of therapeutic and disciplinary measures without a chance of negotiation or withdrawal. This, according to Platt, in fact "consolidated the inferior social status and dependency of lower-class youth" without solving the problem of delinquency.[15] To counter this focus on control and repression Steven Mintz has called for giving greater consideration to the variety of positions among the "child-savers." As he points out, children and their parents not only became subjects of control as new government policies and agencies emerged around 1900, but moreover learned how to use them for their own purposes. Mintz thus interprets the reformers' attempts to universalize the middle-class ideal of a protected childhood devoted to play and education as a break with the past and the creation of new opportunities, rather than a mere transformation of control mechanisms.[16] In other words, they can be seen as providing new social citizenship rights for the young, especially those from the lower classes.

Germany provides a good case in point. As medical concepts came to dominate explanations of deviance around 1910 and the focus of reform shifted to improving the health of young people, particularly those from working-class families, infant welfare stations became established in the big cities. Social Democrats, however, whom the ruling elites excluded from national-level government participation as a threat to the empire, wholeheartedly supported this measure, as it offered meaningful services and knowledge to working-class families. Liberal reformers emphasized that steps such as the introduction of new health services and the improvement of vocational education (now coupled with lessons on citizenship) were intended to better integrate workers in the nation by enabling them to be active participants. Two camps of reformers, one basically liberal "social-managerial" and the other conservative "patriarchalist," as Edward Dickinson has called them, were to be found in the US as in Germany, despite the different political systems in the two countries. Both camps wanted to restore order and elite domination in an increasingly complex society, but they differed in their strategies to achieve this aim.[17] The liberal strategy was certainly ambiguous, as it tied in seamlessly with imperialist policy and, by supporting state intervention and relying on scientific expertise, would in Germany later become compatible with National Socialist policy.[18] But on the eve of the First World War (as in the 1920s), it offered the working classes opportunities for self-improvement and engagement that increased their social and political citizenship rights.

The tensions between the conservative and the liberal reform strategy were apparent not only in the field of juvenile justice (where liberals such as F. W. Foerster in Germany had some mitigating influence on disciplinary methods in the reformatories around 1910),[19] and the ambiguity of liberal reform was tangible not only in the multifaceted activities in the field of child welfare, including the US Children's Bureau, as Katharine Bullard describes in this volume. Similar contradictions were also apparent in schooling, the third major field of reform in the US and in Germany. In the US, school attendance was mandatory in all states by 1918 and the number of pupils grew enormously, particularly in high school but also in kindergarten. Progressive reformers regarded school as the key institution for "Americanizing" the new immigrants from Europe. Americanization meant more than acquiring literacy and numeracy; it aimed at full assimilation, including the adoption of middle-class standards of hygiene and family life. While for many immigrant children (and their parents) school education was an empowering experience they actively sought, for others, such as Southern Italians, it created severe tensions between children and their parents and threatened the stability of the family, whose preservation was one of the chief aims of the reformers.[20]

By the turn of the century in Germany compulsory schooling was well established, albeit somewhat less well-enforced in rural areas. Instruction, especially in Prussia, followed a clearly authoritarian line and was intended to instill obedience to the Prussian monarchical state. Religion and history therefore were key subjects in elementary school. While earlier scholarship stressed the authoritarian thrust of Prussian education policy, more recently countervailing tendencies have been emphasized: many elementary school teachers held liberal political views, and state influence was diluted by local governments, which had to provide funding, and by the churches, the Catholic Church in particular, which remained in charge of supervising elementary schools in the countryside.[21] Moreover, the same working-class people who as children had attended elementary school in Prussia as adults voted in increasing numbers for the Social Democrats, making it the largest party by 1912 and thus thwarting one key goal of Prussian authorities.[22] Schooling apparently helped them develop their own interpretation of their political citizenship rights. Furthermore, when Prussian authorities in their attempt to fully "Germanize" the Eastern provinces decreed a ban on Polish as a language of religious instruction in elementary schools, Polish parents and children protested in large numbers, supported by local clergy.[23] Here too, state policy produced agency rather than discipline. It was not only in the US that ethnic minorities had to come to terms with public education.

Reform pedagogy, certainly part of the liberal camp of the reform movement, had only limited impact on the form and content of school instruction prior to the First World War. In the US, John Dewey developed a concept of instruction centered on holistic, pragmatic experience and democratic cooperation. Though "administrative progressives" proved receptive to translations of Dewey's ideas into proposals for curriculum reform in line with the new structure, as David Tyack has pointed out, they preferred to modernize schools by centralizing control in the hands of well-qualified experts instead.[24] In Germany, methods of school instruction and, as Caroline Kay describes in her essay, of family education remained chiefly stern and discipline-oriented. In Munich and in Hamburg, however, handicraft instruction and working with art were introduced into the high school curriculum by pioneer educators, and a small number of newly founded boarding schools in the countryside experimented with creating self-governing communities of teachers and students. While not pursuing an agenda of overall political democratization, these were both moves away from a school instruction narrowly focused on training the mind.[25]

This concept of young people discovering their own abilities more fully was also the driving force of the German youth movement. It comprised middle-class youth who, dissatisfied with the materialism and stuffiness of their parents' world, wanted to rejuvenate Germany by rediscovering themselves through the experience of nature and by choosing their own leaders.[26] Politically highly ambiguous, this attempt at developing youth's own agency led many participants to volunteer as soldiers in 1914 and later on to join the ranks of the National Socialists. The youth movement first emerged in 1911, a time when conservatives established, along with the Boy Scouts, the League of Young Germany, an association meant to gather "national" youth and provide them with pre-military training to stem the tide of Social Democracy (which was also building up a youth organization at the time).[27] Like juvenile justice and schooling, the organization of youth was marked by the tension between a conservative concept to control and a liberal concept to help Germany's future citizens find their own voices.

From the First World War to the Second

While the First World War did not fundamentally alter concepts and practices of child-rearing and child welfare policies on either side of the Atlantic, it speeded up processes that were already under way. The German revolution of 1918 established political conditions for a general welfare reform that increased the role of the state and expanded social citizenship rights. In contrast, the reform movement in the US lost its momentum and turned from reordering society to remaking families, as psychologists took the lead in defining the "normal" child and strategies to correct deviance.

The war changed the conditions under which children grew up, more so in Germany than in the US as the latter entered the war only in 1917. As many fathers were called to army service, mothers often had to bear the double burden of child-rearing and work in factories or offices. While new allowances were granted by the German state to support families and young mothers, not least in order to boost the declining birth rate, they expanded women's (and children's) social citizenship rights in principle, but eventually failed to make up for the effects of wartime inflation and the deteriorating supply of food, clothing, and fuel. Concerns that youth would become increasingly wayward due to a lack of supervision and new opportunities to earn money by factory work mounted, leading to a host of repressive new regulations such as compulsory savings and curfews.[28] Against such conservative strategies to remain in control of youth, social-managerial reformers, as Edward Ross Dickinson has pointed out, emphasized the need to focus on the flexibility and independence of the young as future soldiers and called for enhancing the role of the state as public guardian of troublesome youth.[29] As Andrew Donson describes in his contribution to this volume, pedagogical reformers stressing the development of independent personalities had greater opportunities to experiment with new curriculum ideas. Discussions about a complete overhaul of youth policy, aimed at centralizing it and giving state governments a stronger role, remained inconclusive until the fall of 1918 due to the resistance of religious charities and municipal governments fearful of losing influence.[30]

The revolution of November 1918 established a new framework for child welfare policies in Germany. It increased social citizenship rights and created more equality in public education, but it did not bring about the radical changes that some hoped for and others feared. Intense political conflicts hampered reform efforts in subsequent years. In the wake of the revolution, coalition governments on the national level and in Prussia, which were headed by the Social Democrats but included the Catholic Center Party as well as the left-liberals, enacted laws that increased the influence of state institutions while preserving the role of religion and religious welfare organizations. In the field of schooling, this meant forcing every child to attend a public elementary school by abolishing their private competitors. However, public elementary schools, especially in rural areas, retained their confessional character, allowing parents to send their children to a school of their faith.

In the field of welfare, the National Child Welfare Act of 1922 brought the reform process of the prewar years to a conclusion in a similar compromise, as it stipulated a general public responsibility for the upbringing of every child but granted religious and other private charities a strong minority voice in the youth bureaus that were to organize and supervise welfare activities in every city and on the state level. While the activities of the municipal bureaus were mainly preventive (i.e., aimed at educating women in hygiene and child-rearing or setting up school lunch programs) and recreational, religious charities regarded them as unwanted competition and increased their own activities. Bourgeois parties and the churches joined forces to legislate against "trash and smut," i.e., literature and movies that might endanger the morality of young people, not least proper sexual mores.[31] Elementary school education saw fierce battles between proponents of compulsory religious instruction and advocates of a purely secular school.

As Charles Israel shows in his essay, in American schools during the same period the place of religion also was a hotly contested issue. German conflicts mirrored these cleavage lines in party politics: conservatives and Catholics on the one side faced socialists and left-liberals on the other in both cases.[32] Academic pedagogues were unable to serve as a mitigating force in these acrimonious debates, as they were split themselves, most of them adopting the position of a philosophical pedagogy that continued the legacy of reform pedagogy but kept aloof from politics.[33] While child welfare became increasingly medicalized as the number of infant health stations and health offices in the cities grew and many schools hired their own doctors, psychoanalysis was still marginalized. Hardly affected by the ideas of pedagogical reformers, these physicians were receptive to eugenic ideas and, as a consequence, to their radicalization under the Nazi regime.[34]

In the United States, the First World War had much less of an impact than in Germany. As Ellen Berg argues in her essay, kindergartens maintained an internationalist approach during the war while implementing a program of Americanization in their institution.[35] Indirectly, the war contributed to a victory for the maternalist progressives, as the passage of the Sheppard-Towner Act of 1921 would hardly have been conceivable had women not gained the right to vote in the wake of the war. Establishing government responsibility for child welfare, the law provided federal matching grants for states to educate mothers in nutrition and hygiene and establish child health institutions. However, in administering the law the US Children's Bureau kept the focus on white children's social citizenship, as Katharine Bullard points out in her essay.[36]

The key development of the 1920s in the US was the "psychologization" of childhood. As Peter Stearns has noted, children were no longer seen as sturdy young creatures who mainly had to be equipped with a good moral education to become upright citizens but as vulnerable beings who needed protection and science-based care to grow up with no lasting "maladjustments."[37] New child guidance clinics provided expert advice and treatment by psychiatrists, psychologists, and social workers. While these (largely male) experts claimed supreme authority in child-rearing matters, thereby denying it to mothers in particular, they also, as Kathleen Jones has shown, competed with one another and faced parents who did not always give in to their demands.[38] These limits to scientific authority notwithstanding, mothers also became the prime target of advice literature on child-rearing. As the preschool phase of child development emerged as particularly crucial, the burden of proper rearing methods weighed heavily on mothers, not least in the behaviorist model of John B. Watson, who prescribed a rigid regimen of positive and negative stimuli and warned against an overemotional tending of the child's needs. Expert advice, meant to support parents, thus ran the risk of paradoxically creating more, not less anxiety, especially among mothers.

While the Great Depression triggered, as Ann Hulbert has noted, a reevaluation of emotional bonds within the family and thus caused the stern behaviorist language to be toned down, mothers remained the target of attacks.[39] In her essay in this volume, Rebecca Jo Plant examines a prominent example of such criticism, Philip Wylie's *Generation of Vipers*, written as the war effort again seemed to necessitate warnings against the dangers of overindulgent mothering. As mothers were singled out in the 1920s and after, family relations changed, primarily in the middle classes. Family life became more intimate, and fathers were supposed to turn from authoritarian disciplinarians into "dads" who spent more time with their children. Children gained more independence with the onset of the consumer society and became more oriented toward their peers as high school attendance rose.[40]

In Germany, child-rearing practices seem to have remained more authoritarian in the 1920s, but more research is needed to substantiate this point.[41] After the onset of the Great Depression and the demise of parliamentary government, child welfare policy saw the continuing rise of eugenic thinking and a growing emphasis on discipline and the family. The Nazi regime initially appeared simply to continue these trends and was therefore welcomed not only by conservatives but also by a number of "social-managerial" reformers, since it adopted such elements of reform pedagogy as an emphasis on leadership by the young themselves in the field of recreational activities. Over the course of the 1930s, however, it became increasingly clear that Nazi youth policy amounted to a break with the past, as Christian charities were pushed aside and eventually banned from participation in the youth bureaus by 1939 and a radical anti-Semitism alongside the exclusion of the "defective" emerged as guidelines.[42] Jewish and leftist pedagogical, psychological, and medical experts were forced out of their positions; many ended up as emigrés in the US.[43]

Nazi school policy, while never entirely consistent, was equally guided by a radical anti-Semitism. Grounded in a basic anti-intellectualism, it also featured an aggressive nationalism and propagated clearly separated gender roles: male students were to prepare for their role as soldiers, female students for theirs as mothers. A mandatory state youth organization, the Hitler Youth, was to further boost the ideological zeal of the young.[44] Disciplining the young even under the auspices of a dictatorship, however, was not entirely successful. While staunch young Catholics and, to a lesser degree, Protestants rejected ideological claims of the regime, cliques of working-class and also bourgeois youth in big cities sought to keep their subcultures free from state interference.[45] Tara Zahra's essay describes the extent to which the claims the Nazi regime made on children and youth were realized in an ethnically mixed area where they faced competition from another nationalism.

During the Second World War, Nazi child welfare and youth policy became further radicalized. Private high schools run by Christian churches had to close, and elementary schools lost their confessional character, despite massive Catholic protest. Eugenic measures turned into outright murder, as children (as well as adults) judged to be severely mentally "defective" were killed in the "euthanasia" program. Jewish children were murdered in the Holocaust. Guided by the principle to instill the willingness to work hard in young people, measures to combat "waywardness" became increasingly harsh and brutal. Not only did the number of children taken from their families to be placed in foster care and reformatories rise during the war; starting in 1940, but the regime established two "youth protection camps" and a system of "work education camps" where German and foreign youth were subjected to a regime akin to that of concentration camps.[46]

In contrast, the New Deal era in the US was marked by a different type of rising state involvement in matters of child-rearing and education. By providing funds for a number of programs, for instance nursery schools for children of unemployed parents, the federal government took responsibility for child welfare on an unprecedented scale. During the war, its involvement increased further, most notably by helping establish the Extended School Services, a before- and after-school program, as well as daylong (in some cases 24-hour) child care centers for younger children, both of which eased the burdens of working mothers. Institutions and programs such as these allayed fears about the deprivations that apparently threatened "latchkey kids" and seemed to pave the way for a comprehensive system of public day care for children. But as prominent child-rearing experts continued to advocate that mothers stay at home with their children in their first years and resistance against federal funding remained strong, the US government discontinued its engagement after the war.[47] The war also triggered concerns about a rise in juvenile delinquency, since many young people preferred employment in the war industries to remaining in high school. In contrast to Nazi Germany, however, such anxieties did not lead to repressive policies but eventually allowed the emergence of the "teenager" as a new type of adolescent consumer.[48] As the war drew to a close, the citizenship ideals that guided German and US education and youth policies could hardly have been more different.

Postwar Successes and Problems

The United States and Germany entered the postwar era under very different conditions, but from the 1960s on, both countries grappled with similar problems and concepts of raising and educating the young. In the US, military victory and the emergence of post-Depression affluence suggested a more relaxed attitude toward child-rearing, epitomized in the first edition of Dr. Benjamin Spock's hugely popular *Common Sense Book of Baby and Child Care*, published in 1946. However, as the basic political conservatism of the 1950s called for citizens who were first and foremost flexible and well-adjusted consumers in an environment marked by "other-directedness" toward one's social reference group, as David Riesman put it, mothers again came under pressure as those responsible for making the nuclear family the core group of all others.[49]

In a similar vein, schools were to follow a "life-adjustment" approach that downplayed traditional and abstract subjects in favor of those relevant for solving practical problems, and replace a teacher-centered style of instruction with one that allowed greater student involvement. Initially meant to implement John Dewey's concept of "democracy in action," the life-adjustment approach became increasingly trivialized and met with growing criticism.[50] As school attendance, particularly in high schools, skyrocketed in the wake of the postwar "baby boom," youth, as Steven Mintz has argued, became more clearly separated from young children as well as from adults. Possessing greater purchasing power and spending more time with their peers than ever before, teenagers, including many from the working classes, developed styles of dress and interests in music that raised concerns when they did not align with middle-class norms. The alleged rise of juvenile delinquency thus became the object of a "moral panic" in the mid-1950s. While rock 'n' roll, one of its triggers, subsequently came to be domesticated, it nevertheless, as Mintz has pointed out, paved the way for a more overtly political youth protest in the following decade.[51]

The two Germanys that emerged from war and defeat redefined the relationship between child-rearing and state policy in very different ways. East Germany, under Soviet domination, attempted to raise socialist citizens by introducing a comprehensive school for all children and concomitant activities organized by state agencies and a new communist youth organization. Family education was to follow goals set by the regime. Cultural influences from the West, in particular rock and then beat music, continued to trigger conflicts and kept many young people at a distance from the regime.[52]

In West Germany, Allied efforts to thoroughly restructure the highly selective school system foundered amidst strong resistance from teachers, administrators, and politicians. While a restoration of the confessional elementary school and the patriarchal family seemed to provide the best antidotes to any form of "totalitarianism" and help contain an emerging consumerist modernity, the 1950s saw more than a mere return to a pre-1933 conservatism. Programs in the field of child welfare and youth policy underwent a huge expansion, including a host of activities in civic education. Concerns about wayward youth turned into a "moral panic" in the mid 1950s in both parts of Germany, preceded and fueled by the panic in the US, leading to a "law for the protection of youth" (*Jugendschutzgesetz*) in West Germany that resembled Weimar attempts to control young people's morality.[53] By the end of the decade, however, youthful unrest became accepted as reflecting psychological needs of the young in the West.[54] Fathers came to be defined here, as Till van Rahden shows in his essay in this volume, as more understanding and playful "dads," while parents began learning to use their rights in the school system, as Dirk Schumann describes in his contribution. Around 1960 there were increasing signs that a democratic spirit had begun to take hold in West Germany.

Driven by the civil rights movement in the US and a growing discontent with the conservative government and the silence about the Nazi past in West Germany, the young on both sides of the Atlantic engaged in open protest and fought successfully for more rights in the 1960s and early 1970s. A radical counterculture denounced sexual repression and called the traditional family structure into question. Child-rearing in experimental family communities and kindergartens (*Kinderläden*) rejected authoritarian methods and encouraged children to develop their own rules.[55] Desegregation of the American school system at first did not make much headway in the wake of the Brown decision of 1954, but from the late 1960s on, this changed with the introduction of court-ordered busing and other proactive policies. Racially mixed schools then helped shift the approach to discipline problems away from punishment and toward understanding underlying social and psychological factors, thus also strengthening the role of experts in and outside the schools.[56]

While US federal legislation gave a boost to programs aimed at ending discrimination against female and disabled students in the schools, Supreme Court decisions granted students the rights of due process and free speech. In a similar development, decisions by higher West German courts ended the "special concept of authority" ("*besonderes Gewaltverhältnis*") in the school system, which had been the basis for restrictions on key basic rights such as free speech.[57] While teachers, particularly in the US, and parents, particularly in Germany, also gained more rights in the school system, as Dirk Schumann shows in his essay, this overall expansion of social and political citizenship came at a price on both sides of the Atlantic. Schools turned into bureaucratic institutions (while also becoming ever larger) in which administrators, teachers, students, and parents constantly fought a multitude of conflicts, often with resort to the courts. Growing public dissatisfaction about the performance of the school system indicated that the institution, regarded more than ever before as central to preparing the young for their role as future citizens, seemed to be failing in this task.[58]

Physicians, psychologists, and experts from other disciplines, whose numbers continued to grow in institutions of child welfare and education, were nevertheless not in a position to provide decisive leadership. As concepts of diagnosis and therapy shifted to treating behavioral problems as part of a system of social relations in the 1970s, experts from the "psy"-sciences themselves came to be seen as part of this system, losing their status as omniscient problem-solvers.[59] This granted more agency to parents and children with problems, but it made therapy more difficult and open-ended. While combating child abuse became an important policy field starting in the 1960s in the US and, conceptually at least, helped secure children's basic rights, vague definitions of the issue, competing interests of experts, parents, and lawyers, and staff shortages and problems of cooperation between the public agencies involved resulted in serious cases getting lost in a bureaucratic maze and amidst the clamor of the "child abuse industry."[60] In her contribution to this volume, Lynne Curry gives an account of the manifold problems inherent in the drive to fight against child abuse since the 1950s. Social and political citizenship rights had expanded considerably since the postwar era, but the institutions and mechanisms implemented to guarantee them spawned unintended consequences that called into question the very successes that seemed to have been achieved.

The Contributions to This Volume

In her essay "Children and the National Interest," Sonya Michel sets the stage by discussing how children's welfare and the national interest became intertwined in the nineteenth century in the US and Western, Central, and Eastern Europe. As nation-states identified the health of their populations as a key resource of state power, they devised policies to improve children's welfare as well as public schooling—policies that became ever more invasive in the "private" sphere of the family. A growing number of internationally connected experts helped formulate and implement these policies. Whereas the American Revolution had been cast as a revolt against a tyrannical father, post-revolutionary public discourse reemphasized obedience. It also called upon women to become "republican mothers" who would inculcate the values of the new state in its future citizens, and advocated state intervention to have the children of the poor raised properly. This discourse, however, largely excluded African Americans and other racial minorities. In France, children came to be seen as a particularly precious national resource, given the country's low birthrate and the manpower it required for its colonial expansion. In the secular moral order that the Third Republic attempted to create, the state would govern through the family. In Britain, too, imperialism as well as international economic competition drove the state to engage in a variety of child welfare measures. While children of the poor were at first treated as if they belonged to a different "race" and were redeemable only if separated from their parents, welfare policies after 1900 put more emphasis on supporting (and reshaping) families.

Child welfare efforts in Germany initially followed a pronounced paternalist model bolstered by religion but with little state interference. Following the foundation of a German nation-state under Bismarck, instruments of state intervention increased considerably, while fears of the rising strength of the Social Democratic Party made national unity the guiding principle of these measures, imbuing them with a clear political mission. In Eastern Europe, where nation-states began to emerge only in the late nineteenth and early twentieth centuries, child welfare measures tended to be pursued by private actors, with limited scope. As was shown by attempts to Magyarize school instruction in Hungary and eugenic policies aimed at strengthening the peasant population in Romania, however, in states with considerable national minorities such measures could trigger severe conflicts. At the outset of the twentieth century, Michel concludes, state intervention in the family sphere had become well established on both sides of the Atlantic and, because of its imbrication with national interests, was set on a course of further expansion.

The first section of the volume, "New Beginnings," examines novel institutions and practices of child welfare and education spawned by the international reform movement in the early twentieth century and how they were reshaped by the First World War. Katherine Bullard describes the ambivalence of a new institution that was a product of progressive reform in her essay "Children's Future, Nation's Future: Race, Citizenship, and the US Children's Bureau." Founded in 1912 and particularly active in wartime, the bureau cast its programs, which provided advice and medical support, as necessary assistance for those representing the future of the nation. Citing several surveys conducted by the bureau, however, Bullard points out that this concept of "social citizenship" was based on an explicit distinction between whites and nonwhites. Representing the standard against which the health of all others was measured, white children were depicted in promotional materials in a clean and prosperous environment, whereas African American and other nonwhite children were portrayed in primitive settings. The bureau ran special programs in the US territories of Puerto Rico, Hawaii, Guam, and the Philippines, justifying them by referring to similar activities in parts of the British Empire—not parts with large indigenous populations, however, but those such as New Zealand that could more easily be portrayed as basically white.

Andrew Donson describes the convergence of reform pedagogy with German nationalism and militarism in his essay "From Reform Pedagogy to War Pedagogy: Education Reform before 1914 and the Mobilization for War in Germany." Prior to 1914, schooling in Germany was marked by an authoritarian style that featured rigid discipline and learning by drill, but as Donson points out, attempts by Wilhelm II and leading officials to inculcate it with an aggressive nationalism had met with resistance from teachers and the academy. The outbreak of war, however, triggered a wave of patriotism that silenced pacifist voices among the teachers and led to ad hoc revisions of curricula and classroom activities that introduced references to the war and materials such as newspapers, previously shunned as too "political." As teachers were encouraged to develop close relationships with their students and to experiment with curricula, key demands of reform pedagogy were fulfilled, albeit in a uniformly nationalistic and militaristic spirit. Drawing upon collections of the new "free" compositions, Donson argues that at least until the end of 1915 most students shared the violent militarism and nationalism taught in German schools at that time.

In her essay, "'Linked with the Welfare of All Peoples': The American Kindergarten, Americanization, and Internationalism in the First World War," Ellen L. Berg refutes the view that wartime kindergarten redefined Americanization as complete and potentially coercive assimilation. Prior to the war, the Americanization movement had discovered kindergarten as a powerful instrument, in particular because it allowed many immigrant mothers to be reached through their children. During the war the term "war work" became shorthand for the broader goals of kindergarten activities, denoting for the most part the teaching of useful habits such as conservation techniques and calls to save for the Red Cross. Traditional Fröbelians, who represented a teacher-centered style of pedagogy, regained some ground against progressive reformers, and the patriotism that kindergarten promoted sometimes turned into jingoism. On balance, however, kindergarten remained committed to a concept of internationalism and world citizenship, symbolized by the fact that the institution's German name "kindergarten" was retained.

The second section of the volume, "Redefining Parents' Roles," investigates how concepts of father- and motherhood changed from the early twentieth century to the era following the Second World War. In Wilhelmine Germany, as Carolyn Kay shows in her essay "How Should We Raise Our Son Benjamin? Advice Literature for Mothers in Early Twentieth-Century Germany," the rise of the sciences coincided with an increase in the number of advice books on child-rearing that acknowledged the pivotal role of the bourgeois family for the strength of the nation. Drawing in particular on the works of pediatrician Adalbert Czerny and pedagogue Adolf Matthias, Kay argues that these books, written by academic experts from various disciplines and directed primarily at mothers, agreed that discipline was the precondition for attaining the other middle-class values. Only a minority of advice-givers, including female authors such as feminist Adele Schreiber, emphasized the primacy of a nurturing environment over stern methods of punishment.

Rebecca Jo Plant examines a fundamental change in the definition of the mother's role in her essay "Debunking Mother Love: American Mothers and the Momism Critique in the Mid Twentieth Century." American experts warned that just as authoritarian fathers had given rise to totalitarianism in Nazi Germany, overly protective mothers would weaken democratic fortitude in the US. Citing the findings of psychoanalysis, they recommended close bonding between mother and child only in the very early years and urged emotional distance thereafter to allow the child to develop its individuality. As letters to popular author Philip Wylie demonstrated, many mothers seemed to agree with the experts' position. Plant argues that this redefinition marked a break with the tradition of "republican motherhood," as it devalued and pathologized mother love and discouraged women from constructing their entire identities around their maternal role.

A redefinition of the father's role is the topic of Till van Rahden's essay "Fatherhood, Rechristianization, and the Quest for Democracy in Postwar West Germany." As early as the late 1950s, he argues, West Germans developed a concept of "democratic fatherhood" as a contribution to creating a democratic culture. Gaining influence in the wake of postwar rechristianization, Catholic and Protestant lay organizations and family experts in the public debate welcomed the shift away from tradition and obedience to mutual trust and basic equality as foundations of authority and applied it to relations in the family. While not calling into question the norm of heterosexual relationships and the separation of gender roles, they advocated a gentle, playful fatherhood that marked a clear break with past concepts of militarized masculinity and would thus help overcome the legacy of the Nazi regime.

The third section of the volume, "Parental Rights and State Demands," discusses interactions and conflicts between parents and state agencies over issues and in fields that lacked a clear demarcation of their respective rights and competencies. Charles A. Israel, placing the infamous Scopes trial of 1925 in a new perspective in his essay "Who Owns Children? Parents, Children, and the State in the United States South," describes conflicts about religious and moral education in the American South. At the turn of the century, this education was seen primarily as the task of parents, not of public schools. As progressive reformers focused their efforts on public schools, which had been established in significant numbers only since the Civil War, conservatives in the South sought to give the Bible a substantial presence in the classroom. William Jennings Bryan, as Israel points out, fought against the teaching of evolution mainly because he regarded it as inspired by a Nietzschean materialism that allegedly had become the hallmark of German education, whose superiority the First World War had called into question. Combining the arguments of the will of the majority and of parental rights, Bryan and his followers cast the state as "creature and servant" of parents and found courts sympathetic to their views.

In her essay "'Children Betray Their Father and Mother': Collective Education, Nationalism, and Democracy in the Bohemian Lands, 1900–1948," Tara Zahra challenges the traditional view that the concept of collective education typically stood in fierce opposition to that of education in the family. Absent a nationalizing policy of the government in Vienna, German and Czech nationalists set up their own networks of educational and child welfare institutions prior to 1914 to make up for deficits of family education and win over children of bi-national origins. As tensions between the two groups grew after 1918, these institutional networks expanded and harnessed the expertise of more academic disciplines, including that of the new discipline of psychoanalysis. Following the Nazi takeover of Bohemia in 1938/39, all of its educational institutions were placed under state control, a measure that fundamentally changed views of collective education. Czech nationalists now called upon families, mothers in particular, to turn their homes into bulwarks of Czech nationalism, and Sudeten Germans, fearing that they might lose their cultural hegemony, likewise wanted their mothers to stay at home. After 1945, attempts to create distance from both Nazism and communism created the myth of an apolitical private sphere that totalitarianism had tried to invade and destroy.

Dirk Schumann argues in his essay "Asserting Their 'Natural Right': Parents and Schooling in Post-1945 Germany" that parental involvement in school affairs contributed to the liberalization of educational methods and to political democratization in West Germany. Once parents' rights were acknowledged as "natural rights" in the new constitution, an active minority of parents began challenging school authorities on all levels by participating in newly formed parents' councils and in face-to-face encounters with teachers and officials starting in the late 1940s and 1950s. Corporal punishment by teachers emerged as a particular source of conflict. Bolstered by debates about educational reform and the political mobilization of the 1960s and 1970s, parents' involvement in school matters became a well-established feature of the educational system. Though it largely failed to increase formal participation rights and grappled with the increasing bureaucratization of schools, parents' involvement contributed in a pragmatic fashion to improving conditions at individual schools.

Lynne Curry examines the tension between calls for better state protection for abused children and deep-rooted notions of the sanctity of the family in her essay "'Special Relationships': The State, Social Workers, and Abused Children in the United States, 1950–1990." Four-year-old Joshua DeShaney suffered severe brain damage and remained partially paralyzed after a number of beatings by his father and the women he lived with in 1983/84. This was not due to negligence on the part of the state agencies involved, however. The reason was instead, as Curry argues, that the social worker who was in charge of the case, and to whom the police deferred, followed a "therapeutic" rather than an "authoritative" model in her actions. This model prioritized keeping a family together and counseling its members over placing a child in state custody to protect it from abuse. Reflecting the guiding principle of the training of social workers in Wisconsin in the 1960s and 1970s, it also exemplified the general weakness of the concept of family preservation that was prevalent at the time in the US.

Taken together, the essays in this volume help conceptualize the "century of the child" as one of overall increasing state and expert influence. This increasing influence, however, was neither to be equated with linear progress nor with growing control but marked by a profound ambiguity. With the exception of the National Socialist and the Communist regimes in Germany, control-oriented and liberal managerial policies and practices coexisted on both sides of the Atlantic from the early twentieth century onwards. While schools as well as kindergartens provided access to education and greater participatory rights to a growing number of the young, they also had the chance to inculcate more and more of them with specific values. In wartime and under a dictatorship, this feature of public education became particularly critical. Teachers as well as parents and children, however, rather than being only passive recipients of state policies, were able to have some influence themselves on educational and welfare institutions. Parents in particular proved able to successfully pursue their own agendas, to some degree even under the adverse circumstances of a dictatorship.

Expert influence enhanced this overall ambiguity. Particularly as authors of advice literature and key personnel in public health institutions, experts sought to establish themselves as ultimate authorities in matters of child-rearing and education. However, they saw their magisterial position erode in the last third of the century, when increasingly bureaucratized welfare states spawned conflicts between their various agencies and experts came to see themselves as individual actors among others in a complex environment. Catholic experts differed from Protestants and laicists, and psychologists quarreled with physicians and pedagogues as well as social workers. While experts assessed and formulated concepts of child-rearing and thus helped determine mainstream ideals as well as the parental roles associated with it, they provided parents with welcome support but also created anxieties, especially among mothers.

Despite these important similarities between the US and German Central Europe, there were also significant differences. More authoritarian and statist by comparison at the beginning of the twentieth century, German educational and welfare policies underwent greater ruptures and the experience of a totalitarian regime before the middle of the century. In addition to delaying a broad public discussion of psychological and psychoanalytical approaches to child-rearing, this resulted in an uneven development of social and political citizenship rights. While the former increased steadily overall—with the crucial exception of Jews and other groups defined as outsiders by the Nazi regime—the latter lost their meaning following the Nazi takeover. When they were formally reestablished in the late 1940s, Germans had to get reacquainted with using them. This process and the statist structure of German school administration (as opposed to the localist one in America) delayed and limited German parents' exercise of participatory rights. Nevertheless, the contributions to this volume suggest that by the 1970s parents' citizenship as well as that of children had considerably expanded on both sides of the Atlantic, with the US and German Central Europe show-ing more similarities than dissimilarities, compared with the beginning of the twentieth century.

It is to be hoped that this volume will help stimulate further comparative and transnational research in the field. Closer attention should be paid to the negotia-tion processes in which standards of corporeal and mental "normality," devised by academic experts of various stripes, were translated into new institutions and practices in schooling and the welfare system in conflict and cooperation with politicians, parents, teachers, social workers, and the young themselves. The second half of the twentieth century in particular seems much less well-explored in this respect than its first half. One specifically interesting aspect in this con-text is how the media, not least through "moral panics" they helped trigger and exploit, contributed to these processes within and beyond national boundaries. It also seems well worth exploring how transnational experiences of experts and, to a growing degree, also of young people and their parents through travel and exchange programs called national concepts of education and welfare into ques-tion and helped the young assert their citizenship rights. Research on questions such as these will help us overcome the national bias still dominating much of the scholarship and throw into sharp relief the profound ambiguities of the "century of the child."

Notes

1. *Verhandlungen des Deutschen Bundestages, 6. Wahlperiode, Stenographische Berichte,* vol. 71 (Bonn, 1969), 27.
2. Ellen Key, *The Century of the Child* (New York, 1909; Swedish edition 1900).
3. Bryan S. Turner, "Contemporary Problems in the Theory of Citizenship," in *Citizenship and Social Theory,* ed. Bryan S. Turner (London, 1993), 1–18, here 2.
4. Access to a variety of resources that are located outside of the political sphere as a precondi-tion for citizenship is emphasized by Ursula Vogel, "Is Citizenship Gender-Specific?" in *The Frontiers of Citizenship,* ed. Ursula Vogel and Michael Moran (London, 1991), 58–85.
5. Thomas H. Marshall, "Citizenship and Social Class," in *Class, Citizenship, and Social Develop-ment,* ed. Thomas H. Marshall (New York, 1964), 65–122.
6. Margaret R. Somers, "Citizenship and the Place of the Public Sphere: Law, Community, and Political Culture in the Transition to Democracy," *American Sociological Review* 58 (1993): 587–620.
7. Linda K. Kerber, "The Meanings of Citizenship," *Journal of American History* 84, no. 3 (1997): 833–854, here 846.
8. Kathleen Canning, "The Concepts of Class and Citizenship in German History," in *Gen-der History in Practice: Historical Perspectives on Bodies, Class, and Citizenship,* ed. Kathleen Canning (Ithaca, 2006), 193–211; Karin Hunn, *"Nächstes Jahr kehren wir zurück …:" Die Geschichte der türkischen "Gastarbeiter" in der Bundesrepublik* (Göttingen, 2005).
9. Seth Koven and Sonya Michel, "Introduction: 'Mother Worlds,'" in *Mothers of a New World: Maternalist Politics and the Origins of Welfare States,* ed. Seth Koven and Sonya Michel (New

York, 1993), 1–42. For a similar argument about the bureaucratization of women's initially emancipatory welfare work in Germany see Canning, "Concepts," 205–206. On the history of the Children's Bureau see Kriste Lindenmeyer, *"A Right to Childhood": The US Children's Bureau and Child Welfare, 1912–1946* (Urbana, 1997).

10. David B. Tyack, *The One Best System: A History of American Urban Education* (Cambridge, MA, 1974), 61; June Edwards, *Women in American Education, 1820–1955* (Westport, 2002); Alan R. Sadovnik and Susan F. Semel, eds., *Founding Mothers and Others: Women Educational Leaders during the Progressive Era* (New York, 2002); Margret Kraul, "Höhere Mädchenschulen," in *Handbuch der deutschen Bildungsgeschichte, vol. IV: 1870–1918: Von der Reichsgründung bis zum Ende des Ersten Weltkriegs,* ed. Christa Berg (Munich, 1991), 279–303, here 281–283; Hartmut Titze, "Lehrerbildung und Professionalisierung," in Berg, *Handbuch,* 345–370, here 363–364.

11. Marshall, "Citizenship," 107–110.

12. Robert H. Wiebe, *The Search for Order, 1877–1920* (New York, 1967); Daniel Rodgers, *Atlantic Crossings: Social Politics in a Progressive Age* (Cambridge, MA, 1998); Axel R. Schaefer, *American Progressives and German Social Reform, 1875–1920: Social Ethics, Moral Control, and the Regulatory State in a Transatlantic Context* (Stuttgart, 2000).

13. Steven Mintz, *Huck's Raft: A History of American Childhood* (Cambridge, MA, 2004), 176–178; Mary E. Odem, *Delinquent Daughters: Protecting and Policing Adolescent Female Sexuality in the United States, 1885–1920* (Chapel Hill, 1995).

14. Edward Ross Dickinson, *The Politics of German Child Welfare from the Empire to the Federal Republic* (Cambridge, MA, 1996), 100–105; Judith Sealander, *The Failed Century of the Child: Governing America's Young in the Twentieth Century* (Cambridge, 2003), 25–31.

15. Anthony Platt, *The Child Savers: The Invention of Delinquency* (Chicago, 1969), here 177.

16. Mintz, *Huck's Raft,* 155–156, 173–184.

17. Dickinson, *Politics,* 6–9.

18. Detlev J. K. Peukert, "Sozialpädagogik," in *Handbuch der deutschen Bildungsgeschichte, vol. V: 1918–1945: Die Weimarer Republik und die nationalsozialistische Diktatur,* ed. Dieter Langewiesche and Heinz-Elmar Tenorth (Munich, 1989), 307–335.

19. Dickinson, *Politics,* 106–110.

20. Tyack, *System,* in particular 182–198, 229–255.

21. Frank-Michael Kuhlemann, "Niedere Schulen," in Berg, *Handbuch,* 179–227; Marjorie Lamberti, *State, Society, and the Elementary School in Imperial Germany* (New York, 1989).

22. Gerhard A. Ritter and Klaus Tenfelde, *Arbeiter im Deutschen Kaiserreich, 1871–1914* (Bonn, 1992), 720–729.

23. Lamberti, *State,* 139–147.

24. Tyack, *System,* 196–197.

25. Ulrich Herrmann, "Pädagogisches Denken und die Anfänge der Reformpädagogik," in Berg, *Handbuch,* 147–178, here 165–166; cf. Wolfgang Scheibe, *Die Reformpädagogische Bewegung 1900–1933: Eine einführende Darstellung* (8th ed. Weinheim, 1982); on the highly selective and largely critical German reception of Dewey up until the 1960s, see Stefan Bittner, *Learning By Dewey? John Dewey und die deutsche Pädagogik 1900–2000* (Bad Heilbrunn, 2001), in particular 73–74; Carsten Müller, *Sozialpädagogik als Erziehung zur Demokratie: Ein problemgeschichtlicher Theorieentwurf* (Bad Heilbrunn, 2005), 207–221.

26. Herrmann, "Pädagogisches Denken," 163–170.

27. Christa Berg, "Familie, Kindheit, Jugend," in Berg, *Handbuch,* 91–146, here 129.

28. Ute Daniel, *The War From Within: German Women in the First World War* (Oxford, 1997).

29. Dickinson, *Politics,* 113–118, 124–136.

30. Ibid., 136–138.

31. Detlef J. K. Peukert, *Grenzen der Sozialdisziplinierung: Aufstieg und Krise der deutschen Jugendfürsorge von 1878 bis 1932* (Cologne, 1986), 175–191.

32. Dickinson, *Politics,* 141–203; cf. Marjorie Lamberti, *The Politics of Education: Teachers and School Reform in Weimar Germany* (New York, 2002).

33. Heinz-Elmar Tenorth, "Pädagogisches Denken," in Langewiesche and Tenorth, *Handbuch*, 111–154, here 118–125.
34. Dickinson, *Politics*, 142–144, 183–184.
35. One aspect of this was the "immigrant gifts" program; see Kristin L. Hoganson, *Consumers' Imperium: The Global Production of American Domesticity, 1865–1920* (Chapel Hill, 2007), chap. 5.
36. Molly Ladd-Taylor, "'My Work Came Out of Agony and Grief': Mothers and the Making of the Sheppard-Towner Act," in Koven and Michel, *Mothers*, 321–342.
37. Peter N. Stearns, *Anxious Parents: A History of Modern Childrearing in America* (New York, 2003), 17–47.
38. Kathleen W. Jones, *Taming the Troublesome Child: American Families, Child Guidance, and the Limits of Psychiatric Authority* (Cambridge, MA, 1999).
39. Ann Hulbert, *Raising America: Experts, Parents, and a Century of Advice About Children* (New York, 2003), 106–151.
40. Mintz, *Huck's Raft*, 214–216; Gary Cross, *An All-Consuming Century: Why Commericalism Won in Modern America* (New York, 2000), 38–46; Paula Fass, *The Damned and the Beautiful: American Youth in the 1920s* (New York, 1977).
41. Adelheid Gräfin zu Castell Rüdenhausen, "Familie und Kindheit," in Langewiesche and Tenorth, *Handbuch*, 65–86.
42. Dickinson, *Politics*, 204–234; Elizabeth Harvey, *Youth and the Welfare State in Weimar Germany* (Oxford, 1993).
43. Mitchell G. Ash and Alfons Söllner, eds. *Forced Migration and Scientific Change: Émigré German-Speaking Scientists and Scholars After 1933* (Cambridge, 1996).
44. Heinz-Elmar Tenorth, "Pädagogisches Denken," in Langewiesche and Tenorth, *Handbuch*, 111–154, here 143–147; Bernd Zymek, "Schulen," in Langewiesche and Tenorth, *Handbuch*, 155–208, here 190–203; Wolfgang Keim, *Erziehung unter der Nazi-Diktatur*, 2 vols. (Darmstadt, 1995 and 1997); Reinhard Dithmar and Wolfgang Schmitz, eds., *Schule und Unterricht im Dritten Reich* (Ludwigsfelde, 2001).
45. Alfons Kenkmann, *Wilde Jugend: Lebenswelt großstädtischer Jugendlicher zwischen Weltwirtschaftskrise, Nationalsozialismus und Währungsreform* (Essen, 1996); Winfried Speitkamp, "Jugend und Protest im Nationalsozialismus," in *Konflikt und Reform: Festschrift für Helmut Berding*, ed. Winfried Speitkamp and Hans-Peter Ullmann (Göttingen, 1995), 276–292.
46. Nicholas Stargardt, *Witnesses of War: Children's Lives Under the Nazis* (London, 2005), in particular 56–79; Frank Kebbedies, *Außer Kontrolle: Jugendkriminalpolitik in der NS-Zeit und frühen Nachkriegszeit* (Essen, 2000).
47. Sonya Michel, *Children's Interests/Mothers' Rights: The Shaping of America's Child Care Policy* (New Haven, 1999), 118–149; William M. Tuttle, Jr., *"Daddy's Gone to War": The Second World War in the Lives of American Children* (New York, 1993), 74–89. See also Emilie Stoltzfus, *Citizen, Mother, Worker: Debating Public Responsibility for Child Care after World War Two* (Chapel Hill, 2006).
48. Thomas Hine, *The Rise and Fall of the American Teenager* (New York, 1999), 227–231.
49. Hulbert, *Raising*, 208–243.
50. Diane Ravitch, *The Troubled Crusade: American Education 1945–1980* (New York, 1983), 43–80; Robert L. Hampel, *The Last Little Citadel: American High Schools Since 1940* (Boston, 1986), 43–51.
51. Hine, *Teenager*, 239–248; Mintz, *Huck's Raft*, 282–302, 308.
52. Sonja Häder and Heinz-Elmar Tenorth, eds., *Bildungsgeschichte einer Diktatur: Bildung und Erziehung in SBZ und DDR im historisch-gesellschaftlichen Kontext* (Weinheim, 1997); Christoph Führ and Carl-Ludwig Furck, eds., *Handbuch der deutschen Bildungsgeschichte, vol. VI. 1945 bis zur Gegenwart: Zweiter Teilband, Deutsche Demokratische Republik und Neue Bundesländer* (Munich, 1998); Alan McDougall, *Youth Politics in East Germany: The Free German Youth Movement 1946–1968* (Oxford, 2004); Mark Fenemore, *Sex, Thugs, and Rock'n'Roll:*

Teenage Rebels in Cold-War East Germany (New York, 2007); Uta Poiger, *Jazz, Rock'n'Roll, and Rebels: Cold War Politics and American Culture in a Divided Germany* (Berkeley, 2000).

53. Heide Fehrenbach, *Cinema in Democratizing Germany: Reconstructing National Identity after Hitler* (Chapel Hill, 1995), 113–116.
54. Dickinson, *Politics*, 251–283; Poiger, *Jazz*.
55. Dagmar Herzog, *Sex after Fascism: Memory and Morality in Twentieth-Century Germany* (Princeton, 2005), 162–174; Mintz, *Huck's Raft*, 311–318.
56. Ravitch, *Crusade*, 168–179; Joseph E. Illick, *American Childhoods* (Philadelphia, 2002), 149.
57. Ravitch, *Crusade*, 267–268, 280–312; Hampel, *Last Citadel*, 95–96; Torsten Gass-Bolm, "Das Ende der Schulzucht," in *Wandlungsprozesse in Westdeutschland: Belastung, Integration, Liberalisierung 1945–1980*, ed. Ulrich Herbert (Göttingen, 2002), 436–466.
58. Ravitch, *Crusade*, 312–320; Hampel, *Last Citadel*, 22–28; Lutz R. Reuter, "Rechtliche Grundlagen und Rahmenbedingungen," in Führ and Furck, *Handbuch*, 35–57.
59. Kurt Aurin, "Zur Geschichte der 'Schulpsychologie' in der Bundesrepublik Deutschland: Entwicklungen und Neuorientierungen," in *Theorie und Praxis der Beratung: Beratung in Schule, Familie, Beruf und Betrieb*, ed. Bernd-Joachim Ertelt and Manfred Hofer (Nuremberg, 1996), 71–93, here 82–89; Terje Neraal, Cordelia Fertsch-Röver-Berger, and Dorit Peh, "Schulpsychologische Beratung im Interaktionsfeld Familie-Schule," *Psychologie in Erziehung und Unterricht* 30 (1983): 299–309.
60. Sealander, *Failed Century*, 61–88.

Part I

FOUNDATIONS

Chapter 1

CHILDREN AND THE NATIONAL INTEREST

Sonya Michel, with Eszter Varsa

As the title of this volume suggests, child-rearing in the twentieth century was not the exclusive province of parents: when it came to raising *citizens,* states were likely to become involved. This was certainly true in the cases discussed in the essays that follow. But this observation also prompts a question about timing: was the nationalization of child-rearing in the US and Europe strictly a twentieth-century phenomenon? Not entirely, in our view. This chapter argues that concerns about the relationship between children and the "national interest" are as old as nations themselves. During the "long nineteenth century," which saw the rise of the modern nations of the West, those concerns came well to the fore. Notably, however, they were less prominent in parts of German Central Europe where nation-states had not yet fully formed.[1] Thus a comparison between the United States and Western Europe, on the one hand, and German Central Europe on the other, throws into relief the degree to which children and nationalism became mutually imbricated, and the ways in which the focus on children served to strengthen nations, and vice-versa.

Nations expressed their interest in children in a variety of ways. Historians have readily linked the rise of public schools with the growth of nations,[2] but they have been less likely to see child welfare policy in the same light. Instead, many contend, shifting approaches to child welfare policy were driven by "internalist" forces—the identification of specific problems, the proliferation of knowledges, the visions and values of reformers, and the professionalization of social services; or by local conditions—a focus on poverty, illness, illegitimacy, crime, or delinquency. Since Anna Davin published her pathbreaking article "Imperialism and Motherhood" in 1978, however, historians have also understood the importance of national interest in reproducing workers, soldiers, and managers of empires; increasing populations and/or improving their quality; and encouraging

Notes from this chapter begin on page 44.

or discouraging the growth of particular racial, class, religious, or ethnic groups. "Healthier babies," Davin wrote, "were required not only for the maintenance of [the British] empire but also for production under the changing conditions made necessary by imperialist competition."[3] Over the course of the long nineteenth century, as she and others have documented in Britain and elsewhere, such imperatives led to greater surveillance of families, the erosion or blurring of presumed boundaries between "public" and "private," and a weakening of parental rights, producing ideologies, policies and practices that affected parents as well as children and "fused" child health and welfare "with the broader political health of the nation."[4]

Adding child welfare policy to education meant that reformers could refine their methods and attempt to mold children as citizens of a specific nation.[5] During the first half of the nineteenth century, the two approaches were often combined in institutions such as boarding schools, orphanages, and houses of refuge, which, according to their promoters, had the advantage of separating children from "unwholesome" parents and environments and thus afforded more latitude for achieving national goals. By the last quarter of the century, however, reformers were turning from institutional toward more individualized—and more invasive—approaches that positioned professionals as authorities in relation to the families they were pledged to preserve.[6]

In the first decades of the twentieth century, as discourses shifted to incorporate the terminology of the new social and behavioral sciences, the national interest remained central, gaining fresh energy from the eugenics movements emerging throughout Europe and the United States.[7] The embrace of eugenics was but one of many parallels in education and child welfare policy across societies. These were not coincidental, but nor were they the result of some sort of inevitable convergence of the forces of modernization. Rather, they emerged from robust international conversations among reformers and professionals that not only served to convey information but produced standards that could serve as useful tools in national debates over policy.[8]

Such developments were inherently political and must be analyzed as such.[9] This is not to say that internalist factors had no impact on conceptions of childhood and trends in child welfare policy; reformers were also interested in creating a nurturing environment for children and in helping them to develop themselves. Rather, these goals frequently became bound up with national and, increasingly, transnational interests that not only shaped views of specific groups of children and skewed welfare policies in certain directions but lent force to demands for greater resources for and state control over children and families. As reformers and politicians across societies asserted that the future of nations lay in children, they came to be viewed as "national assets," a site of "national investment."[10] The linkage between children and the national interest became productive: of "truths" about children;[11] of institutions, bureaucracies and apparatuses; and ultimately of nations themselves. While national interest alone may not have directly shaped reforms or specified their content, it is probably safe to say that major reforms were unlikely to be undertaken if they were perceived as inimical to the national interest. At the same time, in the absence of a strongly articulated national interest (as in much of nineteenth-century Central and Eastern Europe), child welfare and education were likely to develop much more slowly, remaining privatized, often under religious rather than secular auspices.[12]

Reforms dealing with children held particular importance for women, changing the meaning of motherhood and turning "private family responsibilities into political and social concerns."[13] Historians debate whether this shift to "maternalism" actually increased women's political power. Ann Taylor Allen, for example, finds that it had mixed results: "Maternal roles in the family, though in one sense limiting women's possibilities, in another sense provided a model of empowerment and ethical autonomy."[14] While some scholars argue that women played a major role in shaping social policy across Europe and North America,[15] others contend that it was male politicians and officials who ultimately set the public agenda and held the purse strings, more often working *through,* rather than *with,* women.[16] This does not mean that maternalism had no impact on social policy; to the contrary, maternalists often self-consciously tacked to catch the winds of nationalism in their institutional and ideological sails. But nationalism could turn into the doldrums for maternalists who disagreed with its aims.

This chapter examines the relationship between children and the national interest during the nineteenth century in the United States and the countries of German Central Europe. We also discuss more briefly Britain, France, Romania, and the Soviet Union. While this broad range somewhat exceeds the focus of the present volume, the inclusion of the additional cases allows us both to document more fully the pervasiveness of certain patterns and draw attention to continuities and connections across societies. Though this chapter lacks the rich archival texture of those that follow, it is intended to sketch the historical background for the developments that they document.

New Citizens for a New Nation

For Americans, most historians would agree, the focus on children dates back to the very birth of the nation: indeed, the colonists' revolt against the British was closely related to their revolt against stringent Calvinist precepts of child-rearing. Throughout the colonial period Americans used Lockean discourses to challenge the authority of not only actual fathers but their political "father," George III. Soon after the Revolution, however, a search for order, coupled with anxieties sparked by the French Revolution and a rapid rise in immigration, led to a familial counterrevolution, with reformers and cultural leaders seeking ways to restore parental authority over children.[17]

The counterrevolution lasted at least as long as the initial revolt, and although much of its emphasis was on the mother's—rather than the father's—role in child-rearing, its tone was anything but Lockean. To take just one example, the popular author Lydia Sigourney, in her 1838 book *Letters to Mothers,* expressed her anxiety about "the influx of untutored foreigners" to the US and instructed American women as follows:

> Obedience in families, respect to magistrates, and love of country, should … be incul-
> cated with increased energy by those who have earliest access to the mind …. Let [the
> mother] come forth with vigour and vigilance, at the call of her country … like the
> mother of Washington, feeling that the first lesson to every incipient ruler should be,
> "*how to obey.*"[18]

Sigourney's emphasis on obedience was part of her more general insistence that women had a key role to play in producing good citizens. "A barrier to the torrent of corruption, and a guard over the strongholds of knowledge and of virtue, may be placed by the mother, as she watches over her cradled son … The degree of her diligence in preparing her children to be good subjects of a just government, will be the true measure of her patriotism."[19]

Sigourney was but one of a long line of commentators and civic leaders who produced what historian Linda Kerber has called the discourse of "republican motherhood," one that linked mothering directly to the political health of the new nation and imbued women's domestic labors with a significance that extended well beyond the home.[20] This discourse, self-consciously reflective of Rousseau, expressed Americans' more general understanding of the connection between families and the health of the polity, which came into sharper focus after the Revolution. Whether the well-ordered family was seen as the wellspring of good citizenship, as in Sigourney, or a model, either literal or metaphorical, of a good society, American elites regarded it as an essential component of the new political order.[21]

The centerpiece of these model families was, of course, the children—children who would soon take their place in the new nation. From the outset, their futures were both raced and gendered, since the Constitution and the laws of the land barred enslaved African Americans from citizenship and strictly delimited white women's rights. The discourse of republican motherhood assumed that white male children would become rational, self-sufficient adults who could shoulder the responsibilities of participating in a democratic polity, while white female children would grow up to become the kind of mothers who could reproduce good male citizens. The futures of African American and Native American children were not considered.

While the discourse of republican motherhood was implicitly addressed to mothers of the middling and elite classes, another, very different, set of public discourses focused on parents and children of the popular classes, namely, those of poverty relief. From the early nineteenth century on, the numbers and visibility of Americans who were "living poor" grew,[22] and with them public attention to the issue. Poverty troubled civic leaders less because of the suffering it caused than because it rendered citizens—men, that is—economically dependent and therefore incapable of carrying out impartially the responsibilities of political participation.[23] Thus relief was aimed at preventing the poor (especially able-bodied men) from becoming paupers (permanently dependent on the public purse), lest they lose their economic self-sufficiency, which, for the early nationalists, was closely bound up with political autonomy. In keeping with this goal, reformers believed that it was essential to reach children early, in order to put them "on the right path" toward sobriety and self-discipline by training them to make a living (if they were boys) or to support themselves and maintain their respectability until marriage (if they were girls).

Remedies for poverty shifted over time, but the focus on children remained constant. Early in the nineteenth century, reformers preferred to separate children from their families by either assigning them to institutions or "placing them out" as indentured workers or in foster families. Later, they shifted to policies aimed at keeping children at home by reforming their entire families. Such policies dramatically recast notions of privacy and family life carried over from the colonial period.[24] The intact, self-sufficient colonial family had been regarded as the model for institutions such as the poorhouse, not vice versa.[25] Gradually, however, reformers' anxieties about the state of families, especially of the poor, led them to concede that institutions should not merely offer temporary assistance but play a permanent role in the lives of the poor, not only to compensate for the inadequacies of their families but in some cases to replace them altogether. Although family breakdown seemed to be most prevalent among the poor, its occurrence led to a widespread fear that families in general could no longer be regarded as the cornerstones of civil society or the wellspring of citizenship. Thus the nation had to rely on other social institutions—beyond the family—to produce good citizens.

Linking childhood with the national interest meant that children were no longer regarded as the sole responsibility—or the "property"—of their parents, as they had been during the colonial period, but instead increasingly fell under the purview of public officials, reformers, professionals, and the law. This shift had various, and often contradictory, implications for Americans, depending upon race, ethnicity, gender, and class as well as age. For women of the elite and middling classes, it meant not just new duties and stature under the sign of republican motherhood, but also the beginning of what would be an enduring and often troublesome relationship with experts, professionals, and advice-givers of various stripes.[26] In contrast, for men, especially those of the middling and upper classes, it marked the continuation of a decline in patriarchal authority that had begun in the colonial period. The new emphasis on women's role in child-rearing (spurred by not only republican but also sentimental ideologies of motherhood) undermined fathers' familial authority, while developments in the law regarding bastardy, custody, and property rights gave both women and children unprecedented leverage vis-à-vis men.[27] All of this was counterbalanced by men's growing monopoly of breadwinning, but this too would become increasingly constrained by laws regarding desertion and paternal responsibility, starting in the 1890s.[28]

Throughout the nineteenth century, race and ethnicity on the one hand, and education and child welfare on the other, were mutually constitutive. While access to various services and provisions was usually determined by race and ethnicity, those categories were themselves in flux. The long history of miscegenation between African and Euro Americans, particularly in the South, coupled with continuous waves of immigration from all over Europe and East Asia, contributed to what historian Matthew Frye Jacobson has called the "instability of race." This was most apparent with regard to Europeans, many of whom were not immediately presumed to be white but had to gain that status.[29] There was little mobility for African Americans but somewhat more for Native Americans, provided they were willing to enter white society on *its* terms. Education and child welfare became key components of the process by which some ethnic groups would become "whitened" while others remained more or less excluded from the "wages of whiteness."

This harsh method of sorting was evident in reformers' approach to the children of the poor in American cities at mid century. Although white urban street urchins might be denigrated as "street Arabs"—a term intended to mark them as foreigners—they were nonetheless considered "redeemable" if only they could be separated from "unfit" parents and the corrupting influences of the city.[30] Thus, starting in the 1860s, New York City philanthropist Charles Loring Brace, working under the aegis of the Children's Aid Society, organized a series of "orphan trains" that delivered scores of poor white children—mostly boys, many from immigrant households and many who in fact had living parents—to willing foster families in presumably more salubrious rural environments all across America. Widely admired, Brace's scheme attracted many emulators[31] and continued well into the twentieth century, ultimately transporting some 150,000 children from city to countryside.[32]

Similarly, reformers believed that Native American children could be assimilated into white society if they were removed early enough from their families of origin. To this end, starting in the 1870s, both missionaries and government officials set up dozens of "Indian schools" across the country. While some were day schools located on or near reservations or other predominantly Indian communities, reformers preferred to ship Native American children to far-off boarding schools, thereby avoiding parental meddling and continued student contact with native culture.[33] To promote assimilation, the schools' curricula included lessons in patriotism centered around the rituals of flag raising and "American" holidays. They also imparted American gender norms[34] and, to eradicate racial markers, sought to transform their charges' appearance, hygiene, manners, food preferences and bodily comportment. In some cases attendance at these schools was voluntary, in others compulsory, but the upshot, particularly for Native American children who stayed for any length of time, was that they fell into a kind of cultural limbo, alienated from their families and culture of origin yet denied the promised benefits of full American citizenship.[35] Despite these outcomes, the schools were considered so successful that they were subsequently replicated in US colonies in the Philippines and Puerto Rico.[36] There is also evidence that they inspired white Australians' devastating, decades-long policy of removing Aboriginal children from their families of origin and placing them in white families.[37]

For the children of "white" immigrants and Native Americans, then, the cost of assimilation was physical, social, and cultural estrangement from their roots. But for children of other racial groups, assimilation was not really an option, with the result that they had far less access to the benefits—however dubious—of white-directed socialization. In most of the South before the Civil War, enslaved African American children were barred from learning to read and grudgingly given only rudimentary health care—and that for instrumental reasons. After Emancipation, efforts on the part of both African American and liberal white reformers to improve education and child welfare services in black communities were hampered by Jim Crow laws in the South and more subtle forms of racism in the North. Nonetheless, as historian Heather Williams shows, African Americans, both enslaved and free, consistently pursued a quest for literacy and education more generally, relying on self-teaching when other resources were not available.[38]

Children of Chinese extraction also faced school segregation. Restricted in their efforts to form families by the Chinese Exclusion Act (passed in 1882 and not rescinded until 1943), which severely limited the immigration of women and children and denied citizenship to all Chinese Americans, they tended to live within the confines of urban Chinatowns, most notably those in San Francisco and New York City, where local authorities grudgingly provided segregated schools. But Chinese community leaders, fearing that the children would grow up without adequate knowledge of Chinese language and culture, started their own schools, where these subjects were taught.[39] The schools met with much resistance from children, who saw them as efforts to keep them from assimilating. But their parents were not simply being conservative. Rather, having learned from their own bitter experience that no matter how "Americanized" they became they could never gain full acceptance in mainstream white society, they believed it was important to prepare their offspring to function effectively within the transnational Chinese–Chinese American community, where they would find abundant commercial opportunities.[40]

While racial minority children were largely excluded from the dominant vision of the American future, their white counterparts were at the center. For parents and children of the white popular classes in the nineteenth-century United States, this meant that family ties were always tenuous, subject to the vicissitudes not only of the economy but also of the latest ideas about preparing children for their place in society. Depending upon race and ethnicity as well as timing, a poor family ran the risk of being torn asunder by reformers who thought it best to send children to a refuge, a boarding school, or "out west"; or it might be allowed to remain "intact" but under the watchful eye of a friendly visitor or, later, a social worker. While reformers' thinking underwent frequent transformations, much of it was driven by an understanding that their policies would have implications not just for the children of the poor, but for the nation.

(Re)Producing Frenchmen

In France as in the US, the linkage between children and nation may be traced back to its Revolution. And in France, too, leaders of the new society looked to women to prepare children for citizenship. André Amar, a member of the revolutionary Committee on General Security, directed women "to begin the education of men, to prepare the hearts and minds of children for public virtue."[41] By the late eighteenth century, physicians, politicians, and military and public officials were publishing tracts calling for "the preservation of children" in the interest of the nation and demanding improvements in education and child-rearing practices (especially among the wealthy), and in the treatment of foundlings, who by definition were poor.[42]

Here too policies divided along class lines; the welfare of all children was construed as being in the national interest but for different reasons, and in different ways. It was important, for example, to lower mortality rates for foundlings since they could "eventually serve in national endeavors such as colonization, the militia, and the navy, for which they would be perfectly suited owing to their lack of constricting family ties."[43] Clearly, reformers were not weighed down by an excess of sentiment, but by what historian Jacques Donzelot calls "the lack of social economy"—the fact that the state derived little benefit from its investment in foundlings, since many died before they could repay, through military service, the "debt" they had incurred by being kept alive at public expense.[44]

Bourgeois children, by contrast, were highly valued, with the result that their mothers, like their American counterparts, became the darlings of civic leaders and professionals who sought to enlist them as educators of their offspring and guardians of their health. While such duties lent *les mamans* new stature, they were encouraged to carry out their sacred duties under the tutelage of physicians and other professionals (indeed, they were referred to as "medical auxiliaries"). When it came to the poor, French reformers, like the Americans and, as we shall see, the British, gradually shifted from institutionalization to policies designed to shore up "intact" families. Foundling hospitals were replaced by family allowances that permitted poor single mothers to keep their infants (albeit under close medical supervision), while charities as well as academics promoted marriage among the poor—again, to be contracted and carried out under the direction of the authorities. Public housing and labor polices were also designed with an eye toward creating and maintaining order and hygiene among working-class families.

Such policies were closely imbricated with the national interest. In the wake of the Franco-Prussian war, nationalists and "populationists" cast about for scapegoats for the perceived population crisis. Some blamed high mortality rates and malnourishment among infants on the practice, common among urban mothers, of resorting to wet nurses. The 1874 Roussel law, which brought the wet nursing industry under strict state regulation, was the first in a series of measures enacted over the next four decades to mobilize women's reproductive capacities on behalf of the nation. These included protective labor legislation for both girls and women and pregnancy and maternity leave. As a result, according to historian Elinor Accampo, "women's bodies were not their own; to historian Joshua Cole, "motherhood itself dissolved into 'the social.'"[45]

Nationalists were concerned not only about the numbers but also the character of French children. As historian Sylvia Schafer explains, for officials of the Third Republic, *abandon moral*—the failure of families to train and educate their children properly—constituted a problem for the state because it broke down the distinction between the moral child and the deviant, the child who could take his place in civil society and the one who would become marginal or socially deviant. Children who were morally abandoned were not innocent victims but future criminals—prostitutes, alcoholics, radicals—and thus required state assistance if not supervision. Part of the problem arose, of course, from the Third Republic's own adamant anti-clericalism; how could morality be instilled in such a context? In the 1880s, Schafer tells us, Paris, the home of the majority of French children identified as "morally abandoned," became a kind of laboratory for child protection policies. In the interest of creating a *secular* moral order, the state also readily assumed responsibility for education. It was through such policies that the state produced itself—expanding its authority, even presenting itself as a substitute for what it perceived as failed parental authority. In this way, what Donzelot has called the "policing of families" became instantiated, a process whereby the state did not so much control families directly as govern through them.[46]

Imperialism's Children

Britain's interest in children, like that of France, intensified in the last quarter of the nineteenth century, also in response to perceived national crisis. In addition to the Boer War and the burden of maintaining its empire, Britain was also feeling keenly the pressure in international economic competition, much of it coming from the United States.[47] To promote "national efficiency," public officials focused increasingly on children. Children, to be sure, had long received the attention of private philanthropists, and their welfare and education were central to the debates that led to passage of the New Poor Law of 1832,[48] as well as the various factory acts of the 1840s.[49] Both the poor law and philanthropic efforts relied on institutions such as schools and orphanages that were designed to deal with large categories of children in broad strokes, but from the 1870s on, as views of child welfare became more complex, reformers sought other ways to regulate children's minds and bodies, protect them "from uncivilized and neglectful behaviour," and instruct them "in matters of hygiene, personal responsibility, and 'citizenship.'"[50] Many of these policies, which historian Nikolas Rose has dubbed "neo-hygienism,"[51] were undertaken in the name of national efficiency. According to the Liberal Prime Minister H. H. Asquith, it was necessary to "safeguard England's 'raw material.'"[52] It was not just a matter of providing factory workers for domestic industry, but, as Anna Davin has demonstrated, of ensuring that the administrative and military elites needed to maintain "imperial domination" would comprise competent officers and officials.[53]

Britons' awareness of their imperial status also heightened standards for citizenship. Although the country followed the rule of *jus soli*—determining citizenship by place of birth rather than parental nationality (*jus sanguinis*)—this did not mean that elites automatically regarded every child born on its soil a full-fledged member of English society. In nineteenth-century England, class, of course, was the great line of social cleavage, often sharpened through expression in racial terms. As historian Lydia Murdoch has noted,

> Reformers ... used racialized language to separate poor children from the broader English social body, drawing on a confused mixture of national, ethnographic, anthropological, biological, and even zoological terminology. Like the urban poor in general, poor children were often construed as a separate race from the English.[54]

Observers routinely used epithets like "wild savages," "a tribe of national encumbrances," "the most curious motley of zoological specimens possible," and, of course, the familiar "street Arab," to describe this group. Nonetheless, reformers believed that poor children were redeemable, if only they could be separated from the environments, and particularly the parents, who had turned them into savages. Like the Americans with their orphan trains, English reformers practiced "philanthropic abduction,"[55] in this case sending children to suburban institutions whose purpose, according to Murdoch, "was to create an alternative world to the existing culture."

By the turn of the century, and even more by the time of the Great War, attitudes toward poor and working-class parents became somewhat more conciliatory. In keeping with a widespread sense that the country required solidarity, first to maintain its empire and compete effectively against other industrial nations, and then to win the war, reformers now believed that it made sense to enlist all parents in efforts to assist their children. In part, this shift was an attempt to address Conservative fears that the services Liberals were promoting, such as school meals and early childhood education, would "undermine parental responsibility." Many parents expressed gratitude for the services and material resources that were made available to their children,[56] but some learned the bitter lesson that the state's interest in them and their children could be double-edged. If they were perceived to have "failed in their duty to provide ... a proper childhood, the state as over-parent could punish them and remove their children."[57]

Children into Germans

Around the turn of the nineteenth century, the dominant view in the states that would come to constitute the German nation was that children and their welfare were properly the concern of parents. But parental responsibility was characterized in such a way that it was difficult to maintain its exclusivity. According to historian Rebekka Habermas, the "sacralization" of motherhood, based on assumptions of parental disinterest and self-sacrifice that had become prevalent, paved the way for its eventual professionalization.[58] This tendency was amplified by growing Christian concern about the "spiritual waywardness" produced by a collapse of traditional communal and social structures, itself the result of a trend toward modern rationality and individualism. As in the United States during this period, the middle-class family was central to conservative religious visions of society, so it was the family that became the focus of efforts to stem the tide of social collapse through religious revival. But when such efforts failed, more dramatic intervention might be required.

In the 1820s, reformers began to focus on cities as the source of youthful immorality. Wilhelm Heinrich Riehl, a Bavarian journalist and academic, claimed that young people seeking their fortunes in urban environments became "intoxicated, confused, and discontented."[59] The only alternative was to rescue children from their impious surroundings and ensure proper upbringing by placing them in a "house of salvation" (*Rettungshaus*) such as those founded by southern and central German pietists in the 1820s or, most famously, in Hamburg in 1833 by Johann Hinrich Wichern, a teacher and former Protestant theological student. Unlike American institutions of the period (and anticipating the "cottage system" that would appear later in both the US and Britain), Wichern's *Rettungshäuser* were intended to "[reproduce] the structure of the preindustrial patriarchal family."[60] However, as historian Edward Ross Dickinson describes them, this was a family in which women, curiously, appeared to be absent:

> Each was under the direction of a "house father" and was staffed by lay "brothers," and the spiritual reformation of the child was accomplished by the enforcement of strict obedience, by constant admonition and moral instruction, by the example of Christian life provided by the staff, and by the beneficial influence of supervised agricultural and artisanal labor.[61]

Under Wichern's leadership, a *Rettungshaus* movement took shape, establishing more than 300 houses across Germany by 1869 and serving as the core of an expanding Protestant reform initiative centered on children and run under the aegis of an organization called the Central Commission for Domestic Missions, or the "Inner Mission," as it became widely known.[62]

Secular liberals also mobilized around child reform, though their efforts emphasized self-help and enlightenment values rather than religious revival and child rescue. Through schools for factory children as well as adult education, they sought to help the working classes become self-sufficient yet adaptable and skilled enough to flourish within the "new capitalist-commercial social order."[63] Despite their self-presentation as advocates of modernity, these liberals were, Dickinson argues, similar to their conservative counterparts in key respects. They held values that were little more than secularized versions of religious tenets and, instead of "divine authority," embraced "paternal rationality."[64] Most significantly (and in sharp contrast to the Social Democrats), both movements were firmly opposed to state intervention into childhood or family life, and until the 1870s they managed to keep the state at bay except when it came to control of public schools.

Unification under Bismarck did little to alleviate concerns about social unrest in Germany; in fact, the new focus on nationalism exacerbated fears that local authorities' firm grip on the social order was being undermined and national culture was weakening religious faith. But while conservatives sought to restore traditional structures and values, liberals began calling for more state intervention. With their somewhat conflicted support, the Prussian parliament passed two key pieces of legislation: the Legal Guardianship Code of 1875, which increased state control of previously semi-autonomous legal guardianship, and the Law on Compulsory Correctional Education of 1878, which allowed the state to institutionalize children who had committed a crime (previously, the law had permitted removal of children from families only when their parents were deemed unfit).[65]

In the ensuing decades, German liberals would have reason to question the role they had played in ushering the state into the once-private sphere of family and child welfare provision, as conservative public officials, citing rising rates of juvenile delinquency and nonmarital births, pushed through a series of increasingly draconian social measures. An 1886 law passed in the state of Baden, for example, allowed removal of children to reformatories or foster families *before* they had even committed crimes (that is, when their behavior "indicates that the authority of the parents ... and the disciplinary power of the schools is not sufficient to prevent [his or her] complete moral ruin").[66] In 1901, a Leipzig physician named Max Taube instituted a highly restrictive system of oversight for unwed mothers and their children with the goal of reducing high rates of both illegitimacy and infant mortality among illegitimate children. The first, according to Taube, resulted from "the unconstrained life and the too-early independence of the female sex"; the second, from the fact that young unwed mothers lacked both the knowledge and resources to rear their offspring properly.[67] Taube also denounced young men for being ignorant of "the dangers for honor and body"[68] that premarital sex exposed them to, and fumed that their refusal to take responsibility for the children they sired revealed their callousness and lack of moral fiber. Bypassing the "normal" patriarchal family altogether, Taube created what Dickinson calls "a thoroughly modern, rational, bureaucratic mass institution for the care of a specific disadvantaged social group. Accepting the terms imposed by modern industrial society, [he] sought to order that society according to modern 'industrial' principles."[69]

But Taube's was not the only approach to the perceived problem of immorality among the young during this period. More liberal Protestants, particularly women, were also raising their voices over this issue and promoting a different vision of reform.[70] Figures like Hanover's Paula Müller, an educated and highly motivated middle-class officer of the German Protestant Women's League, denounced the "indecency" and "moral deficiency" of her day, but she looked to mothers as the remedy, exhorting them to serve as unimpeachable role models for their children, particularly with regard to sexual matters. Those who lived in big cities, she said, bore a special responsibility to counter the "vulgar" and "frivolous" values their children were likely to encounter.[71]

Liberal Protestant men like Walther Classen, Viktor Böhmert, and Johannes Tews also proposed anodyne responses to the problems of youth. Classen, who was trained in theology but opted for a career in social work in Hamburg, promoted the idea of using settlement houses as centers from which he and his colleagues could organize clubs, classes, cultural events, and outings for boys and girls.[72] Classen had been influenced by London's Toynbee Hall, which he visited in 1900, and he was also familiar with the *Volksheime* (people's houses) that Böhmert had founded in Dresden in the 1880s. Böhmert, known as the "workers' friend," was particularly concerned with the needs of working-class mothers and children, but instead of seeking to regulate them directly, as Taube did, he called for protective labor legislation, urging Germany to follow the Swiss example by outlawing all work for children under age fourteen. Such measures would, he asserted, safeguard "the bodily, intellectual, and moral health of the children's world."[73]

While Classen and Böhmert emphasized voluntary initiatives, Tews placed his faith in public schools, which, he held, could produce well-balanced individuals who had not only the mechanical intelligence needed by an advanced industrial economy, but also the moral fiber and cultural development to sustain a satisfactory life.[74] In opposition to the Social Democrats, Tews asserted that education should be used not "to isolate and control members of minorities who might be viewed as threats to national cohesion," but to promote "non-partisanship and inclusivity."[75] This stance would have put him out of step not only with the majority of Germans, who accepted the principle of *jus sanguinis,* but also with many of his American educator contemporaries.

The leading reformers of the new German nation, like their French and American counterparts, increasingly spoke in broad political terms, viewing "the social question," particularly when it came to the problems of youth, within a national context. To many, as historian Andrew Lees notes, young people's failure "to become healthy and productive workers, … parents, [and] law-abiding citizens" meant that those "who ought to form the locus of hope for the nation's future seemed instead to portend a slackening . . . of [both] the energies and of the cohesion that had apparently inhered in the empire during the heady days of enthusiasm that followed its establishment in 1871." [76] A Bavarian writer named Otto Fleischmann declaimed: "Everyone knows what a scourge growing vagabondage and crime have become for our fatherland. Our streets are filled with roaming youths, our prisons consume ever larger amounts of money. Friends of humanity wrack their brains trying to figure out how this evil can be controlled."[77] For Fleischmann, the disorder of youth was just one aspect of the city's threat to the nation.[78]

In response to this perceived crisis, some conservative "friends of humanity" abandoned the language of religious revival, individual rescue, and salvation in favor of an organicist vision that subordinated individuals to the greater social good but promised the benefits of integration in exchange. Hugo Appelius, a prominent jurist who focused much of his considerable energy on children and youth and subsequently became a proponent of establishing juvenile courts based on the American model, called for an unprecedented degree of state intervention in the private sphere (for example, in families where both parents worked outside the home), but he also asserted that citizens could, in a sense, "domesticate" the state or bring it down to their own scale through voluntary participation. Writing in 1892, he explained:

> We too often make the old mistake of regarding the state as something foreign, something antagonistic to us; and yet, we are all members of the one great whole, which we all make up. Everyone who acts as even a tiny cog in the great machine acts on behalf of all of society, the well-being of which in turn benefits the individual. The more the state recruits its citizens, within the limits of their capacities, to help solve the common tasks, the more the sense of belonging together, the sense of solidarity with the interests of the state, will become and remain lively.[79]

As Dickinson comments, "If the state had to be more active in society, the citizen had to become more active in the state."[80]

Writing around the same time, another reformer, Franz Pagel, a German schoolteacher who took a great interest in the futures of "fatherless" children, also called upon individuals to participate actively in the state: "[T]he state is an organic whole, a social organism ... In it there is a rich articulation and unbreakable interdependence of the individual parts ... Each part is important for the whole, just as in a clock even the smallest wheel cannot be missing."[81]

Citizens' specific task, according to Pagel, was to "[facilitate] the healthy development of every individual": "If society ... ensures the natural development of the physical and mental powers of its members, then it creates factors which create and transmit value, which will serve the personal well-being of the individual and the well-being of the nation."[82]

Despite the emphasis on the joys of national unity in these quotations, it is difficult to avoid noticing that the price of inclusion was conformity. Both Pagels and Appelius were implicitly calling upon one group of Germans—the "normal" ones, those who stood on the right side of the law—to monitor another group, the deviants. Though promoted in the name of benevolence, this was, in a sense, little more than a kind of vigilantism. While conformity to specific norms and an emphasis on unity certainly runs through the rhetoric of the other nations we are discussing, none of them sought to enlist the citizenry in enforcing those norms in the manner urged here.

As a society based on *jus sanguinis,* Germany accepted as citizens only the children of citizens (as opposed to all children born on its soil) and thus tended to remain more racially homogeneous than its *jus soli* counterparts, Britain and the United States. Yet, as the discussion of American and British developments reveals, the latter two nations were hardly models of indiscriminate integration and sought to limit citizenship in a variety of ways outside the law. Middle-class Germans do not appear to have used the kind of vivid racializing language that scholars have discovered in the other two nations[83] (though we cannot claim an exhaustive review of the German historical scholarship), yet their call to carry out an Inner Mission to the poor and working classes may have had the same exoticizing and distancing effect that the British achieved with their rhetoric of empire.

Child Welfare without National Interest

Many of the patterns we have traced in Western Europe and the United States appeared somewhat later in Central and Eastern Europe, with the rise of national-ism in those regions. However, as historians Sabine Hering and Berteke Waaldijk point out, "the histories of social work are not always 'national' histories. The responsibility of the nation state for the welfare of its citizens is just one of the forms social welfare can take. For many of the countries in Eastern Europe the national solution of the 'social question' was not even an option during long periods of their history" when they were "part of multi-national empires (whether Austrian-Hungarian, Russian, or Turkish), ... ruled by foreign occupying powers (fascist, communist, or otherwise) or ... part of a federation that united several nations."[84] Although scholarship on the history of social welfare in Central and Eastern Europe is still sparse,[85] there are already indications of important com-parisons to be made with the trajectory of child welfare policy in the US and Western Europe.

Prior to the emergence of nation-states, much of the child welfare that existed was organized under local, private, and often religious auspices. In mid nine-teenth-century Warsaw, for example, a growing population of orphans was cared for by a range of denominational charitable institutions—the only ones allowed by tsarist authorities—supervised by a body called the Main Custodian Coun-cil, established by tsarist decree. The council was in place from 1830 to 1870, when it was dissolved as the "result of post-uprising repressions." In the ensuing years, state support dried up, but the charitable organizations, "despite enor-mous bureaucracy and obstacles created by the Russian authorities, developed extremely vigorously."[86]

Nationalism was not entirely absent from this seemingly privatized form of child welfare; these organizations, in addition to their work with orphans, also "pursued patriotic activity under the cover of philanthropic aid."[87] In this instance, national interest was not embodied in the agencies or policies of a nation-state but persisted outside of government, where it remained covert, not even leaving rhetorical traces. Moreover, because the impact of these organiza-tions remained almost entirely localized, their ability to act as agents of national-ism was highly circumscribed. Throughout much of the nineteenth century, rural children in Poland grew up in the bosom of an "autonomous traditional peasant culture" that was primarily oriented toward reproducing itself and virtually immune from outside influences, other than the church.[88] At the same time, the children of bourgeois elites in Warsaw were being raised according to the modern principles of hygiene and nutrition that their parents imbibed through popular publications, but these child-rearing projects were highly individualized and not conceived in terms of any sort of national interest. The parents were "virtually all ... of non-Polish extraction with roots in Jewish and German tradition," and some "of Swiss and French origin"; this meant that their orientation was, if anything, cosmopolitan.[89]

Policies toward children—specifically, education—did become an important vehicle for nationalism within the context of the Austro-Hungarian Empire. Historian Tibor Frank notes that "educational reform, together with the judicial and administrative reforms, became one of the cornerstones" of the post-Compromise Hungarian state.[90] The Nationality Law accepted by the Hungarian Parliament in 1868 stipulated that Hungary would not recognize the existence of separate nationalities, and it denied them collective national rights or political institutions. The liberal leadership privileged the idea of creating a unitary Hungarian national state, and they looked to education as a likely place to implement their vision. Although the first Primary School Education Law, which came into effect in the same year as the Nationality Law, promulgated only voluntary "Magyarization" by not making Hungarian language instruction compulsory, the nationalists used village schools and especially secondary schools to turn the intellectuals of the various nationalities into Hungarians.[91] From 1879 onwards, it became obligatory to teach Hungarian in all state-run elementary schools, and according to Frank, from the 1880s onwards "Magyarization was pursued much more openly and forcefully, and Hungarian nationalism emerged clearly in its forceful impatience."[92] Although there is no in-depth research on the connection between Hungarian nationalism and child welfare reform, the intensity of Hungarian nationalism may explain why, as historian Susan Zimmermann has shown, the state took the lead in child welfare policy in the eastern (Hungarian) half of the empire, while in the western (Austrian) half, it remained under the aegis of municipal authorities[93]—more along the lines of Poland.

In other parts of Central Europe, child welfare policy also developed slowly until the late nineteenth or early twentieth century, when, in several cases, it leapt dramatically. The Bohemian lands discussed by Tara Zahra in her essay in this volume offer one case in point;[94] another is Romania, where the crisis of identity provoked by the creation of "Greater Romania" at the end of the First World War prompted the state to take desperate eugenicist measures. Writing about the eugenics campaigns in Romania, historian Maria Bucur notes that, unlike in Germany, England, and the United States, where eugenics "addressed perceived crises of development within populations with an already well-defined sense of national identity,"[95] the Romanian movement developed at a moment of great political change. Bucur compares the case of Romania, where "a new nation was patched together practically overnight, beyond the aspiration of its constituent parts,"[96] to that of the Soviet Union, where the radical politics of identity building required a fusion of nationalism and eugenics. "Soviet eugenicists," Bucur writes, "attempted to construct the new Homo Sovieticus according to the laws of hereditary determinism and evolution much as Romanians attempted to construct an entirely new model for a typical, healthy Romanian."[97]

Like the Soviet Union but unlike most of the West, Romania was compelled to adapt its eugenics policy to the largely rural conditions in which more than three quarters of the new nation's population lived, and there was a staggering rate of illiteracy. The absorption of Transylvania, Bukovina, Bessarabia, and the Banat into Romania as a result of the war greatly expanded the country's urban middle class but presented a conundrum for the nationalists. As Bucur puts it, "If it were true that the middle class had the greatest intellectual hereditary capabilities, this would imply that the Hungarian and German populations in Transylvania, who made up the great majority of the urban middle classes, were in fact superior to the Romanian population."[98] The eugenicists, who were aware of this issue, claimed that peasants "represented the 'biological reservoir of all the strata that lay on top of it'" and called for more "rigorous ethnic selection of the middle classes and an increased effort to educate peasants across the board."[99] They also focused on the issues of infant mortality, venereal disease, alcoholism, tuberculosis, and immunization against epidemic diseases, expanding the state's responsibilities in public health care but at the same time aiming to control spousal selection and reproduction. The eugenicists' goal was to convert these previously marginal issues into central ones for the state. The establishment of the Ministry of Health Care in 1922, for example, was seen as essential for the "qualitative development of the entire population."[100] "The welfare of mother and child was considered intimately linked to the welfare of the nation. Thus the most developed field of social assistance was children's welfare."[101]

Although admittedly sketchy, this account of educational and child welfare policy in nineteenth-century Central Europe offers several insights that reinforce our general points about the imbrication of child-rearing and the national interest. On the one hand, where fully formed nation-states and a strong sense of nationalism were absent, child welfare tended to remain privatized and parochial. On the other, child welfare and education presented nationalists with suitable vehicles for their aims, and while their often rapidly undertaken policies brought efficiency, increased resources, and, undeniably, certain benefits to children, some also entailed harsh and exclusionary consequences.

Conclusion

Thus the idea that children and childhood were important to the nation was not a new one for either Americans or Europeans at the turn of the twentieth century. Yet the "high modern state," to use James Scott's term, was still under construction.[102] Both schools and states were still relatively rudimentary. Though most industrializing societies had by this time established some form of public education, linkages between schools and social services were yet to be established. Almost everywhere, maternal and child welfare were still largely funded and administered by private charities, not public agencies. Just emerging were the new social and behavioral sciences that would not only offer fresh rationales for binding children more closely to the national interest but also help produce the state apparatuses and professional corps needed to carry out the task. Imperial powers were only beginning to use their colonies as laboratories for social and medical experiments, many of them involving children,[103] and most of the wars that would provide impetus for advances in child welfare policy in the metropole had not occurred. Moreover, some of the most powerful terms for labeling, treating, isolating, and institutionalizing children—hypersexuality, delinquency, maladjustment, abnormality, attention deficit disorder[104]—were not yet in use; this volume will allow us to put together a comprehensive list.

But by 1900, if not decades before, children and childhood had already become matters of national interest in the US and much of Western Europe, and Central and Eastern Europe were soon to follow. Throughout the long nineteenth century, reformers already had at their disposal elaborate vocabularies of control—idleness, intemperance, degeneracy, pauperism, feeblemindedness, *abandon moral,* even eugenics—vocabularies that could be and were used to categorize children, separate them from their parents, "place" them in institutions or households meant to "improve" or "rehabilitate" them, or allow them to remain in supervised family settings. The "happy" child, the untouched child, one who was somehow out of history, did not exist. In fact, all children—not just the poor and abandoned ones—were already only "historical," and already inextricably linked to the national interest, whether for good or for ill.

Notes

Eszter Varsa provided research for much of this chapter and was the main author of the sections on Hungary and Romania.

1. See Larry Wolff, "Revising Eastern Europe: Memory and Nation in Recent Historiography," *Journal of Modern History* 78, no. 1 (2006): 93–118; and Sabine Hering and Berteke Waaldijk, *Guardians of the Poor – Custodians of the Public: Welfare History in Eastern Europe, 1900–1960* (Opladen and Farmington Hills, 2006), 28–29.
2. The classic example would be Lawrence Cremin, *American Education: The National Experience, 1783–1876* (New York, 1980); for France and Germany, see Detlef Müller et al., eds., *The Rise of the Modern Educational System: Structural Change and Social Reproduction, 1870–1920* (New York, 1987); and for Britain, Michael Sanderson, *Education, Economic Change, and Society in England, 1780* (Houndsmill, Basingstoke, Hampshire, 1991).
3. Anna Davin, "Imperialism and Motherhood," *History Workshop Journal* 5 (1978): 49.
4. Harry Hendrick, *Children, Childhood, and English Society, 1880–1990* (New York and Cambridge, 1997), 5. See also Deborah Dwork, *War Is Good for Babies and Other Young Children:*

A History of the Infant and Child Welfare Movement in England, 1898–1918 (New York, 1987); Anna Davin, *Growing Up Poor* (London, 1996); Lydia Murdoch, *Imagined Orphans: Poor Families, Child Welfare, and Contested Citizenship in London* (New Brunswick, NJ, 2006); Ann Laura Stoler, *Race and the Education of Desire* (Durham, NC, 1995); Pablo Mitchell, *Coyote Nation: Sexuality, Race, and Conquest in Modernizing New Mexico, 1880–1920* (Chicago, 1995); and Katherine Bullard, "Saving the Children: Discourses of Race, Nation and Citizenship in America" (PhD diss., University of Illinois at Urbana-Champaign, 2005); as well as many of the other works cited in the course of this chapter.

5. One might also look at children's culture—toys, books, games, modern media, and the like—but this is beyond the scope of this chapter.

6. For a useful comparative catalogue of policies and their dates of inception, see Rachel Fuchs, "France in a Comparative Perspective," in *Gender and the Politics of Social Reform in France, 1870–1914,* ed. Elinor Accampo et al. (Baltimore, 1995), 163–165.

7. Ibid., 175–177; see also Mark H. Haller, *Eugenics: Hereditarian Attitudes in American Thought* (New Brunswick, NJ, 1984); Edward Ross Dickinson, *The Politics of German Child Welfare from the Empire to the Federal Republic* (Cambridge, MA, 1996), chap. 8; and Alexandra Minna Stern, *Eugenic Nation: Faults and Frontiers of Better Breeding in Modern America* (Berkeley, 2005). There has been considerable debate about the relationship between the American eugenics movement and Nazi racial policies; see Stefan Kühl, *The Nazi Connection: Eugenics, American Racism, and German National Socialism* (Oxford, 1994).

8. Daniel T. Rodgers, *Atlantic Crossings: Social Politics in a Progressive Age* (Cambridge, MA, 1998), esp. chap. 6; Thomas Bender, *A Nation Among Nations: America's Place in World History* (New York, 2006), chap. 5. Ann Taylor Allen points to the significance of international ties in expanding and sustaining the kindergarten movement in "The Kindergarten in Germany and the United States, 1840–1914: A Comparative Perspective," *History of Education* 35, no. 2 (1995): 173–188. In many cases, the exchanges had a specifically political agenda; see Ulla Wikander, "'Some Kept the Flags of Feminist Demand Waving': Debates at International Congresses on Protecting Women," in *Protecting Women: Labor Legislation in Europe, the United States, and Australia, 1880–1920,* ed. Wikander, Alice Kessler-Harris, and Jane Lewis (Urbana, 1995).

9. In relation to this issue, the historian Edward Ross Dickinson urges scholars of child welfare policy (particularly feminist historians) to "address the formal constitution of political power in Western societies." Dickinson, *Politics,* 2.

10. Fuchs, "France in Comparative Perspective," 162; and Hendrick, *Children, Childhood,* 37.

11. I am using this in the Foucauldian sense; notably, however, Foucault does not focus on nationalism as a force in the shaping of policy. See n. 21 below.

12. Hering and Waaldijk, *Guardians of the Poor,* 28–29; see also Kurt Schilde and Dagmar Schulte, eds., *Need and Care: Glimpses into the Beginnings of Eastern Europe's Professional Welfare* (Opladen and Bloomfield Hills, 2005).

13. Elinor Accampo, "Gender, Social Policy, and the Formation of the Third Republic: An Introduction," in Accampo et al., *Gender and the Politics of Social Reform,* 3.

14. Ann Taylor Allen, *Feminism and Motherhood in Germany, 1800–1914* (New Brunswick, NJ, 1991), 2.

15. Seth Koven and Sonya Michel, eds., *Mothers of a New World: Maternalist Politics and the Origins of Welfare States* (New York, 1993); Theda Skocpol, *Protecting Soldiers and Mothers: The Political Origins of Social Policy in the United States* (Cambridge, 1992); Gisela Bock and Pat Thane, eds., *Maternity and Gender Policies: Women and the Rise of European Welfare States, 1880s–1950s* (London, 1991).

16. Accampo, "Gender, Social Policy," 21–22; Fuchs, "France in Comparative Perspective," 162. Fuchs argues that "[w]omen's activities help explain the rise of the welfare state in Western Europe to a lesser extent than in the United States" (184).

17. Jay Fliegelman, *Prodigals and Pilgrims: The American Revolution Against Patriarchal Authority, 1750–1800* (New York and Cambridge, 1982). Whether or not patriarchy was already waning

at the time of the Revolution remains a subject of debate, but Fliegelman himself concedes that a counterrevolution did occur.

18. Lydia Sigourney, *Letters to Mothers* (New York, 1838), 8–9.

19. Ibid., 9.

20. Linda K. Kerber, *Women of the Republic: Intellect and Ideology in Revolutionary America* (Chapel Hill, 1980).

21. According to Michel Foucault, "prior to the emergence of population [his term for the nexus of individual sexuality and reproductivity with national interests], it was impossible to conceive of the art of government except on the model of the family." But by the mid eighteenth century, he argues, "the family becomes an instrument for the government of the population, and not the chimerical model of good government." Michel Foucault, "Governmentality," in *The Foucault Effect: Studies in Governmentality,* ed. Graham Burchell et al. (Chicago, 1991), 99–100. For the United States, I would date this shift at least half a century later, to the period when the new nation was taking form; Foucault does not refer to nationalism in this regard.

22. The term is Gary Nash's; see his chapter "Poverty and Politics in Early American History," in *Down and Out in Early America,* ed. Billy G. Smith (University Park, PA, 2004).

23. Seth Rockman, *Welfare Reform in Early America* (Boston, 2003), Introduction.

24. Those views are captured succinctly in the title of John Demos's study *A Little Commonwealth: Family Life in Plymouth Colony* (New York, 1970; rpt. 2000).

25. Shirley Samuels, "The Family, the State, and the Novel," *American Quarterly* 38, no. 3 (1986): 386, paraphrasing David Rothman, *The Discovery of the Asylum: Social Order and Disorder in the Early Republic* (Boston, 1971), 42–43.

26. Barbara Ehrenreich and Deirdre English, *For Her Own Good: 150 Years of Experts' Advice to Women* (Garden City, NY, 1978); see also Elizabeth Rose, "Taking on a Mother's Job: Day Care in the 1920s and 1930s," in *"Bad" Mothers: The Politics of Blame in Twentieth-Century America,* ed. Molly Ladd-Taylor and Lauri Umansky (New York and London, 1998).

27. Michael Grossberg, *Governing the Hearth: Law and Family in Nineteenth-Century America* (Chapel Hill, 1985).

28. Michael Willrich, "Home Slackers: Men, the State, and Welfare in Modern America," *Journal of American History* 8, no. 2 (September 2000): 460–489; Anna Igra, *Wives Without Husbands: Marriage, Desertion and Welfare in New York City, 1900–1935* (Chapel Hill, 2007).

29. Matthew Frye Jacobson, *Whiteness of a Different Color: European Immigrants and the Alchemy of Race* (Cambridge, 1998); David Roediger, *The Wages of Whiteness: Race and the Making of the American Working Class* (London, 1991); and Noel Ignatiev, *How the Irish Became White* (New York, 1995).

30. Bullard, "Saving the Children," chap. 2.

31. Some emulators ran into problems; see Linda Gordon, *The Great Arizona Orphan Abduction* (Cambridge, 1999).

32. Bullard, "Saving the Children," chap. 2; Stephen O'Connor, *Orphan Trains: The Story of Charles Loring Brace and the Children He Saved and Failed* (Boston, 2001).

33. Mitchell, *Coyote Nation,* 28.

34. Margaret D. Jacobs, *Engendered Encounters: Feminism and Pueblo Cultures, 1879–1934* (Lincoln, NE, 1999), chap. 1. See also Brenda J. Child, *Boarding School Seasons: American Indian Families, 1900–1940* (Lincoln, NE, and London, 1995).

35. The theme of liminality is a constant in memoirs by Native Americans who attended such schools and is also prevalent in both the autobiographical and fictional literature of African Americans and immigrants from all corners of the world. Similarly, it may be found in the memoirs of British children of this period; see Davin, *Growing Up Poor,* chap. 11.

36. Pedro A. Cabán, *Constructing a Colonial People: Puerto Rico and the United States, 1898–1932* (New York, 1999), chap. 4.

37. Margaret D. Jacobs, "Maternal Colonialism: White Women and Indigenous Child Removal in the American West and Australia, 1880–1940," *The Western Historical Quarterly* 36, no. 4 (2005): 453–476.

38. Heather Andrea Williams, *Self-Taught: African American Education in Slavery and Freedom* (Chapel Hill, 2005); see also Jacqueline Jones, *Soldiers of Light and Love: Northern Teachers and Georgia Blacks, 1865–1873* (Chapel Hill, 1980); and James D. Anderson, *The Education of Blacks in the South, 1860–1935* (Chapel Hill, 1988).
39. Him Mark Lai, "Teach Chinese Americans to be Chinese: Curriculum, Teachers, and Textbooks in Chinese Schools in America during the Exclusion Era," in *Chinese American Transnationalism: The Flow of People, Resources, and Ideas between China and America during the Exclusion Era,* ed. Sucheng Chan (Philadelphia, 2006), 194–210.
40. Xiao-Huang Yin, "Writing a Place in America: The Sensibilities of American-Born Chinese as Reflected in Life Stories from the Exclusion Era," in Chan, *Chinese American Transnationalism,* 211–236.
41. Quoted in Accampo, "Gender, Social Policy," 12; here Amar is, of course, echoing Rousseau. For a somewhat different but provocative interpretation of the relationship among children, the family, and the French Revolution, see Lynn Hunt, *The Family Romance of the French Revolution* (Berkeley, 1993).
42. Jacques Donzelot, *The Policing of Families* (Baltimore, 1997), 10.
43. Ibid.
44. Ibid.
45. Quoted ibid., 8.
46. See n. 16 above.
47. See, for example, William T. Stead, *The Americanization of the World, or, The Trend of the Twentieth Century* (New York, 1901; rpt. 1972), which, despite its title, focuses on fears of the American domination of Britain.
48. Harry Hendrick, *Child Welfare: Historical Dimensions, Contemporary Debate* (Bristol, 2003), 40–46.
49. Anna Clark, *The Struggle for the Breeches: Gender and the Making of the British Working Class* (Berkeley, 1995), 219–221. As Clark explains, the Factory Acts were passed largely at the behest of the male-dominated labor movement, not of reformers, though labor activists did invoke ideals of domesticity in their efforts to restrict the working hours and conditions of women and children.
50. Hendrick, *Children, Childhood,* 41.
51. Nikolas Rose, *The Psychological Complex: Psychology, Politics and Society in England, 1869–1939* (London, 1985), 85–89.
52. Quoted in George K. Behlmer, *Child Abuse and Moral Reform in England, 1870-1908* (Stanford, 1982), 220.
53. Davin, *Growing Up Poor,* 49.
54. Murdoch, *Imagined Orphans,* 26.
55. Ibid., 164.
56. Ibid., 165.
57. Davin, *Growing Up Poor,* 214.
58. Rebekka Habermas, "Parent-Child Relationships in the Nineteenth-Century," *German History* 16 (1998): 43–55.
59. Quoted in Andrew Lees, *Cities, Sin, and Social Reform in Imperial Germany* (Ann Arbor, 2002), 26.
60. Dickinson, *Politics,* 13.
61. Ibid.
62. Ibid., 13–14.
63. Ibid., 14. This position may be explained, at least in part, by the fact that a number of the founders of the main liberal reform organization, the Central Association for the Welfare of the Working Classes, were business leaders "who sought to extend the achievements of the infant industrial economy and protect it from the dangers of social revolution by ameliorating the lot of the working classes" (ibid., 14).
64. Ibid., 15.

65. Ibid., 20.
66. Quoted ibid., 22.
67. Quoted ibid., 25.
68. Ibid.
69. Ibid., 27.
70. The most insightful discussion of women's role in reform remains Allen, *Feminism and Motherhood.*
71. Lees, *Cities, Sin*, 107; see also Allen, *Feminism and Motherhood*, 193.
72. Lees, *Cities, Sin*, chap. 7.
73. Quoted ibid., 220.
74. Quoted ibid., 232.
75. Ibid., 233.
76. Ibid., 259.
77. Ibid., 138.
78. Ibid., 36.
79. Quoted in Dickinson, *Politics*, 24.
80. Ibid.
81. Quoted ibid., 28.
82. Quoted ibid.
83. See, for example, Murdoch, *Imagined Orphans*; Seth Koven, *Slumming: Sexual and Social Politics in Victorian London* (Princeton, 2004) and Bullard, "Saving the Children."
84. Hering and Waaldijk, *Guardians of the Poor*, 28–29.
85. Hering and Waaldijk's collection is the first in any language to offer a relatively comprehensive compendium of studies of welfare history, including child welfare, in the region. The collection is drawn from a larger project on the history of social welfare in Eastern Europe that covered Bulgaria, Romania, Croatia, Slovenia, Hungary, Poland, Russia and Latvia; a companion volume, Schilde and Schulte's *Need and Care*, is drawn from the same project.
86. Elżbieta Mazur, "Care for Orphans in Nineteenth Century Warsaw," *Acta Poloniae Historica* 79 (1999): 124.
87. Ibid., 123.
88. Włodomierz Mędrzecki, "The Shaping of the Personality of Peasant Youth and Its Start in Life in Central Poland, 1864–1939," *Acta Poloniae Historica* 80 (1999): 102.
89. Mariola Siennicka, "Child in Wealthy Warsaw Bourgeois Family: Second Half of the 19th and the Early 20th Century," *Acta Poloniae Historica* 79 (1999): 135.
90. Tibor Frank, "Hungary and the Dual Monarchy, 1867–1890," in *A History of Hungary*, ed. Peter F. Sugar, Péter Hanák, and Tibor Frank (Bloomington and Indianapolis, 1990), 254–258.
91. The first debate of the bill, in 1848, ended in a proposal to mandate Hungarian as the language of instruction in state primary schools.
92. Frank, "Hungary and the Dual Monarchy," 255.
93. Susan Zimmermann and Gerhard Melinz, "Gyermek- és ifjúságvédelem Budapesten és Bécsben a dualizmus korában" [Child and Youth Protection in Budapest and Vienna during the Austro-Hungarian Monarchy], in *Gyermeksorsok és gyermekvédelem Budapesten a Monarchia idején* [The Lives of Children and Child Protection in Budapest during the Austro-Hungarian Monarchy], catalogue for A Fővárosi Szabó Ervin Könyvtár Budapest Gyűjteményének kiállítása [Exhibition by the Budapest Collection of the Municipal Ervin Szabo Library] (Budapest, 1996).
94. Tara Zahra, "'Children Betray Their Father and Mother': Collective Education, Nationalism, and Democracy in the Bohemian Lands, 1900–1948," in this volume.
95. Maria Bucur, *Eugenics and Modernization in Interwar Romania* (Pittsburgh, 2002), 8.
96. Ibid.
97. Ibid., 9.
98. Ibid., 162.

 99. Ibid.
100. Ibid., 191.
101. Roxana Cheschebec and Silvana Rachieru, *History of Social Work in Romania, 1900–1960: Romania Final Report*, Volkswagen Project on Social Work in Eastern Europe (Siegen, 2005), referred to in Hering and Waaldijk, *Guardians of the Poor*, 119.
102. James C. Scott, *Seeing Like a State: How Certain Schemes to Improve the Human Condition Have Failed* (New Haven, 1998).
103. Stoler, *Race and the Education of Desire*.
104. And, of course, the murderous racial policies of the National Socialists were yet to come.

Part II

NEW BEGINNINGS

Chapter 2

CHILDREN'S FUTURE, NATION'S FUTURE
Race, Citizenship, and the United States Children's Bureau

Katharine S. Bullard

In the late nineteenth and early twentieth centuries, a growing consensus among the population of the United States began to coalesce around the notion of a national interest in the childhood of all Americans, whether or not they were materially advantaged. Based in the conviction that the future of all children was as citizens and that citizenship required particular nurturing and training, numerous local governments and charities had already begun programs to provide material and educational assistance to children. Advocates for children and the White House conferences on childhood called for a national plan to assist children, seeing this as a more consistent expression of their belief in children's importance to the whole nation. One of the results of this was the formation of the United States Children's Bureau in 1912 to investigate the condition of women and children throughout the country and to promote their health and well-being. The development of programs to promote the welfare of all children helped to establish a nominal social citizenship[1]—the right to material assistance as a part of membership in the national community—for American children. However, in the United States, the height of progressive reform in this period also coincided with a general white, middle-class consensus on the biological basis of racial divisions and the drawing of internal racial boundaries. As many historians have suggested, racial boundaries were drawn through violence, but also through legal and visual means of defining the national community and its citizens.[2] In this essay I will demonstrate that the ways in which the bureau went about its work and presented it helped to define the racialized child citizen.

In the United States, assistance for poor children and families was the province of private organizations for most of the nineteenth century. Displaying a general sense that poverty was a moral failing, charity organizations mainly ministered

---

Notes from this chapter begin on page 65.

to spiritual rather than material needs. As the nineteenth century progressed, children began to occupy a special place in the national imagination as innocent victims of their parents' failings.[3] By mid-century the sentimentalization of childhood as a time of play and education in the middle class was helping to drive reformers like Charles Brace to turn their attention to the children of the urban poor, whose work and play often took place on the streets. Efforts by charitable organizations like Brace's Children's Aid Societies in New York reflected the preoccupation with Americanization and middle-class culture and were focused on the children of Irish and German immigrants.

By the end of the century, many of those concerned with poor women and children argued that their well-being was of national concern and that they had a right to community support. Drawing on the sense that women had a special role in rearing and educating children, women progressives in particular argued that mothers deserved community financial support to perform this task. The development of mother's pension programs in cities like Chicago illustrated the growing power of that argument. The architects of these programs conceived of motherhood as a national service that deserved similar compensation to military service.[4]

Despite the universalist language of the program, the mother's pension programs were not for everyone. Generally programs were limited to mothers who fit a particular behavior profile—widowed rather than single, not employed, and living in homes that the middle-class administrators deemed appropriate. In part because of this "suitability" requirement, mother's pensions rarely went to non–English speakers or women of color. Additionally, in the South, mother's pensions were often denied in order to keep African American women working in the fields.[5]

At the same time that localities were beginning to institute mothers' pension programs, activists were also advocating the establishment of the federal bureau for children. Boosters for the bureau also argued that women and children were a national resource that needed to be conserved by national intervention as a right of citizenship. Lillian Wald and Florence Kelley, two prominent progressive women, noted that agriculture had its own bureau and that children, being a far more important national product, also needed an agency of their own to study their needs and provide information about their care.[6] In situating children as a national product, the bureau was building on the eugenics movements that argued for material and educational assistance as a way to strengthen white, middle-class motherhood and reproduction, and it is this heritage that helped to define the bureau's activities.[7]

With the establishment of their own federal department, children became the result not just of familial reproduction, but also national reproduction and strength. The first two directors of the bureau, Julia Lathrop and Grace Abbott, shared with Wald and Kelley a background in the settlement house movement and in the social sciences among a group of women that was also arguing for mothers' pensions. As one of the early publications of the Children's Bureau put it: "Each death at childbirth is a serious loss to the country. The women who die from this cause are lost at the time of their greatest usefulness to the State and to their families; and they give their lives in carrying out a function which must be regarded as the most important in the world."[8] Women, in this quote, were not merely engaged in a private enterprise but were giving birth to a valuable commodity that was needed if the United States was going to compete on a world stage.

Since children were important to more than their own families, mothers needed specific instructions on how to ensure children were raised correctly. Unlike earlier periods, when only poor families were thought to need guidance on child-rearing, the professionals of the bureau would provide materials for everyone, believing that all families need some guidance to ensure the best results. However, because of their focus on all children—including middle-class, white children—the bureau would not, unlike the Bureau of Indian Affairs, for example, work in the homes of individual families investigating their circumstances or providing financial aid. The focus of their work would be on educating mothers about their job. Pamphlets like *Infant Care* (1914) and *Prenatal Care* (1913), sponsoring fairs for "better babies," and commissioning studies of infant mortality and poverty were in line with this mission.

The staff of the bureau was mostly women, but not necessarily mothers. Their qualifications came from experience in the settlement house or charitable movements, or from education in sociology or social work. These were areas where women were able to carve out a place for themselves as professionals.[9] In the preface to both pamphlets, Julia Lathrop, the bureau director, assures the reader that the author, Mrs. Max West, has "university training" and is a mother of young children, and that the pamphlet "has been read and criticized by a large number of well-known physicians and nurses, and by many mothers."[10] Despite the fact that Mrs. West was a mother, it was her university training and advice from medical professionals that made the pamphlets authoritative.

The consequences of not caring for the child properly according to expert advice were very grave. A cartoon used in child health exhibits around the country shows an innocent-looking child under attack by the forces of "poverty," "ignorance," and "bad surroundings." Using war imagery, the cartoon demonstrates the risks that parents were taking (including death), by raising their child without the assistance of experts who could help to protect their child. While poverty was included in this list of dangers to childhood, the bureau did not (and could not) provide any material support; nor would there be much financial assistance on the local level. Instead, these evils were to be combated with information and guidance.

While the feeding of children was a private, family matter, the bureau had an interest in its impact on the formation of the future citizen, and science could provide the best guidance in determining that feeding. As the professionals of the bureau knew, the healthy, civilized baby could not tolerate spicy, immigrant food; rather, clean milk should be the foundation of her diet. Food, in this sense, was a metaphor for the larger cultural issues of Americanization. The Children's Bureau pamphlet *Milk, Indispensable Food for Children,* written by a female physician, reminded its readers that "intellectual and moral abnormality are largely influenced by physical health and a period of malnutrition among the children of America may easily be followed by a period of intellectual and moral deterioration." Malnutrition was a direct result of unscientific feeding of babies.[11]

The standards of child care could be very specific in order to create the best future citizen. In their discussion of nutrition and other issues, the Children's Bureau was by extension creating an image of the future citizen. Parents needed expert advice on nutrition to promote the healthy development of their children. But at least in some sense the nation also required that this advice be available to all. Physical and mental health was important even for the children of immigrants. These children had previously been left to eat inappropriate food (unless living within range of a local charity or social service bureau), but with a federal bureau available to all parents, they too could have the nutritional support required to help them be good citizens. In attempting to intervene in the lives of all children—at least by pamphlet—the bureau was signaling the inclusion of these immigrant children.

Despite the critiques that I make of the bureau's policies and ideologies in this essay, the benefits of the work of the Children's Bureau were quite tangible and important for women. It brought information and advice and often some free access to medical care. As one woman put it in her letter to the bureau, the pamphlets on prenatal and infant care were "valuable" and gave "good advise [sic]."[12] For women, the government's concern for their children made their role valuable not only to their own child, but to the larger society. In their letters to the bureau, women made clear how grateful they were and asked for advice after getting their first round of pamphlets.[13] For the women who received information, free exams for their infants, or other kinds of assistance from the bureau, the help was a mark of their importance to the nation.

In its purview to provide information to all Americans, the published material of the Children's Bureau assumed that readers would not be stymied by lack of access to medical care or other material benefits because of racial segregation, poverty, or other barriers. Mrs. Max West insisted in *Prenatal Care* on the need for a physician to verify pregnancy and to be involved in care,[14] which was nearly impossible in rural areas—or, for black women, in the Jim Crow south, where few doctors would examine African American patients. The bureau eventually encouraged the use of midwives for African American women but considered them unacceptable as birth attendants for whites.[15]

Pamphlets on child-rearing also assumed an audience of white readers whose position afforded them some movement around the growing American empire. Care manuals included advice on protecting their children from exotic environments. Mrs. Max West's pamphlet on infant care included a section on "Infant Feeding in the Tropics" that advised women living in the Canal Zone and the Philippines on how to raise their children as healthy Americans.[16] This publication, written only in English and distributed mainly in the United States, focused on spreading the bureau's methods of child-rearing to Americans everywhere.

The bureau was chartered to work with all children, and while many of its publications covered topics that would be of concern to all mothers, their visual representations of children were exclusively white. It is an adorable white baby who is under attack by "Baby's Foes." Baby-week information for parents was decorated with a photo of a smiling, pink-cheeked white baby who was obviously well nourished and well cared for. This was displayed through the baby's attractive clothing and round face, a mark of the excellent care that it was receiving. Its material privilege was obvious from its white clothing and general nutrition. Pamphlets on infant care came with similar figures. This was indicative of a growing sentimentalization of white childhood in the nineteenth century as children became less important to the family economy, but more important emotionally.[17]

In campaigns against child labor by the bureau and by other groups, it was the white child whose future was endangered. An early twentieth-century image, Lewis Hine's famous poster "Making Human Junk," which showed the effect of factory work on children, was an example of the use of the figure of the sentimentalized white child in the campaign against child labor. The "before" pictures shows white children arranged in a school photograph standing upright and looking right at the camera. The "after" photo shows bent, dirty children whose eyes are downcast—"Human Junk."

Viviana Zelizer argues in *Pricing the Priceless Child* that as children lost economic value in the family in the nineteenth century and gained in sentimental value, child labor became more socially unacceptable. Although it is unspoken in her analysis, her argument only works for white children—imagined as precious and valuable—as is visible in the poster "Making Human Junk." This is not to say that individual nonwhite families did not value their children, but rather that there was no social investment in their childhood. Children continued to work in migrant labor in the Southwest and in sharecropping in the South.

Similarly, as the Children's Bureau turned its focus to child labor and stressed the potential damage to the nation's resources, African American and Mexican migrant children were not the target of reports on child labor. The bureau's reports stressed the danger of accidents and health problems that would plague children into adulthood, calling labor a "waste of childhood."[18] While the campaign against child labor was phrased in general terms, the focus of the bureau's studies that were intended to prove the dangers of child labor centered on particular areas of the country and professions that were predominately white. Studies of coal mining in Pennsylvania, child labor in North Dakota, and indenture in Wisconsin as well as the administration of child labor laws in the states that already had them focused the attention of the bureau on white children.[19] Some African Americans showed up in studies of cotton-picking areas, but the majority of the subjects of the studies were white, despite the fact that far more African American children were working in Southern cotton fields.[20] Migrant farm workers, particularly Mexican farm workers, also do not figure in the bureau's analysis of child labor, and barely show up in the child welfare studies of this period as well.

In these reports, the body of the child takes center stage. Descriptions of children's working conditions emphasized the difficult physical conditions and their impact on the child's body. The imagery of these descriptions invokes the importance of protecting children and the inappropriateness of their work. In one cannery the bureau studied, "some as young as 5 or 6 were found at work in cold, damp, drafty sheds, their hands cut by sharp oyster shells, shrimp thorns, and the knives they used in the work."[21] The physical details in this quote (their cut hands) were meant to invoke the protective parental instincts in readers, making the child in the shed a member of their own community rather than a stranger.

In this same discussion of child labor, the director of the bureau (Grace Abbott) goes on to remind her audience of the need to "conserve the health and intelligence of our future citizenship."[22] In order to accomplish this, it was important for children to spend their early years in school, rather than in the workplace, according to the bureau. Education would help to mold the children of even the poorest and most "degraded" families into responsible voters and participants in the life of the nation. This was not just the opinion of the Children's Bureau, according to Abbott: "public opinion in the United States responding slowly to a century of education as to the evils resulting from the premature employment of children is finally registering the conviction that the years of childhood should be years of play and training."[23] School, along with exemption from wage-earning, would allow America's children to take on the burdens of citizenship later in life.

Rural work in general, for the bureau, was not as great a concern as urban employment; in part this was because of the focus on the model white child. For the bureau, the greatest danger was the loss of school time. Rural work, because it did not "completely shut the child out of school," was preferable to factory work.[24] Despite director Grace Abbott's references to paid work, however, in the same letter she still refers to "farm boys and girls," suggesting more an idyllic family farm than sharecropping or migrant farm work. Sharecropping and migrant farm work, while certainly practiced by whites, disproportionately affected non-whites, whose children would most likely lose a great deal more school time or attend inadequate schools.

While the descriptive studies of the bureau were important, the bulk of their publications focused on developing a statistical picture of American childhood. Like other social scientists of their time and with the same training, the bureau's studies took as their basis the division of the races. For the staff, the only questionable part of this was how to ensure that localities were keeping careful records of their population by race and ethnicity. The use of race in the census, on birth certificates, and in the reports of the bureau gave it a reality beyond the visual. African Americans in particular were a source of difficulty for progressive social scientists interested in developing models of American society based on assimilation.[25]

Studies that did not focus on race still used it as a means of organizing their findings. Reports using these records to study infant or maternal mortality (for example) broke down their findings by race. While this seems obvious in a way to us today, we need to think about the implications of racializing the population at the level of statistics. Every study done by the bureau breaks down its population by race. Studies such as *Social Study of Mental Defectives in New Castle Co., Del.* (1917), a study on playgrounds for children in Washington, D.C. (1917), and one on maternity care in Mississippi (1921) all divided the populations they studied based on race.

In the more general publications of the bureau that attempted to provide parents and doctors with expectations of children's development, the standard was taken as white. The publication *Average Heights and Weights of Children under Six Years* contains tables that break down the children by white and "Negro" and by gender. Although the data collection includes a space for examiners to note the place of birth of mother and child, the ethnic origin of children is not a determining factor in its average height and weight. The longer version of this study, *Statures and Weights of Children under Six Years of Age,* does include some information on children of various ethnic groups, but it is only African American children that are completely isolated from the "white group."[26]

One could argue that by creating racial categories in their reports, the bureau was documenting the social impact of segregation and hoped to ameliorate it. African Americans would have less access to playground facilities, for example, because of Jim Crow laws. Higher poverty rates among African Americans would have an impact on their ability to access medical care and would then raise the mortality rate for mothers and babies. The first bureau director, Julia Lathrop, refers to the bureau's extra focus on training midwives for the African American population in the South as an alternative to ensuring the care of medical doctors.[27] Yet the African American child, as well as the Native American child, remained an aberration compared to the "average" American, i.e., white child. In dividing the population based on race, the Children's Bureau was not only recording but also codifying race. As a federal agency, and of course not the only one that did this, its use of racial categories had particular power. It brought segregation from a visual to a statistical realm, declaring in some sense that there was a biological difference in children that was clear from their race.

Descriptions of nonwhite communities reinforced the sense of biological destiny. One study done in 1918, *Rural Children in Selected Counties of North Carolina,* focused on the African American population. The tone of this study was quite different than those that focused on white, even immigrant, populations. Unlike whites, the population of African Americans was labeled by their race—"Negro." The report also presented an anthropological view—"The negro is by nature gregarious and revels in social gatherings"[28]—that was absent when the bureau analyzed the condition of other populations.

While the bureau did not label populations "white" in the narrative sections of their reports (as they did with nonwhite communities), they used other kinds of racialized terminology. Bureau did make reference to the benefit of its programs to "the race," which indicated a focus on the expanding population of whites.[29] As a pamphlet on the importance of milk for babies reminded mothers, "ultimate victory can come only to the nation that carefully conserves the stamina of its children, upon whom depends the future of the race."[30] Wendy Kline argues in *Building a Better Race* that although some have suggested that the term race had a more benign "human race" connotation, it cannot be separated from the larger context of race in America. In her analysis of the eugenics movement, positive eugenics (i.e., the development of a good stock of mothers and therefore children) was focused on white, middle-class women, as was the Children's Bureau.[31] Similarly, in the publication put out recounting a 1919 conference on child welfare, a bureau author noted in the summary that childhood is crucial to "civilization of a race."[32] This publication also included a talk by Professor Kelley Miller of Howard University on "Racial Factors," in which the professor insisted that "the Negro is part of the body politic."[33] This paper, however, was drowned out by rest of the talks from the conference, which continued to segregate the population they studied.

The Sheppard-Towner Act, the premier prenatal legislation of the Children's Bureau's tenure, best exemplifies the focus on white children's social citizenship—the right of children to have their well-being a matter of national interest. The act (passed in 1921) provided funds for education for mothers around the country, particularly in areas that were not well served by the medical profession. Although this legislation was set up to benefit the entire American population, its priorities reflected the racial makeup of the ideal citizen. In addition, the implementation of the act differed depending on the location. States were to administer the act; therefore, in the territories of the US, Hawaii, Puerto Rico, and the Philippines its implementation was quite different. Focusing on race and place allows us to unpack the assumptions about social citizenship made in this program.

In the Sheppard-Towner Act, the bureau showed particular concern for rural areas. Many historians have commented on the bureau's focus on rural America in their Progressive-era work. Molly Ladd-Taylor, in her monograph on child welfare, *Mother-Work,* suggests the importance of a shared vision of motherhood between the activists of the bureau and the mothers they worked with. She argues that the focus on rural women mirrored the background of the women of the bureau, the Midwestern origins of Lathrop and Abbott being just two examples of this. However, there was more in play than simply the background of the staff—and Abbott and her staff would certainly have taken offense at the charge that they were favoring particular women. They saw their programs as universal (at least for American citizens).

The Sheppard-Towner Act best exemplifies the development of a notion of social citizenship—the right of children to a basic standard of care that ensured well-being—in the activities of the bureau. Its programs provided funding to educate *all* women on maternal and infant hygiene. It did not include provisions to test the needs of particular women or demand some other qualification to access its programs. The act provided for developing materials to be distributed by mobile health units, working with state agencies to bring public nurses to various underserved areas, and assisting states in developing their own programs to reduce infant mortality. Sheppard-Towner exemplified the goals of the bureau, letting mothers and children know that their health was a national priority and that they had a right to some kind of care from the state and federal government.

The administration of Children's Bureau programs in the territories and reservations of the United States was fundamentally different from that in the states. Legislation authorizing the program had to include a special sanction to extend the program to Hawaii, Puerto Rico, and Alaska.[34] Federal employees generally organized and staffed programs in Puerto Rico and the Philippines, and the Bureau of Indian Affairs employees staffed programs conducted on reservations, as opposed to state programs, which used their own employees and the local organizations.

The child welfare activities undertaken in the territories under Sheppard-Towner in many ways echo the work with African Americans in the states. Both involved experts from outside and of a different "race" instructing locals on child-rearing, and the attitude toward the local populations was similar. As the bureau's report on child welfare in Puerto Rico in 1923 put it condescendingly, "it has been difficult to teach the people to use vegetables."[35] The report went on to point to improvements in literacy and sanitation since Americans took over the island through the use of American officials and some Puerto Rican employees.[36]

In administering these programs, the Children's Bureau demonstrated an anthropological attitude about the residents of the territories similar to that used in describing African American communities in the South. For example, their report on child welfare regarded the racial makeup of the island as an intricate part of the improvement of child welfare. "While some families have prided themselves upon preserving their blood unmixed the population in general is a product of the mixture of races. The prevailing type is Spanish, with occasional evidence of the addition of Indian or negro blood."[37] This comes in the section of the report that outlines the history and culture of the island but relies on the author's visual evidence of racial difference. It is difficult to see why such an observation was included in a report on child welfare work, but it is indicative of a general equation of race and the possibility of civilization. Work with children also came with a host of other interventions meant to modernize and civilize the island's residents in such spheres as sanitation, diet, and housing, but it was not always clear that this uplift was possible.[38]

The difference between the administration of Sheppard-Towner in the white population of the states and that in the territories and African American regions of the South reflects larger conceptions of race and citizenship in America. White children took center stage in the programs of the Children's Bureau because they were the valuable future citizens of the American nation. The children of African American sharecroppers, Puerto Ricans, or Mexicans were not brought into citizenship because they did not share the European heritage of the nation. As Grace Abbott reveals in a 1930 letter about the effect of the Depression on Puerto Rico: "Unfortunately the appeals for our local situation are almost sure to interfere with it [campaigns for funds for Puerto Rican children], because while the Porto Rican [*sic*] children belong to us, they do not seem to do so directly as the children of the unemployed."[39] Unlike the "children of the unemployed," who were not specified in terms of race or origin, the Puerto Rican children remained outside of the imagined community of the nation.

Campaigns for children's health included state-sponsored "Better Baby" contests and health fairs, which focused on children's bodies. At these events, children would be weighed and measured and compared against one another by their overall health score. Each child's relative measurement was based upon his or her "familial and racial types."[40] The majority of these events were single-"race"—meaning that they needed to be white or nonwhite. A few health fairs were also held by the Bureau of Indian Affairs on reservations.

The materials the Children's Bureau used to promote the Sheppard-Towner Act and other activities to reduce infant mortality and improve children's health featured images of healthy, rosy-cheeked white children being cared for by white doctors and nurses. These children were literal pictures of health and an example of what the bureau could achieve for the nation as a whole. The promotional materials on the child health conferences and other activities included photos of the ideal health conference and past activities: in one, a white child is being fussed over by an official-looking, uniformed nurse and a doctor, with a well-dressed mother beaming at the child. The exam itself is watched through glass by other attendees at the conference. At the conference as well as in the photograph, the baby's body is on display to promote the health of all babies.[41]

Most important, however, is that the image displayed the white baby as the standard ideal of what a baby should be. The display of childhood—of the healthy normal baby—is also a model of what the nation can and should produce for itself. As Shawn Michelle Smith has recently argued in *American Archives*,[42] pictures of children functioned as a way of proving the wealth and privilege of a family in the nineteenth century. Used in the context of a federal publication, photos of children were a display of the material successes of the American nation in the twentieth. The images in the Children's Bureau materials displayed the white child, and pointedly not the nonwhite child, as a product of the civilized society.

In contrast, the photographs of child welfare conferences on African Americans and of "natives" (American, Puerto Rican, or Hawaiian) are primitive-looking and emphasize the general unfitness of the lives of their families. A photograph of "An examination at a Negro conference" from *Maternity and Child Care in Selected Rural Counties of MS* (1921) shows an African American mother and child with a white woman examining the baby. Unlike the previous photo from a child health conference, this appears to take place outside, with little other interest in the baby. In the first photo, all of the attention is on the baby itself, including an audience behind the window; in this mother and baby are focused on the camera and the child is not attended by extra professionals. A photograph from Puerto Rico's Baby Week shows a baby clinic held in a schoolhouse—again, a location not normally used for health work. This photo shows mothers, some fathers, and uniformed nurses proudly holding babies for the camera. The accompanying text informs the reader that "the nurses made regular follow-up visits and taught the mothers how to prepare food for their babies, and other elements of child care,"[43] instructions that not all mothers apparently needed.

The reality of health fairs in Puerto Rico recalls that the American dominion included not only the states, but also the territories. By the time the bureau was founded, the US claimed Puerto Rico, the Philippines, Guam, and Hawaii in addition to the reservations of American Indians. The administration of the programs of the Children's Bureau in the territories of the United States was fundamentally different from that in the states. In contrast to state programs, federal employees generally staffed programs in Puerto Rico and the Philippines. Bureau of Indian Affairs employees staffed programs held on reservations. Presumably these areas did not have the experts necessary to run such programs, which in fact became part of the larger rationale for holding these areas as part of the American empire.

In arguing for new programs in general, the bureau drew comparisons between the United States and other civilized nations. Britain in particular was called upon to show what America was not doing. As Lathrop put it: "naturally enough Great Britain and her colonies present to this country the most accessible and abundant material upon every subject in the field of child welfare."[44] Canada, New Zealand, and Australia are also specifically named by Lathrop as examples of what Americans can do for children in wartime. Importantly, she does not specify what British colonial possessions such as India or those in Africa are doing to maintain standards of labor for women and children, only areas marked as white.[45]

New Zealand has a special place in the history of progressive reform as a model as well as a settler colony. Peter Coleman argues in his monograph *Progressivism and the World of Reform* that New Zealand's undertakings in infant mortality prevention, minimum wage, and labor were all crucial to the American progressive project. For him, the incidence of intellectuals conducting research on New Zealand and using it for advocacy made the role of this nation pivotal.[46] The Children's Bureau published several studies that detailed the work New Zealand had done in improving the lives of infants and children.[47] The symbolism of New Zealand and its history as a white, settler colony is important for understanding its impact on the relationship between progressivist reform and racialized citizenship, although Coleman does not deal with this. New Zealand, with its population of indigenous but unmentioned Maori, shared with the United States segregation built on racial hierarchies. In the studies of New Zealand's welfare system, as well as in Coleman's analysis, racial difference does not even merit a mention. Rather, race was rendered invisible and the society of the island was portrayed as idyllic.[48] The New Zealander was simply white.

In the decades that followed the implementation of the Sheppard-Towner Act, the Children's Bureau declined in importance. The final version of the Social Security Act assigned administration of Aid to Dependent Children (ADC) to local agencies, rather than to the Children's Bureau. Each locale had its own rate of monetary compensation, and each bureau was subject to the whims of its staff in terms of who was "fit" for assistance. Unlike the old age pension system or even the unemployment benefit system under the Social Security Act, where monetary benefits were given when individuals met defined criteria, ADC required an investigation of potential recipients' moral fitness in many places, including "suitable home" and "fit mother" requirements.[49] Left to ADC were the single mothers and women whose husbands did not qualify under the programs of the Social Security Act—migrant workers, illegal aliens, and the descendents of slaves. As political scientist Suzanne Mettler and others have effectively argued, ADC functioned as a catch-up program for those who did not fit the other security programs. Since it was at the whim of local authorities, it was also subject to the needs of local landowners and farmers.[50] Historian Linda Gordon notes in *Pitied But Not Entitled* that African American women were routinely denied ADC to keep them in the field during the harvests.[51]

In her recent monograph *The Failed Century of the Child,* Judith Sealander argues that American public policy in the twentieth century failed in its stated goals to guarantee a decent standard of health and security to all of its children. She points to what she terms contrary tendencies in American culture and thinking about childhood. While Americans wanted small government, they were willing to accept some intervention for the sake of improving childhood. Children were rhetorically supported, but those who worked with them—i.e., teachers, day care workers, etc.—were underpaid. In theory all children were supported, but in reality racist policies determined who received good services and who did not.[52] Despite her critiques of the welfare state as a whole, she maintains a faith in the idea of social support in the basic way it has been practiced and a sense that racism was to some degree separate from the welfare state. Racism, according to Sealander, interfered with its proper functioning, but was not constitutive of it.

In examining the work of the Children's Bureau, we can see the ways in which instituting care for children was based on the model, white, future citizen. This discursive, statistical, and material construction is vital to understanding the racial content of welfare. In order to help to parse out the current obsession with the welfare dependency and with the burden of illegal immigrants, we must look at the history of race and status in child welfare work. It is these populations— Mexican and African American—that particularly do not fit into the conception of citizenship envisioned with these programs. This discussion also helps us to consider the ways in which race and migration are built into the very foundations of assistance to childhood.

Notes

1. This term, "social citizenship," was coined by British scholar T. H. Marshall in his essay "Citizenship and Social Class" in *Citizenship and Social Class and Other Essays*, ed. T. H. Marshall (Cambridge, 1950).

2. See for example Gail Bederman, *Manliness and Civilization: A Cultural History of Gender and Race in the United States, 1880–1917* (Chicago, 1995); Tracey Boisseau, *White Queen: May French-Sheldon and the Imperial Origins of American Feminist Identity* (Bloomington, 2004); and Laura Wexler, *Tender Violence: Domestic Visions in an Age of US Imperialism* (Chapel Hill, 2000).

3. See Viviana Zelizer, *Pricing the Priceless Child: The Changing Social Value of Children* (Princeton, 1994).

4. See Joanne Goodwin, *Gender and the Politics of Welfare Reform: Mother's Pensions in Chicago, 1911–1929* (Chicago, 1997); and Molly Ladd-Taylor, *Mother-Work: Women, Child Welfare and the State, 1890–1930* (Champaign, 1994), 135–166.

5. Ladd-Taylor, *Mother-work*, 149 and Gwendolyn Mink, *The Wages of Motherhood: Inequality in the Welfare State, 1917–1942* (Ithaca, 1995).

6. Kriste Lindenmeyer, *"A Right to Childhood": The U.S. Children's Bureau and Child Welfare, 1912–1946* (Urbana, 1997), 10.

7. Wendy Kline, *Building a Better Race: Gender, Sexuality, and Eugenics from the Turn-of-the-Century to the Baby Boom* (Berkeley, 2001), especially chap. 1.

8. Grace L. Meigs, MD, *Maternal Morality from All Conditions Connected with Childbirth in the US and Certain Other Countries*, Children's Bureau Publication (Washington, D.C., 1917).

9. See Seth Koven and Sonya Michel, eds. *Mothers of a New World: Maternalist Policies and the Origins of Welfare States* (New York, 1993) and Kathryn Kish Sklar, *Florence Kelley and the Nation's Work* (New Haven, 1995).

10. Letter of transmittal by Julia Lathrop, in Mrs. Max West, *Prenatal Care* (Washington, D.C., 1913), 5.

11. Dorothy Reed Mendenhall, *Milk, Indispensable Food for Children* (Washington, D.C., 1918), 29.

12. Letter from G.W. Missouri to Mrs. West dated 29 May 1918 in Molly Ladd-Taylor, ed., *Raising a Baby the Government Way: Mothers' Letters to the Children's Bureau, 1915–1932* (New Brunswick, NJ, 1986), 61.

13. See Ladd-Taylor, *Raising a Baby the Government Way.*

14. West, *Prenatal Care*, 7.

15. Bruce Bellingham and Mary Pugh Mathis, "Race, Citizenship and the Bio-Politics of the Maternalist Welfare State: 'Traditional' Midwifery in the American South Under the Sheppard-Towner Act, 1921–29," *Social Politics* 1, no. 2 (1994): 157–189.

16. Mrs. Max West, *Infant Care* (Washington, D.C., 1914), 50. On standards of American health in the tropics see also Warwick Anderson, "Immunities of Empire: Race, Disease and the New Tropical Medicine, 1900–1920," *Bulletin of the History of Medicine* 70, no. 1 (1996): 94–118.

17. Zelizer, *Pricing the Priceless Child.*

18. Grace Abbott, "Looking Fore and Aft in Child Labor," *The Survey* 63 (1929): 333.

19. See Children's Bureau publications *State Child Labor Standards* (Washington, D.C., 1924); *Administration of Child Labor Laws* (Washington, D.C., 1924); *Work of Children on Truck and Small-fruit Farms in Southern NJ (Washington*, D.C., 1924); *Child Labor in North Dakota* (Washington, D.C., 1923), and *Child Labor and the Welfare Anthracite Coal Mines* (Washington, D.C., 1922).

20. See Sonya Michel, *Children's Interests/Mothers' Rights: The Shaping of America's Child Care Policy* (New Haven, 1999), 102–104. Michel also notes that bureau workers thought agricultural

work was less dangerous that machine work (102), but I believe it also has to do with who was performing agricultural labor in certain areas of the country.

21. Grace Abbott, "A National Minimum of Protection for the Working Child," Central Files: 1921–1924, Box 222, Folder: 8-4-1, Record Group 102, Records of the United States Children's Bureau, National Archives, College Park, MD (hereafter USCB), 2.

22. Ibid.

23. Grace Abbott, "Child Labor Since 1929," sent to *Encyclopedia Britannica* 4-29-37, Box 25, Folder 2, in papers of Grace and Edith Abbott, Special Collections, Regenstein Library, University of Chicago, Chicago, IL (hereafter GEA papers), 1.

24. Grace Abbott to Mrs. Maud J. Mills, Secretary, Columbia County Farm Bureau, Oregon, 1 April 1924, Box 40, Folder 11, GEA papers, 1.

25. See Dorothy Ross, *The Origins of American Social Science* (Cambridge, 1991), in particular chap. 5, "The Liberal Revision of American Exceptionalism."

26. Robert Morese Woodbury, *Statures and Weights of Children under Six Years of Age* (Washington, D.C., 1921).

27. Julia Lathrop, "Mothers to the Rescue: What Should the Government Do to Protect Maternity and Infancy?" *The Woman's Journal* 14, no. 2 (1929): 9. On African American midwives see Bellingham and Mathis, "Race, Citizenship and the Bio-Politics of the Maternalist Welfare State."

28. Frances Sage Bradley, MD, and Margaretta Williamson, *Rural Children in Selected Counties of North Carolina* (Washington, D.C., 1918), 55.

29. For more on the expansion of "whiteness" see Matthew Frye Jacobson, *Whiteness of a Different Color: European Immigrants and the Alchemy of Race* (Cambridge, 1998).

30. Mendenhall, *Milk*, 29.

31. Kline, *Building a Better Race*, 5.

32. *Standards of Child Welfare, Report of Children's Bureau Conference May and June 1919* (Washington, D.C., 1919), 11.

33. Ibid., 67.

34. "Administration of the Maternity and Infancy Act," Central File 1921–1924, Box 240, File 11-0, USCB.

35. Helen Barry, *Child Welfare in the Insular Possessions of the United States, Part I Porto Rico* (Washington, D.C., 1923), 16.

36. Ibid., 5.

37. Ibid., 3.

38. See Laura Briggs, *Reproducing Empire: Race, Sex and US Imperialism in Puerto Rico* (Berkeley, 1998) and Eileen Findlay, *Imposing Decency: The Politics of Sexuality and Race in Puerto Rico, 1870–1920* (Durham, 1999).

39. Grace Abbott to Dr. S.J. Crumbine, American Child Health Association, 4 November 1930, Central File 1929–1932, Box 403, File: 7-3-0-7-4, USCB, 1.

40. Ada Schweitzer, MD, "Better Baby Contest at State Fair," Central File 1921–1924, Box 246, File 11-16-2 USCB.

41. Photograph in Anna Louise Strong, *Child Welfare Exhibits: Types and Preparation* (Washington, D.C., 1915).

42. Shawn Michelle Smith, *American Archives: Gender, Race and Class in a Visual Culture* (Princeton, 1999).

43. Barry, *Child Welfare in the Insular Possessions of the United States*.

44. Julia Lathrop, "The Children's Bureau in War Time," *North American Review* 206, no. 744 (1917): 735.

45. Ibid., 739.

46. Peter Coleman, *Progressivism and the World of Reform: New Zealand and the Origins of the American Welfare State* (Lawrence, 1987).

47. See Etta Goodwin, *New Zealand Society for Health of Women and Children: Examples of Methods of Baby Saving Work in Small Towns and Rural Districts* (Washington, D.C., 1914) and *Infant Mortality and Preventative Work in New Zealand* (Washington, D.C., 1922).

48. Antoinette Burton, "New Narratives of Imperial Politics in the Nineteenth Century," in *At Home With Empire*, ed. Catherine Hall and Sonya Rose (Cambridge, 2007).

49. Suzanne Mettler, *Dividing Citizens: Gender and Federalism in New Deal Public Policy* (Ithaca, 1998), 164.

50. See Robert Lieberman's *Shifting the Color Line: Race and the American Welfare State* (Cambridge, 1988) for more on the ways in which ADC was granted and withdrawn in order to keep African American women in fields.

51. Linda Gordon, *Pitied But Not Entitled: Single Mothers and the History of Welfare* (Cambridge, 1994), 276.

52. Judith Sealander, *The Failed Century of the Child: Governing America's Young in the Twentieth Century* (Cambridge, 2003).

Chapter 3

FROM REFORM PEDAGOGY TO WAR PEDAGOGY
Education Reform before 1914 and
the Mobilization for War in Germany

Andrew Donson

In North America and Western Europe at the end of the nineteenth century, optimism and rising prosperity inspired a host of teachers, politicians, students, activist women, state officials, and self-professed pedagogues to found institutions and get laws passed to make young people more reliable and productive. Germany applied special vigor to these efforts. Graduates of its world-renowned universities pioneered new spheres of social sciences, such as adolescent psychology, that produced spirited reformers and lent rational legitimacy to their claims. Because of its long tradition of founding clubs, Germany also had more private and professional associations than other countries, and these groups were in position to organize support for progressive change. At the turn of the century, Germany also had more journals and institutes devoted to the science of raising reliable and productive youth, and professors, teachers, private researchers, and youth advocates produced a wide-ranging and prodigious body of criticism and practical suggestions. Today scholars refer to this corpus as reform pedagogy (*Reformpädagogik*).

Before the First World War, advocates of this reform pedagogy often clashed with the conservatives who controlled the highest positions of power. Wilhelm II and his ministers wanted pliant subjects and spent political capital to rebut reforms aimed at empowering citizens. Trying to please their superiors, education administrators and many teachers in elementary and secondary schools accordingly favored conservative methods and curricula, such as liberal use of corporal punishment and staid textbooks extolling the Hohenzollern dynasty. Such approaches to instruction tended to smother pupils' individuality and free thinking and prevent challenges to established authority.

Notes from this chapter begin on page 81.

During the war, however, the disputes over education reform subsided because the advocates of change convinced officials, and Germans more generally, that their child-centered (*vom Kind aus*) teaching methods reinforced patriotism. The reformers and the teachers who carried out their ideas subsequently spearheaded a political mobilization that emboldened Germans to hold out for military victory, helping to fulfill the army's goal using all possible resources available for the war effort (youth and children made up close to half of the civilian population). Under a movement that became known as war pedagogy (*Kriegspädagogik*), teachers encouraged boys to fantasize about themselves as soldiers and urged girls to be willing to sacrifice for Germany without complaint. The combination of nationalism and child-centered teaching methods is perhaps surprising in a militarized society subject to mass conscription and martial law, but because of the *Burgfrieden* (party truce of August 1914) and the perception of unity around the war among the political parties, most administrators trusted that teachers and pupils were reliable patriots. Under war pedagogy, officials permitted teachers to implement reform teaching methods, such as writing autobiographical essays, which had been controversial before the war because they mitigated the authority of the teacher and gave schoolchildren opportunities for individual self-expression. Though the heyday of war pedagogy lasted only sixteen months, teachers following its methods arguably reinforced commitment to the war for far longer. Their experiments with teaching methods also heartened them to undertake more extensive reforms after the war.

Educational Reform before 1914

Scholarship on education has lagged behind other fields in the history of turn-of-the-century Germany and remains dominated by an interpretation that supposes teaching methods were especially stern, even cruel, and that the curriculum glorified the military and Germany's increasingly aggressive nationalism.[1] While evidence from memoirs and books by turn-of-the-century foreign observers support that schools were authoritarian, the charge that schools were jingoist and militarist is harder to substantiate. Furthermore, although German teaching methods (with some notable exceptions) remained authoritarian until 1914, numerous writers criticized them in the reform pedagogy movement.

The severity in schools was in part a response to the state's imperative to instill obedience in Germany's youngest citizens who might as adults turn to Social Democracy and reject the constitutional monarchy. The severity also had to do with the rank of secondary school teachers as state officials, a status that gave parents little recourse to challenge. The Prussian state under Wilhelm II never gave elementary school teachers recognition as full civil servants, a privilege that secondary school teachers enjoyed, but this inferiority only motivated them to be strict in the hopes of proving they were reliable executors of the state's will and thus deserving of promotion. In many elementary (*Volksschulen, Gemeindeschu-*

len, etc.) and secondary schools (*Gymnasien, Realgymnasien,* etc.), disparaging and physically maltreating pupils were accepted practices. American observers of German schools were generally appalled at the endless drills and rote memorization that required pupils to reproduce their teachers' views exactly. German memoirists recalled how they feared their teachers and were enervated by the monotonous repetition in school. This approach to schoolchildren was far from universal—female elementary school teachers, who enjoyed one of the most distinguished careers available to women, harbored less resentment and were less strict. But the teaching profession in Germany was overwhelmingly male: whereas female elementary school teachers composed 80 percent of the profession in England and 60 percent in France, in Germany they accounted for just 20 percent. Schooling bore the general imprint of a male culture that valued giving orders and having them obeyed. Elementary and secondary school teachers generally aimed to get pupils to accept authoritarian ways and social hierarchies in Germany. By most assessments, they achieved this goal.[2]

Some evidence suggests that teachers and education officials also aimed to instill, in addition to blind obedience, crass nationalism and militarism. Secondary school teachers were far overrepresented as a profession in radical nationalist groups like the Pan-German League and tended to be enthusiasts of imperialism. Many were reserve officers, and almost all were devoted to the German army and navy. Likewise, though elementary school teachers generally voted for the left-liberal Progressive Party, they too clamored for the privilege of becoming reserve officers, along with the opportunities and social prestige the appointment bestowed. Few in the government doubted their patriotism or their respect for the military. Many descriptions of school curricula in autobiographies note the emphasis on German superiority and the legitimacy of the Hohenzollern dynasty. War was cast as a valid instrument to achieve political aims and as an exercise in manliness, and the army was described as a prestigious institution that could unite a conflicted nation. Indeed, after the ascension of Wilhelm II in 1890, schools at all levels devoted more time to national holidays, gave more emphasis to war in history curricula, and introduced songs in music instruction that praised soldiering and the sacrifice of life for the nation.[3]

However, the introduction of more militarism and nationalism faced resistance from educators who found brash imperialism distasteful and respected the old curricula. The number of weekly hours devoted to German (as opposed to the classical or modern languages) in the secondary schools rose just barely or not at all after 1890. In many elementary school curricula, the number of hours of German even declined. Even though turn-of-the-century German historians wanted to establish the legitimacy of the German Empire and the Kaiser, they generally refused to write excessively nationalist history textbooks. They preferred a sober and objective style and did not glorify war itself. Furthermore, increasing numbers of self-professed pedagogues, some openly pacifist, braved censure and repulsed attempts by the far right to introduce jingoist texts into school libraries and curricula. In sum, German schooling before 1914 was arguably authoritarian and severe in its methods but only moderately nationalist and militarist in its content. Some advocates of reform pedagogy before 1914 opposed this jingoism, but most did not care one way or another. Like the German middle class more generally, most were moderately nationalist.[4]

Reform-minded pedagogues' primary goal was to revive and put into practice the educational theories pioneered by early nineteenth-century education theorists like Johann Pestalozzi and Friedrich Fröbel. They hoped to thereby redress the severe teaching styles that stifled creativity, self-esteem, and critical thinking. Many took inspiration from the Swedish pedagogue Ellen Key, whose *Century of the Child* was translated into German in 1902 and called for a child-centered pedagogy that respected and nurtured a pupil's individuality.[5]

Their suggestions on how to achieve this goal were innovative and wide-ranging. Some, like Georg Kerschensteiner, the chair of the municipal school board in Munich and a Progressive Party delegate in the Reichstag, and Hugo Gaudig, a director of a girl's secondary school in Leipzig, criticized the drill teaching methods for spoon-feeding knowledge rather than developing skills and character. Both suggested an alternative "activity school" (*Arbeitsschule*) that would raise schoolchildren to be productive and responsible citizens in a constitutional state. In 1909 Kerschensteiner founded such a model school in a working-class neighborhood in Dortmund. In the first months of school, pupils established trust with their teacher through games, songs, and storytelling and only afterward began learning reading and arithmetic. The schools also had laboratories, aquariums, natural lighting, and other features that made them lively and stimulating. Other reformers, like Berthold Otto, wanted to create an environment more conducive to learning by making schools more like families. In Otto's model "home teaching school" (*Hauslehrerschule*) teachers were free from any prescribed curriculum and taught according to the wishes of their pupils. The schoolchildren expressed their interests in a weekly one-hour "community education" (*Gesamtunterricht*), during which they decided on their own themes for instruction for the following week. Like Gaudig's and Kerschensteiner's activity schools, Otto's home teaching school granted pupils some authority to self-govern. Pupils decided how to discourage and discipline absenteeism, for example.[6]

Beyond these pedagogues, scores of other theorists and practitioners proposed different ways to raise more creative, productive, and good-natured youths. Their ideas ranged from making art the centerpiece of education to encouraging pupils to write autobiographical essays and fiction. These reformers had considerable support, in particular from the professional societies of elementary school teachers, who sponsored conferences and appealed to school administrators to allow them to put the new pedagogical ideas into practice. But outside more progressively liberal regions like the states of Baden, Thuringia, and Württemberg and cities like Berlin, Hamburg, and Leipzig, they had little support. Until the First World War, the conservatives running the education bureaucracies generally saw little reason to permit a child-centered pedagogy. To them it was soft, unmanly, ineffective, and politically dangerous because the methods could potentially stimulate working-class challenges to state authority. Among rural and small-town elementary school teachers notable for their conservatism, reform pedagogy was far from the mainstream.

War Pedagogy

In the months following the outbreak of war in August 1914, German schooling at all levels underwent an unprecedented change in goals, tenor, content, and methods. The militarist and nationalist content of the curriculum in most classrooms took a quantum leap. In many cases, war pervaded *all* subjects in schools—German, history, religion, gymnastics, natural science, handwork, even mathematics. Because martial law silenced antiwar critics, and most Germans believed that supporting national defense trumped everything else, teachers in elementary and secondary schools could introduce the new content—letters by soldiers, war sermons by clergy, eulogies to fallen heroes, songs with violent lyrics, and graphic descriptions of battles—without criticism from the left.

This content was graphic, jingoist, and bellicose. Letters from the front were supposed to excite students about the thrill of war. Religious instruction presented the conflict as a holy war, an undertaking willed by God to purge Germany of modern sin and apostasy. Favored passages from the Bible included the Old Testament stories about the warriors Joshua, Samson, David, and the Maccabees. To practice arithmetic, teachers on occasion had their pupils calculate the tons of ammunition needed to annihilate a French division.[7] Whole assemblies of teachers and schoolchildren celebrated with speeches, songs, and slide shows of the front.[8] In art class, schoolchildren drew violent pictures of combat and submitted them to exhibitions and competitions.[9] History instruction did away with the tiresome narratives of German kings and focused almost wholly on either past wars or the present war's origins, weapons, tactics, strategies, and heroism.[10] Pupils brought into class examples of the millions of popular war poems published by ordinary citizens.[11] On plaques, in speeches, and during moments of silence, schoolchildren honored fallen soldiers, their fighting teachers, and winners of the Iron Cross, the army's award for bravery.[12]

Although teachers and pedagogues agreed that gender should shape learning, the curriculum for boys and girls under war pedagogy was often the same. Over 60 percent of elementary schoolchildren in Prussia learned in coeducational classrooms, particularly in small cities, towns, and the countryside. The boys and girls sat on opposite sides of the room, but they had the same lessons and read the same material. By law until 1916 they also uniformly had male teachers. There was more possibility to create curricula specific to gender in big city schools with enough rooms to segregate the sexes, but under war pedagogy the female teachers who taught most of the all-girl classes regularly used the same material and methods as the male teachers in the coed or all-boy classes. The female teachers encouraged girls to read the daily reports of the High Command, study maps of the war, and bring both to school for discussion.[13] Schoolgirls also compared Roman strategy in the Punic Wars to contemporary British naval policy; studied battleships, torpedo boats, and submarines; wrote essays about the siege of Antwerp and the fall of the fortress at Liège; and kept war diaries that chronicled the battles and victories of the German army.[14] Such activities were in accordance with orders by the Prussia provincial governors, such as the one in Stettin in October 1914 that asked teachers to instruct boys as well as girls in topography and military strategy.[15] In their war compositions, girls and boys alike fantasized about combat. In memoirs and oral histories, even schoolgirls who later opposed the war greeted the militarism and nationalism enthusiastically in 1914 and 1915.[16]

Most teachers and pedagogues nonetheless thought that because boys would become soldiers and girls wives tending the home front, the war accentuated differences in gender roles. Lessons on writing original compositions and interpreting war poems and stories accordingly encouraged boys to imagine becoming fearless soldiers, prepared to die or endure wounds and privation for Germany's victory. This ultimate sacrifice for country was for boys in the future, but for girls the moment was now to show the ultimate feminine virtues in war: selflessness, thriftiness, and steadfast, cheerful support of men and Germany, whatever the hardship. The lessons targeting girls with these ideas were sometimes practical and to the point, as when a teacher had her schoolgirls calculate the number of wheat rolls a family could save weekly if everyone had oatmeal for breakfast.[17] Other times they embraced a larger moral imperative of making deep sacrifices and accepting suffering in order to bring about victory. For example, a Catholic schoolteacher read to her pupils the poem "Heroine," about a woman who endured the hardship of the war and ultimately the death of her husband, who "sacrificed his life for freedom! / Died in the Father's name for the Reich and Throne." The teacher emphasized that the father died in peace because he knew his wife would devote herself to her children.[18]

War pedagogy's most peculiar trait was that the education officials softened their demands that teachers maintain the old authoritarian methods. Their reasons were several. First, after thousands of administrators and tens of thousands of teachers left their posts for the army, it was practically impossible to maintain the peacetime school regulations. Bureaucratic oversight weakened, and the depleted ranks of administrators recognized that the few remaining teachers had to adapt their classroom practices to new burdens, such as increased class size and pupils whose attention was distracted by the excitement of the war mobilization.[19]

Second, officials believed that because of the extraordinary political unity around the allegedly defensive war under the *Burgfrieden,* the danger lessened that reform teaching practices—ones that encouraged self-expression in young people—would result in schoolchildren voicing anti-militarist or anti-nationalist sentiment. In addition, the conservative press, which had hounded the education bureaucracies before the war to introduce more nationalist curricula, was elated with war pedagogy and urged administrators and the public to refrain from criticizing teachers.[20]

Lastly, school officials were comforted by the absence of opposition to the war in the public sphere. Though the silence was in part a result of self-censorship and the threat of government action against critics, it seemed to officials—they in fact claimed this repeatedly in their decrees and reports—that German youth were universally patriotic. Before 1914, many administrators had criticized the methods that encouraged schoolchildren's personal expressions because the ideas of young people were mundane sentiments about pets and weather, not valuable concepts about geography, history, religion, or any of the other subjects the pre-scribed lessons plans required instructors to teach. But now schoolchildren were engaging with what officials believed were more valuable subjects: nationalism, military strategy and tactics, the organization of the army, and the self-sacrifice of ordinary citizens for a national cause. School administrators saw the war as an excellent opportunity to instill in German youth patriotism and respect for national unity. It also seemed inappropriate for teachers to be haughty and aloof when so many schoolchildren were patriotic, committed to the war, and had fathers and brothers risking their lives in the army.[21]

The provision that enabled teachers to experiment with new methods and content was the abandonment of formal lessons plans (*Lehrpläne*). Enforced by state school inspectors before the war in Prussia and other states, the lesson plans were the primary way that government regulated what happened in the class-room. They stipulated topics and hours to be spent on them. Not surprisingly, the debates over curricula always centered on the efficacy of the lesson plans.[22] The most progressive-minded teachers and reformers wanted the plans to be more flexible to enable pedagogical experimentation. But few in the bureaucracy were willing to budge on them. That obstinacy ended in August 1914. Impro-visation resulted in part from dealing with the practical difficulties of running schools in wartime. More deeply, the Prussian Ministry of Education recognized the benefits of pedagogical experimentation for the national mobilization.[23]

The use of newspapers in classrooms during the war is a good example of how the war permitted the introduction of reform methods. Before the war, most administrators banned newspapers in classrooms because they were believed to expose schoolchildren to the sordidness of German class politics. But the end of political dissent made patriotism appear hegemonic in newspapers. In this situation, administrators permitted reform-minded teachers to ask pupils to cull articles from newspapers. Teachers now regularly used them in class to develop research skills and direct the curriculum toward schoolchildren's interests about the war.[24]

Another example of the reform aspects of war pedagogy was the physical envi-ronment of the classroom. Almost all descriptions of classrooms in elementary and secondary schools before 1914 painted a gloomy atmosphere. Classroom walls were bare and gray. Without decoration, they looked like military barracks. This dullness, foreign observers argued, reinforced the general pedagogical goal of breaking the individuality of pupils and encouraging conformity.[25] A goal of most reformers before the war was to remedy the blandness of the school environment, and in the war pedagogy classroom, the physical environment of classrooms indeed took on a more festive and colorful air.[26] The walls were adorned with maps of the front, flags marking the battles, photos of pupils on collection drives, and pictures of generals, trenches, machine guns, airplanes, and submarines, all cut from magazines and assembled into posters. Ribbons from victory holidays remained in classrooms after the celebrations. Many schoolchildren's own artwork—architectural drawings of trenches, depictions of dogfights and the like—hung in classrooms.[27] Images of war were not exactly what the reformers had in mind when they sought to enliven the classroom before 1914, but teachers under war pedagogy certainly adopted the reformers' principles. Teachers innovated by combining the reformers' suggestions with militarism and nationalism. In general, the war implemented the goals of two educational movements, movements that had been separate before 1914: reform teaching methods and militarist and nationalist curricula.

Schoolchildren's War Compositions

Evidence of how writing lessons changed under war pedagogy provides the richest and most detailed illustration of how educational reform coalesced with nationalist and militarist goals. Before the war, the dominant way of teaching writing was to use so-called fixed compositions (*gebundene Aufsätze*). In this method, the teacher provided, either orally or schematically, not only the composition's content but also its thesis, style, structure, evidence, development, and conclusion. The resulting compositions, foreign observers remarked, were highly uniform.[28] Defenders claimed that fixed compositions were the proven way to produce essays that were elegant, logical, orderly, and syntactically correct. In truth, writing instruction in the German lands had been far less constrained until the mid nineteenth century. The dominance of fixed compositions was a consequence of the expansion of public elementary schooling and the controls states hoped to exert over the populace. By the 1870s they had become dominant in secondary schools as well.[29]

In the decade before the war, many wanted to replace fixed compositions with so-called free ones (*freie Aufsätze*)—that is, personal narratives, fictional stories, or expository essays in which the pupils independently chose the subject, conceived the form, or developed their own line of argument. The most sensational advocates of free compositions, the Hamburg elementary school teachers Adolf Jensen and Wilhelm Lamszus, charged that a pupil could not learn to write "with the teacher's tongue sticking out and his whip behind him."[30] This advocacy of free compositions was a particularly sharp attack on the authoritarianism of Germany under Wilhelm II: the movement demanded that the state raise schoolchildren who could think for themselves rather than follow the orders of their teachers. It also came from below. Its most spirited proponents were almost exclusively elementary school teachers, who had not attended university. In this way, it contrasted with the other movements within reform pedagogy, whose innovators were usually university professors or university-trained researchers. Notably, most proponents of free compositions were pacifists; Lamszus was later dismissed for publishing his terrifying and prophetic *Das Menschenschlachthaus* [The Human Slaughterhouse] (1912), a novel about the nature of the coming industrial war.[31]

Opponents of free compositions countered that children's ideas were illogical, dull, and meaningless. In their favor, they could point to published collections of free compositions that addressed only the most mundane themes of everyday life—dogs, rainstorms, furniture, sunsets, Santa Claus, and the like.[32] Implicit in their criticism was also that free compositions were a departure from the benefits to the state of the authoritarian relationship between teacher and pupil. While some school districts allowed students to write them now and then, they were in general disparaged, particularly by principals and school inspectors. Older schoolteachers resisted them as well.[33]

However, the outbreak of the war generated new reasons to champion free compositions. Schoolchildren were witnessing the extraordinary mobilization of German military might, reading about the victories of the army, observing a time of putative national unity, and seeing common Germans sacrifice for their nation—all experiences that, administrators, reformers, and teachers agreed, were worth putting down on paper. Furthermore, because of the absence of public dissent and the perception of universal patriotism—a result of the *Burgfrieden*—political subjects, such as the organization of the military or the battles of soldiers, no longer raised controversy. Provincial administrators believed they helped preserve in pupils' memories "the great times."[34] With these encouragements and all prohibitions lifted, teachers openly experimented with free compositions.[35]

The result was that hundreds of free compositions written primarily in 1915 wound up in the hands of researchers studying the effect of the war on schoolchildren. For those interested in schoolchildren's voices, these compositions—altogether I found 1,286 personal and expository essays, fictional stories, and short autobiographical accounts—provide some of the richest material available to historians. To be sure, though their authors came from a variety of regions and social classes, they were not a representative sample of schoolchildren's views. With the exception of one researcher, collectors were biased in wanting to show how the methods and content of school curricula had changed in a way helpful for the war. Yet at the very least, the compositions show that many teachers experimented with free compositions to support the war and the national mobilization. They also provide a window into the ideology that teachers tried to instill under war pedagogy: an unwavering commitment to the war and the nation and an indulgence in the heroism of soldiers and the violence of battles.

The designation "free" needs to be placed into context: these compositions were written in schools under the supervision of teachers and selected for publication to show support for the war. Pupils never had complete freedom in choosing their topics, and it is impossible to measure the degree that pupils really believed what they wrote in these compositions. Suggestions of topics for free compositions invariably accorded with the nationalist agenda of war pedagogy, steering pupils toward jingoism and belligerency, as the following selection of the crassest topics shows:

How I Play War
Why I Would Like to Enter the War
Our Volunteers in the Army
Why Do We Hate England?
England's Jealousy
France's Old Hate and Desire for Revenge
The Apotheosis of Prussia in 1813 and the Mobilization in 1914
The Pious Cannot Remain in Peace When Evil Neighbors Do Not Fall
To What Extent Has the World War Produced an Upsurge in National Consciousness?[36]

Yet pupils could write what they wished under the rubrics. While this may not seem innovative to us today, it was in 1914 and 1915 in a German educational system that had previously stifled creativity and individuality. Because of the new pedagogical freedoms, pupils had more opportunity than before to take an original point of view and thereby take ownership of their writing.

By having pupils develop a positive perspective on the war in their own words, teachers under war pedagogy avoided crass indoctrination while still carrying out their aim of mobilizing their schoolchildren patriotically. Not surprisingly, in over 17 percent of the essays (209), the pupils described early victory celebrations (Liège, Tannenburg, Sedan Day 1914, Masurian Lakes) or asserted that a new patriotic spirit among soldiers and the population marked August 1914.[37] An additional 29 percent (367) described the front as an exciting war of movement with infantry that stormed trenches, zeppelins that dropped bombs on Paris, and generals like Hindenburg who took tens of thousands of Russians prisoners. Their battle scenes described impersonalized heroism. They detailed victories in blood, boots, and flying shrapnel but avoided the emotions of the war and accordingly anticipated the stylized cold soldier popularized after 1918 by Ernst Jünger.[38]

The compositions were venues in which boys and sometimes girls could fantasize, often graphically, about combat. The framing of their fantasies in the first person shows that teachers under war pedagogy encouraged or tacitly approved identification with the destruction of enemy property and life. Of the compositions my research located, over one fifth indulged in this violent masculine fantasy. They imagined themselves the subjects of the brutality:

If I were 18 years old, I would join the infantry … I would most like assault attacks. You can call out firm hurrahs during attacks. I would plunge into everything that came in my way with my bayonet.[39]

The gruesome details of killing were usually not spared:

> I only wish that I could be a soldier. Then I would like to stand across from the English, whose skulls I would smash with my rifle butt so that they would lose their hearing and sight.[40]

A fiction fantasized about catching an enemy patrol:

> Two French came near to me; with my sword I split the skull of the first. The other, who was already wounded, begged me for mercy.[41]

These fantasies highlighted youth's prowess, fearlessness, and superhuman strength.[42] Male schoolchildren wished for justice in the form of brutal physical punishment, particularly of the Russians and English.[43] The expressions sometimes came in poetic form. This one was written by a girl:

> Dear good Hindenburg, pound the Russians thoroughly
> Drive them into the sea, then they will scream and beg for mercy.[44]

One left-liberal researcher who analyzed the compositions claimed that these expressions represented an "actual emotional infection," but in their introductions all the other editors were all exuberant about the positive effect of the war on schoolchildren.[45] In my research in the pedagogical press I discovered only one other teacher who agreed that the compositions were "excessive in their rage."[46] War pedagogy may not have alone caused such hateful and violent fantasies— they were also a product of a more general climate of intensified nationalism and militarism—but it certainly encouraged them.

The pedagogy varied, of course, by region and individual teacher. Its reform methods were far more favored by urban elementary school teachers than rural ones or secondary school teachers. But even in areas considered most progressively liberal, such as Berlin and Leipzig, the content of the militarism and nationalism in the school curricula ratcheted up. The acceptance of war pedagogy was extraordinary: until January 1916, there was not a single outright criticism published in the pedagogical press.

A curriculum centered on the war was a phenomenon in all the belligerent nations. But Russian pedagogical theorists warned teachers about the risks to the psychological development of youth posed by violent war images.[47] Evidence suggests that English schools showed more restraint in using graphic images of warfare, as well.[48] French schools likewise reoriented lessons around the war, carrying out "a veritable revolution in content and methods." At the start of the 1914/15 school year, the French minister of public instruction issued a circular, asking teachers to engage pupils in the war and "salute the heroism of those who are pouring out their blood for liberty, for justice, for human rights." War was supposed to be at the center of the curriculum. But manuals for French elementary school teachers urged them to "love France and hate war." Teachers were supposed "to show children that war is odious and ignoble, a scourge that sows ruin and death." Furthermore, far more teachers took part in the peace movement in France than in Germany. The war imagery in the French curricula depicted enemy German soldiers as fierce and aggressive. The soldiers of the French Republic were the enlightened champions of progress and law. By contrast, in German war pedagogy the soldiers most often depicted as fierce and aggressive on the Western front were not French but German.[49]

The situation in Germany was most analogous to that in Italy, which in 1915 also instituted a system of "war education" with the goal of raising patriotic children. Schoolchildren read military bulletins, studied war geography, and did other patriotic activities. The national organization of Italian schoolteachers in fact constituted the main producer of prowar propaganda, which they undertook voluntarily without any direct order from above. As in Germany, elementary school teachers pushed for territorial expansion and democratic reform.[50]

War Pedagogy beyond 1915

Because of the stalemate on both the Eastern and Western fronts, teachers after 1915 no longer benefited from the cadence of military victories and their opportunities to celebrate the present. The novelty of war pedagogy—its new subjects, methods, activities, and media—gradually wore off. Teacher shortages made it increasingly difficult to maintain a normal school regime. Even worse for morale, limited supplies of food and coal weakened pupils and teachers alike. Almost all suffered from the agony and trauma brought on by the deaths and casualties of millions of soldiers: by April 1917, one out of ten prewar male teachers in Prussia was dead. Under these conditions, the war was less a "great teacher" and cheerful spirit than a leveler and Grim Reaper. Many teachers and school directors no longer cared about creative nationalist classroom practices. Most who used them did not try to make pupils enthusiastic for war but just prepared them to endure hardship. After 1915, articles endorsing the methods and content of war pedagogy declined steadily in the most influential journals, like *Pädagogische Zeitung* and *Leipziger Lehrerzeitung*. Elementary school teachers in particular returned to the prewar curriculum and sympathized, in July 1917, with the Reichstag Peace Resolution signed by the Progressive, Center, and Majority Social Democratic Parties, who called for an immediate end to the war without annexations or reparations.

Nevertheless, most teachers continued with war pedagogy in the sense that they summoned pupils to hold out to achieve a total military victory and reject a negotiated peace. Though teachers devoted fewer lessons to the war because of the shortened school day, to varying degrees many retained a curriculum that focused on the present and suggested that war was necessary and honorable. Like almost all Germans, teachers hoped Germany would win and gain something for its sacrifices. In contrast to the heyday of war pedagogy, war was rarely a central theme of instruction after 1915. In the context of death, mutilation, and deprivation, few teachers treated it as the miracle that rejuvenated the nation. But poems, dictations, free compositions, Bible stories, and mathematical exercises about war continued to have a place in the repertoire of many teachers. Most teachers still found stories of heroism useful for instilling the patriotism necessary to hold out for a military victory.

The teachers who turned against the war—typically urban elementary school teachers who suffered especially under the escalating inflation and sympathized with the starving and exhausted urban populations who wanted peace—were mostly silent about the war curriculum after 1915. Far more vocal in the press in support of the war and German territorial expansion were school officials, secondary school teachers, rural elementary school teachers, and female teachers of all sorts, as well as some better-off or particularly patriotic urban elementary school teachers. Even suffering elementary school teachers could reluctantly support a curriculum to help military victory—for example, during and immediately after the negotiations of the favorable treaty of Brest-Litovsk in January 1918 and the military offense in the spring of 1918, when it seemed for one last time that Germany could win the war.[51]

The push for progressive reform did not end with the introduction of war pedagogy. After implementing changes in methods and curriculum ad hoc, elementary school teachers attacked the far more intractable problem of inequity, demanding with ever greater conviction that the government grant them the privilege of attending university, eliminate the elitist clerical school inspectors, and advance pupils into secondary schools based on merit, not ability to pay. Because they felt indebted to the lower-middle class for its support of the war and recognized that the war had revealed a dearth of talent among government officials, even some conservative-minded teachers in Germany's exclusive secondary schools were hard pressed to find counter-arguments that such reforms were fair and necessary. Discussion of reform did not wane after 1916, despite the hunger, overburdening, and millions of casualties on the front. The personnel to run schools and the coal to heat them dwindled, making it impossible to maintain regular instruction, let alone carry out further progressive change. But the liberal and conservative press recognized the work teachers did to get their pupils to hold out for victory. Few teachers liked the war after 1915, but most hoped desperately for a victory. Only a handful ever publicly opposed it, in part because they assumed that their commitment and sacrifice for Germany would justify reforms during peacetime. This was especially true after the chancellor agreed, in 1917, to hold a government conference, which convened in 1920, on how to reform the education system after the war.

The immediate legacy of the war for German elementary school education was that it became less controversial to experiment with child-centered methods that nurtured the pupil's individuality and mitigated the teacher's authority. After the unexpected and disastrous defeat, elementary school teachers seemed to forget their experiments with the national mobilization under war pedagogy. But they did adapt the reform spirit of August 1914 to an era of peace under the liberal laws of the Weimar Republic. Thousands were able to open new schools that eschewed the strict drill method, forbade insulting and beating pupils, fostered candid dialogue in the classroom, worked closely with parents and communities, and reduced the distance between teachers and pupils through field trips and festivities.[52]

Notes

1. Hans Ulrich Wehler summarized this scholarship in *The German Kaiserreich 1871–1918* (Lemington Spa, 1985), 120–124, and few have since challenged this view.

2. Heidi Rosenbaum, *Formen der Familie: Untersuchungen zum Zusammenhang von Familienverhältnissen, Sozialstruktur und sozialem Wandel in der deutschen Gesellschaft des 19. Jahrhunderts* (Frankfurt a. M., 1982), 168–173; Folkert Meyer, *Schule der Untertanen: Lehrer und Politik in Preussen, 1848–1900* (Hamburg, 1976), 200–203; Rainer Bölling, *Volksschullehrer und Politik: Der Deutsche Lehrerverein 1918–1933* (Göttingen, 1978), 25–26; Rainer Bölling, "Elementarschullehrer zwischen Disziplinierung und Emanzipation: Aspekte eines internationalen Vergleichs (1870–1940)" in *Bildung, Staat, Gesellschaft im 19. Jahrhundert: Mobilisierung und Disziplinierung*, ed. Karl-Ernst Jeismann (Stuttgart, 1989), 331, 337; I. L. Kandel, "Germany," in *Comparative Education: Studies of the Educational Systems of Six Modern Nations*, ed. Peter Sandiford (London, 1918), 124–130; Rudolf Pörtner, ed., *Kindheit im Kaiserreich: Erinnerungen an vergangene Zeiten* (Düsseldorf, 1987), 105, 115; and *Statistisches Jahrbuch für den preußischen Staat*, ed. Preußisches statistisches Landesamt, 14 (Berlin, 1917), 222–223, and 15 (Berlin, 1918), 229.

3. Rainer Bölling, *Sozialgeschichte der deutschen Lehrer* (Göttingen, 1983), 51–52, 129; Bölling, *Volksschullehrer*, 9–10, 19, 24–25, 74–75; Heinz Lemmermann, *Kriegserziehung im Kaiserreich: Studien zur politischen Funktion von Schule und Schulmusik, 1890–1918* (Bremen, 1984); Jakob Vogel, *Nationen im Gleichschritt: Der Kult der "Nation in Waffen" in Deutschland und Frankreich 1871–1914* (Göttingen, 1997), 75–77, 89, 144–162; and Horst Joachim Frank, *Geschichte des Deutschunterrichts: Von Anfängen bis 1945* (Munich, 1973), 511–518, 528–531, 544–557.

4. James Albisetti, *Secondary School Reform in Imperial Germany* (Princeton, 1983), 254–256, 282; and James Olson, "Nationalistic Values in Prussian Schoolbooks Prior to World War 1," *Canadian Review of Studies in Nationalism* 1 (1973): 51.

5. On the wide-ranging research activities within reform pedagogy, see Peter Dudek, *Jugend als Objekt der Wissenschaft: Geschichte der Jugendforschung in Deutschland und Österreich 1890–1933* (Opladen, 1990), 21–133.

6. Wolfgang Scheibe, *Die Reformpädagogische Bewegung (1900–1932)* (Weinheim, 1974), 81–109, 171–254.

7. See, for example, n. a., "Lehren des Krieges für Erziehung und Unterricht," *Katholische Zeitschrift für Erziehung und Unterricht* 65 (1916): 344; H. Kölling, "Die Aktualität des Unterrichts," *Pädagogische Zeitung* 43 (10 September 1914): 690–691; Eduard Stemplinger, "Kriegsjahresberichte 1914/15 der bayerischen gymnasialen Anstalten," *Deutsches Philologen-Blatt* (1914): 747–749; and Bernd Moiske, "Formeln, Schüler, Krieg: Mathematisch-naturwissenschaftliche Fachpädagogik um die Zeit des ersten Weltkrieges," in *Lehrer helfen siegen: Kriegspädagogik im Kaiserreich*, ed. Arbeitsgruppe "Lehrer und Krieg" (Berlin, 1987).

8. See, for example, n. a., "Helden und Kinder," *Vossische Zeitung*, 9 September 1915.

9. N. a., "Krieg und Zeichenunterricht," *Der Volksschullehrer* 9 (9 December 1915): 576; and Paul Hildebrandt, "Wie unsere höheren Schüler den Krieg erleben," in *Wie Deutschlands Jugend den Weltkrieg erlebt*, ed. Wilhelm Müller (Dresden, 1918), 65.

10. See the decree by the Kaiser announced by von Trott zu Solz, "Stoffverschiebungen im Geschichtslehrplan zugunsten der neuesten Geschichte," *Zentralblatt für die gesamte Unterrichtsverwaltung in Preußen* (2 September 1915): 693–700.

11. N. a., "Das Kriegsgedicht in der Schule," *Preußische Volksschullehrerinnen-Zeitung* 10 (15 May 1916): 38.

12. N. a., "Jahresberichte der höheren Schulen," *Deutsches Philologen-Blatt* 23 (6 January 1915): 16.

13. Elisabeth Seifarth, "Der Unterrichtserfolg in der Kriegszeit," *Die Lehrerin* 32 (18 December 1915): 297–298; n. a., "Auch für den Krieg," *Monatsschrift für katholische Lehrerinnen* 28 (May 1915): 296–297; and n. a., "Unsere Schulen und der Krieg," *Die höheren Mädchenschulen* 27 (26 October 1914): 412–418.

14. Olbrich, "Kriegsaufsätze der Oberprima einer Studienanstalt," *Frauenbildung* 14 (1915): 62; Jo Mihaly [Piete Kuhr], *There We'll Meet Again: A Young German Girl's Diary of the First World War* (Gloucester, 1982), 54, 96; n. a., "Freie Aufsätze für die Kriegszeit", *Monatsschrift für katholische Lehrerinnen* 28 (June 1915): 343–344; and Anny Schulze "Kriegstagbücher," *Die Lehrerin* 32 (1 May 1915): 34–36.

15. N. a., "Verfügung der Schulabteilung der Regierung Stettin, 23.2.1915," *Amtliches Schul-Blatt für den Regierungs–Bezirk Stettin* 28 (1915): 13, as reprinted in Klaus Saul, "Jugend im Schatten des Krieges: Dokumentation," *Militärgeschichtliche Mitteilung* 34 (1983): 127–128.

16. N. a., "Eine Schlacht an einem heißen Sommertage 1870," in *Kinderaug' und Kinderaufsatz im Weltkriege*, ed. O[tto] Karstädt (Leipzig, 1916), 249–50 (quotation); and Pörtner, *Kindheit*, 99–102, 138, 143, 177–197.

17. N. a., "Rechenaufgaben zur Brotfragen," *Preußische Volksschullehrerinnen-Zeitung* 8 (15 March 1915): 181.

18. Luise Hesse, "Aus der Zeit für Schule und Leben," *Monatsschrift für katholische Lehrerinnen* 28 (February 1915): 86–88.

19. Over a third of administrators and teachers in Prussia were in the army by the end of the 1914/15 school year. Geheimes Staatsachiv Preußischer Kulturbesitz (GStA) Rep. 76. VI Sec. I Gen. z: 243 Bd. I, Bl. 25.

20. Education Minister, Munich, 9 October 1914, Staatsarchiv Munich RA Nr. 53885; Schepp, "Unsere Schulen in der Kriegszeit," *Lehrer-Zeitung für Ost- und Westpreußen* 45 (3 October 1914): 812; n. a., "Krieg und Volksschule," *Katholische Schulzeitung für Norddeutschland* 31 (17 September 1914): 614–615; and n. a., "Der Krieg und die Schule," *Deutsche Tageszeitung*, 16 February 1915, in Bundesarchiv-Lichterfelde 8034 II 6938, Bl. 144.

21. "Verfügung der Schulabteilung," 127–128; Werner Dackweiler, "Der große Weltkrieg im Dienst unseres Aufsatzes," *Naussische Schulzeitung* 13 (15 April 1915): 58–59; n. a., "Aus dem Kriegsschuljahre 1914/1915 der Volksschule Lörrach," *Badische Schulzeitung* 53 (5 June 1915): 179; and Blanckenhorn, "Lehrplan und Krieg," *Der Volksschullehrer* 9 (26 August 1915): 40.

22. Paul von Glizycki, Stadt- und Kreisschulinspektor in Berlin, "Das Volksschulwesen," *Das Unterrichtswesen im Deutschen Reich*, vol. 3: *Das Volksschulwesen und das Lehrerbildungswesen*, ed. Wilhelm Lexis (Berlin, 1904); and Scheibe, *Reformpädagogische Bewegung*, 72.

23. Deputy of Education Minister, 10 August 1914, GStA Rep. 76 VI Sec. I Gen. z: 243 Bd. I, Bl. 9. In 1911, the education minister scolded teachers for refusing to follow the *Lehrplan*. See decree from 23 October 1911 in *Quellen zur deutschen Schulgeschichte seit 1800*, ed. Gerhardt Giese (Göttingen, 1961), 227–228.

24. N. a., "Zeitung und Schule," *Der Volksschullehrer* 9 (9 December 1915): 576; and Julius Krause, "Das erste Jahr des Weltkrieges im Geschichtsunterricht der Tertia," *Monatsschrift für höhere Schule* 14 (1915): 408.

25. Thomas Alexander and Beryl Parker, *The New Education in the German Republic* (New York, 1929), 3; William Learned, *An American Teacher's Year in a Prussian Gymnasium* (New York, 1911), 351; and C. H. Leppington, "Some Characteristic Differences between English and German Education," *Charity Organization Review* 13 (1903): 189.

26. Scheibe, *Die reformpädagogische Bewegung*, 70, 91–92, 140–142.

27. N. a., "Das Kriegsbild in der Schule," *Der Volksschullehrer* 9 (8 July 1915): 319; n. a., *1914–1918: Kriegs-Gedenkschrift des Andreas-Realgymnasiums* (Berlin, 1919), 6–8; and Paul Matzdorf, "Wie wir den Krieg miterleben," in Müller, *Deutschlands Jugend*, 48–49.
28. Thomas Alexander, *The Prussian Elementary Schools* (New York, 1918), 334.
29. H. Stern, "Noch einmal Aufsatz und Niederschrift," *Pädagogische Zeitung* 42 (27 November 1913): 884, 882–885; Otto Ludwig, *Der Schulaufsatz: Seine Geschichte in Deutschland* (Berlin, 1988), 275–276, 288–291; and Abigail Green, *Fatherlands: State-Building and Nationalism in Nineteenth-Century Germany* (New York, 2001), 191–192.
30. Adolf Jensen and Wilhelm Lamszus, *Unser Schulaufsatz ein verkappter Schundliterat: Ein Versuch zur Neugründung des deutschen Schulaufsatzes für Volksschule und Gymnasium* (Hamburg, 1910), 10.
31. Karolina Fahn, *Der Wandel des Aufsatzbegriffes in der deutschen Volksschule von 1900 bis zur Gegenwart* (Munich, 1971), 75–78; Ludwig, *Schulaufsatz*, 306–307, 314; Marieluise Christadler, *Kriegserziehung im Jugendbuch: Literarische Mobilmachung in Deutschland und Frankreich vor 1914* (Frankfurt, 1979), 306–316; Scheibe, *Die reformpädagogische Bewegung*, 150–154; Horst Joachim Frank, *Geschichte des Deutschunterricht: Von Anfängen bis 1945* (Munich, 1973), 361–371; and Wilhelm Lamszus, *Das Menschenschlachthaus: Bilder vom kommenden Krieg* (1912), ed. Johannes Merkel and Dieter Richter (Munich, 1980).
32. K. Foltz, "Niederschriften und Aufsätzen," *Pädagogische Zeitung* 43 (1 August 1914): 646; and Karl Linke, *Der freie Aufsatz auf der Unterstufe, Mittelstufe, und Oberstufe* (Braunschweig, 1916), 5–9, 168–210. Despite a publication date of 1916, all the essays in this collection were written in 1913 and early 1914.
33. Fahn, *Aufsatzbegriff*, 54–59; and Willy Müller, "Zur Einführung in den neuen Grundlehrplan für die Volkschulen Groß-Berlins," *Pädagogische Zeitung* 43 (30 April 1914): 349.
34. For some of the various decrees of the Prussian regional authorities, see Blanckenhorn, "Lehrplan und Krieg"; Peters, "Kriegspädagogik in der ländl. Fortbildungsschule," *Hannoversche Schulzeitung* 50 (27 October 1914): 690–691; and "Verfügung der Schulabteilung."
35. Karstädt, *Kinderaug' und Kinderaufsatz*, 1 (quotation); Max Engel, *Leipzigs Volkschulen im Zeichen des Welkriegs: Auf Grund von Einzelberichten und unter Mitarbeit von Lehrern und Direktoren* (Leipzig, 1915), 27–28; n. a., "Laßt die Jugend die große Zeit erleben," *Der Volksschullehrer* 8 (15 October 1914): 634–35; n. a., "Aus dem Kriegsschuljahre 1914/1915 der Volksschule Lörrach," *Badische Schulzeitung* 53 (5 June 1915): 180; and Dackweiler, "Der große Weltkrieg," 58–59.
36. Gustav Spiegelberg, *Über 800 Aufgaben über den Weltkrieg 1914/15 zu freien Aufsätzen und Niederschriften in Schulen* (Halle, 1915), 33; n. a., "Freie Aufsätze für die Kriegszeit," *Monatsschrift für katholische Lehrerinnen* 28 (June 1915): 343–344; Friedrich Brücker, "Die Konzentration des Unterrichts im Weltkriege," *Katholische Zeitschrift für Erziehung und Unterricht* 65 (1916): 39; Fritz Elsner, "Die Schule und der Krieg," *Für unsere Mütter und Hausfrauen* 26 (17 September 1915): 101, reprinted in Saul, "Jugend," 132–134; E. Leupolt, "Der Krieg und der Schulaufsatz," *Hannoversche Schulzeitung* 51 (28 September 1915): 467–468; and Hildebrandt, "Kriegs-Themata im Schulaufsatz," *Berliner Vossische Zeitung*, 2 April 1915.
37. Hanna B., "Die ersten Kriegstage in einem Dorfe an der französischen Grenze," in *Das Buch Michael: Mit Kriegsaufsätzen, Tagebuchblättern, Gedichten, Zeichnungen aus Deutschlands Schulen*, ed. Hermann Reich, 2nd ed. (Berlin, 1918), 156.
38. On the warrior image before Jünger, see George Mosse, *Fallen Soldiers: Reshaping the Memory of the World Wars* (New York, 1990), 115, 122–125.
39. Müller, "Ich stieße alles nieder!" in Karstädt, *Kinderaug' und Kinderaufsatz*, 53.
40. Untitled, in *Jugendliches Seelenleben und Krieg*, ed. William Stern (Leipzig, 1915), 91.
41. "Ein Feldbrief aus dem Jahre 1813," in *Aus eiserner Zeit: Freie Kriegsaufsätze von Meeraner Kindern*, ed. Arthur Fröhlich (Leipzig, 1915), 116–119.
42. See, for example, K. Bernhardt, "Wo hast du den Weihnachtsbaum bekommen?" in Karstädt, *Kinderaug' und Kinderaufsatz*, 95–96.

43. See untitled in *Das Kind und der Krieg: Kinderaussprüche, Aufsätze und Zeichnungen*, ed. Max Schach, (Berlin, 1916), 35, and the two untitled compositions in Stern, *Jugendliches Seelenleben*, 88, 107.
44. Schorschel, untitled in *Die Kinder und der Krieg: Aussprüche, Taten, Opfer und Bilder*, ed. Hans Floerke (Munich, 1915), 144–145.
45. Alfred Mann, "Die Aufsätze von Kindern," in Stern, *Jugendliches Seelenleben*, 91.
46. E. Hylla, "Krieg und jugendliches Seelenleben," *Pädagogische Zeitung* 44 (26 August 1915): 407.
47. Aaron Cohen, "Flowers of Evil: Mass Media, Child Psychology, and the Struggle for Russia's Future during the First World War," in *Children and War*, ed. James Marten (New York, 2002).
48. David Parker, "'Talent at Its Command': The First World War and the Vocational Aspect of Education, 1914–1939," *History of Education Quarterly* 35 (1995): 237–259.
49. Stéphane Audoin-Rouzeau, *La guerre des enfants 1914–1918* (Paris, 1993), 24–37 (first quotation on 25); Stéphane Audoin-Rouzeau, "Children and the Primary Schools of France," in *State, Society and Mobilization in Europe during the First World War*, ed. John Horne (Cambridge, 1997), 41–42 (second two quotations); Jacques Ozouf and Mona Ozouf, "Le thème du patriotisme dans les manuels primaires," *Le Mouvement social* 49 (October–December 1964): 15 (fourth quotation); and Mona Siegel, *The Moral Disarmament of France: Education, Pacifism, and Patriotism, 1914–1940* (New York, 2004), 18–50.
50. Andrea Fava, "War, 'National Education,' and the Italian Primary School," in Horne, *State, Society and Mobilization*, 53–69.
51. G. Gille, "Durchhalten und siegen!" *Deutsche Blätter für erziehenden Unterricht* 44 (12 January 1917): 124–126; n. a., "Gebot der Stunde," *Katholische Schulzeitung für Norddeutschland* 33 (23 November 1916): 469–470; and Andrew Donson, "War Pedagogy and Youth Culture: Nationalism and Authority in Germany in the First World War" (PhD diss., University of Michigan, Ann Arbor, 2000), 188–199.
52. Bölling, *Volksschullehrer*, 126–129, 227–228; Marjorie Lamberti, *The Politics of Education: Teachers and School Reform in Weimar Germany* (New York, 2002) , 60–61, 106–122, 133–143, 245–246; and Wilhelm Flitner, *Der Krieg und die Jugend* (Stuttgart, 1927), 316–320.

Chapter 4

"LINKED WITH THE WELFARE OF ALL PEOPLES"

The American Kindergarten, Americanization, and Internationalism in the First World War

Ellen L. Berg

Introduction

The beginning of the First World War and the United States' subsequent entry into combat reignited American concerns about national identity. During the 1910s, a virtual national obsession with "Americanization" programs intended to create reliable American citizens informed educational programs, including those of the burgeoning kindergarten movement. Kindergarten teachers' pedagogical literature and records of their daily interactions in the classroom reveal that they were engaged in the project of preparing for life after the war. In doing so, they were trying to resolve two important questions: What does it mean to be an American? And how should Americans relate to the world? By examining the kindergarten movement's views on Americanization and internationalism, this essay will show that many kindergarten teachers maintained ideals that were at odds with the jingoism with which we often associate the era. Instead of viewing Americans in opposition to the rest of the world, many kindergartners imagined a community beyond national borders, encouraging visions of world citizenship and internationalism.

After 1880, a mass migration of so-called "new immigrants" had altered the demographics of the country. Whereas previous migrants originated primarily from Northern and Western Europe, now first- and second-generation immigrants, who comprised one third of the country's population, more often traced their origins to Southern and Eastern Europe. The increasing industrialization and urbanization of the country added to native-born Americans' sense of disorientation. Responses to this new immigration varied. Some Americans turned toward nativist organizations and "scientific" racism; indeed, the severe immigration restrictions enacted in 1921 and 1924 demonstrate the strength of anti-immigrant sentiment. Simultaneous with the xenophobia, however, was a more measured response from other native-born Americans and previous immigrants who believed that new arrivals could become reliable citizens. Led in many cases by middle-class women, who coordinated their work through women's clubs and religious sisterhoods, institutions such as social settlements, aid organizations, and religious charities sought to teach immigrants what it meant to be Americans.

One of the most popular institutions through which to reach immigrants was the kindergarten. By 1892, over 100,000 children attended American kindergartens, about half in public schools and half in private institutions. The latter included both fee-charging kindergartens and "free kindergartens," which offered low- or no-cost classes through kindergarten associations, religious institutions, and social settlements.[1] A German immigrant brought Friedrich Fröbel's kindergarten to the United States in 1856, and English speakers subsequently adopted and developed it. Even as American "kindergartners," as kindergarten teachers were known, altered the curriculum in the late nineteenth and early twentieth centuries, they maintained Fröbel's emphasis on the importance of play to children's development, using songs, stories, and games in their classrooms.[2]

The kindergarten proliferated in large part because contemporary reformers believed it to be one of the most effective ways to integrate immigrants into American life.[3] Kindergartners and their supporters had several reasons to claim their institution's suitability for Americanization work.[4] First, immigrants and second-generation Americans were pervasive in the kindergarten: a study of immigrants in industrial cities found that 58 percent of the public- and parochial-school kindergarten students had foreign-born fathers.[5] Second, educators described children aged four to six as being particularly "impressionable" and thus more open to the work of Americanizers.[6] Third, kindergartners had seemingly unique access to foreign-born mothers (and thus to immigrant homes) because they shared a common interest in the young children.[7]

Additionally, the kindergarten espoused a paradigm of democracy within the classroom that gained renewed respect during the First World War from Americans who feared that modern society overemphasized individualism.[8] For example, the exigencies of wartime caused psychologist G. Stanley Hall to suggest that a too-extreme focus on "individuality" might "lead to caprice, to self-indulgence, and lack of control."[9] The kindergarten's view of democracy as a community of equals, exercising their own rights while ensuring that they did not trample on the rights of others, thus drew attention.[10] Indeed, kindergartners and their supporters claimed that "the kindergarten is the best exemplification of a true democracy that can be found, in the school system."[11] Kindergartners, proud of the attention their views on democracy received during wartime, redoubled their emphasis on individual subordination of desires to the needs of the group.[12] After all, they argued, the ideals of brotherhood and unity offered hope for postwar generations.[13]

Kindergartners were probably drawn to the label of "Americanization" work because of the popularity of the movement and their own uncertainty about the kindergarten's future in the face of war. During the 1910s, the growth of kindergartens, particularly in public schools, led to classroom spaces for approximately 365,000 children. However, kindergarten supporters fretted that the total percentage of four- to six-year-olds served was leveling off at 12 percent of the population.[14] The impact of the war was ambiguous. While Elizabeth A. Woodward, supervisor of the Brooklyn Free Kindergarten Society, observed increased interest in new kindergarten programs, others worried about vulnerable kindergartens; for example, coal shortages in 1917 led to temporary school closures affecting some kindergartens in Boston and Worcester, Massachusetts. Kindergartners and their allies objected to these measures, arguing that they should be a last resort after "saloons, clubs and places of amusement were compelled to suspend their activities, and all other means of coal conservation were exhausted."[15] Joining the Americanization movement might have seemed like a way to safeguard the ongoing work of the kindergarten during wartime.[16]

Americanization Lessons in the Kindergarten

The goals of participants in the Americanization movement varied greatly, with kindergartners holding their own well-developed conception of what it meant to be an American child during the First World War. Like other Americanizers, they prioritized national harmony over ethnic identity; thus, although they did not see the two as mutually exclusive, their curricula challenged ethnic group unity and immigrant ways of life. However, the kindergartners' principles and curricula did not reflect the extreme side of the Americanization movement—which was at times quite nativist and coercive.[17] Notably, kindergartners did not make major revisions of the kindergarten curriculum, nor did they suggest great changes for children's lives. Instead, Americanization as conceived and practiced by kindergartners was expansive and flexible, even as it met the goals of the larger Americanization movement.

Historians have long emphasized Americanization work related to housekeeping and child-rearing; for instance, Eileen Boris quotes the General Foundation of Women's Clubs' plan to teach "American ways of caring for babies, ventilating the house, [and] preparing American vegetables, instead of the inevitable cabbage."[18] While kindergartners carried out home economics work during the 1910s, they had already incorporated domestic lessons in their curricula for decades before, particularly in their work with mothers.[19] Though some observers suggested that kindergartners' wartime work with mothers in "the preparation and conservation of food and clothing" represented a broadening of their work, in fact the attachment of the label "war work" to this domestic education merely formalized long-standing activities of the kindergarten.[20] Kindergarten work in this area in the 1910s reflected stated attempts, not to change the cultural traditions of immigrants but rather to teach them how to cope with shortages. Kindergartners were instructed: "Ask the foreign mother to acquaint you with her foods and dishes, then assist her in finding food substitutes which will nearly correspond to the diet upon which she has been dependent."[21]

More important than home economics lessons, in the Americanization work of kindergartners, were issues of American identity, English language acquisition, and American patriotism. Though vague on methods used to promote American identity, supporters of the kindergarten looked for evidence of success in their Americanization work. For example, they highlighted examples of children labeling themselves as Americans. The Bureau of Education's *Americanization Bulletin* reported in 1918 that "we have today no foreign children in our country, at least judging from the attitude of our kindergartens." It explained:

> If you don't believe it, go and ask them and watch the scorn in the four and five and six years old eyes. Are you Russian, are you Polish, are you Italian, are you Greek? 'I'm 'Merican!' is the answer. Are you German, little Ruth? 'No, I'm 'Merican!' But your name is German; is your mother a German? 'No, she's 'Merican'—a little defiantly. And your father, persists the teasing questioner, is he a German?
>
> Her yellow head drooped and her face flushed a little, 'Yes, he's a German'—she said it very low, then looking up bravely and happily she said, 'but he's a good German, he don't like the Kaiser! And I'm ALL a 'Merican!'
>
> Who can say this four year old has not grasped the full significance of the times?[22]

Kindergartners also emphasized examples in which parents identified their children as American, many of them demonstrating that the development of an American national identity began well before kindergartners became involved. Marie J. Schuetze, who taught at San Francisco's "cosmopolitan" Emma Marwedel Kindergarten, reported in 1917 that during a "game of spring flowers," she had assigned roles to her students. "'Now you are a buttercup,'" Schuetze told one girl, whose response was telling: "'No, no,' she protested, 'I ain't; I'm American.'" Schuetze used this example to show that "[o]ccasionally the parents make an effort to impress their children with the knowledge of their citizenship."[23] In 1915, her fellow San Franciscan, Anna Manning of the Adler Kindergarten, had written that a mother visited the kindergarten and told the teacher of her son: "'He no more Guiseppe [sic]. In Italia that alla right, alla right. Now he one Americano, my man, he say Joe more better for style, see? Good bye, teacha.' With many gestures and bows she departed, fully convinced that she had taken decisive steps toward the naturalization of the future citizen." Manning concluded, after Giuseppe/Joe's mother left, that "the man who desires an American name for his son is reasonably sure to take some pride in his family and their future status in the land of his choice."[24] Of course, such examples do not reveal fully the perspectives of the parents and their motives for instilling American identities in their children.

Yet parallel to this emphasis on children's Americanness, kindergartners simultaneously expressed appreciation for so-called "immigrant gifts." Sometimes their interest in other cultures was diffuse, as when *The Kindergarten and First Grade Magazine* published a series of folk tales of various cultural origins, including English, Slavonic, Danish, Japanese, Southern United States, and Biloxi Indian. (It also included a story by the Brothers Grimm but, likely because of the war, did not mention that they were German.)[25] At other times, teachers drew deliberately on the origins of the communities they served. One kindergartner incorporated her students' Syrian folk game into classroom play, and workers at the University of Chicago Settlement invited "a neighborhood man who played the concertina and knew all the old country dances" to perform at parties, delighting immigrants who did not "know American dances."[26] In 1917, Olive Wills of Cheyenne, Wyoming, suggested a new twist on the usual flag-waving exercises to honor presidents Washington and Lincoln in February. She proposed "a study of the flags of those nations across the water that are so absorbing our attention just now. Also of the nationalities represented by the little ones in our class, perhaps German, Italian, English, French, Greek or Dutch or Bulgarian, Roumanian or Belgian."[27] Implied in activities that succored ethnic identity was a conviction that immigrants should nonetheless consider themselves as Americans foremost. One teacher of a Boston kindergarten class of second-generation Jewish children reminded them that "one can be a good Jew and a good American at the same time, and that we loved the American flag best of all the flags."[28] Furthermore, despite the kindergartners' expansive rhetoric and isolated attempts to incorporate immigrant culture into their activities, they did not articulate a clear program for how immigrants could maintain a dual identity, except, perhaps, in becoming bilingual.

Kindergartners firmly believed in the importance of English language education. Some of this interest was purely practical, for teachers often encountered children who did not understand English.[29] Kindergartners advocated training in English as an aid to first grade teachers, reducing "retardation" of immigrant children in school and allowing them to be promoted with their peers.[30] They also endorsed English language acquisition as a sign of Americanization as well as an aid to subsequent Americanization work. The Pasadena, California, Board of Education reported on the perceived successes of its work with Mexican children: "Scarcely a child can speak a word of English when he enters kindergarten and for weeks is too timid and diffident to try. Gradually by entering into the kindergarten games and activities, and with unrestricted use of the kindergarten materials, he forgets himself and speaks English almost as readily as his own native tongue. He has had his first course in Americanization."[31] The symbolic importance of language to the kindergartners is evidenced by a 1918 article by Woodward:

Little Secunda, aged four, had spent most of his winter in the kindergarten and his Spanish mother had faithfully attended the weekly mothers' meetings. One morning, in a sudden burst of confidence, he joyfully announced to his teacher, "I speak American, my mother learn speak American, my father learn speak American,—then my father puts on soldier suit and goes to fight the Germanies."[32]

The perceived progression from foreigner to American through use of English language, as suggested by this anecdote, could serve as a valuable marketing tool for the kindergarten.

Kindergartners seemed more confident about the ultimate acquisition of English by immigrant children than by their parents. Kindergartners generally presumed that children would easily learn English in other settings, if not in the kindergarten. Thus they seemed unconcerned by alarmist claims such as that by Fred Clayton Butler, an Americanization proponent, who argued that some third-generation immigrants were still so isolated in their own "colonies" that they "studied only their own language and never heard English spoken."[33] First-generation immigrants, however, seemed to have fewer opportunities to learn English, particularly immigrant women, who were less involved in American culture than their husbands and children.[34] Some kindergartners recommended English classes to the women, occasionally teaching the classes themselves.[35] Others observed that kindergarten children could bring home the English they learned at school, though they worried that children placed in the role of missionary to the rest of the family would lose respect for their parents.[36] Kindergartners were largely sympathetic to the difficulties these mothers might have in learning English, and they believed that language acquisition was ultimately a minor—and perhaps even inconsequential—step in the process of Americanization. Gertrude Stone, of the University of Chicago Settlement Kindergarten, concluded, "It is not such a vital necessity that the parents should speak the English language as that they should get the true American ideals."[37]

This preference for substance over form also played itself out in a wartime debate over the German origins of the word kindergarten. Generalized anti-German sentiment in the United States renewed a previous debate over changing the kindergarten's name, possibly to "Play School, Sub-Primary, Early Elementary, Beginner's Class, Preparatory Primary" or similar terms.[38] American kindergartners on both sides of the debate agreed that the kindergarten had already become "thoroughly naturalized" in the United States and that the institution had no practical connection to contemporary Germany. In fact, they publicized the fact that Germany had banned the kindergarten temporarily in the nineteenth century because of what Almira Winchester described in 1918 as the perceived threat of "self-activity, freedom, and respect for individuality ... to the success of military autocracy."[39] Proponents of the name "kindergarten" thus argued that to keep the name was to honor the traditional values of democracy that Germany had abandoned.[40] Their opponents, on the other hand, tended to use pedagogical arguments about the "organic" connection of the kindergarten to the primary school and the perceived need for a name that reflected this fact. A few kindergartners used contemporary anti-German attitudes—allegedly not their own, but those of others—as reasons to abandon the name kindergarten.[41] Proponents of the term, on the other hand, vehemently denounced this argument, refusing to be cowed by "the clamor of somewhat blatant patriots," in the words of Mabel L. Culkin of the State Normal School, La Crosse, Wisconsin.[42] Those who opposed the name change ultimately won, of course; no other name "so aptly and euphoniously" represented the work of the institution, in Winchester's words.[43] Kindergartners were more concerned about the content of ideas than the language in which they were expressed. According to Catharine R. Watkins, the director of public kindergartens in Washington, D.C., those wanting to change the name of the kindergarten used arguments that were "petty and unworthy of the broad patriotism which America demands."[44]

Patriotism and Internationalism during Wartime

Watkins's language raises a final aspect of Americanization that was taught within the kindergarten: patriotism. Patriotism had many different meanings to Americans during this period.[45] Many teachers saw patriotism primarily as a manifestation of duty toward others.[46] This vision of patriotism was thus not exclusively fixed upon the United States. In 1896, leading kindergartner Kate Douglas Wiggin had denounced "particularistic" patriotism in favor of a "wider and a more inclusive study" that was more universalistic in nature.[47] This idea of broader patriotism continued to shape kindergartners' understanding of the place of the United States in the world during the early twentieth century, even as the United States moved toward war. Kindergartners had long been opposed to militarism, which contradicted their principle of peaceful resolution of conflicts. They opposed corporal punishment in the classroom, to the wonder of many parents accustomed to controlling their children through threatened or actual beatings. In the minds of teachers trained in kindergarten methods, children should experience the "brotherhood of mankind" through their interactions within the classroom. Yet clearly this theory created a tension between lessons of patriotism and universalism in kindergarten classrooms, particularly during wartime.

Historians have identified several different varieties of internationalism during the Progressive era.[48] Alan Dawley has recently studied the path of the "new internationalism," as developed by individuals such as Jane Addams, with a focus on world cooperation rather than the imperialist motivations of other so-called internationalists.[49] Prior to the First World War, progressive internationalists such as Addams believed "that they could be both good citizens of the United States and cosmopolitan citizens of the world."[50] Members of the kindergarten movement were often internationalists, as well. As a diverse group, some kindergartners no doubt leaned toward cultural imperialism. For example, Angeline Brooks, formerly of Teachers' College, wrote in 1916 of the "growing realization of the organic unity of the human race" and the resulting tendency toward "the larger view of world-citizenship which calls for wider sympathies and involves great obligations—sympathies that must include every race and creed." While

Brooks was concerned with maintaining "moral leadership among the nations," others in the kindergarten movement prioritized ideals of world cooperation for less imperialistic reasons.[51]

At the beginning of the war, kindergarten publications urged kindergartners to continue to teach about the universality of all people. Bertha Johnston, a columnist for the *Kindergarten-Primary Magazine,* wrote consistently on this subject. In October 1914, after the onset of war in Europe, she recommended that teachers could paraphrase "The Last Lesson" by Alphonse Daudet for their students. The original story sentimentalizes the demise of French-language education in an Alsatian village after the Franco-Prussian War. Despite the clear parallels to German militarism during the current war, Johnston recommended that teachers not name the countries in relating the story to their students, in order to "keep strictly to the spirit recommended in President Wilson's advice as to neutrality and the avoidance of antagonism between citizens of different races."[52] Instead of laying blame on Germany, teachers could employ the story as a lesson in antimilitarism more generally. Johnston's subsequent columns continued to emphasize the universality of all people, a principle that kindergartners hoped would advance international peace. In 1915, she urged teachers to discuss Esperanto, a language intended "to unite peoples," with their students.[53] The next year she appealed for teachers to instill in their students the attitude "that every race has contributed imperishable gifts to mankind ... The negative, hate-producing side of this terrible world-convulsing tragedy must not be allowed to take root in the consciousness of little children especially here in America, which owes so much to the people of all races."[54] She also bemoaned the war's effect upon "the many unhappy children in the far-away, warring countries, whose devoted parents have been unable to save them from the onslaught of the cruel foe and who awaken to terror and starvation after nights of nervous sleep. Poles, Russians, Germans, French, Belgians! Oh, the horror of it! It is said that there are no children left in Poland under seven years of age."[55]

The wider American kindergarten movement, embodied in the International Kindergarten Union (IKU), initially took a stand against the war. Peace advocates had recently founded many new organizations in the United States, and female reformers, kindergartners among them, played a key role in this phase of the peace movement. For example, three sisters prominent in the kindergarten movement—Mari Ruef Hofer, Amalie Hofer Jerome, and Andrea Hofer Proudfoot—helped to organize the 1912 American tour of a Nobel Peace Prize winner, Baroness Bertha von Suttner.[56] The executive board of the IKU sent delegates to a January 1915 meeting of the Women's Movement for Constructive Peace at the behest of Addams, who sought participation from women's organizations.[57] At the meeting, Addams spoke on the particular way in which women valued life, because they "have been responsible for the care of children and the aged and all that class which needed especial care." Thus, the death of soldiers was of particular concern to women and represented "the wanton destruction of their life's work," for women had helped to nurture those men through childhood as mothers and teachers.[58] The meeting, attended by kindergarten representatives, resulted in the founding of the Woman's Peace Party (later the Women's International League for Peace and Freedom).

Within the kindergarten movement, the newly established Peace Committee of the IKU vowed to work toward "elimination of war-toys and picture-books of warfare" and to "encourage the use of a different kind of history text-book in schools."[59] This committee, sometimes referred to as the Committee on Affiliation with the Woman's Peace Party, also organized a special afternoon meeting following the close of the IKU's annual meeting in August 1915, a "Program to Promote Peace," with talks by a member of the American School Peace League, a moderate peace organization, as well as by the president of the National Education Association.[60]

Despite espousing neutrality and international peace, American kindergartners, like the rest of the country, began to rally against Germany. For instance, in a discussion of carpentry published in January 1915, Jenny B. Merrill belied her support for the Allies in her suggestion that teachers could chronicle how people in London used crates to build cradles "for the little Belgian babies whose homes were burned."[61] Furthermore, concerns about the American kindergarten movement's official stance of neutrality and condemnation of the war arose from kindergartners in Canada, which, as part of the British Empire, was already at war. At the annual IKU meeting in August 1915, the Toronto Froebel Society protested "against affiliation with the Woman's Peace Party."[62]

Although the IKU did not immediately act on those concerns, the United States' ensuing move toward war led the organization to pull further away from its official alliance with pacifists. In November 1915, Wilson announced his support for "a full preparedness program." The Woman's Peace Party equated preparedness with militarization and became a public voice for anti-preparedness, opposing increased military spending and the use of public schools for military training.[63] The IKU, however, sided with Wilson and left the peace movement, reassuring the dissenters from Toronto in February 1916 that the IKU's affiliation with the Woman's Peace Party "was entered into for the year 1915, that no new chairman has been appointed for the committee, and that there is no cause for anxiety."[64] Some kindergartners did begin to use the language of preparedness, as when Winchester wrote: "A vast army of little children has entered the doors of our school buildings this year. They are already the army of the future ... No captain is more important in the army than is the kindergartner at her post."[65]

While *Kindergarten-Primary Magazine* continued to publish advertisements from pacifist organizations, it did not subsequently address the subject in its own articles.[66] The collapse of the official connection between the IKU and the peace movement occurred just at the height of the Woman's Peace Party, which reached a peak membership of 40,000 in February 1916.[67] Thus, the kindergartners predated other liberal reformers' retreat from pacifism, though not by long. Once the United States joined the war in April 1917, few pacifist dissenters remained in the United States to resist "the lure of Wilson's insistent crusade to 'make the world safe for democracy.'"[68] No kindergartners were known to violate "community standards for appropriate patriotic behavior" during the war, and none were among the public school teachers dismissed because of accusations of disloyalty.[69]

The IKU's initial union with the Woman's Peace Party and subsequent departure demonstrates that although kindergartners valued peace and universal understanding extremely highly, they were also practitioners in charge of classrooms rather than merely philosophers. Pacifism was, for them, an important part of their beliefs but not the main thrust of their work. David S. Patterson has characterized three types of peace activists in the early twentieth century. While "world federationists" and "legalists" supported the development of an international government and an international court, respectively, the "generalists" were more vague in their goals, "urging their government to promote international good will in its foreign policies" but not specifying the nature of international organization.[70] The kindergartners certainly fit in this latter group. Allegiance to both a national and an international community had previously seemed possible to them, but the war made it appear less so. Theoretically, the kindergartners still supported international brotherhood, but they could not envision a workable solution to the international conflicts of their day.

An extension of their own methods of discipline would have called for disruptive, aggressive parties to be excluded from the larger community until they chose to participate peacefully, yet what could be done in the case of an aggressor who could not be contained and who imperiled the community? The kindergartners' eventual support of the First World War parallels their own occasional weakening of another core ideal, their staunch prohibition against corporal punishment. Most kindergartners would not countenance the spanking of unruly children, but an 1898 article, "Shall Chastisements Come by the Hand or the Rod? My Confession," demonstrates how one teacher's values eroded under pressure. Faced with Charlie, a small boy whose violence and lack of repentance "threatened to demoralize the kindergarten entirely," Connecticut public school kindergartner Marion Van Vliet concluded that "he was at that stage of moral development where nothing but brute force appealed to him." Thus, although "[i]t was against all my kindergarten theories ... and I shrank very much from such an act," Van Vliet screwed up her courage and whipped him. Afterward, Charlie gradually became "our most interested pupil," a cooperative contributor to the classroom community. Although the kindergarten philosophy opposed corporal punishment, Van Vliet, a soldier in the trenches, so to speak, applied her "common sense" to the situation in the hopes that it would achieve her aim of peace in the classroom.[71]

Just as Van Vliet still advocated peaceful modes of discipline whenever possible, kindergartners did not rush to militarism upon leaving the peace movement. Uncomfortable with teaching about the physical reality of war, some teachers preferred to emphasize the abstract dedication to one's country that soldiers embodied. Thus, though some teachers initiated soldier games among their students, other kindergartners worried about the violent implications of such play, focusing instead on the soldiers' willingness for self-sacrifice over their military exploits.[72] Patriotic displays were probably more prominent during the war than previously.[73] However, the manifestations of patriotism within classrooms were not particularly militaristic. For example, kindergartners taught their students various pledges of allegiance. Johnston advocated the use of the "well known salute" in its original form: "I pledge allegiance to my flag and to the Republic for which it stands—one nation, indivisible, with liberty and justice for all," while a Boston public school kindergarten used another popular pledge imbued with religious meaning: "We give our heads and our hearts to God and our country— one God, one country, and one flag!"[74] Kindergartners also labeled war work, particularly that for the Red Cross, as a manifestation of children's patriotism as well as a step toward Americanization.[75] Here, then, patriotism was presented to the children as a sacrifice toward others in the United States and beyond.

Some kindergartners continued to promote internationalism even after Americans joined the war. Fanniebelle Curtis in particular put these ideas into practice. Curtis had been one of the IKU's representatives at the foundational meeting of the Woman's Peace Party. Even though the kindergarten movement had departed from the peace movement, Curtis continued to echo the idea of a "new internationalism," which the now-vilified Addams had dubbed "cosmic patriotism."[76] At the IKU's annual meeting in 1917, Curtis called for "a new Internationalism—a higher Internationalism which will establish a standard of social service, a common end where brotherhood prevails, where the greater shall not oppress the weak, where all little children shall live in Republican States and only God is King."[77] Curtis subsequently solicited support for kindergarten work for French and Belgian refugees to be undertaken by the IKU in Europe at the war's conclusion, urging funders to consider "Not only our Nation's Children but the Children of the World."[78] In addition to donations by adults, the generosity of American kindergarten children responding to this campaign gave kindergarten proponents hope for the future of international relations.[79]

Articles by kindergartners suggested other ways to share a sense of internationalism with children, making them feel connected to the greater world. The kindergartens of Pasadena explicitly aligned American citizenship with world citizenship:

> As in our past year our adult consciousness has broadened until we feel that the happenings in any part of the world touch us, that our welfare is linked with the welfare of all peoples, so the kindergarten child's interests have reached to other countries. The interest in the children of France and Belgium has given added value to stories of children in other lands and has made giving a natural happy act. In the singing of patriotic songs, in saluting the flag, in making gardens, the kindergarten children have learned to feel that they are a part of a great country. But in the making of citizens for the United States and the world we have not forgotten that well developed muscles, capable hands, trained senses, the love of the beautiful, happy helpfulness and co-

operation must be worked for every day if the children are to become complete, well rounded individuals.[80]

This focus on not only American but also world citizenship suggests the continued strength of the kindergarten tenet of teaching children to appreciate the universality of all people even in the midst of unprecedented international conflict. Kindergartners bemoaned the failure of adults across the world in bringing about the war. Grace Barnard wrote, "We have been forced to realize the lack of brotherhood" internationally, thus, "to train a generation to ideals of brotherhood, a challenge comes to us to think world thoughts and live international lives."[81] Henry Neumann, leader of the Brooklyn Society for Ethical Culture, expounded on the importance of kindergartners at their national convention in 1916: "Is there anything so very big about teaching a roomful for little ones how to live together? It becomes big as soon as we remind ourselves how sadly the grown-up world still needs that lesson of living together aright—person with person, group with group, nation with nation."[82]

Countering their lofty ideals about universalism, kindergarten teachers encountered young students already imbued with belligerence and national bias. In researching Minneapolis's Wells Memorial House social settlement, Howard Karger found chilling examples of wartime jingoism among children. According to the head resident, Margaret Chapman, "The martial spirit exists from kindergarten up." She cited an example of a four-year-old girl who, on the first day of kindergarten, "strode to the center of the circle, and in no uncertain tones said: 'I am here; I can lick this whole bunch of kids; I can—' and making a dramatic sweep around with her hand, 'I can swipe the head off every kid here just like the Germans.'" In another example, Karger quotes Chapman as "proudly" reporting on the source of a commotion. The children explained to the kindergartner: "'Why,' they piped up, 'don't you see, we are striking the heart of the Kaiser.' A large heart had been drawn on the side of a barn and their baby fingers with sticks and stones were striking at the heart."[83] These examples demonstrate that children arrived at the kindergarten already thinking a great deal about the war; thus, teachers had to determine how to address the issue in the classroom. Although the Bureau of Education recommended that teachers "inject American ideals rather than war ideals into all games and stories both for the children and the mothers," it did not elaborate on this vague advice, thereby leaving teachers to develop their own approaches.[84]

Articles written by active kindergartners gave more detailed descriptions of how the war might enter children's play in the classroom. Culkin advised that "[c]hildren are profoundly interested in the manifestations of this great dramatic upheaval going on about them. It is not profitable to forbid or evade war plays and war discussions in the kindergarten. This is only to postpone such activities until after kindergarten hours." Instead, she contended, permitting children to play at war would allow their "strong sense of justice" to come out as well as to encourage "[s]ympathy and unselfishness."[85] In this same vein, Mary R. Dooling of West Newton, Massachusetts, suggested a new game about "Red Cross Workers," sung to the tune of "The Roman Soldiers," in which boy soldiers asked the girl Red Cross workers if they had provisions to offer, thereby demonstrating the gendered nature of the kindergarten ideals.[86] Dorothy A. Wall reported on developing activities based on her Washington, D.C., students' interests. Their play led to drills utilizing the flags of all of the allies, and, ultimately, of Germany:

> Finally the game was so organized that the children marched until the piano signaled by a bugle call the time of the Allies' attack, that is, the time to be vigilant, while Germany's plan was to get out of the room. All this was done in march time to marching music. It was interesting to see the nations line up at the doors and others gradually press Germany into the position of not being able to move.[87]

This dramatization of the war within the kindergarten classroom was likely not an isolated case, as other classroom teachers similarly struggled with the choice of how to allow children to assimilate the realities of the war.

Conclusion

The debates within the kindergarten movement during the First World War—over what it meant to be an American and what Americans' relationship to the world should be—are distillations of much wider societal debates of the time. For kindergartners, they were not merely issues of pedagogy but opportunities to envisage an idealized United States. They staunchly believed that after the war ended, as generation after generation of children and parents absorbed this model of living from the kindergarten setting, they could subsequently apply it to the rest of their lives.

While American nationalism in the guise of Americanization found a temporary home in the kindergarten, the objectives of the kindergarten actually remained very much the same as before, for kindergartners continued to promote an optimistic vision of the unity of all people rather than American superiority. Kindergartners' conception of core American values included goals of self-sacrificing democracy and a broad sense of international patriotism that incorporated not just other Americans but also citizens of the world. For this community of teachers, patriotism was not limited by national boundaries but was part of developing a wider sense of international unity. Even after the United States had joined the war, many kindergartners maintained an ideal of internationalism. Instead of pitting Americans against the rest of the world, they looked beyond national borders, envisaging the students as future world citizens, a surprising stance in what is usually seen as a conservative era in the development of conceptions of nationalism. Though universalist tendencies surely did not rule every kindergarten, the overwhelming focus of most leaders in the kindergarten movement was not merely American citizenship but world citizenship, suggesting a distinct vision of children's proper socialization during the early twentieth century.

Notes

1. Susan Elizabeth Blow, *Symbolic Education: A Commentary on Froebel's "Mother Play"* (New York, 1894), 8; "Field Notes," *Kindergarten Magazine* 5 (October 1892): 152.
2. Barbara Beatty, *Preschool Education in America: The Culture of Young Children from the Colonial Era to the Present* (New Haven, 1995); Michael Steven Shapiro, *Child's Garden: The Kindergarten Movement from Froebel to Dewey* (University Park, 1983); Evelyn Weber, *The Kindergarten: Its Encounter with Educational Thought in America* (New York, 1969).
3. Nina Catharine Vandewalker, *The Kindergarten in American Education* (New York, 1908), 121.
4. Earl Barnes, *How the Kindergarten Makes Americans*, U.S. Department of the Interior, Bureau of Education Kindergarten Circular No. 9 (Washington, D.C., 1923); "Local Efforts," *Foreign-Born* 1 (November 1919): 22; Bessie Locke, *Manufacturers Indorse the Kindergarten*, U.S. Department of the Interior, Bureau of Education Kindergarten Circular No. 4 (Washington, D.C., July 1919); "Mobilized Women Establish Kindergartens," *Americanization* 2 (1 September 1919): 4; *The Kindergarten and Americanization*, U.S. Department of the Interior, Bureau of Education Kindergarten Circular No. 3 (Washington, D.C., November 1918).
5. Ellen L. Berg, "Citizens in the Republic of Childhood: Immigrants and the American Kindergarten, 1880–1920" (PhD diss., University of California, Berkeley, 2004), 4; United States Immigration Commission, *The Children of Immigrants in Schools*, 5 vols, in Reports of the Immigration Commission, 41 vols (Washington, D.C., 1911).
6. "Americanization Should Begin Early," *Americanization* 1 (1 January 1919): 5; Bessie Locke, "Kindergarten Legislation in Behalf of Americanization," *Americanization* 1 (1 March 1919): 2; Locke, *Manufacturers Indorse the Kindergarten*, 1; Elizabeth Ash Woodward, "The Children's Year and the Opportunity of the Kindergarten for Conservation Work in Congested Cities," *The Kindergarten and First Grade* 3 (November 1918): 366-370.
7. Catherine R. Watkins, "The Kindergarten as a Profession," in *Proceedings of the Twenty-Seventh Annual Meeting of the International Kindergarten Union*, (1920): 143, Association for Childhood Education International (ACEI) Archives, Special Collections, University of Maryland Libraries; S. E. Weber, *The Kindergarten as an Americanizer*, U.S. Department of the Interior, Bureau of Education Kindergarten Circular No. 5 (Washington, D.C., December 1919); Elizabeth Ash Woodward, "Americanization Work of the Kindergarten: Abolition of Racial Prejudices, Barriers, and All that Keeps the People in America Apart," *The Kindergarten and First Grade* 5 (March 1920): 90.
8. Mary D. Bradford, "The Contribution of the Kindergartens to the Elementary Schools," in *Proceedings of the Twenty-Seventh Annual Meeting of the International Kindergarten Union*, (1920), 117, ACEI Archives.
9. Mary C. Shute, "The Practice of Democracy in the Kindergarten," *The Kindergarten and First Grade* 3 (March 1918): 90; Lucy Wheelock, "Report of Educational Committee," *The Kindergarten and First Grade* 2 (November 1917): 393.
10. Jenny B. Merrill, "Continued Report of IKU Opening Session, Monday, 8 P.M.," *Kindergarten-Primary Magazine* 32 (September 1919): 1; "Editorial Assault on the 'Play Spirit': Henry Sabin Answers Editor Kasson—Argument by Dr. Luther Gulick," *Kindergarten Magazine* 11

(December 1898): 261; John A. Thompson, *Reformers and War: American Progressive Publicists and the First World War* (Cambridge, 1987), 52–56.

11. Bradford, "The Contribution of the Kindergartens to the Elementary Schools," 118; Gertrude Stone, "Americanization in a Settlement Kindergarten," *The Kindergarten and First Grade* 4 (December 1919): 398; Lucy Wheelock, "Report of Committee of Nineteen," in *Proceedings of the Twenty-Seventh Annual Meeting of the International Kindergarten Union,* (1920), 53, ACEI Archives.

12. Almira M. Winchester, *Kindergarten Education* (Washington, D.C., 1918), 5. See also Luella Palmer, Grace E. Mix, and Catherine Walkins, "How the Kindergarten Provides Education," *Kindergarten-Primary Magazine* 29 (January 1917): 18–19.

13. Winchester, *Kindergarten Education,* 393.

14. Mary Dabney Davis and National Education Association of the United States, Department of Kindergarten Education, *General Practice in Kindergarten Education in the United States* (Washington, D.C., 1925), 13; Marvin Lazerson, "The Historical Antecedents of Early Childhood Education," in *National Society for the Study of Education: 21st Yearbook* (Chicago, 1972), 41; Nina Catharine Vandewalker, *Kindergarten Progress from 1919–20 to 1921–22,* U.S. Department of the Interior, Bureau of Education Kindergarten Circular No. 16 (Washington, D.C., 1924): 1.

15. "Report of Sub-Committee on Education of Committee of Nineteen," in *Proceedings of the Twenty-Fifth Annual Meeting of the International Kindergarten Union,* (1918), 85, ACEI Archives; Lella M. Ayres, "Neighborhood Food Conservation Classes," *The Kindergarten and First Grade* 3 (September 1918): 280; Hetty B. Schriftgiesser, "Training the Foreign Child for American Citizenship," *The Kindergarten and First Grade* 3 (November 1918): 365.

16. Grace Eldridge Mix, "International Kindergarten Union: Report of the Propaganda Committee," *The Kindergarten and First Grade* 3 (December 1918): 440; Pioneer Kindergarten Society, *Annual Report* (San Francisco, 1918), 20; Mary Melinda Kingsbury Simkhovitch, *Neighborhood: My Story of Greenwich House* (New York, 1938), 190; University of Chicago Settlement, "University of Chicago Settlement Kindergarten," (Chicago, 1918), 1; Lucy Wheelock, "A Message from the Educational War Activity Committee," *The Kindergarten and First Grade* 3 (December 1918): 443; Wheelock, "Report of Educational Committee," 392.

17. For a contrasting argument, see Barbara Beatty, "'The Letter Killeth': Americanization and Multicultural Education in Kindergartens in the United States, 1856–1920," in *Kindergartens and Cultures: The Global Diffusion of an Idea,* ed. Roberta Lyn Wollons (New Haven, 2000), 53–54.

18. Eileen Boris, "The Power of Motherhood: Black and White Activist Women Redefine the 'Political'," in *Mothers of a New World: Maternalist Politics and the Origins of Welfare States,* ed. Seth Koven and Sonya Michel (New York, 1993), 233.

19. Berg, "Citizens in the Republic of Childhood," 81–85.

20. "Report of Sub-Committee on Education of Committee of Nineteen," in *Proceedings of the Twenty-Fifth Annual Meeting of the International Kindergarten Union,* (1918), 85, ACEI Archives.

21. *The Kindergarten and Americanization,* 3.

22. Laura E. Whitney, "'Mericans' All," *Americanization Bulletin* 1 (December 1, 1918): 6.

23. Pioneer Kindergarten Society, *Annual Report* (San Francisco, 1916), 25.

24. Pioneer Kindergarten Society, *Annual Report* (San Francisco, 1915), 17.

25. The introduction to this 1918–1919 series is Gertrude Maynard, "A Year of Folk Tales," *The Kindergarten and First Grade* 3 (September 1918): 288–289.

26. "Practical Suggestions That Have Proved Their Worth," *The Kindergarten and First Grade* 4 (January 1919): 25; Stone, "Americanization in a Settlement Kindergarten," 399.

27. Olive Wills, "February," *Kindergarten-Primary Magazine* 29 (February 1917): 143.

28. Schriftgiesser, "Training the Foreign Child for American Citizenship," 264.

29. Berg, "Citizens in the Republic of Childhood," 150; Mary Florence Hay, "Americanization of the Foreign Child," *Kindergarten and First Grade* 6 (May 1921): 181.

30. Edna Dean Baker, "Value of the Kindergarten," *Child-Welfare Magazine* 13 (September 1918): 9; Maybell G. Bush, "The First School Days of the Non-English Child," *The Kindergarten and First Grade* 4 (June 1919): 215; Edna K. Haupt, "English in the Kindergarten," *The Kindergarten and First Grade* 1 (April 1916): 159; Mildred J. Surdam, "A Plan for Increasing the Vocabulary of Foreign-Speaking Children," *The Kindergarten and First Grade* 3 (May 1918): 190; Winchester, *Kindergarten Education*, 5; Elizabeth Ash Woodward, "Americanization Work of the Kindergarten: The Acquirement of a Common Language," *The Kindergarten and First Grade* 5 (February 1920): 45.

31. Pasadena (Calif.) Board of Education, *Pasadena Kindergartens, 1901–1919* (Pasadena, 1919), 18–21. See also Ruth Austin and Gads Hill Center, *Annual Report* (Chicago, 1919), 2.

32. Woodward, "Children's Year," 367.

33. Fred Clayton Butler, "America's Duty to the Next Generation," in *Proceedings of the Twenty-Sixth Annual Meeting of the International Kindergarten Union,* (1919), 169, ACEI Archives.

34. Social Service During the War Committee of the International Kindergarten Union, "More Suggestions for Social Service," *The Kindergarten and First Grade* 3 (February 1918): 79.

35. John Daniels, *America via the Neighborhood* (New York, 1920), 252; Elizabeth Ash Woodward, "Americanization Work of Kindergartners," *The Kindergarten and First Grade* 4 (April 1919): 129; Woodward, "Acquirement of a Common Language," 47. In one case, a Yugoslavian kindergartner in Oakland, California, offered classes "in English and the fundamentals of American institutions" to fathers. "American Press Comments," *Foreign-Born* 1 (April 1920): 12. However, most kindergartners appeared to believe that fathers had ample opportunities for Americanization, both informally and formally, through their workplaces and social service institutions. See, for example, Elizabeth Harrison, "The Kindergartner's Opportunity in the Problem of Americanization," *The Kindergarten and First Grade* 3 (June 1918): 221.

36. Baker, "Value of the Kindergarten," 9. See also Bradford, "The Contribution of the Kindergartens to the Elementary Schools," 114; "Why the Kindergarten Is a Vital Americanizing Agency," *Child-Welfare Magazine* 13 (April 1919): 234; Woodward, "Acquirement of a Common Language," 47.

37. Stone, "Americanization in a Settlement Kindergarten," 399. See also Woodward, "Abolition of Racial Prejudices, Barriers, and All that Keeps the People in America Apart," 91.

38. Merrill, "Continued Report of IKU Opening Session, Monday, 8 P.M.," 2–4; Shapiro, *Child's Garden,* 187.

39. Winchester, *Kindergarten Education,* 7.

40. "Shall the Name 'Kindergarten' Be Changed?" *The Kindergarten and First Grade* 4 (January 1919): 28; "Shall the Name 'Kindergarten' Be Changed?" *The Kindergarten and First Grade* 3 (December 1918): 432.

41. "Shall the Name 'Kindergarten' Be Changed?" *The Kindergarten and First Grade* 4 (March 1919): 108; "Shall the Name 'Kindergarten' Be Changed?" *The Kindergarten and First Grade* 4 (February 1919): 67.

42. "Shall the Name 'Kindergarten' Be Changed?" *The Kindergarten and First Grade* 4 (May 1919): 204.

43. Winchester, *Kindergarten Education,* 8.

44. Catharine R. Watkins, "Is It Advisable to Change the Name 'Kindergarten?'" in *Proceedings of the Twenty-Sixth Annual Meeting of the International Kindergarten Union* (1919), 158, ACEI Archives.

45. See Cecilia Elizabeth O'Leary, *To Die For: The Paradox of American Patriotism* (Princeton, 1999).

46. "Teaching Patriotism," *The Outlook* 55 (30 January 1897): 376.

47. Kate Douglas Smith Wiggin and Nora Archibald Smith, *The Republic of Childhood,* 3 vols., vol. 3: *Kindergarten Principles and Practice* (Boston, 1896), 63.

48. For internationalist viewpoints, see Sondra R. Herman, *Eleven against War: Studies in American Internationalist Thought, 1898–1921* (Stanford, 1969).

49. Alan Dawley, *Changing the World: American Progressives in War and Revolution* (Princeton, 2003). For discussions of the more imperialistic varieties of internationalism, see Eldon J. Eisenach, *The Lost Promise of Progressivism* (Lawrence, 1994); Eldon J. Eisenach, "Progressive Internationalism," in *Progressivism and the New Democracy*, ed. Sidney M. Milkis and Jerome M. Mileur (Amherst, 1999).

50. Dawley, *Changing the World*, 35–38.

51. Angeline Brooks, *Religious Education in the Public Schools* (1916), ACEI Archives.

52. Bertha Johnston, "The Committee of the Whole," *Kindergarten-Primary Magazine* 27 (October 1914): 59.

53. Bertha Johnston, "Additional Mother-Play Suggestions," *Kindergarten-Primary Magazine* 27 (April 1915): 259; Bertha Johnston, "Mother Play: The Bridge," *Kindergarten-Primary Magazine* 27 (May 1915): 276-277.

54. Bertha Johnston, "Mother Play—The Thumb Is One; Or Naming the Fingers," *Kindergarten-Primary Magazine* 29 (September 1916): 18–19.

55. Bertha Johnston, "Hints and Suggestions," *Kindergarten-Primary Magazine* 29 (November 1916): 65.

56. Charles E. Beals, "The Baroness von Suttner's Tour," *Advocate of Peace* 75 (January 1913): 9–10.

57. Kathryn Kish Sklar, "'Some of Us Who Deal with the Social Fabric': Jane Addams Blends Peace and Social Justice, 1907–1919," *Journal of the Gilded Age and Progressive Era* 2 (January 2003): 80–96.

58. Linda K. Schott, *Reconstructing Women's Thoughts: The Women's International League for Peace and Freedom before World War II* (Stanford, 1997), 43.

59. International Kindergarten Union, "Minutes of the Executive Board of the IKU, February 21–27, 1915," 213, ACEI Archives; International Kindergarten Union, "Minutes of the Mid-Year Meeting of Executive Board of the IKU, Dec. 29, 1914–Jan. 2, 1915," 208, ACEI Archives.

60. *Proceedings of the Twenty-Second Annual Meeting of the International Kindergarten Union* (1915), 157, 162, ACEI Archives.

61. Jenny B. Merrill, "Practical Suggestions for January," *Kindergarten-Primary Magazine* 27 (January 1915): 143.

62. International Kindergarten Union, "Minutes of the Executive Board of the IKU, August 16–21, 1915," 216, ACEI Archives.

63. Harriet Hyman Alonso, *Peace as a Women's Issue: A History of the US Movement for World Peace and Women's Rights* (Syracuse, 1993), 70; David M. Kennedy, *Over Here: The First World War and American Society* (Oxford, 1980), 30; Robert H. Zieger, *America's Great War: World War I and the American Experience* (Lanham, 2000), 140.

64. International Kindergarten Union, "Minutes of the Executive Board of the IKU, February 14–15, 1916," 221, ACEI Archives.

65. Winchester, *Kindergarten Education*, 392.

66. See, for example, Jane W. Bartlett, "There Is a Better Way," *Kindergarten-Primary Magazine* 29 (September 1916): n.p.

67. Alonso, *Peace as a Women's Issue*, 65.

68. Frances H. Early, *A World Without War: How US Feminists and Pacifists Resisted World War I* (Syracuse, 1997), 3.

69. H. C. Peterson and Gilbert C. Fite, *Opponents of War, 1917–1918* (Madison, 1957), 110.

70. David S. Patterson, "An Interpretation of the American Peace Movement, 1898–1914," in *Peace Movements in America*, ed. Charles Chatfield (New York, 1973), 23.

71. Marion Van Vliet, "Shall Chastisements Come by the Hand or the Rod? My Confession," *Kindergarten Magazine* 11 (October 1898): 92–96.

72. Berg, "Citizens in the Republic of Childhood," 175–176.

73. See, for example, Bertha Johnston, "Hints and Suggestions," *Kindergarten-Primary Magazine* 29 (May 1917): 239; Jenny B. Merrill, "Suggestions by Weeks," *Kindergarten-Primary Maga-*

zine 29 (February 1917): 146; Pioneer Kindergarten Society, *Annual Report* (San Francisco, 1918), 13.

74. Teresa R. Flaherty, "Americanizing the Immigrant Child," *The Kindergarten and First Grade* 3 (October 1918): 315; Johnston, "Hints and Suggestions," 239.

75. "N.E.A. Meeting Not To Be Postponed: President Wilson Sees No Reason Why This Should Be Done," *Kindergarten-Primary Magazine* 29 (June 1917): 243; Pasadena (Calif.) Board of Education, *Pasadena Kindergartens, 1901–1919*, 29–30; Pioneer Kindergarten Society, *Annual Report* (San Francisco, 1918), 21; "Social Service" in *Proceedings of the Twenty-Fifth Annual Meeting of the International Kindergarten Union*, (1918), 102, ACEI Archives.

76. Jane Addams, *Newer Ideals of Peace* (New York, 1915), 237.

77. Fanniebelle Curtis, "War Time," in *Proceedings of the Twenty-Fourth Annual Meeting of the International Kindergarten Union*, (1917), 148, ACEI Archives.

78. Fanniebelle Curtis, "The Kindergarten Unit in France," *The Kindergarten and First Grade* 3 (December 1918): 395–402; Elizabeth Harrison, "The Children of the World," *The Kindergarten and First Grade* 4 (February 1919): 76–78; "Report of Committee of Nineteen" in *Proceedings of the Twenty-Fifth Annual Meeting of the International Kindergarten Union*, (1918), 82–84, ACEI Archives; Annie Laws, "Committee on Foreign Affairs," in *Proceedings of the Twenty-Fourth Annual Meeting of the International Kindergarten Union* (1917), 150–151, ACEI Archives.

79. "How the Spirit of Giving Developed in Two Kindegartens [sic]," *The Kindergarten and First Grade* 4 (February 1919): 82.

80. Pasadena (Calif.) Board of Education, *Pasadena Kindergartens, 1901–1919*, 14.

81. Grace Everett Barnard, "The Report of Committee on Foreign Correspondence," in *Proceedings of the Twenty-Third Annual Meeting of the International Kindergarten Union*, (1916), 69, ACEI Archives.

82. Henry Neumann, "The Wisdom of Life and the Experiences of Children," *The Kindergarten and First Grade* 1 (September 1916): 279.

83. Quoted in Howard Jacob Karger, *The Sentinels of Order: A Study of Social Control and the Minneapolis Settlement House Movement, 1915–1950* (Lanham, 1987), 32.

84. *The Kindergarten and Americanization*, 2.

85. Mabel L. Culkin, "The Kindergarten and the War," *The Kindergarten and First Grade* 3 (June 1918): 236.

86. "Practical Suggestions That Have Proved Their Worth," *The Kindergarten and First Grade* 3 (December 1918): 426.

87. Dorothy A. Wall, "What Are We Going to Do with the War in the Kindergarten? A Unit of Work Developed through the Project Method," *The Kindergarten and First Grade* 3 (October 1918): 322.

Part III

PARENTAL RIGHTS AND STATE DEMANDS

Chapter 5

How Should We Raise Our Son Benjamin?
Advice Literature for Mothers in Early Twentieth-Century Germany

Carolyn Kay

In early twentieth-century Germany, bourgeois ideals of childhood became the popular subject of a wide range of advice books for parents and experts, written by doctors, psychologists, pedagogues, pastors, and feminists. While advice literature on child-rearing had existed in German society since the early modern period, as Steven Ozment and Gerald Strauss have shown,[1] and while prescriptive notions of parental discipline and children's obedience remained fairly consistent (with the exception of the more tolerant Enlightenment era), the modern views were nonetheless distinct and illuminating in ways that have not been explored by many historians. Closer study of these advice books reveals a greater emphasis upon the expert as the source of child-rearing advice (doctors and pedagogues especially); furthermore, in much of the literature there is a sacralization of the mother as the caregiver of young children. Indeed, the importance of the mother's role in child-rearing is acknowledged by such experts, and her self-sacrifice urged as a means of securing the stability of the family and the security of the nation.[2] The "bad" mother, on the other hand, is castigated by these experts as a destructive influence upon the nation's young children. Specifically, the experts attacked disinterested parenting by scolding mothers for mistakes such as selfishness in refusing to breastfeed, or the weak indulgence of children's bad behavior. The positive and correct development of the bourgeois child, meaning the civilizing of the child according to bourgeois norms, became the ideal—and the experts directed their "a-b-c's" of proper parenting almost exclusively at mothers. Advice literature in Imperial Germany highlights, then, the popular status of the expert, the new emphasis upon "correct" mothering, the gender divisions within the

Notes from this chapter begin on page 119.

bourgeois family of the industrial age, and the centrality of the family within the new German nation.

Analysis of this literature also allows the historian to approach prevailing bourgeois ideals of the era as enunciated by the experts—including the importance of self-mastery, productive work, adherence to authority, and orderliness—ideals that would ensure that the child emerged as a successful member of bourgeois society in the new Germany, civilized and obedient to distinct gender roles.[3] The failure of parents (especially mothers) to adhere to this advice, warned the experts, would result in willful, selfish, and dependent children who would weaken the *Volk* and ultimately the nation. The immense popularity of advice books in Imperial Germany suggests that, at the very least, mothers (and some fathers) felt compelled to consult the experts on raising children. In this article, I consider several examples of child-rearing literature by experts (professional or self-proclaimed), including two renowned doctors (Adalbert Czerny and Livius Fürst), a best-selling author and pedagogue (Adolf Matthias), feminist writers (Adele Schreiber and Laura Frost), and religious authors (Clara Heitefuss, Berta Mercator and Nikolaus Faßbinder). My research thus far—based upon a select sample of popular texts—considers the kinds of advice given as a barometer of prevailing social views held by bourgeois experts and the educated public.

In Imperial Germany, the family was the essential component of society—much more significant than the individual.[4] It was the chrysalis of future generations, able to nurture productive sons and marriageable daughters, and it fostered early notions of citizenship and thus national consciousness. Throughout Europe, the rise of the bourgeoisie and the division of work and home into separate spheres meant that the family became a haven for private emotions and "natural" morality. Acting, according to Peter Gay, "as the organizer of unruly passions, the preserver of cherished beliefs, and the chosen instrument of socialization,"[5] the bourgeois family engaged in what Mary Jo Maynes has called "an engrossing and contentious enterprise" to establish a proper family life.[6] Domesticity was welcomed, as the bourgeoisie set itself apart from other classes socially, culturally, and economically. The private home became the ideal setting for domesticity in prescriptive literature of the era, showcasing for the public a world filled with orderly children and loving parents. More emphasis was placed upon the mother, now responsible for bearing, protecting, and rearing the children (including teaching the little ones before they entered school). Definitions of motherhood shifted too, so that mothers were assessed not by how many children they bore and raised, but by how well they reared their children. A domestic ideology, clearly influenced by ideas of romanticism, took sway as men and women developed a quasi-religious reverence for family life. Family occasions—birthdays, christenings, and weddings—became commonplace, and Christmas celebrations were enormously popular, especially in Germany. The family portrait—captured by an artist or photographer—became as common as a Sunday stroll in the Tiergarten.[7]

Considering how prevalent middle-class notions of the sacrosanct family became, it is not surprising that such values extended beyond the middle class in Germany, or in Britain for that matter. Gunilla-Friederike Budde's comparative study of the nineteenth-century *Bürgertum* in both nations shows that while the middle class numbered somewhere between 5 and 16 percent of the population, its ideals of marriage and family had a profound effect on the attitudes of other classes.[8] Working-class memoirs of childhood in Imperial Germany, for example, often express anger and sadness at how the authors were deprived of loving domestic environments and the kinds of celebrations— especially at Christmas— that would have meant toys, turkey, and pudding. Thus, as Maynes has stressed, writers like Adelheid Popp "compared the hardships of their lives with the ideal notion of childhood along middle-class lines."[9] And it was not just workers who succumbed to romantic notions of the family: earlier in the nineteenth century public attitudes about the monarchy, in both Britain and Germany, extolled the importance of a good family, and the aristocracy came under attack for its scandalous habits and sham marriages. As Catherine Hall summed it up: "sexual licentiousness was out; marriage and the family were definitely in."[10]

At the center of this family was the child. In the period between 1890 and 1920 families in Germany became smaller as fertility declined (especially in urban areas).[11] Whether this change was due to a conscious decision by parents to limit the size of their households because of the expense of raising children, or because of the desire for a more intimate family unit,[12] the result was the same: the ideal size of the bourgeois family shrank to mother, father, and two or three children.[13] The satirical magazine *Simplicissimus* took great joy in parodying this bourgeois arrangement.[14]

With the change in family size we also see evidence of much closer bonds between parents and children, and particularly between mother and child. Bourgeois children lived longer (as did parents), especially as infant mortality rates declined for this class, in contrast to the high rates of infant death for the working and rural classes. Children of the middle class received close attention and care as love and affection, or at least duty, drew families together.[15] When tragedy did strike and a child died of disease or accident, parents expressed enormous sadness, equal to the suffering experienced at the loss of an adult family member.[16] Earlier in the century the high incidence of child mortality had left middle-class mothers forlorn and grief-stricken, evidence that deep connections with individual children already existed at this time;[17] as the century progressed such bonds intensified. Families in Germany and France used the familiar forms of address (*du* and *tu*) with their children; they lavished affection on tiny sons and precious daughters, recording every step, word, and growth.[18] Bourgeois children did not have to work outside the home and thus spent long hours of the day with mama; the parent-child bond had a much greater chance of deepening under these conditions. Indeed, by the time of the *Kaiserreich* middle-class Germans expressed a strong desire for children, seen as an essential part of any family, and they invested tremendous amounts of money, affection, and attention on their offspring.[19]

Furthermore, the notion of the child and of childhood became sentimentalized in memoirs, autobiographies, and fiction.[20] Budde notes, for example, that many German autobiographies of nineteenth-century middle-class life depict childhood positively as a sunny land of loving mothers and joyful homes where children were cared for, protected, and gently nurtured.[21] Parents of the era were equally guilty of indulging in sentimental approaches to the child: small children were tiny buds of joy in the garden of the family, sweet and full of blossoming promise.[22] At the same time the idea of children as independent beings who could see, hear, and feel in their own ways became more commonplace: this led to the conception of the child as separate from adult experience.[23] Children's nurseries, furniture, toys, and clothing appeared;[24] artists like Fritz von Uhde celebrated the unique world of the *Kinderstube*; and *Struwwelpeter* as well as *Max and Moritz* became enormously popular books in the burgeoning production of children's literature.[25]

In nineteenth-century Germany, middle-class attitudes to child-rearing also went through some distinct and fascinating shifts, as evidenced in Ann Taylor Allen's *Feminism and Motherhood in Germany, 1800–1914*. At the start of this century child-rearing was very much a public issue, and the writings of eighteenth-century pedagogues prevailed among the educated elites of the upper and middle classes, urging fathers to raise their children, including toddlers.[26] Rousseau's *Emile* was a model for this kind of approach, stressing the significance of male authority for the development of the child's character. But beginning with the writings of Pestalozzi and the romantic author Jean Paul, the role of the mother assumed greater significance. Pestalozzi, for example, believed that the love between mother and child helped to nurture the kind of relationship that would engender the child's sense of fraternity with others, and thus evoke in children a sense of moral responsibility to society.[27] His many writings extolled women's importance in rearing children, giving less weight to the notion of the mother's biological function and more to her moral and social guidance of the young. Thus, as Allen has argued, to Pestalozzi a mother's work had a "central culture-producing significance."[28] Jean Paul's approach, heavily influenced by romantic thought, praised a mother's innate ability to nurture and love her children; he argued that because of these qualities women must take responsibility for child-rearing in the home. To him, children were divine creatures, close to God, innocent and naturally good—and he believed that women were best able to raise these children because they resembled children in their emotionality.[29] Jean Paul's writings on child-rearing confined women to the private world of the home and excluded them from responsibility for public life—but he did acknowledge their crucial role in child-rearing.

Beginning with the kindergarten movement of the mid-nineteenth century (and the theories of Fröbel), new ideas of rearing and educating children took sway, and early feminists such as Bertha von Marenholtz-Bülow became involved.

Allen has called this development the emergence of spiritual motherhood: an ideology of social activism based upon the idea that education could improve and unify German society.[30] Fröbel praised the mother-child bond as loving and positive; he aimed to change children's education so that the end result would be adults who accepted the order of society freely and constructively. Thus he encouraged children's natural and free play, and a sense of belonging based upon love rather than fear of authority or force. Group games with other children and play with toys such as colorful blocks and balls could help the child's construction of order and reinforce the importance of cooperation.[31] As Fröbel's ideas spread among the educated middle class, more women sought to establish kindergartens in towns and cities, but it was not until the 1870s and 1880s that private kindergartens and kindergarten training programs were established in large numbers. What is particularly fascinating about Allen's study is her argument that German feminists saw the issue of motherhood and child-rearing as vitally important to German society and women's public activism. While historians like Richard Evans have argued that this emphasis upon the home revealed the conservatism of German feminism, Allen shows that German feminists connected the home with the public world, basing their social vision upon an ideal conception of the family and maternal love.[32]

Scientific Child-Rearing in Imperial Germany

From the last few decades of the nineteenth century onward, Imperial German society experienced yet another shift in ideas about children as the private world became increasingly public: the rise of scientific child-rearing. Experts on childhood (usually male)—pedagogues, psychologists, and doctors—weighed in on the debate over what sort of child-rearing produced the best results. Many books, pamphlets, journals, and newspaper articles appeared at this time, escalating in number after the turn of the century; while some were written by experts for experts, a larger number were directed at the public and became part of the popularizing trend of child-rearing advice. Most of the authors dedicated their ideas to the public at large and made some reference to workers and rural dwellers, but their advice was clearly intended for mothers who would stay at home and care for their children—bourgeois women. Moreover, despite the economic, social and cultural distances that separated rural from urban women, and workers from aristocrats and the female bourgeoisie, child-rearing experts tended to hold up the model of one kind of mother who used similar goals and methods to raise good, productive children: the firm, loving, and sensible bourgeois mother.[33]

In Imperial Germany advice books by doctors dominated the lists of child-rearing manuals, with German doctors assuring mothers that physicians knew best how to raise healthy children—especially in the modern world. This was certainly the approach taken by Dr. Adalbert Czerny, an acclaimed pediatric physician and professor. He was the author of *Der Arzt als Erzieher des Kindes* [The Physician as Child

Educator], which was first published in 1908 and remained in print, through nine editions, up until 1942.[34] Czerny acknowledged that in the past parents had successfully brought up their children by using the tried and true methods of their own parents' generation. "For typical parents," he pointed out, "textbooks or journals on child rearing were never a great necessity."[35] But according to Czerny, this tradition of parenting could only continue if the child were reared in the same conditions as his parents, a situation increasingly uncommon in modern Germany. Directing his comments to a bourgeois audience, Czerny stressed that most parents of his era had seen a steady increase in wealth, such that their children were brought up in luxury, with all sorts of opportunities. Parents now sought not just a good early education for their loved ones, but the best type of child-rearing—yet they had lost the ability to measure what was appropriate or helpful for this purpose.[36] As a result, Czerny concluded, doctors were being called upon more and more for direction in modern child-rearing, so that parents did not fall prey to doing too little or too much in bringing up their children.

Another popular text from this era was Dr. Livius Fürst's *Das Kind und seine Pflege* [The Child and His Care].[37] Fürst, like Czerny, was a respected physician of child medicine in Berlin. While he acknowledged in the book's foreword (for the edition in 1897) that popular texts on child-rearing were not viewed favourably by "scholarly circles," he nonetheless stressed the importance of a good book by an expert (a designation earned, in his own case, by thirty-three years of professional work). He offered the book to a general audience, reminding his readers that "every loss of a child is a loss of the nation's power."[38] Fürst's readers were likely women of the *Bürgertum,* as the kind of close and constant attention he prescribed for German mothers and the harsh criticism he reserved for working-class parents (whom he accused of neglect) make it likely that he was attempting to preach to his own class.

When we consider the books by Czerny and Fürst, along with other popular advice manuals in Imperial Germany—by doctors Christian Hufeland, Philip Biedert, and Friedrich Ammon, for example—the information on the physical care of the child is progressive and, by today's standards, often medically sound. Notably, all of these doctors advocated breastfeeding as the best and most natural method of feeding one's child,[39] evidenced in the lower infant mortality rates among mothers who breastfed (as opposed to those who used wet nurses or cow's milk). And all these authors complained that too many women refused breastfeeding out of fear or selfishness. Ammon, Fürst, and Hufeland also advised pregnant mothers to avoid alcohol, to get exercise and fresh air, to wear comfortable clothing (no restrictive corsets), and to eat a good mixture of vegetables and fruits.[40] Once the child was born, he or she needed regular feedings, lots of rest, fresh air both outside and inside his room (and no smoking!), frequent examinations by a doctor, vaccination against smallpox within the first year, and tender love from his devoted mother.[41]

For the historian considering these works, the bourgeois attitudes of the doctors—revealed particularly in their advice on how mothers should attempt to shape children's character—are striking. The virtues of cleanliness, orderliness, ethical behavior, self-improvement, and obedience to rules are praised as qualities to be nurtured in the child from the earliest days. Doctors were unable to escape their culture in the nineteenth and early twentieth centuries, as Peter Gay has noted in *The Bourgeois Experience*: "they were husbands and fathers, worried like other bourgeois about the precarious sanctity of their homes."[42] To Gay this is revealed in the medical literature on sexuality, and especially on masturbation (considered disturbing and dangerous), but we can also see bourgeois attitudes in the kind of child-rearing that many doctors, along with leading pedagogues of the era, advocated.

Above all, what appears again and again in the literature is the central role of the "good" mother in helping the child to develop in such a way as to practice self-mastery over his worst impulses, while also obeying and indeed revering his parents' authority. Most of the writers suggest or state outright that the child's nature tends towards the bad, and that given the chance by weak mothers he or she will be obstinate, contrary, and mischievous. Thus Czerny warns of the tyranny of young children who are coddled by mothers, or more commonly by older mothers and grandmothers, so that every caprice and wish of the infant is granted. He sees this as particularly dangerous in the first year of the baby's life, when so many habits are already being formed. Indulging the baby can only lead to the mother's loss of power, and by age two or three the child will terrorize the household[43] and will also refuse to eat properly or to heed the doctor's advice.[44] Fürst attacks *"Affenliebe"* (doting love), defining this slavish devotion as a central ingredient in weak parenting. Children with such mothers become "bad-tempered creatures" with "hateful characters."[45] Instead, mothers must be loving and firm—demanding obedience. Thus they need to learn to recognize the different cries and squeals of their babies, so that "vulgar" impulses and desires, such as willfulness, rage, and impetuosity, can be stifled as soon as possible.[46] Mothers should simply ignore the infant's demands by, for example, leaving a crying baby that is fed and dry to cry it out. In all cases, the offending child should be dealt with calmly and kindly, Fürst asserts, using corporal punishment as a last resort. "The child," he reminds his readers,

> quickly learns to recognize and return affection to the friendly face and loving hand. Alone, the child has a minor disposition to tyranny. He tries to carry through his wishes and greed, and later his will, by means of tears, crying, and temper tantrums. Here it becomes clear that from the beginning one must work against becoming the slave of the child. One should let him cry, delay giving him the demanded nourishment, ignore his tears and bad temper—and the child will soon notice that he will not achieve his aims in this way. He will put aside his practice of bad behavior unaffected by entreaties or order. He will thus learn to submit to a certain conformity and regularity, and will already feel the influence of education—while also not loving his mother any less.[47]

On the issue of punishment of the child by the mother, these writers are clear: the discipline should follow the bad action immediately, be just and fair—according to the severity of the child's act—and end with the mother reminding the child how much he or she is loved (thus stressing that the punishment was given out of love for the child's welfare). Hitting and slapping are accepted as appropriate responses to a child acting up, though not always as a first option. Instead, Fürst, for example, urges the mother to quietly and firmly correct the child, and when this does not work, to ignore the infant's screams and ultimately make clear to the child by facial features and raised voice that she is very displeased.[48] Czerny also advises the use of verbal warnings, as well as denial of the child's wishes or requests, but he makes clear that if a child repeatedly shows disobedience and noncompliance, corporal punishment must be used (is "essential"), and it must hurt to be effective. He does add, however, that such punishments should be quick and never excessive.[49] Fürst, too, concedes that hitting a child may be the best option for a parent seeking to correct bad behavior, although only the face, back, and hands should be struck and the parent should remember the delicate constitution of young children. Other punishments approved include shaming the child, removing comforts, and rebuking him or her.[50]

What Czerny and Fürst advocate, then, is the mother's careful manipulation of the child's will, so that only those actions that are deemed appropriate by the parent and do not in any way challenge her authority (or the father's) will be chosen by the child and become second nature. Czerny argued that children had to be taught to practice "self-mastery" as early as possible, to coincide with the child's subordination to the will of the parent. "The child not only learns to understand that he cannot have this or that," says Czerny, "he also learns to appreciate that what is done comes from the wish or order of the person who is responsible for his education."[51] As part of this process, correct and sometimes hard discipline is not to be shunned. However, both doctors also emphasize the crucial role of the loving mother in the rearing of children. Fürst declares that care of the child lies naturally in the hands of mothers—who are the center of every household and who offer love, care, and self-sacrifice.[52] Indeed, it is stressed that the child requires an environment of love and deep devotion from a gentle, nurturing mother (not from a nanny, or child nurse, or wet nurse, or any other member of the house staff). And the ideal image in each of these advice books is that of the loving bourgeois home in which affection is an essential element of the mother-child bond.

Czerny's approach to raising a child, made evident in *The Physician as Child Educator*, was fundamentally shaped by the rise of professional medicine and thus of pediatrics. He saw the child as a biological entity driven by the nervous system—and thus argued that the infant or toddler had to be protected from such excitable influences as excessive cuddling from his mother.[53] He states outright that the child needs to be taught self-discipline by the mother and that this can be realized most effectively if a baby is subjected from its earliest days to scientifically founded rules—i.e., a rigid system of feeding, potty training, nighttime sleeping, and personal cleanliness. As noted, the emphasis here was upon subjugating the child's will to that of the mother (through daily behavior), such that the child came to accept obedience and submission as natural to his or her development. Thus, Czerny's prescription for the socialization of the child, according to Reinhard Spree, "was to lead to self-control (control of the emotions and desires) which in turn should promote the two most important secondary aims: subordination to authority and social accommodation."[54] Spree believes that the ideas of Czerny and other pediatricians in Imperial Germany were very influential and encouraged the notion of the parent-child relationship as a kind of science, where the child became a machine, the parent an engineer.[55] Indeed, within this approach to rearing children, the individuality of the child—including his or her emotions, spontaneity, and unique character—was pushed aside, and thus children's needs were ignored. Spree goes as far as to suggest that such notions of child-rearing may have helped to create the authoritarian, intolerant, and insecure personality common to some followers of Nazism: "it could be argued," he states, "that the path to National Socialism was smoothed by quasi-scientific prescriptions for child socialization."[56]

Popular Pedagogy on Child-Rearing in Early Twentieth-Century Germany

The most popular child manual in early twentieth-century Germany was a book written by a professor of pedagogy: Adolf Matthias. He too called for discipline and love in the modern family. In 1896, Matthias's *Wie Erziehen wir unsern Sohn Benjamin?* [How Should We Raise Our Son Benjamin?] appeared in print, and in the foreword to a later edition of 1906 the author explained his interest in child-rearing. "In these days of unassuming and simple greatness on the battle-field we have become a strong and mighty people; the roots of that power to victory lie nowhere else than in our healthy family life and in our good rearing of children."[57] Making reference to the French defeat in 1871, Matthias intoned that "history teaches that a healthy family life forms the measure of the health of the entire nation, and that the decline of family life and children's upbringing constitutes an unmistakable sign of impending ruin." He lamented the influence of child-rearing practices that created flabby and haughty children. "We must protect our most precious gift, so that everywhere and always we will remain a vigorous people ready to defend ourselves."[58]

Matthias directed his best-selling book (which went through ten editions from 1896 to 1916) at mothers and fathers; indeed, he emphasized the crucial role of both parents in the upbringing of the child. His attacks on bad parenting often focused upon the mother, however, and singled out "*Affenliebe*"—spoiling the child—as a terrible mistake. The goal of educating Benjamin was to produce a moral, orderly, well tempered, resolute, physically strong, and obedient child—in other words, a child of good character and powerful self-control who respected authority. While it was crucial to help Benjamin to learn to direct himself—through self-mastery—parents were the essential guides in this process. Thus Matthias argued that although mothers could provide the love and care that were critical for any young child, fathers imparted a purposeful sense of power, seriousness, and authority; without the participation of the father in child-rearing, parents risked producing children that were too soft and indulgent.[59] But if both parents cooperated in raising their children, and if they supported each other at times when hard discipline was required, Benjamin would flourish. Like many authors, Matthias equated "the child" with the male child—here named after the youngest and most troublesome son of the biblical Jacob—although the advice given was meant to be beneficial for the rearing of both male and female children.

For Matthias, parents' responsibility for educating their children started early—in the first year of the infant's life. "From the first day, from the first breath of the child, one should govern the baby's tidiness and good habits as a first expression of authority over the rearing of the child—especially as one must exert an early instructional impression upon the spirit of the child."[60] By the fifth or sixth month parents could impose their will, since a baby at this point would be able to respond to tones of voice, a particular look, or even words. Little Benjamin could tell if his mother was happy or sad, angry or friendly. Thus parents could impose punishments by indicating they were angry, or—if it was necessary—by slapping the baby.[61] (Matthias justified slapping babies by arguing that if such punishment was not given early, the older child would more likely have to be thrashed severely.)

The author argued forcefully that parents must direct the child to choose what is right and good rather than what is bad, suggesting that the child's nature is inherently naughty. If disciplined early (when obeying one's parents is more natural) the baby would come to act in a good way as though this was second nature; if the parents did nothing, the child would later be unable to stop himself from being bad. Matthias set great store in the idea that the first year of a child's life would determine his future, and constantly reminded the reader that discipline problems would only escalate if they were not resolved as early as possible. Above all, he urged parents to stick to a strict schedule in caring for the child, to avoid catering to the many whims of a young baby, to encourage the child to be orderly and tidy, and to emphasize the necessity that the young child obey. "Early on, through practice, one must determine who will be the master."[62]

In two separate chapters on the child's will and on punishment of the child, Matthias lays bare his belief that parents must tame the child's impulses and shape behavior to what they find acceptable. One section in particular—on disciplining the child by refusing to speak to him or her—bears quoting, as it was selected by Alice Miller in her book on violence and child-rearing (*For Your Own Good*):

> A very fine and worthy position is assumed by silent punishment or silent reproof, which expresses itself by a look or an appropriate gesture. Silence often has more force than many words and the eye more force than the mouth. It has been correctly pointed out that man uses his gaze to tame wild beasts: should it not therefore be easy for him to restrain all the bad and perverse instincts and impulses of a young mind? If we have nurtured and properly trained our children's sensitivity from the beginning, then a single glance will have more effect than a cane or gentler influences ... For whom the Lord loveth, he correcteth.[63]

Miller points out that here the child is being asked to view parents as sharing in the divine omnipotence of God. And indeed, Matthias argues that children are happier and recognize it is a blessing "when they do not have to follow their own unrefined and uncertain will, but the honest, strong and unbending will of adults."[64]

Debates on Child-Rearing At the Turn of the Century

When Ellen Key wrote *The Century of the Child* (released in Germany in 1902), she attacked child experts who "continue to educate as if they believed still in the natural depravity of man, in original sin, which may be bridled, tamed, and suppressed" and who worked "to suppress the real personality of the child, and to supplant it with another personality."[65] Her attack on prevailing notions by experts such as those considered above found resonance in Germany, where her book had many readers. "Even men of modern times," she pointed out, "still follow in education the old rule of medicine, that evil must be driven out by evil."[66] This evil, of course, was corporal punishment—which Key equated with torture. For Key the solution to the dilemma of raising children was to allow each child to develop naturally, without force or deception, and to give the child respect and consideration just as one would another adult. The child's inherent characteristics were to be allowed free expression, as long as they did not injure another person or the child herself.

Key's provocative argument found supporters among child educators in early twentieth-century Germany, as the issue of child-rearing split those concerned into camps of disciplinarians and child advocates. This was the era of generational conflict—of the Youth Movement, or *Wandervogel*—which embraced ideas of independence, the spiritual regeneration of German society, and the superiority of youth. Authority was suspect, not only within the family, but also within the nation's political life. Moreover, new authors on child-rearing, influenced by Social Democratic ideas, began writing for working-class audiences. They urged parents to dispense with physical punishment and to allow their children to develop freely, respecting and nurturing the child's inherent qualities. A fascinating example of this approach is Julian Borchardt's *Wie sollen wir unsre Kinder ohne Prügel erziehen?* [How Should We Educate Our Children Without the Rod?], which first appeared in 1919.[67] Among these child advocates of the early 1900s were groups such as the Dürerbund, which released the journal *Am Lebensquell* [At the Source of Life] in 1909, 1913, and 1917. The essays in the edition for 1917 encourage frank and open discussions of sexuality with one's children and begin with the reminder that "[a] small child is, in truth, neither moral or immoral: he is simply amoral, without knowledge of good or evil."[68]

Taking a similar position, the two-volume *Das Buch vom Kinde* [The Book of the Child] released in 1907 and edited by feminist and socialist sympathizer Adele Schreiber, offered the latest research on the physical and emotional development of the child. In the forward to volume one, Schreiber attacked "*Erzie-*

hungsdespotismus" (educational despotism) and all those who sought to break and enslave youth.[69] This point was taken up by Laura Frost in her article entitled "Allgemeine Charaktererziehung im frühen Kindesalter" [The General Education of Character in Early Childhood]. She rejects the presumption in most advice manuals that education of the child, beginning from birth, should result in the infant's complete submission to the power and superiority of her or his parents as early as the end of the first year. Noting how this approach involves breaking the will of the child, Frost argues

> We also demand good and well behaved children, but we don't want this result to be achieved through forcing the child's personality; instead there should be sympathetic guidance and development of children's natural tendencies ... The child is not a piece of our property with whom we can do as we like—according to our wishes—or on whom we should imprint a rubber stamp of our personality. A child is an independent small being, and as such must be treated with understanding.[70]

Mothers needed to create a nurturing environment in the home, offering positive reinforcement of the child's accomplishments and characteristics in order to produce a happy, strong, sensitive, and intelligent person. Love, not fear or punishment, was to be offered consistently. And while Frost did acknowledge that discipline of the child was sometimes necessary, her solution was to place the child in her or his room for an hour's rest, since the quiet would do the child good and likely allow her or him to reflect on what was done wrong.[71] A time-out, instead of the rod, was the way of the future.

There were female writers on child-rearing who rejected these views. Clara Heitefuss, for example, the wife of an evangelical minister and founder of the Pfarrfrauen-Schwesternbund, wrote in *Mutter und Kind* [Mother and Child] (1913) that respect for authority was on the decline and it was essential for the Christian mother to raise her children to be obedient, pious, and selfless. Her argument skewers the selfishness of modern times, including the pursuit of material wealth and personal comfort; in contrast, Heitefuss calls for cohesion, love, and hierarchy in the family. Recalcitrant wives must respect their husbands, bad children their mothers and fathers. She directs mothers to take on the duty of punishing the children physically, reminding them that a Christian mother has the highest authority on her side, and that if the child has chosen evil, "holy love" can punish because it is just and right.[72] Berta Mercator's *Was braucht mein Kind?* [What Does My Child Need?][73]—published in 1906—also supports corporal punishment, including striking the infant for not using the potty correctly. Like Matthias, Mercator stresses domination of the child by the parent, such that the will of the child is subordinate. At the same time she encourages calm and caring affection between mother and child, and reminds the reader how ennobling and significant motherhood is for all women—a blessing from God. In both of these advice books we see the conservative influence of German Protestantism, particularly in the authors' defense of patriarchy and discipline within the family.

Catholic authors raised similar themes. A Catholic headmaster in Trier, Niko-laus Faßbinder, wrote a wartime text entitled *Am Wege des Kindes: Ein Buch für Eltern und Erzieher* [Along the Children's Path: A Book for Parents and Teachers] (1915). This work paints a very romantic portrait of the devoted, loving mother and of her responsibility to nurture her children. Mother-love, he argues, is the greatest and the most important kind of love in human life. A mother who truly cares for her children will choose between the base desires of the child and the higher goals that will provide a good education. She will be selfless, and direct her love for the true benefit of the child.[74] As a contrast to this good woman, Faßbinder laments the kind of mother who inflicts grave harm upon the child—and thus he speaks of the "unnatural mother"—child murderers or mothers who neglect their children.

Yet, for Faßbinder, the far greater problem is that of the indulgent mother, a woman who gives in to what he calls "women's weaknesses." As examples of such mothers Faßbinder lists a number of types: mothers who cannot bear to hear their children cry, and so feed them on demand. Or mothers who ruin children's teeth and stomachs with sweets. Mothers who know their children have delicate constitutions and yet let them use swings or kiss them too much—which over-stimulates them. He also criticizes mothers who threaten and threaten but do not punish, and mothers who always find excuses for their sons.[75] Here we see, once more, the notion of "*Affenliebe*"—of the doting mother who will ruin her child through too much love and permissiveness. Again, the idea that good mothers must be tough and must discipline their children, even while offering them love, is the model most experts prescribe for women to follow.

The Experts on German Child-Rearing: Discipline or Love?

In her book on American child-rearing in the twentieth century, *Raising America,* author Ann Hulbert argues that experts on children have consistently faced one essential problem: "as children—and just as important, their mothers—prepare to meet the pressures and the allures of an increasingly materialistic and meritocratic mass society, is it more discipline or more bonding that they need at home?"[76] In Imperial Germany the experts tended to recommend more discipline, although they did not deny the significance of close relationships between parents and chil-dren. There is plenty of evidence of support for mother-centered child-rearing, with love and affection considered by the experts a natural and indeed essential part of the family. Parental love for the child was praised as the most beauti-ful and moral form of affection, and care of the child was said to teach parents equally valuable qualities: self-renunciation, patience, persistence, and devotion to others.[77] Here we see examples of the cultural shift in nineteenth- and early twentieth-century bourgeois attitudes to the child, and the acceptance by experts of close emotional bonding between parents and their offspring.

However, experts on the child also attacked mothers who doted too much on their children, or who through overindulgence produced selfish and lazy youth. The advice seems to have been that love is good, but too much love can be dangerous. And in some of the most popular books on child-rearing, mothers were warned to keep their babies to a rigid schedule of feeding and sleep, and to discipline them as early as possible. The goal here was to produce children who were organized, orderly, productive, self-disciplined, respectful to parents (and later to schoolteachers), and obedient: in other words, the children were to be civilized, and thus made ready to enter middle-class society. Gender roles were given emphasis by the end of the first year, when boys were offered more opportunity for outdoor activity, and when toys (dolls for girls, soldiers and trains for boys) began to accentuate gender-specific characteristics. Nonetheless, experts did not stress gendering the child in its early years; rather, this became a stronger theme in the advice literature on parenting children from ages seven and up.

While it is true that advice literature on child-rearing cannot reveal to the historian what parents actually did within the home—whether they rejected or took to heart the advice they read—there is still much to be learned here. Indeed, advice literature offers information on the culture of advice giving—on attitudes and beliefs shared by the experts—and on socially constructed ideals of the family. In the German case we see several important aspects. First, there is the increase in the number of popular books on child-rearing coinciding with the ascent of science and medicine in the Wilhelmine era and indicative of growing interest in these disciplines among professionals and the lay public alike. One might assume that the prestige and stature of these experts endowed their recommendations on child-rearing with considerable power to prescribe norms and standards that parents felt pressure to emulate. A strategy repeatedly used by authors of this advice literature was to present parents with the specter of the bad mother (coddling or overindulging the infant) and of the failed child who became lazy, defiant, and selfish. The message to parents was that such mistakes would cause enormous harm to the family if this advice was not heeded.

Second, the advice literature of this period makes clear the crucial role of the mother in the German family and places significant pressure upon her to raise sensible, learned, and orderly children. Third, we see several of the predominant values of bourgeois culture—self-mastery, responsibility, and productive activity—echoed in the advice of the child-rearing manuals. Middle-class parents turning to these books learn that preparing their child to become an industrious, successful, and cooperative member of bourgeois society is a worthy and indeed crucial task, and will ultimately strengthen the nation and the *Volk*. Fourth, we see a conflict between advice given by doctors, pedagogues, and religious authors, emphasizing the importance of discipline and subordination of the child, and the critics of such an approach (Ellen Key, Adele Schreiber, Laura Frost) who advocate a much freer development of the child's natural characteristics.

In this conflict we see the rise of hereditarian thought, contained within the early study of eugenics.[78] According to psychologists such as Wilhelm Preyer (author of *Die Seele des Kindes* [The Mental Development of the Child], 1881) children's characteristics are set by hereditary traits, and cannot be educated. The role of the mother, then, is to allow these characteristics to develop naturally, not to attempt to mold or shape them through restrictive child-rearing.[79] Ellen Key accepted such ideas (she was a supporter of Darwinian thought), and her views extended to books like Adele Schreiber's *Das Buch vom Kinde*. In the twentieth century the battle over nature versus nurture would continue to be central to notions of the child. Finally, the popularity of advice books asking "How do I educate my child?"—written by middle-class experts protecting bourgeois values—offers the historian more evidence of the centrality of bourgeois culture, and indeed of the bourgeois family, within Imperial Germany.

Notes

1. Steven Ozment, *When Fathers Ruled: Family Life in Reformation Europe* (Cambridge, MA, 1983); Gerald Strauss, *Luther's House of Learning: Indoctrination of the Young in the German Reformation* (Baltimore, 1978). See also Joel F. Harrington, "Bad Parents, the State, and the Early Modern Civilizing Process," *German History* 16, no. 1 (1998): 16–28.
2. See Rebekka Habermas, "Parent-Child Relationships in the Nineteenth-Century," *German History* 16, no. 1 (1998): 43–55.
3. See Christa Berg, "Rat Geben: Ein Dilemma pädagogischer Praxis und Wirkungsgeschichte," *Zeitschrift für Pädagogik* 37, no. 5 (1991): 709–734.
4. Thomas Nipperdey, *Deutsche Geschichte 1866–1918*, vol. 1 (Munich, 1990), 43. See also Ingeborg Weber-Kellermann, *Die deutsche Familie* (Frankfurt a. M., 1974), 102–118.
5. Peter Gay, *Education of the Senses*, vol. 1 of *The Bourgeois Experience* (New York, 1984), 423.
6. Mary Jo Maynes, "Class Cultures and Images of Proper Family Life," in *Family Life in the Long Nineteenth Century 1789–1913*, ed. David Kertzer and Marzio Barbagli (New Haven, 2002), 195.
7. Angelika Lorenz, *Das deutsche Familienbild in der Malerei des 19. Jahrhunderts* (Darmstadt, 1985), viii–ix.
8. Gunilla-Friederike Budde, *Auf dem Weg ins Bürgerleben: Kindheit und Erziehung in deutschen und englischen Bürgerfamilien 1840–1914* (Göttingen, 1994), 25.
9. Maynes, "Class Cultures and Images of Proper Family Life," 214.
10. Catherine Hall, "The Sweet Delights of Home," in *A History of Private Life*, vol. 4, ed. Michelle Perrot (Cambridge, MA, 1990), 50.
11. Kertzer and Barbagli, *Family Life in the Long Nineteenth Century 1789–1913*, xxiii–xxiv.
12. Ibid., xxiii–xxviii.
13. Budde, *Auf dem Weg ins Bürgerleben*, 56–57. In the twentieth century, workers and agricultural laborers would also limit the size of their families: Kertzer and Barbagli, *Family Life in the Long Nineteenth Century 1789–1913*, xxiv.
14. Budde, *Auf dem Weg ins Bürgerleben*, 56.
15. Loftur Guttormsson, "Parent-Child Relations," in Kertzer and Barbagli, *Family Life in the Long Nineteenth Century 1789–1913*, 265. On parent-child relations in Germany see also Habermas, "Parent-Child Relationships in the Nineteenth-Century" and Nicholas Stargardt, "German Childhoods: The Making of a Historiography," *German History* 16, no. 1 (1998): 1–15.
16. Michelle Perrot, "Roles and Characters," in Perrot, *A History of Private Life*, vol. 4, 212.

17. Ann Taylor Allen, *Feminism and Motherhood in Germany, 1800–1914* (New Brunswick, NJ, 1991), 47.

18. Nipperdey, *Deutsche Geschichte,* 56; Perrot, "Roles and Characters," 208; Budde, *Auf dem Weg ins Bürgerleben,* 193.

19. Nipperdey, *Deutsche Geschichte,* 54–55; Guttormson, "Parent-Child Relations," 265.

20. Maynes, "Class Cultures and Images of Proper Family Life," 213.

21. Budde, *Auf dem Weg ins Bürgerleben,* 22, 194. Reminiscences of childhood by German Jews also took on a nostalgic character, emphasizing the happy and prosperous years of the *Kaiserreich* era: see Ursula Blömer and Detlev Garz, eds., *"Wir Kinder hatten ein herrliches Leben": Jüdische Kindheit und Jugend im Kaiserreich, 1871–1918* (Oldenburg, 2000).

22. C. Michael, "Vernünftige Gedanken einer Hausmutter: Glückliche Jugend," *Die Gartenlaube* 33 (1879): 548–549.

23. Budde, *Auf dem Weg ins Bürgerleben,* 193.

24. See Ingeborg Weber-Kellermann's *Die Kindheit* (Frankfurt a. M., 1979), 100–156; 192–230.

25. For a list of the most popular children's books in nineteenth-century Germany, see Budde, *Auf dem Weg ins Bürgerleben,* 129.

26. Allen, *Feminism and Motherhood in Germany,* 20–21.

27. Ibid., 24.

28. Ibid., 26.

29. Ibid., 29.

30. Ibid., 66.

31. Ibid., 38.

32. Ibid., 59. A more recent book by Allen highlights the importance of motherhood to German feminists of this era: see Ann Taylor Allen, *Feminism and Motherhood in Western Europe, 1890–1970* (New York, 2005). Also see Richard Evans, *The Feminist Movement in Germany, 1894–1933* (London, 1976).

33. Irene Hardach-Pinke, "Zwischen Angst und Liebe: Die Mutter-Kind Erziehung seit dem 18. Jahrhundert," in *Zur Sozialgeschichte der Kindheit,* ed. Jochen Martin and August Nitschke (Freiburg, 1986), 541.

34. Adalbert Czerny, *Der Arzt als Erzieher des Kindes* (Leipzig, 1908; rpt. 1942). On Czerny see Albrecht Peiper, *Chronik der Kinderheilkunde* (Leipzig, 1992), 287–289. In the United States, too, scientific child-rearing became very popular at the *fin-de-siècle,* with doctors Emmett Holt and Stanley Hall the most famous writers on the subject. See Ann Hulbert, *Raising America: Experts, Parents, and a Century of Advice About Children* (New York, 2003), 19–93.

35. Czerny, *Der Arzt als Erzieher des Kindes,* 1.

36. Ibid., 1–2.

37. Dr. Livius Fürst, *Das Kind und seine Pflege* (Leipzig, 1886; rpt. 1897). Other well-known child-rearing manuals by doctors include Dr. Friedrich August von Ammon's *Die ersten Mutterpflichten und die erste Kindespflege* (Dresden, 1827), which by 1898 was in its 36th printing; Dr. Georg Drechsler, *Mutterfreuden, Muttersorgen: Pflege dein Kind!* (Aachen, 1898); Dr. Christian Hufeland, *Guter Rath an Mütter über die wichtigsten Punkte der physischen Erziehung der Kinder in den ersten Jahren* (Leipzig, 1865; rpt. 1803); Th. Goerges, *Das Kind im ersten Lebensjahr* (Berlin, 1902); and Dr. Philip Biedert, *Das Kind, seine geistige und körperliche Pflege von der Geburt bis zur Reife* (Stuttgart, 1906).

38. Fürst, *Das Kind und seine Pflege,* 4.

39. Ammon, *Die ersten Mutterpflichten und die erste Kindespflege,* 35–37; Fürst, *Das Kind und seine Pflege,* 5–7, 52; Hufeland, *Guter Rath an Mütter,* 13–14.

40. See, for example, Ammon, *Die ersten Mutterpflichten und die erste Kindespflege,* 5–52.

41. Hufeland, *Guter Rath an Mütter,* 19, 36. On the other hand, advice that babies should sleep through the night by six months, endure daily cold washes, and be potty trained within the first year seems indeed to belong to the historical past.

42. Gay, *Education of the Senses,* 316. On physicians' anxiety regarding masturbation, see 294–318.

43. Czerny, *Der Arzt als Erzieher des Kindes*, 19.
44. Ibid., 19–21.
45. Fürst, *Das Kind und seine Pflege*, 188–189.
46. Ibid., 188.
47. Ibid.
48. Ibid., 187–190, 224.
49. Czerny, *Der Arzt als Erzieher des Kindes*, 37–41.
50. Fürst, *Das Kind und seine Pflege*, 225.
51. Czerny, *Der Arzt als Erzieher des Kindes*, 29.
52. Fürst, *Das Kind und seine Pflege*, 15.
53. Reinhard Spree, "Shaping the Child's Personality: Medical Advice on Child-Rearing from the Late Eighteenth to the Early Twentieth Century in Germany," *Social History of Medicine* 5 (1992): 331–332.
54. Ibid., 331.
55. Ibid., 332.
56. Ibid., 335.
57. Dr. Adolf Matthias, *Wie erziehen wir unsern Sohn Benjamin?* (Munich, 1896; rpt. 1911), xiii–xiv.
58. Ibid., xiii–xiv.
59. Ibid., 8–9.
60. Ibid., 4.
61. Ibid., 4.
62. Ibid., 4.
63. Ibid., 101, 105. The translated passage appears in Alice Miller, *For Your Own Good: Hidden Cruelty in Child-Rearing and the Roots of Violence*, trans. Hildegarde and Hunter Hannum (New York, 1984), 37–38.
64. Matthias, *Wie erziehen wir unsern Sohn Benjamin?* 76.
65. Ellen Key, *The Century of the Child* (New York, 1909; rpt. 1900), 107, 108. The German edition is entitled *Das Jahrhundert des Kindes* (Berlin, 1902).
66. Ibid., 107.
67. Julian Borchardt, *Wie sollen wir unsre Kinder ohne Prügel erziehen?* (Berlin, 1919). On the *Wandervogel* see Robert Wohl, *The Generation of 1914* (Cambridge, MA, 1979), 43–47 and Peter Strachura, *The German Youth Movement, 1900–1945* (London, 1981).
68. Dürerbund, *Am Lebensquell: Ein Hausbuch zur Geschlechtlichen Erziehung* (Dresden, 1917), 3.
69. Adele Schreiber, ed., *Das Buch vom Kinde*, 2 vols. (Leipzig, 1907), vol. 1, iii–iv.
70. Laura Frost, "Allgemeine Charaktererziehung im frühen Kindesalter," in Schreiber, *Das Buch vom Kinde*, vol. 1, 42.
71. Ibid., 50.
72. Clara Heitefuss, *Mutter und Kind* (Barmen, 1913), 44–45.
73. Berta Mercator (real name Berta Josephson), *Was braucht mein Kind? Fragen und Antworten für Mutter von einer Mutter* (Potsdam, 1906). This book went through 8 editions, and was published up to 1935.
74. Nikolaus Faßbinder, *Am Wege des Kindes: Ein Buch für Eltern und Erzieher* (Freiburg, 1915; rpt. 1923), 25–26.
75. Ibid., 37–38.
76. Hulbert, *Raising America*, 7.
77. See for example C. Michael, "Unsere Kinder als der Eltern Erzieher," *Die Gartenlaube* 4 (1879): 65–67.
78. Allen, *Feminism and Motherhood in Germany*, 156.
79. Ibid., 157. Wilhelm Preyer, *Die Seele des Kindes: Beobachtungen über die geistige Entwickelung des Menschen in den ersten Lebensjahren* (Leipzig, 1881).

Chapter 6

DEBUNKING MOTHER LOVE
American Mothers and the Momism Critique in the Mid Twentieth Century

Rebecca Jo Plant

Almost 19 years ago, on my 25th birthday, I gave birth to a son. I remember lying in the hospital bed and thinking what a terrible responsibility that was. Projecting myself forward, I saw myself at forty: one of those white haired, charming, terrible octopus women in a smart lilac colored suit, violets, and immaculate gloves. I was sitting in a fashionable restaurant with a handsome young man, and we were celebrating "our" birthday. That vision frightened me. I saw how easily I could forge a chain out of the accident of these simultaneous birthdays. I imagined how he could be summoned from school, from his job, and later from his own family, because it was "our birthday, and we have always celebrated it together." And I made a quiet vow there and then that where ever else I succeeded or failed in motherhood, this was one tragedy I would not bring about.[1]

In 1957, Mrs. O. of Napa, California, recollected the thoughts that had passed through her mind after giving birth to her son in the 1930s. Contemplating her new role, she had immediately envisioned an image of the type of mother that she did *not* want to become. That image was vivid in details: a middle-aged woman who relied on the accessories of respectable femininity—violets and white gloves—to conceal her "terrible octopus" nature. Such a woman would regard her handsome young son as but another accessory, and she would exploit the fact that they shared a birthday to strengthen her hold over him. To be a truly good mother, as opposed to the type of mother that society lauded, Mrs. O. believed that she would need to resist the temptation to cultivate an intimate relationship that might prove gratifying for her, yet detrimental to her son.

Why was a new mother in the late 1930s haunted by the fear that her love for her helpless newborn would one day prove harmful? Or, granting the sug-

---

gestible character of memory, why did a middle-aged mother in the late 1950s recall having had such ominous postpartum reflections? The historical specificity of Mrs. O.'s account appears in sharper focus when contrasted with that of Sarah Huntington, a middle-class Bostonian who wrote the following diary entry after giving birth to her first child in 1820: "Deeply impressed with a sense of the vast importance of a mother's duties, and the lasting effect of youthful impressions, I this day resolve to endeavour, at all times, by my precepts and my example, to inspire my children with just notions of right and wrong, of what is to be avoided and what pursued, of what is sacredly to be deserved and what unreservedly depreciated."[2] Although both women experienced an overwhelming sense of responsibility upon becoming mothers, their fears as to how they might fail their children could scarcely have differed more. Sarah Huntington, anxious that she would not be mother *enough,* pledged to follow a course of self-vigilance and intervention, molding her newborn and future children into virtuous adults. Mrs. O., fearful that she would mother *too much,* vowed to practice self-restraint, lest she stymie her son's ability to function as an unfettered and autonomous adult.

The striking difference between these two women's reflections points to a dramatic transformation in the cultural construction of maternal affectivity that significantly influenced middle-class mothers' behavior and emotional lives. In the wake of the First World War, the ideal of mother love that had taken root in Sarah Huntington's day came under vigorous assault.[3] Cultural critics and psychological experts rejected three tenets of moral motherhood with special vehemence: the conviction that mother love was the purest of all human sentiments, entirely unrelated to sexual desire; the notion that motherhood entailed tremendous self-sacrifice and that children incurred debts to their mothers that could never be repaid; and the belief that mothers should forge emotionally intense relationships with their children to keep them on the path of virtue.[4] By the 1940s and 1950s, these views had been all but inverted. Recasting motherhood as the pinnacle of "feminine fulfillment," psychological experts and their popular exponents jettisoned the concept of maternal self-sacrifice and reversed the trajectory of indebtedness between mother and child. They warned that maternal attachment could be narcissistic, and that women's unmet sexual desires could easily—and disastrously—become misdirected toward their children, especially their sons. Finally, they insisted that, after a period of intense attachment during the child's first few years, mothers should restrain their maternal impulses in order to encourage separation and emotional independence. Particularly in the two decades following the Second World War, commentators and experts betrayed a wariness of mothers and maternal influence that Victorian Americans could scarcely have fathomed.

It is difficult to reconcile the extent and intensity of postwar mother-blaming with standard views of the era as one that glorified suburban domesticity and motherhood. Until recently, women's historians have portrayed the domestic ideology that flourished after the Second World War as a virtual resurgence of Victorian gender ideals, updated to reflect contemporary sexual mores. "Women were directed right back to where they had been a century earlier—in captivity of the cult of motherhood," historian Mary Ryan wrote in 1983. "All the sophisticated involutions of clinical and popular psychoanalysis only served to direct the American woman back to familiar roles, exiling her not only to the bedroom and the maternity ward, but to the kitchen, nursery, and dressing table."[5] Historian Joanne Meyerowitz and others subsequently challenged this narrative by arguing that all women were "not June Cleaver" and that popular culture in fact frequently lauded women's "nondomestic activity, individual striving, and public success."[6] But scholars have yet to recognize how radically the postwar maternal ideal itself departed from the past. Not only was domestic ideology less hegemonic than previously assumed, it also promoted a strikingly new view of motherhood premised on a rejection of past ideals and practices. Rather than an era that resurrected Victorian ideals of motherhood, the 1940s and 1950s should be seen as a period in which the demystification of mother love achieved dominance in mainstream American culture.

I advance this argument through a new interpretation of the "momism critique"—a curious mixture of psychological diagnosis and cultural analysis first articulated by the popular writer Philip Wylie in his sensational bestseller of 1942, *Generation of Vipers.*[7] Employing a style that veered between biting satire and apocalyptic jeremiad, Wylie warned that maternal dominance was eroding American individualism and masculine fortitude, leaving the nation vulnerable to external threats and internal decay. Though modernist writers and psychological experts had been railing against overbearing mothers since at least the 1920s, Wylie's critique stood out for its extraordinary venom and for the linkages that he drew between momism and other "isms" that threatened the nation's democratic order, namely fascism and communism.[8] Throughout the 1950s and into the 1960s, "momism" remained an influential diagnosis of the white, middle-class American family—a term that conjured up images of domineering and shrewish mothers, henpecked fathers, and maladjusted children who drifted toward homosexuality or juvenile delinquency.[9]

Scholars have often viewed the momism critique as a byproduct of, or a kind of counter-reaction to, a more dominant gender ideology that glorified motherhood. In contrast, I argue that it helped to establish the narrow limits within which maternal influence could be unequivocally celebrated.[10] To be sure, leading child-rearing experts in the 1940s and 1950s, including the phenomenally successful Benjamin Spock, perceived maternal care as absolutely essential to healthy development.[11] However, they did not praise mothers for acting as vigilant moral guardians of their children's souls, as in Victorian times, nor for conscientiously following rigid schedules, as in the immediately preceding decades. Instead, psychological experts of various schools urged women to follow their "natural" instincts by gratifying infants' needs and desires. Only constant and loving maternal care in infancy and early childhood, they repeatedly stressed, could instill the sense of "security" that would allow children to develop into autonomous adults and democratic citizens. As scholars have noted, this new permissive child-rearing ideology intensified maternal obligations by tethering mothers closely to young children and by enhancing their responsibility for psychological as well as physical development.[12] What has been less recognized, however, is that the very same prescriptions simultaneously delimited the maternal role. Not only did experts portray the benefits of maternal care as concentrated in the very earliest years of life, they also demoted "mother love" to "maternal instinct"—a powerful psychobiological drive. By stigmatizing prolonged mother-child (especially mother-son) intimacy as pathological, they urged women to adopt a more self-conscious and wary stance toward their maternal feelings and impulses.

The momism critique comprised only a single chapter of *Generation of Vipers*—a mere nineteen pages—but reviewers and many readers singled it out as the most provocative and compelling part of the book.[13] The chapter resonated in large part because Wylie infused a familiar caricature—the priggish and provincial American matron—with new and sinister meaning. "Never before," he thundered, "has a great nation of brave and dreaming men absent-mindedly created a huge class of idle, middle-aged women."[14] Whereas previously, mom had "folded up and died of hard work somewhere in the middle of her life," she now emerged from her childbearing years with prodigious energy, which she poured into shopping and a host of meddlesome activities.[15] Wylie's attack on "moms" did not focus exclusively, or even primarily, on their behavior as parents, for he also decried their influence as clubwomen, citizens, and consumers. At base, he challenged the idea that women should be seen as entitled to special influence and prerogatives, in either the public or the private realm, because of their status as mothers.[16] Once psychiatrists and social scientists began appropriating the term in works of their own, however, "momism" came to be understood more narrowly—as a quasi-diagnosis of a certain type of pathogenic mother.

Though the momism chapter reads more like a satirical sketch than a fully developed argument, Wylie leveled several damning accusations at moms in their capacity as child-rearers. First, he insisted that maternal "self-sacrifice" was in truth a selfish and manipulative strategy designed to keep children trapped in emotional bondage. Second, he claimed that the resulting infantilization prevented sons from redirecting their affective energies away from their mothers, which in turn rendered them incapable of forming mature, heterosexual relationships. As he scathingly wrote in *Generation of Vipers*:

> "Her boy," having been "protected" by her love, and carefully, even shudderingly, shielded from his logical development through his barbaric period, or childhood … is cushioned against any major step in his progress toward maturity. Mom steals from the generation of woman behind her (which she has, as a still further defense, also sterilized of integrity and courage) that part of her boy's personality which should have become the love of a female contemporary. Mom transmutes it into sentimentality for herself.[17]

And finally, Wylie alleged that, in order to establish and maintain an exclusive mother-son dyad, moms purposefully undermined paternal authority. To illustrate this process, he described how a seemingly prosaic domestic scene became laden with fateful overtones:

> Thus, the sixteen-year old who tells his indignant dad that he, not dad, is going to have the car that night and takes it—while mom looks on, dewy-eyed and anxious—has sold his soul to mom and made himself into a lifelong sucking-egg. His father, already well up the creek, loses in this process the stick with which he had been trying to paddle. It is here that mom has thrust her oar into the very guts of man.[18]

According to Wylie, a boy could become a man only by first submitting to paternal authority and identifying with his father; if he rejected his father's authority prematurely, he not only unmanned his father, but also unwittingly effeminized himself. Thus, when moms declined to support their husbands and allied with their sons, they poisoned the father-son relationship and barred the path to mature manhood.

Although Wylie's language was extreme, the charges that he leveled were hardly new. By the time he published his critique, anxieties about overweening mothers and ineffectual fathers had been a dominant theme of child-rearing literature for at least two decades.[19] As historian Kathleen Jones has shown, psychoanalysts and behaviorists alike developed a "stinging critique of American motherhood" in the 1920s that practitioners within child guidance clinics readily embraced.[20] Scholars have linked the growing attacks on mothers to an array of developments, such as the professionalization of social service work, the backlash against maternalist reformers, and the modernist repudiation of Victorian sentimentality.[21] But what seems indisputable is that emotionally intense "mother love" came to be widely viewed as pathological in the aftermath of the First World War. Psychological experts of various theoretical orientations routinely indicted a certain type of woman: the "over-protective" or possessive mother who stymied her son's psychological development while relegating her husband to the sidelines. Behaviorists, who dominated child-rearing advice in the 1920s and early 1930s, believed that the solution resided in strict, scientific schedules that introduced an element of distance and rationality into the mother-child relationship.[22] (As the psychologist and early childhood educator Ada Hart Artlitt put it, the home should be governed not by "mother love," but rather by the "kitchen time-piece."[23]) In contrast, psychoanalytically oriented experts tended to emphasize the need to rectify imbalanced relationships between husbands and wives, for according to the Freudian model, a boy had to repress his desire for the mother and identify with his father in order to successfully negotiate the momentous Oedipal complex—a developmental feat that proved difficult if the father was too weak or too forbidding, or if the mother's influence proved overwhelming.

Although Wylie clearly echoed interwar experts who condemned sentimental mother love, his momism critique also represented a new departure, in that he connected the dangers of widespread maternal pathology to the political and military threats facing the nation. As historian Mari Jo Buhle has shown, his book in key respects resembled more scholarly works associated with the "national character" school of anthropology, which sought to explain how particular child-rearing practices and attitudes generated distinctive character types that in turn produced particular political cultures.[24] In the 1940s and 1950s, both American and European-born experts helped to construct a portrait of the American mother as a national type that reflected the nation's unique historical trajectory; indeed, it is striking how many prominent émigré psychoanalysts lent support to an exceptionalist view of the American family. "If it is true that in Europe the authoritative father is the main psychological problem of the family," the psychoanalyst Frieda Fromm-Reichmann asserted in 1940, "it holds that the corresponding family problem of this country is the child's fear of his domineering mother."[25] Likewise, the psychoanalyst Erik Erikson characterized the American "mom" as a powerful cultural "prototype," akin to the authoritarian German father.[26] Such arguments surfaced in the popular press as well: in 1945, an article in *Better Homes & Gardens* informed readers that a nation's behavior could be attributed to the "relative degree of mother or father influence" and asserted, "In this country ... the growing domination of American mothers of the 'mom' type is the more immediate menace to our security."[27]

The notion that American moms emasculated the nation's men and threatened its security seemed confirmed in the immediate postwar period, when revelations concerning the high incidence of psychological problems among American draftees and servicemen began to circulate widely in the press. Censored for most of the war, statistics showed that the Selective Service had rejected over 12 percent of all recruits on neuropsychiatric grounds, and that an astonishing 49 percent of all medical discharges had been for neuropsychiatric reasons.[28] To explain this phenomenon, Edward Strecker, chair of the Department of Psychiatry at the University of Pennsylvania and one of the nation's most prominent psychiatrists, appropriated the concept of momism in a bestselling book, *Their Mothers' Sons: A Psychiatrist Examines an American Problem*.[29] According to Strecker, "moms" who had "failed in the elementary mother function of weaning [their] offspring emotionally as well as physically" could be blamed for a large percentage of "immature" men rejected or discharged from service.[30] Though he wrote for a popular audience in a style almost as sensational as that of Wylie, Strecker's work lent the momism critique a new degree of professional credibility. Even an article that criticized commentators who "rant against 'momism'" bowed before the psychiatrist's authority by conceding, "Still, you can't laugh it off ... Not when Dr. Edward A. Strecker ... points to the 2 million men rejected or discharged from the services for neuro-psychiatric reasons and says they're Mom's handiwork."[31] Well into the 1950s, commentators continued to cite Strecker's "findings" as evidence that the nation suffered from faltering masculinity and widespread maternal pathology.[32]

Yet even as experts continued to caution against overprotection, they also increasingly decried the effects of "maternal rejection" and "deprivation." In the wake of fascism, the behaviorist view of infants as blank slates to be molded by all-powerful parents no longer appeared as a positive good—an opportunity to engineer a modern society freed from the inhibitions of the past. Instead, postwar psychological experts invested their hopes for the future in a view of the infant as a nascent individual who would naturally develop into a reasonable, democratic citizen, provided that his or her earliest needs were lovingly met. The withholding of maternal solicitude, which had been widely regarded as a sound approach to the irrational impulses of mother and child alike, thus came to be perceived as a denial of a legitimate need—a denial that actually produced the dependent tendencies that it sought to prevent. The dilemma that presented itself was this: How could experts prescribe a style of mothering that allowed for infantile bonding, without reverting to a sentimental and moralistic notion of mother love?

For most, the solution resided in a notion of maternal instinct that effectively naturalized maternal love by envisioning it as a physical substance—one that was all but secreted from the mother's body.[33] "Mother love is a good deal like food," the psychoanalyst Margaret Ribble explained in 1943. "It has to be expressed regularly so that the child expects it; a little at a time, and frequently, is the emotional formula. When it is given in this way, independence, rather than dependence, is fostered."[34] Or as Dr. Spock patiently explained, "Every baby needs to be smiled at, talked to, played with, fondled—gently and lovingly—just as much as he needs vitamins and calories." Only through a nourishing relationship to the mother, experts agreed, did the child acquire the "security" that allowed him or her to develop into an autonomous being. According to their formulations, loving physical care during infancy and early childhood was the only reliable antidote to the serious political dilemmas of the modern era

Scholars of postwar child-rearing literature have often argued that, in the wake of wartime studies about the consequences of maternal deprivation, motherhood came to be conceptualized as an all-consuming role. Yet while psychiatrists did indeed emphasize the need for intensive maternal care and mother-child bonding in the very young years, thereafter they regarded maternal influence as highly problematic. In essence, they urged mothers to refrain from attempting to mold their children and to serve instead as a loving, yet blank background against which children could define themselves. The extent to which motherhood came to be defined negatively is well illustrated by a passage from Ferdinand Lundberg and Marynia Farnham's 1947 bestseller, *Modern Woman: The Lost Sex,* an antifeminist polemic that presented motherhood as the pinnacle of female accomplishment. Women's historians have often cited this book as a classic articulation of the postwar "feminine mystique," yet they have not noted how radically the maternal ideal that its authors advocated differed from prior conceptions. Consider how Farnham and Lundberg described the ideal, truly "feminine mother":

> Is she so very wise? No, hers is not wisdom in the sense of intellectual knowledge. She just likes her children … Being in balance, she feels no need to inquire into every detail of their lives, to dominate them. Instead, she watches with somewhat detached interest to see what each one takes … She can tell, without reading books on child care, what to do for the children by waiting for them to indicate their need. This method is infallible. She does not fuss over them. If they are too cold, too hot, too wet, hungry

or lonesome, they let her know it and she meets the need. Otherwise she leaves them pretty much to their own devices, although keeping a watchful eye on them.[35]

Here, the mother emerges as a curiously affect-less figure, the very antithesis of the Victorian matron who sought to bind her children with "cords of love" in order to scrutinize the state of their souls. In fact, Farnham and Lundberg seemed determined to avoid all reference to maternal "love": their ideal mother merely "liked" her children and offered them "reassuring support" in infancy and early childhood, thereafter viewing them with greater emotional detachment. She followed her children's lead, making herself available to meet their physical and emotional needs, but otherwise remaining in the background.[36]

The notion that the woman who mothered least mothered best surfaced even in an article that sought to counter the barrage of hostile attacks on American mothers in the postwar press. Published in *Better Homes & Gardens* in 1947, the article featured 72-year-old Janette Murray, a "kindly but unsentimental" woman who raised five successful children while contributing to a wide array of maternalist initiatives.[37] As the writer approvingly noted, Murray "never had time to bind her children in emotional coils." Instead, she earned praise because she acted as a constant but unobtrusive presence; in her daughters' words, she was "always there, in the background, to help out in an emergency, to greet our friends, or to set out breakfast for the school friend who stayed overnight." Describing the Murrays' child-rearing philosophy, the writer succinctly articulated what one astute commentator would dub the new "fun morality": "They shared their lives with their children in whatever they did. It was no sacrifice. It was just more fun."[38] Interestingly, Murray herself struck a rather different note, as evidenced by one of the few passages that quoted her directly: "Love your children and share your life with them, and they'll come out all right," she advised. "Share the work, the sacrifices, the burdens and the joys—everything—and you won't have to worry." In other words, although Murray spoke an older language that recognized "sacrifices" and "burdens" as an inevitable part of motherhood and family life, the article transformed her into an exemplar of the new child-rearing ideology, in which notions of maternal self-sacrifice had little or no place.

Throughout the 1940s and 1950s, experts repeatedly condemned "self-sacrificing" mothers by portraying them as misguided worriers at best, attention-seeking neurotics at worst. "The mother who devotes herself exclusively to her child may have the satisfaction of playing the martyr," warned the psychiatrist David Levy, "but she may dangerously handicap her offspring."[39] Similarly, in *Their Mothers' Sons*, Strecker argued that those women whom the "community lauds and smiles upon" should be regarded with skepticism: although they were "spoken of as 'giving their lives' for their children," in truth they demanded "payment in the emotional lives of their children."[40] Writing for *Ladies' Home Journal* in 1950, the psychiatrist Herman Bundesen singled out one such a mother—a woman "known as an unselfish, devoted parent," whose neighbors would frequently comment, "'She gives her whole life to that boy!'" But according to Bundesen, this seemingly selfless mother was in fact responsible for her son's myriad behavioral problems. "It is typical of the overprotective mother," he remarked, "that she denies herself many normal interests and relationships in order to devote herself unstintingly to the child."[41] These and other psychological experts disparaged maternal "self-sacrifice" in large part because they no longer perceived it as genuinely selfless: what appeared to be self-sacrificing behavior, they suspected, actually represented the mother's attempts to fulfill her own unmet emotional needs.

To ensure that women did not end up directing their frustrated desires toward children, psychological experts and popular writers urged women to cultivate identities beyond that of "mother."[42] Psychologist Anna Wolf, for example, argued in 1941 that the woman with a "strong" personality needed "larger worlds to conquer than her home and family," if only because "[h]er energies need deflection."[43] Similarly, Zuma Steele, writing for *Good Housekeeping* in 1945, alerted readers that confining women's interests to the home could lead to "inbred and unhealthy love." "The woman who gives up everything for her home is doing herself and her home a disservice," she stressed.[44] In 1956, a psychoanalyst quoted in the middlebrow publication *American Weekly* went so far as to suggest that, if a mother felt confined by homemaking, she should seek full-time employment. "If staying home is depressing her and failing to stimulate her creatively, then I believe her husband and children are better off if she gets herself a job outside the home for eight hours a day," Ruth Mouton asserted. "She can't try to please friends, neighbors or relatives. She has to please herself *first,* then try to please others."[45]

As these sources suggest, many writers and experts in the 1940s and 1950s advised women that they should *not* focus solely on their children and their homes. This is not to imply, however, that the postwar cultural climate should be regarded as more favorable for women than feminists and scholars have previously suggested. Rather, what such sources indicate is that the widespread discontent among middle-class women cannot be attributed solely to a "feminine mystique" that exiled women to the domestic realm. Instead, the dilemma that such women confronted is better understood as a vicious double bind. Still largely barred from constructing their identities as autonomous individuals, able to compete on equal terms with men in the public realm, they were also discouraged from constructing their identities as selfless nurturers, entitled to emotional rewards for their sacrifices. Rather, experts and popular culture urged women to embrace the dominant therapeutic ethos by insisting (somewhat paradoxically) that motherhood allowed women to achieve self-fulfillment as *individuals.* Thus, when *Life* celebrated "the American Woman" in 1947, it praised the outlook of a young, middle-class mother of three young children as follows: "Because as an individual she likes the job that she does, she has no problem right now. Like most busy housewives, however, she gives little thought to the future—to satisfactory ways of spending the important years after her children have grown up and left home."[46] No longer a sacred calling, homemaking had become a "job" that would ultimately end. Of course, the problem with this view was that motherhood and homemaking remained very different from other jobs, not least because the homemaker performed unremunerated labor. In truth, the demands of caring for a family often did require mothers to subordinate their own interests and desires, yet they were increasingly prohibited from seeking recognition for their sacrifices, or even from viewing them as such.

The large collection of letters that Philip Wylie received from readers provide insight into how one group of women—primarily white, middle-class, and favorably disposed to psychological expertise—responded to the demystification of mother love.[47] Some women hotly contested Wylie's portrait of American mothers, and many others objected to his tone. Yet from a contemporary vantage point, what is most striking about these letters is how seriously women readers took Wylie's screed, and how many of them conceded that domineering or over-protective mothers constituted a genuine problem. Indeed, many who wrote to Wylie viewed his diatribe as entirely compatible with the new, permissive child-rearing methods promoted by Spock and others. Such women read *Generation of Vipers* as if it were an advice book that could sit comfortably alongside *The Common Sense Book of Baby and Child Care:* whereas the latter outlined a positive model to emulate, the former held up a negative model to avoid.

Young women tended to be particularly enthusiastic about the momism critique, for they correctly interpreted it as an indictment of their mothers' generation rather than their own. One young woman, who signed her letter "Daughter-in law of a Mom," wrote in 1950, "I am striving to be worthy of being included in your category of young women starting out in Motherhood, who have observed Momisn [*sic*] in action have sworn the holy oath [to avoid becoming moms]!"[48] Other youthful readers interpreted the momism critique as lending support to central tenets of postwar domestic ideology, such as the benefits of large families, more engaged fathers, and cooperative marriages. For instance, a 25-year-old mother attributed the phenomenon of momism to the low birth rates of the 1920s and 1930s, when "it was fashionable as well as an economic necessity to have only one or two children and women, who should produce children, mothered what they did produce almost out of existence." Continuing, she explained: "I have, so far, one son and every day of his seven months I have prayed that I will have the strength to allow him his independence. I think the answer is to have a huge family which we are going to do."[49] Similarly, a 23-year-old mother of two expressed her sense of belonging to a new generation of mothers, determined to avoid the failures of their predecessors: "We're doing our best, my husband and I, together, to bring our children up to be good citizens, reliable and independent … When the children attend school all day, I hope to do part-time work, not for bringing in money principally but so I will not become stagnant and dowdy and most of all, complacent, like so many older mothers I've met."[50]

In contrast to these readers, women who felt less confident as to whether they could exempt themselves from Wylie's critique scrutinized their attitudes and behaviors for traces of momism. "I am not so much of a 'mom' as some, but I could detect a trace here and there," wrote a mother of four children in 1944. "However," she added, "both of my sons are married and in far-away cities, so I cannot do them much harm now."[51] In 1946, a woman who had "laughed and gasped" upon first reading the momism chapter grew more sober after rereading it "paragraph by paragraph" to determine if it applied to her. "Alas, it did!" she confessed. "Thereupon I set about trying to eradicate those characteristics, with what success time will tell."[52] Another woman reported that Wylie's book had given her pause, "which was all to the good, since I have three sons. I hope your diatribe against 'Moms' kept me from smothering them entirely."[53] Anxious to dissociate themselves from such an unflattering caricature, and fearful of damaging their children, these women vowed to be more self-reflective and self-policing in fulfilling their maternal role.

Some women who concurred with Wylie's charges made a point of disavowing the notion that motherhood guaranteed women a special place in their children's hearts. Rather than expecting love and affection as a matter of course, they stressed their determination to win their children over through their personal attributes and actions. As one 25-year old woman wrote: "I'm trying to give my children a better deal all the way around. I figure that they had nothing to do with me being their mother. They didn't pick me out. Therefore it is up to me to earn their love and respect."[54] Other women expressed similar views by emphasizing their willingness to be judged by their children. "I am the mother of a fourteen year old son, not a Mom, I hope," wrote one woman. "At any rate, I want him to read your book, when he is older, and make up his own mind."[55] These women disliked the notion that the mother-child relationship should be structured according to proscribed roles that reflected a generic view of maternal duties and children's needs. Instead, they preferred to think of themselves and their children as individuals who interacted according to their unique personalities.

One woman who shared this view found the cultural ideal of "Mother" so distasteful that she attempted to recast her relationship with her three sons in alternative ways. As she explained to Wylie:

> I started weaning my sons at the instant of birth. I was bitterly afraid of "mother love," though God knows how I love them. They are now as completely independent of me as humanly possible. They enjoy my ideas, regard me as a useful encyclopedia, and like me as a friend. They make up their own decisions, minds, act on their own decisions, even if completely opposite to my expressed opinion, knowing I won't bat an eye, cheerfully telling me later if I happened to be right ... But what now for me? I've done my job, and done it well. But it's done. I can do nothing further for my sons but mess into their lives and fiddle with their souls. Actually they have absolutely no need for me.[56]

Alert to the debilitating effects of "mother love," this woman preferred for her sons to regard her as a "friend" or even an inanimate "encyclopedia" than as a mother. Her entire parenting philosophy centered on the idea that she should strive to make herself unnecessary as early as possible—a goal that she believed had been achieved. But now, although her youngest son was still a ten-year-old child, she could no longer foresee a positive role for herself as a mother. Her maternal interest and concern, she feared, would henceforth prove irritating if not dangerous.

Like this respondent, many mothers felt the full force of the momism critique only as their children grew more independent and they themselves approached middle age. Women who had heartily endorsed Wylie's critique in their youth, often in rebellion against their own mothers, sometimes found themselves having second thoughts as their lives progressed. In 1958, one such woman sent Wylie an unpublished essay, entitled "What Philip Wylie Really Thinks about Women," recounting how her views had evolved since 1942, when she first encountered *Generation of Vipers*. At the time, she was "single and childless, a young woman just graduated from the Smith School of Psychiatric Social Work, full of professional jargon, in the midst of my own analysis." Her job at the Children's Bureau, where she counseled "disturbed" and "inadequate" mothers seeking child guidance and foster home placement, combined with her "hostility" toward her own mother, "which is always present in the midst of one's own analysis," made her receptive to Wylie's critique: "I embraced Mr. Wylie's philosophy regarding our cannibalistic matriarchy avidly, in my youthful unsophistication taking all that he said as a literal condemnation of motherhood in its entirety." But after she married, gave up her career, bore four children in four years (including a set of twins), and found most of her contacts "limited to other moms," she began to "re-evaluate" her views and to resent "the ever increasing hostility towards American mothers exhibited by most males." Attributing her initial enthusiasm for the momism critique to her youthfulness and her immersion in psychiatry and psychoanalysis, she now believed that her fluency in psychoanalytic "jargon" had allowed her to adopt a harshly critical attitude toward American mothers that, in retrospect, struck her as misguided and unjust.

This writer ultimately faltered, however, in her attempt to articulate a critique of anti-maternalism. As she went on to explain, she had approached the editors of a national magazine, who encouraged her to pursue her idea for an article entitled "In Defense of American Women." But she could not bring herself to finish the piece. Instead, she did a remarkable and self-defeating thing: she turned her material over to the very man whose ideas she hoped to challenge. "Mr. Wylie started the thing, I thought. He had the reputation, the experience, the male point of view," she wrote in the essay that she sent to Wylie. "People listen to him and care what he thinks." Her defense of American womanhood thus collapsed into an appeal for exoneration, as she implored Wylie to assure her cohort of mothers that they had succeeded where their own mothers had failed: "I had to see for myself what a man of his great literary gifts and powers of perception really thinks about American women as a whole. Are we to him a lost cause?"[57] Sadly, this woman seemed unable to challenge Wylie's "expert" authority, even though she possessed the professional accreditation that he lacked. Because anti-maternalism was so closely associated with the rejection of Victorian sentimentality and moralism, women who avidly embraced the tenets of the dominant therapeutic culture had difficulty articulating their opposition to the momism critique, even when it left them discomfited. The fact that Wylie seemed happy to oblige such women, reassuring them that they were not "moms," did not diminish the pernicious influence that his critique continued to exert through the 1950s and into the 1960s.[58]

Conclusion

During the 1960s and 1970s, the momism critique gradually waned.[59] Its decline can be attributed in part to the easing of cold war tensions, which rendered the critique's animating concerns about male effeminacy and national weakness less pressing, as well as the emergence of new social movements that challenged the gender ideals of the 1940s and 1950s. In her groundbreaking 1963 bestseller, *The Feminine Mystique,* Betty Friedan drew out the feminist implications that had been lurking within the momism critique all along.[60] Although certain passages of her book conveyed skepticism about psychiatric studies of maternal pathology, Friedan did not dispute the notion that pernicious mothering had become endemic within the American middle class. Instead, she used the findings of psychiatrists like Edward Strecker to support her claim that women needed to lead full and self-realized lives, beyond the narrow confines of the home. Such feminist appropriations, which shifted the focus of attention from children's to mothers' well-being, pointed to the broader cultural and political changes that would render the momism critique an anachronism.

However, the decline of the momism critique cannot wholly be attributed to political developments, for it also reflected changes in the way that middle-class women structured their lives and mothered their children. In 1940, fewer than 10 percent of all American mothers with children under the age of six worked outside the home; by 1975 that number had risen to 39 percent.[61] As more mothers entered the workforce and anxieties came to center on a perceived *lack* of maternal involvement, attacks on cloying and overbearing mothers appeared increasingly misplaced. Moreover, though much harder to measure, it seems clear that maternal attitudes and practices also changed. As middle-class mothers absorbed the lessons of the therapeutic culture, they focused less on molding children into virtuous characters whose appreciation of maternal sacrifice kept them bound tightly to family and home. Instead, the "modern" mothers of the mid-twentieth century focused more on equipping children with a sense of emotional "security" by providing them with unconditional love, particularly in their earliest years. During the 1940s and 1950s, many readers had embraced the momism critique because they felt that they actually knew "moms"—women who viewed motherhood as an exalted and noble state, talked openly about their suffering and sacrifices, or intervened without hesitation in their adult children's lives. But by the 1970s, Wylie's caricature no longer elicited widespread recognition as an essentially accurate, albeit overdrawn and mean-spirited, portrait of a certain type of American mother.

Middle-class women who raised families after the Second World War did so in a cultural climate that vehemently repudiated sentimental ideals of motherhood and regarded maternal impulses with deep suspicion. In the 1940s and 1950s, the fear of pathological "mother love" grew so pronounced that the ideal mother was often defined negatively, with the emphasis falling on her ability to refrain from certain objectionable behaviors: she did not undermine her husband's authority, guilt-trip her children, pry into their personal lives, or look to them to meet her emotional or physical needs. As a result, even the mother who managed to raise successful, "mature," and well-adjusted children might be left with little sense of personal accomplishment. For if she believed the experts, once she had equipped them with a sense of "security" during their very earliest years, her most important contribution had been to stay out of their way.

Notes

Acknowledgments: I would like to thank Frank Biess, Frances Clarke, Carolyn Eastman, Rachel Klein, Robert Moeller, and Dirk Schumann for their extremely helpful comments on this essay. I am also grateful to the Radcliffe Institute for Advanced Study for its support, and to the 2005/06 fellows who participated in the Tuesday writing group.

1. Mrs. O. to Philip Wylie, 16 May 1957, Fldr. 7, Box 245, Philip Wylie Papers, Firestone Library, Princeton, New Jersey (hereafter PWP).

2. Quoted in Linda A. Pollock, *Forgotten Children: Parent-Child Relations from 1500 to 1900* (Cambridge, 1983), 117.

3. Historian Peter Stearns has argued that "Victorian motherlove died … during the 1920s and 1930s." Stearns connects the repudiation of sentimental "motherlove" to a much broader shift in the history of emotions that occurred in the second quarter of the twentieth century—a shift marked by a "growing aversion to emotional intensity" and the imposition of new forms of emotional restraint. Peter N. Stearns, *American Cool: Constructing a Twentieth-Century Emotional Style* (New York, 1994).

4. For discussions of the sentimental idealization of motherhood that began in the late eighteenth century and flourished in the nineteenth century, see Ruth H. Bloch, "American Feminine Ideals in Transition: The Rise of the Moral Mother, 1790–1815," *Feminist Studies* 4 (June 1978): 100–126; Nancy F. Cott, *The Bonds of Womanhood: "Woman's Sphere" in New England, 1780–1835* (New Haven, 1977); Sylvia D. Hoffert, *Private Matters: American Attitudes toward Childbearing and Infant Nurture in the Urban North, 1800–60* (Urbana, 1989); Jan Lewis, "Mother's Love: The Construction of an Emotion in Nineteenth-Century America," in *Social History and Issues in Human Consciousness: Some Interdisciplinary Connections,* ed. Andrew E. Barnes and Peter N. Stearns (New York, 1989), 209–229; Mary P. Ryan, *Cradle of the Middle Class: The Family in Oneida County, New York, 1790–1865* (Cambridge, 1981) and Mary P. Ryan, *The Empire of the Mother: American Writing about Domesticity* (New York, 1982).

5. Mary P. Ryan, *Womanhood in America: From Colonial Times to the Present,* 3rd ed. (New York, 1983), 266. Likewise, in her history of the concept of maternal bonding, Diane Eyer argued that the Victorian "hearth angel" ideal "reemerged" in a new guise after the Second World War,

transformed by Freudian psychology into the "feminine mystique." Diane Eyer, *Mother-Infant Bonding: A Scientific Fiction* (New Haven, 1992), 9.

6. Joanne Meyerowitz, "Beyond the Feminine Mystique: A Reassessment of Postwar Mass Culture, 1946–1958," *Journal of American History* 79 (March 1993): 1455–1482; and Joanne Meyerowitz, ed., *Not June Cleaver: Women and Gender in Postwar America* (Philadelphia, 1994). Other important revisionist accounts of postwar domesticity and gender roles include Jessica Weiss, *To Have and to Hold: Marriage, the Baby Boom and Social Change* (Chicago, 2000); Eva Moskowitz, "'It's Good to Blow Your Top': Women's Magazines and a Discourse of Discontent," *Journal of Women's History* 8, no. 3 (fall 1996): 66–98, and Eva Moskowitz, *In Therapy We Trust: America's Obsession with Self-Fulfillment* (Baltimore, 2001), chap. 5; and Susan E. Myers-Shirk, "'To Be Fully Human': U.S. Protestant Psychotherapeutic Culture and the Subversion of the Domestic Ideal, 1945–1965," *Journal of Women's History* 12 (spring 2000): 112–136. For an earlier, highly influential of postwar domesticity, see Elaine Tyler May, *Homeward Bound: American Families in the Cold War Era* (New York, 1988).

7. Philip Wylie, *Generation of Vipers* (New York, 1942). In 1955, to mark the twentieth printing, Wylie published a new annotated edition of *Generation of Vipers*, 2nd ed. (New York, 1955), in which he linked momism to McCarthyism.

8. For an account of literary modernists who attacked the "late Victorian matriarch" in the 1920s, see Ann Douglas, *Terrible Honesty: Mongrel Manhattan in the 1920s* (New York, 1995), chaps. 1 and 6.

9. For an astute analysis of the racial politics of mid-century mother-blaming, see Ruth Feldstein, *Motherhood in Black and White: Race and Sex in American Liberalism, 1930–1965* (Ithaca, 2000). Other important works that discuss the momism critique in relationship to psychiatric and social scientific literature include Mari Jo Buhle, *Feminism and Its Discontents: A Century of Struggle with Psychoanalysis* (Cambridge, 1998), chap. 4; and Jennifer Terry, "'Momism' and the Making of Treasonous Homosexuals," in *"Bad" Mother: The Politics of Blame in Twentieth-Century America*, ed. Molly Ladd-Taylor and Lauri Umansky (New York, 1998), 169–190.

10. In particular, my interpretation differs from that of Michael Paul Rogin. In an influential essay on cold war cinema, Rogin proposed that the momism critique should be viewed as "the demonic version of domestic ideology." By encouraging "maternal surveillance," he argued, postwar domesticity heightened anxieties about "boundary invasion, loss of autonomy and maternal power"—anxieties that then became manifested in demonic representations of mothers. In developing this interpretation, Rogin portrayed postwar domestic ideology as a continuation or extension of Victorian domesticity, which centered on the moral mother who "entered the self, formed it, understood its feelings, and thereby at once produced it and protected it from corruption." The problem with this formulation is that postwar experts, in marked contrast to their Victorian forebears, strongly *discouraged* "maternal surveillance," emphatically insisting on the need for psychological boundaries between mothers and their children, especially sons. Michael Paul Rogin, "Kiss Me Deadly: Communism, Motherhood, and Cold War Movies," *Representations* 6 (spring 1984): 1–36.

11. For an overview of the psychological professions and psychological thinking from 1940 through 1970, see Ellen Herman, *The Romance of American Psychology: Political Culture in the Age of the Experts* (Berkeley, 1995). On the rise of psychoanalysis in particular, see Nathan G. Hale, Jr., *The Rise and Crisis of Psychoanalysis in the United States: Freud and the Americans, 1917–1985* (New York, 1995); and John C. Burnham, "The Influence of Psychoanalysis Upon American Culture," in *Psychoanalysis: Origins and Development*, eds. Jacques M. Quen and Eric T. Carlson (New York, 1978), 52–69.

12. Benjamin Spock, *The Common Sense Book of Baby and Child Care* (New York, 1946), revised and reissued in 1957 and subsequent years, was by far the most influential child-rearing manual in the postwar years. Insightful discussions of the book and its impact appear in Nancy Pottishman Weiss, "Mother, the Invention of Necessity: Dr. Benjamin Spock's *Baby and Child Care*," *American Quarterly* 29 (winter 1977): 519–546; Michael Zuckerman, "Dr. Spock: The

Confidence Man," in *The Family in History,* ed. Charles E. Rosenberg (Philadelphia, 1975), 179–207; William Graebner, "The Unstable World of Benjamin Spock: Social Engineering in a Democratic Culture, 1917–1950," *Journal of American History* 67 (December 1980): 612–629; Henry Jenkins, "The Sensuous Child: Benjamin Spock and the Sexual Revolution," in *The Children's Culture Reader* (New York, 1998), 209–230; Julia Grant, *Raising Baby by the Book: The Education of American Mothers* (New Haven, 1998), chap. 7; Rima D. Apple, *Perfect Motherhood: Science and Childrearing in America* (New Brunswick, NJ, 2006), chap. 5; and Ann Hulbert, *Raising America: Experts, Parents, and a Century of Advice about Children* (New York, 2003), chap. 8.

13. The review in *Time,* for example, devoted seven of its nine paragraphs to a discussion of "Mom" and her younger counterpart, whom Wylie dubbed "Cinderella." *Time* 41 (18 January 1943): 100.

14. Wylie, *Generation of Vipers,* 187.

15. Ibid., 186.

16. For a more detailed analysis of Wylie's critique as a whole, see Rebecca Jo Plant, *The Transformation of Motherhood in Modern America* (Chicago, 2010), chap. 1.

17. Wylie, *Generation of Vipers,* 196.

18. Ibid., 197.

19. Historian Julia Grant has convincingly argued that such fears first emerged in the 1890s and grew pronounced in the 1920s, when psychologists and psychiatrists came to view childhood, rather than adolescence, as the period during which boys acquired their sexual orientation and "masculine characteristics." Julia Grant, "A 'Real Boy' and not a Sissy: Gender, Childhood, and Masculinity, 1890–1940," *Journal of Social History* 37, no. 4 (2004): 829–851. According to historian Maxine Margolis, "The major tenet of child-rearing literature in the 1920s and 1930s was that mothers are dangerous, dangerous to the health and well being of their children and ultimately to society at large." Maxine L. Margolis, *Mothers and Such: Views of American Women and Why They Changed* (Berkeley, 1984), 56.

20. Jones traces the "professional history" of mother-blaming by highlighting its functions within child guidance clinics, where clients were overwhelmingly mothers and children. She argues, "Mother-blaming came to dominate the field of child mental health because, along with its availability in the research literature, its appeal to psychoanalytically oriented practitioners, and its 'fit' with larger cultural concerns, it seemed to work in the clinic." Kathleen W. Jones, *Taming the Troublesome Child: American Families, Child Guidance, and the Limits of Psychiatric Authority* (Cambridge, MA, 1999), chap. 7 (quotations from 175, 186–187).

21. For the rise of psychiatric social work, see Regina G. Kunzel, *Fallen Women, Problem Girls: Unmarried Mothers and the Professionalization of Social Work, 1890–1945* (New Haven, 1993). For the backlash against maternalist reformers in the 1920s, see Molly Ladd-Taylor, *Mother-Work: Women, Child Welfare, and the State, 1890–1930* (Urbana, 1994); and Robyn Muncy, *Creating a Female Dominion in American Reform, 1890–1935* (New York, 1991). The decline of a sentimental emotional culture is discussed in John C. Spurlock and Cynthia A. Magistro, *New and Improved: The Transformation of American Women's Emotional Culture* (New York, 1998), chap. 5; and Douglas, *Terrible Honesty.*

22. Childrearing experts in the Progressive era had also advocated strict schedules, but behaviorists in the 1920s and 1930s tended to view the figure of the mother in a more antagonistic manner, as "an impediment to the scientific upbringing of the young, and even worse, a potential threat." Weiss, "Mother, the Invention of Necessity," 530.

23. Quoted in Jenkins, "The Sensuous Child," 213–214.

24. As Mari Jo Buhle has noted, the study of national character had roots in the Culture and Personality school of the 1920s and 1930s. However, whereas earlier works by anthropologists like Ruth Benedict and Edward Sapir focused generally on child-rearing and "cultural conditioning," the national character studies of the 1940s concentrated more intensively on maternal behavior and attitudes. Buhle, *Feminism and Its Discontents,* 140–146.

25. Frieda Fromm-Reichmann, "Notes on the Mother Role in the Family Group," *Bulletin of the Menninger Clinic* 4 (1940): 132–148.

26. Erik Erikson acknowledged that professionals' assessments of mothers often lacked an objective, scientific tone: "There is in much of our psychiatric work an undertone of revengeful triumph, as if a villain had been spotted and cornered. The blame attached to the mothers in this country … has in itself a specific moralistic punitiveness." Nevertheless, he proceeded to elaborate upon the momism critique by enumerating the unpleasant characteristics of the composite American "mom" and tracing her historical evolution. Erik Erikson, *Childhood and Society* (New York, 1950), 247–256. See also Geoffrey Gorer, *The American People: A Study in National Character* (New York, 1948), 50–51.

27. Amram Scheinfeld, "Are American Moms a Menace?" *Ladies' Home Journal* 62 (November 1945): 135, 138.

28. While 163,000 of these men were dishonorably discharged for reasons such as drug addiction, alcoholism, homosexuality, and psychopathic personality traits, 386,000 received honorable discharges under a variety of diagnoses, the most common being "psychoneurotic." For a more detailed discussion of statistics regarding neuropsychiatric rejections and casualties, see Herman, *The Romance of American Psychology,* 88–99. See also Hans Pols, "War Neurosis, Adjustment Problems in Veterans, and an Ill Nation: The Disciplinary Project of American Psychiatry During and After the Second World War," *Osiris* 22 (2007): 72–97.

29. Edward A. Strecker, *Their Mothers' Sons: A Psychiatrist Examines an American Problem* (New York, 1946). A lengthy excerpt of the book ran in advance of publication: "What's Wrong with American Mothers?" *Saturday Evening Post* 21 (26 October 1946): 14–15, 83–104. For background on Strecker, see Lauren H. Smith, "Edward A. Strecker, M.D.: A Biographical Sketch," *American Journal of Psychiatry* 101 (July 1944): 9–11; and "Dr. E. A. Strecker, a Psychiatrist, 72," *New York Times*, 3 January 1959, 17. The most detailed analysis of Strecker's work appears in Terry, "'Momism' and the Making of Treasonous Homosexuals."

30. Strecker, *Their Mothers' Sons,* 13.

31. Walter A. Adams, "You Can't Talk That Way about Mother!" *Better Homes & Gardens* 25 (June 1947): 45.

32. Strecker's book was widely reviewed and cited. See, for example: "Mama's Boys," *Time* 48 (25 November 1946): 80; and "Nervous in the Service," *Newsweek* 28 (26 November 1946): 64–65.

33. For an excellent study that traces changing scientific conceptions of maternal instinct, see Marga Vicedo, "The Maternal Instinct: Mother Love and the Search for Human Nature" (PhD diss., Harvard University, 2005).

34. Margaret Ribble, *The Rights of Infants: Early Psychological Needs and Their Satisfaction* (New York, 1943), 14.

35. Ferdinand Lundberg and Marynia F. Farnham, *Modern Woman: The Lost Sex* (New York, 1947), 320.

36. Nina C. Leibman has argued that 1950s television programs relegated mothers to the periphery of the family circle and "'solve' the 'problem' of mothers' all powerful and harmful influence … by decisively reconfiguring the father as *the* crucial molder of his children's psyches." See Leibman, "Leave Mother Out: The 50s Family in American Film and Television," *Wide Angle* 10 (1988): 24–41 and *Living Room Lectures: The Fifties Family in Film and Television* (Austin, 1995), chap. 6.

37. Adams, "You Can't Talk That Way about Mother!"

38. Martha Wolfenstein, "Fun Morality: An Analysis of Recent American Child-Training Literature," in *Childhood in Contemporary Cultures*, ed. Margaret Mead and Martha Wolfenstein (Chicago, 1955), 168–179.

39. David M. Levy, "Clinical Evidence of Changing Parenthood," n.d., Fldr. 10, Box 6, David M. Levy Papers, Oskar Diethelm Library, Weill Medical College of Cornell University, New York.

40. Strecker, *Their Mothers' Sons,* 160.

41. Herman N. Bundesen, "The Overprotective Mother," *Ladies' Home Journal* 67 (March 1950): 243–244.

42. As Kathryn Keller has shown, in the 1950s popular culture for the first time began to condone mothers' employment outside the home on the grounds that it would benefit children. Keller identified three versions of this basic argument: "Children are more independent as a result of the mother working; mothers who are satisfied with their jobs are happy and raise happy children; and children need the companionship of other children, which they could attain if they went to day care." Kathryn Keller, *Mothers and Work in Popular American Magazines* (Westport, 1994), 21.

43. Anna W. Wolf, *The Parent's Manual: A Guide to the Emotional Development of Young Children* (New York, 1941), 285.

44. Zuma Steele, "Love and Let Me Go," *Good Housekeeping* 120 (February 1945): 37, 76–79.

45. Maurice Zolotow, *American Weekly* (2 September 1956): 10.

46. "The American Woman's Dilemma," *Life* 22 (16 June 1947): 105.

47. In 1945, Wylie reported that over 5,000 people had written him in response to *Generation of Vipers;* by 1955, he was claiming to have received between 50,000 to 60,000 letters. Other evidence in Wylie's papers suggests that both these estimates are likely inflated. However, there are roughly 1,000 surviving letters in the Philip Wylie Papers from the years 1942 to 1946 alone. Wylie's correspondents did not represent a cross-section of the American public, for they were overwhelmingly white, middle-class, and relatively well educated. In general, they appear drawn from that segment of the population most likely to read child-rearing literature and embrace contemporary psychological theories, at least in popularized forms. Most appear to have been Protestant or from Protestant backgrounds, though a small number identified themselves as Jewish. While nearly two thirds of Wylie's correspondents were men, the majority of letters referring to the momism critique were written by women, for women were more than twice as likely as men to refer to this particular issue. (Roughly a third of all the letters from women discussed the momism critique.) In addition to the letters Wylie received in response to *Generation of Vipers,* I have also cited letters written in response to popular articles on momism that Wylie published in the 1950s. For a more extensive discussion of the Wylie's fan mail, see Rebecca Jo Plant, "The Repeal of Mother Love: Momism and the Reconstruction of Motherhood in Philip Wylie's America," (PhD diss., Johns Hopkins University, 2001).

48. N.a. to Wylie, 9 November 1950, Fldr. 2, Box 240, PWP.

49. M.J.S. to Wylie, n.d., Fldr. 7, Box 6, PWP.

50. Mrs. J.A.S. to Wylie, 11 November 1950, Fldr. 2, Box 241, PWP.

51. M.D.G. to Wylie, 22 February 1944, Fldr. 9, Box 231, PWP.

52. Name illegible to Wylie, 28 June 1946, Fldr. 5, Box 235, PWP.

53. Mrs. W.J.A. to Wylie, 7 July 1949, Fldr. 5, Box 240, PWP.

54. B.I. to Wylie, 9 December 1944, Fldr. 1, Box 233, PWP. Wylie replied, "You are obviously one of the non-vipers, and I suspect your children have picked the right mother after all." Wylie to B.I., 26 December 1944, Fldr. 1, Box 233, PWP.

55. L.R.O. to Wylie, 31 August 1943, Fldr. 4, Box 232, PWP.

56. E.B.M. to Wylie, 18 November 1946, Fldr. 6, Box 235, PWP.

57. N.a. to Wylie, Fldr. 2, Box 156, PWP.

58. In 1957, Wylie published an article in which he argued, "Mothers *are* growing less liable to 'momism'—by millions—in all parts of the nation … For the *modern* young mother … knows that if she truly loves her children, her aim will be, not to make them ultimately mere mirrors of a fatuous, reciprocal adoration, but *independent, self-confident, detached individuals.* She knows her job is essentially, to bring them up in such a fashion that they can live perfectly *without her* and without 'dad.'" Magazine clipping, Wylie, "Mom Is Improving," *This Week Magazine* (n.d., 1957), Fldr. 27, Box 132, PWP.

59. The last serious discussion of momism as a social problem appears to have been the psychologist Hans Sebald's study, *Momism: The Silent Disease* (Chicago, 1976). In 1977, historian Christopher Lasch depicted momism as an obsolete phenomenon. "Recent evidence," he

argued, "suggests that American children, far from becoming overly dependent on their mothers, form strong attachments to neither parent." Lasch, *Haven in a Heartless World: The Family Besieged* (New York, 1977), 74–75.

60. Betty Friedan, *The Feminine Mystique* (New York, 1963), 189–205. Friedan did not explicitly refer to Wylie, but she used the term "momism" and quoted Edward Strecker and other psychiatrists at length. For a more extensive discussion of Friedan's appropriation of the momism critique, see Plant, *The Transformation of Motherhood in Modern America*, chap. 5. The parallels between Wylie and Friedan are discussed in Robin Keehn, "Dialetics of Containment: Mothers, Moms, Soldiers, Veterans and the Cold War Mystique," (PhD diss, University of California, San Diego, 1998), chap. 1; and Christy Erin Regenhardt, "The Psychology of Democracy: Psychological Concepts in American Culture," (PhD diss, University of Maryland, 2006), chap. 4.

61. F. Ivan Nye and Lois Wladis Hoffman, *The Employed Mother in America* (Chicago, 1963), 8; and U.S. Department of Labor, Bureau of Labor Statistics, "Mothers in the Labor Force, 1955–2004," http://www.infoplease.com/ipa/A0104670.html, accessed 13 March 2010.

Chapter 7

Fatherhood, Rechristianization, and the Quest for Democracy in Postwar West Germany

Till van Rahden

"Nazis—not wanted," "Jews—undesirable," and "half-weak fathers": these were the topics that *Der Männer-Seelsorger* [Spiritual Guidance for Men], a monthly Catholic journal, listed as "hot potatoes" in West Germany in 1964.[1] The third of these catch phrases was obviously meant as a retort to the widespread image of the "half-strong youth." But more than that, it pointed to one of the obsessions of West Germany in its early years: discovering what kind of paternal authority was possible and desirable after the catastrophe of National Socialism and the war of extermination. Of course, the debate on the "society without the father" also gave voice to deep-seated anxieties about the changing nature of gender relations.[2] But above all, this longing for new kinds of fatherhood gives us insight into the West German quest for democracy from the early 1950s to the late 1960s.

The history of Germany in the twentieth century moves between the two extremes of its fall in war and genocidal dictatorship, on the one hand, and its return to peace and democracy on the other. Precisely if we view the postwar years as an era after a "rupture with civilization," then we must ask ourselves how a democratic society could emerge from this shadow of violence. Common historical interpretations of the Federal Republic explain its liberalization of political life as a byproduct of the economic miracle and its connection to the West. In the following, by contrast, we will focus primarily on West Germans' quest for a democratic existence and culture. Such a change in perspective draws on Tocquevillian political theory, namely the insight that democracy depends as much on cultural and social practices as on the governing skills of the elite.[3]

Horst Möller has recently argued that viewing democracy as "in the end the origin and goal of history" expresses a political ethos that should in no way be confused with a historical consideration of this system of government—including its opportunities, risks, and fragility. Historians should remain independent of normative views and perceive democracy as improbable and in need of explanation—just as much so as monarchy, aristocracy, and dictatorship. Paradoxically, those for whom the survival of representative democracy and the liberal, constitutional state is most important are the very people who ought to dispense with clichéd declarations about it, but often fail to. The rector of Friedrich Schiller University in Jena, for example, claimed that "really bringing the strength of democracy ... into fruition" had been "reserved for the twentieth century."[4] In the astounding success story of West European postwar democracy, one must not forget that the ups and downs of a democratic polity depend not only on the institutional and economic framework. Only where a genuinely democratic culture and lifestyle have been able to develop is it possible to sustain the democratic form of government even in times of economic and political crisis.

Against this backdrop, the increasingly questionable status of the ideal of the patriarchal father in the 1950s proves to be especially instructive for the early history of the Federal Republic. A good decade before 1968, women and men had begun to develop new notions of what it meant to be a good father. These were encapsulated in such catch phrases as the "democratic family" and "democratic fatherhood"[5]—by which contemporaries meant a gentler kind of manliness that emphasized emotions and trust rather than a spirit of order and obedience. They perceived this to be a prerequisite for a democratic family as well as a democratic society. In talking about "the democratic father," West Germans sought an outlook that allowed them to see the Federal Republic not only as their fate, but as an opportunity to experiment with "democracy as a way of life."

In order to substantiate my thesis, I shall pursue, above all, two questions: how did postwar West Germans redefine the father's place within the family in the 1950s and 1960s, and what broader political significance did they attach to the issue of paternal authority? I rely in my research primarily on publications and periodicals close to the Catholic and Protestant Churches rather than on left or left-liberal publications. It is precisely an analysis of the more conservative spectrum of West German popular culture, the side associated with the Christian democratic parties, that provides an excellent measure of how dramatically the dominant conceptions of paternal authority changed in this period.

Moreover, the early Federal Republic experienced an epoch of "re-Christianization" among Protestants and especially Catholics, which was reflected in the considerable influence of confessional publications. With regard to their organizational structure and their moral legitimacy, the churches were almost the only larger social and cultural institutions perceived to have survived intact the catastrophe of National Socialism.[6] To be sure, the popularity of Christian ethics turned out to be above all an expression of the longing for moral certainties in light of the evils that had manifested themselves in the war of extermination and genocide. In retrospect, it becomes apparent that this new interest in questions of religious morality and the ubiquity of Christian rhetoric in the late 1940s and

1950s often remained superficial and temporary. Yet the experience of a "religious revival" in the immediate postwar years continued to figure prominently in churches' and lay organizations' self-understanding and contributed to their missionary zeal into the early 1960s. True, the belief that the "Zero Hour" was an "Hour of the Church" turned out, in the long run, to be false. Still, against the backdrop of this "self-delusion of the church" about its public support, we can understand the tremendous fervor with which the laity especially embarked upon a search for democracy grounded in Christianity.[7]

We must take this religious discourse seriously if we want to understand how West Germans began to search for a democratic order after their experience of violence and genocide in the 1930s and 1940s. In the 1950s, 60 percent of nominal Catholics attended mass regularly and another 20 percent sporadically, a higher percentage than at any time since the *Kulturkampf* of the 1870s and its immediate aftermath.[8] At the time, church periodicals such as *Frau und Mutter: Monatsschrift für die katholische Frau in Familie und Beruf* [Wife and Mother: Monthly for the Catholic Woman in Family and Career] or *Mann in der Zeit* [Contemporary Man], edited by the Catholic Hauptarbeitsstelle für Männerseelsorge (Main Office of Men's Spiritual Guidance) had circulations of about half a million copies, which was about as high as that of the popular magazines *Der Spiegel, Quick,* and *Stern* .[9] The churches' influence was particularly marked in public debates about the family and paternal authority, as well as in federal and state policies.

Interpreting early West German history as a period of re-Christianization directs our attention not only to the church hierarchies' considerable influence on federal family policies but also to the salience of religious rhetoric in the public sphere. Even those who emphatically embraced the idea of an independent laity to free themselves from the guardianship of the clerics frequently utilized Christian arguments. Up to now, research has neglected this moment of democratic awakening, focusing instead on the conservative restoration carried out in a Christian spirit. At its core, this line of research merely appropriates the criticism of the "clericalization of politics" already widespread in the 1950s.[10] My focus, however, is less on the well-known nexus between conservative politicians and the church hierarchy that often advocated patriarchal conceptions of the family until well after Vatican II.[11] Instead, I am primarily interested in the wide range of Catholic, Protestant, or ecumenical family organizations, as well as Catholic and Protestant family experts, be they theologians and clergymen or sociologists, psychologists, and pediatricians loosely affiliated with the churches.[12]

In light of the "powerful awakening" of Christian lay organizations, the Catholic moral theologian Bernhard Häring believed that a "great era of the Lay Apostolate" had come.[13] On the Protestant side, Hans Hermann Walz, who would later become General Secretary of the German Evangelical Church Congress, claimed as early as 1952 that the lay congresses and movements these people gathered in, which emphasized their lay character, were symptomatic of a "new awakening in the depth of Christian consciousness." Rather than an "unhealthy spirituality," the laity embodied the "fundamental solidarity of the church with the world." Therefore they were "particularly well-suited to act as a progressive element in the church" and to advocate "necessary improvements ... in social, political, and professional relations."[14] In this context, it is hardly surprising that many Catholic and Protestant laypeople in the 1950s used religious arguments to criticize patriarchal conceptions of gender relations and turned to the question of how the relationship between the sexes and the internal order of the family could be newly determined in a democratic polity.[15]

At the same time, the criticism of the patriarchal family ideal and the concomitant search for new forms of paternal authority are closely connected to the renaissance of democratic culture in postwar West German society—something observers both inside and outside the country had barely believed possible. As Volker Berghahn has noted, we have come to learn a great deal about how Germans got into the Nazi dictatorship yet know very little about how they "emerged from the experience of the Third Reich."[16] Beyond the success story of the Federal Republic, we must not forget how weak democratic consciousness was in the new republic after the catastrophe of National Socialism and genocidal warfare. Public opinion surveys at the time attested to early West Germans' skepticism toward the idea of democracy. In 1950, when asked which German had done the most for his country, 10 percent of them still named Hitler, another 14 percent emperors and kings, and 35 percent Otto von Bismarck, whereas only 6 percent opted for "democratic and liberal politicians." West Germans in the two decades after the war were, as Theodor Heuss put it in 1946, "ABC pupils of democracy."[17] In 1966, Karl Markus Michel, in the spirit of leftist opposition to the government, called the early Federal Republic a "young and inept democracy" that had grown out of the "ruins of the state of Hitler, Eichmann, [and] Globke." This thesis certainly would have been considered a truism in the 1950s and early 1960s.[18]

Independent of other differences, many pundits remarked on the great extent to which the shadow of total war, genocide, and moral catastrophe beyond compare lay over the new democracy. "Whoever lived through the 30s and 40s as a German," the melancholy conservative Golo Mann said in a speech before the Jewish World Congress in August 1966, "can never again fully trust his nation; he cannot trust democracy any more than any other system of government; he can never again fully trust humanity, and least of all trust what optimists used to call the 'meaning of history'. Regardless of how hard he may and should try, he will remain sad in the depths of his soul until he dies."[19]

Paternal Authority and the Search for Democracy in the Shadow of Violence

The question of whether and how authority and democracy could be conjoined figured prominently in West Germany's political culture of the 1950s and 1960s.

Within these debates the father soon occupied an emblematic status, as Heide Fehrenbach and Robert Moeller have noted.[20] It is, of course, tempting to interpret the West German obsession with "authority" as indicative of a lack of democratic thinking and as a fixation on authoritative government that was not overcome until the social changes of the late 1960s and early 1970s, that is, until the anti-authoritarian moment of 1968.[21] Yet such a reading of West German political culture fails to take into account that the meaning of authority was already changing between the early 1950s and the mid 1960s.

Around 1950, a hierarchical conception of authority based on tradition and the spirit of order and obedience still prevailed, but in the mid 1950s it began to give way to an idea of authority based on trust embedded in egalitarian social relationships. Thus, the 1963 edition of the *Evangelisches Soziallexikon* [Evangelical Social Encyclopedia] warned against confusing authority and power. "Authority lives from the *trust* it can be given." This trust, the encyclopedia continued, should not be "blindly bestowed" but required "critical vigilance," which "true authority depends on." Such an understanding of authority was consistent with "the idea of partnership." Partnership, in fact, was the "prerequisite of all authority and not just its (dialectical) supplement."[22] A central precondition for partnership, in turn, was "the partners' maturity" (literally their *Mündigkeit*), their "equality," and that "both individuals and groups break away from a patriarchal-authoritarian order."[23] Such ideas can be found in both highbrow and popular literature. In 1965, the *Kirchenzeitung* of Aachen warned readers not to confuse authority "with the right of the mightier or with military commanders, who could force their subordinates to perform the most undignified actions." As so many people at this time had had "bad experiences with the abuse of authority," a new kind of authority was urgently needed, one no longer based on "power and fear" but on "love and trust."[24]

This shift in the meaning of authority accompanied an epochal break in the history of West German democracy—one that has not received the attention it perhaps deserves. This pivotal move becomes particularly apparent when one considers a notion characteristic of the West German public since the Adenauer era, namely that the private sphere constituted the alpha and the omega of a democratic polity. This argument was not just an invention of the late 1960s, when revolutionary fantasies of redemption held sway. To be sure, even today some historians argue that the New Left put an end to Adenauer's authoritative state in "1968," once it recognized that "freedom from a past that is perceived as living on in the present" required a "change in the behavioral dispositions of the individuals and institutional structures of society."[25]

However, this argument fails to account for the fact that in the "motorized Biedermeier period" similar ideas were already widespread. Adolf Schüle, for example, maintained in 1952 that democracy "in politics is only possible when the people who live within it act democratically in their private relationships as well." Otherwise, a democratic polity was "condemned to die." According to the secretary of the Mannheim Chamber of Commerce, the quest for democracy could only succeed if one kept in mind that this form of rule did not end with the system of government but was also a question of a "personal way of life." This was exactly what "the well-known English saying" meant: "democracy begins at home."[26] Schüle conceded that "these things cannot be described in detail or completely." Yet whoever had "breathed the air of a real democracy that reaches into the last branches of private life" would "be able to understand what is meant."[27] From the 1950s and on into the 1970s, the premise remained the same for this Mannheim theorist of democracy, as well as for many others in various contexts, even in oppositional political and cultural milieus: the true foundation of the political was not to be found in hostility or competition, nor in peace or the common good, but in the private sphere.

In the early 1950s, family experts had already begun arguing that neither authoritarian fathers nor a militaristic model of masculinity were compatible with the idea of democracy. Reconceptualizing paternal authority, in fact, was a central concern in a society forced to confront the legacy of National Socialism and authoritarian militarism. Although from today's perspective such interpretations of Nazism seem overly simplistic, they indicate how intensely and earnestly the public of the early Federal Republic discussed the origins of dictatorship and genocide.[28] Fathers could not acquire "the courage to raise children" by relying on an authority that was "merely formal," exhorted Heinrich Bödeker (1911–1998), a pastor from Detmold, in the Protestant monthly *Kirche und Mann* in September 1959. All complaints about the "youth of today" and all longing "for 'the good old times'" could not disguise the fact that many fathers in the new republic were "the heirs of an evil past" who had "helped to shape it." The path to a modern form of paternal authority and child-rearing "for a meaningful future" would remain closed if one attempted "to embellish his personal past and that of his people with lies and evasions." Rather, the courage to raise children required the courage to tell the truth: "the truth in all things, including the past."[29]

Similar ideas circulated in Catholic publications, revealing the extent to which the Federal Republic stood in the shadow of genocide and the war of extermination. In January 1952, *Der Männer-Seelsorger*, for example, published an article entitled "Democracy Begins in the Family." Its author, a Catholic priest, argued that "the father should not make autocratic decisions according to the *Führerprinzip*." Now that West Germans lived in a democratic society, the "patriarchal family" was "no longer in keeping with the times." Instead, "the spirit of good democracy" should make itself felt "in every modern family."[30] In November 1952, the leading Catholic monthly, *Mann in der Zeit*, with a circulation of 400,000, advised fathers not to be "icy-militaristic" (*eiskalt-militärisch*) with their sons and daughters. Paternal authority could not be won by making one's children "stand to attention" (*Strammstehen*) or by ordering them around in "a sergeant-major's voice" (*Kasernenhofton*). Although a certain distance between fathers and sons should be preserved, filial deference should "result from true respect and deep love" rather than pseudo-militaristic obedience.[31]

In the same year, Karl Borgmann, the editor of the magazine *Caritas* and a key figure in the Catholic laicization movement, argued that many Christians continued to support an ideal of the family that was "modeled on bygone conceptions of the state, in which citizens were governed from above and thus sentenced to enforced inactivity." In the January issue of the Catholic monthly *Frau und Mutter,* which boasted more than half a million subscribers at the time, Borgmann emphasized that for children to learn to "experience freedom and to live by" this ideal early on, the family should not take its cues from the ideal of "absolute monarchy" or, worse, "dictatorship." Whoever defended patriarchal-authoritarian forms of child-rearing pretended not to know that those responsible for Nazi crimes had come from "'orderly' families and not from the margins of society." Fathers who had raised their children with "authoritarian ... and violent methods" had been the midwives of the Nazi dictatorship. Those who kept treating their children "wrongfully" had to be aware that these children would themselves "turn into oppressors" as adults, Borgmann cautioned: "Some henchmen of the concentration camps came evidently from so-called 'orderly' families.'"[32]

Around 1960, arguments circling around the association between new concepts of paternal authority and the quest for democracy increasingly received the blessing of Catholic moral theologians such as Bernhard Häring (1912–1988). Similar to Borgmann, Häring believed that the question of the "connection between love and authority in the marriage and family" was urgent. In his study *Ehe in dieser Zeit* [Marriage in This Age], Häring focused on two considerations: "How is Hitler's authoritarian regime reflected in the structure of the family? Does democracy in Germany have a chance of survival considering the structure of the family?"[33] According to Häring, recent history had shown that "in a society that accepts tyranny, dictatorship, or a totalitarian regime without opposition" the family was "the playing field for a man's uninhibited appetite for power." Over time, it was inevitable that the head of the family would come to "rule arbitrarily over his dependents." Thus it was all the more important to realize that a "healthy democracy" could only be "conceivable if the exercise of authority in the family" had an expressly democratic character. Only children who were "raised to be mature members within it" could later be expected "to participate responsibly in social and political life."[34] Against this backdrop, it was encouraging that "the youth of today" rebelled against "child-rearing methods" that smacked of "animal training" and demanded instead "real (democratic-friendly) authority in their upbringing."[35]

Christianity and Democracy:
On the Religious Foundation of the Political Order

Among those who set the tone in criticizing a patriarchal conception of paternal authority on religious grounds were the Catholics who had already belonged to

Left Catholic circles in the 1920s and early 1930s. A particularly interesting and influential member of this group was the lay theologian, sociologist, and psychologist Ernst Michel (1889–1964).[36] In light of his own reading on the sociology and theology of the family, he explicitly rejected the natural law conception of patriarchy that was official church doctrine; this conception had also been reaffirmed by the papal encyclica *casti connubii* of 1930 and a 1953 pastoral of the German Episcopal Conference.[37] Although the Catholic Church also put Michel's study *Ehe: Eine Anthropologie der Geschlechtsgemeinschaft* [Marriage: An Anthropology of Gender Relations] on its Index, the book was favorably reviewed by a number of family experts, including even some Catholic moral theologians.[38] By the early 1950s, Michel had established himself as a leading authority on the crisis of paternal authority; in 1954, he was invited to give the keynote address at a conference on "The Problem of the Father," which was part of a conference series to foster dialogue between physicians and theologians.[39]

In keeping with the mainstream family sociology of the time, Michel subscribed to the ideal of polarized gender roles in the family. Yet his emphasis on the "historical-social" character of fatherhood led him to criticize patriarchal conceptions of paternal authority.[40] Because of the father's presence within it, the family was a "human-cultural" rather than a natural institution; it did not stand outside of history but rather was a product of it.[41] To ensure its continuing relevance, therefore, the family had to reinvent itself continually. According to Michel, the contemporary crisis of the family resulted from the fact that too many fathers were holding on to forms of authority grounded in "legal powers or in moral and religious dogmas," which he considered outmoded since they were based in "brute force" (*Zwangsgewalt*).[42] Contrary to the Church Bishops Conference's calls for the restoration of patriarchy, meaningful paternal authority in contemporary Germany could no longer be based on laws or dogmas, but solely on mutual "trust" and "love."[43]

The ideas of French Left Catholics whose attempts to reconcile Christianity with political modernity shaped Catholic political thought on both sides of the Atlantic in the 1940s and 1950s also resonated in early West German Catholic debates about the relationship between democracy and paternal authority. Along with Emmanuel Mounier (1905–1950), Jacques Maritain (1882–1973), and Gabriel Marcel (1889–1973), Jean Lacroix (1900–1986), a philosopher, sociologist, and co-founder of the magazine *Esprit,* was particularly influential.[44] In his 1948 book *La force et les faiblesses de la famille* (published in German in 1952 with the title *Hat die Familie versagt?*) Lacroix pointed out that both advocates and opponents of the family had committed the fallacy of regarding "paternal authority as the model of any authority." As a result, "they conceive of … the head of state and ultimately of God in terms of the archetype of the Father, whose sovereign figure is in turn understood as the *Paterfamilias.*"[45] In this context, it was almost inevitable that the "contemporary democratic movements" defined themselves "by patricide," Lacroix continued.[46] Since Rousseau, he argued, modern democracy had perceived itself as the product of "a threefold yet single murder: of the king, of God, and of the father."[47] However, this logic of patricide—which was becoming ever more radical—rested on the false assumption that the "values of brotherliness" could only be obtained by "suppressing the values of paternity."[48]

With the experience of the violence of war, as well as the collaboration and capitulation of nearly all European democracies in the face of fascism behind him, Lacroix remarked that a viable form of democracy, a "démocratie massive," could only be developed if its foundational idea of brotherliness did not get distracted by patricide and revolt against God. Instead, he recalled an "esoteric tradition" within Catholicism, the doctrine of the "three realms of the Father, the Son, and the Brother," an idea Lacroix configured as a phase model of progress. First, in the realm of the Father, mankind lived "solely in the idea of fatherhood" and formed "a unitary family under one patriarch." Then followed the realm of the Son, in which "childhood" dominated: "In each group ... the firstborn son possesses the authority. This is the epoch of hereditary monarchy." Since in the realm of the Son authority was no longer derived from the Father but lay in the "totality of all members of the community," the epoch of hereditary monarchy had to make room for the realm of the brother: "Then it is the brothers who choose their leader, and authority works from the bottom up, from the diverse brothers to the single leader." This constituted "the victory of democracy."[49] In response to a 1936 study by a French priest, *Le Règne du frère,* Lacroix noted that democracy was defined not only by the fact that "the brothers, now come of age, claim their right to elect whomever they deem most worthy as their leader." Rather, the epoch of democracy was also the "*realm of the Brother,* in which Christ has become a brother to us, thanks to a more abundant emanation of the gifts of the Holy Ghost."[50]

A pluralistic model of democracy as a forum for antagonistic interests may have seemed very out of place within Lacroix's understanding of democracy as a community of brothers. Yet he succeeded in reconciling two political traditions that had been largely hostile to one another since the French Revolution: the Christian language of brotherliness and the revolutionary language of *la fraternité*. For Lacroix, this reconciliation bore considerable consequences for the question of the relationship between family and political order. Measured against his ethics of democratic brotherliness, the family itself had not failed, but rather just the patriarchal conception of the family. However persuasive the theological substance of Lacroix's Three Realms doctrine may have been, his arguments were perceived by German Catholics "as very open-minded and thought-provoking" (Jakob David) and as "noteworthy" (Georg Scherer).[51]

A Catholicism in Lacroix's sense could be established in good conscience in the "realm of the brother" and thereby affirm the idea of democracy, egalitarian gender order, and, accordingly, a post-patriarchal conception of paternity. Paternity, as understood by Lacroix, stood "in the service of brotherliness." Its purpose was to develop "that brotherly friendship" that could "only achieve fulfillment and autonomy when paternity disappears." "Is it not the actual purpose of the family," Lacroix asked, "to ensure that the children, who at first exist only through their parents, eventually learn to exist through themselves and, by virtue of their equal rights, bring each other into being?" To ask this question meant to answer it. "Paternal power," the philosopher and sociologist concluded, destroyed itself by striving toward "a society of equals among brothers and sisters." Fathers who relinquished the use of physical force to maintain their authority spared their children "the murder … that otherwise would have seemed to be the only way for them to gain their freedom."[52]

Such attempts to devise a genuinely Christian foundation for democracy were by no means restricted to Catholic publicists. At the height of Adenauer era, Protestants voiced similar opinions. In February 1957, Hans Hermann Walz argued that the purpose of the church was to overcome "the indifference of clerics charged with monarchical resentment toward the democratic state" in order to develop a "theology of democracy" in its place. Walz, an assistant to the president of the German Protestant *Kirchentag,* found this task to be all the more urgent, since any community had "as much moral backbone" as did "those groups that constitute it." Thus the Federal Republic was "just as democratic or authoritarian as its individual groups are democratic or authoritarian." Admittedly, Christianity was not the founder of the state; however, its task was "to design it from within" and to advocate democracy with "emphasis."[53] In the same year, the high-volume journal *Kirche und Mann* [Church and Man] exhorted its readers to "become democrats." According to the author, "neither sophistic critics nor fair-weather democrats know, but responsible citizens do: We are all in the same boat, which has difficult journeys ahead." A lead article in the *Monatsschrift für Männerarbeit der Evangelischen Kirche in Deutschland* [Monthly for Men's Work by the Protestant Church in Germany] concluded with a phrase that would have delighted Tocqueville: "put democracy into our hearts and fill it with meaning."[54] Anglo-American theologians took up the role for the Protestants that Lacroix played for the Catholics. As early as May 1950, Heinz-Horst Schrey (b. 1911) encouraged West German Protestants to examine Reinhold Niebuhr's "theological foundation of democracy." His significance for political life in the early Federal Republic and for the ideal of a "free fellowship of citizens" should not be underestimated. The American theologian showed "that democracy was not just any form of government but the only possibility for modern man to preserve a dignified existence between the extremes of anarchy, which comprises only freedom, and tyranny, which comprises only order and coercion."[55] Ten years later, the journal *Kirche und Mann* brought some British considerations regarding the relationship between church and democracy to the discussion. In the context of an event in the Palatinate State Church (*pfälzische Landeskirche*), a group of English Protestants had pointed out that the New Testament contained "dogmatic and ethical passages that … had the potential to found a responsible democracy". These were formulated as "theological insights" above all in the writings of the radical Puritans. The purpose of the continental church consisted in "abandoning the hierarchical model of Church and society" and in embracing the Puritan foundation of democracy as a genuinely Christian form of government.[56]

Gentle Fatherhood instead of Militarized Masculinity

The new models of domestic masculinity, so central to the early West German quest for democracy, soon found their way into the prescriptive literature on child-rearing and parental guidance. Increasingly, advice was directed straight at fathers.[57] Of course, these publications do not indicate just how often fathers actually pushed prams, changed diapers, or hugged their children. But considering the typically wide circulation of these texts and the fact that they were designed to appeal to a wide audience, they can nevertheless provide a reliable measure of the longing for an "ideal family," that is, a specific image of the family that was hardly less "real" than the daily life of the family.[58]

A brochure entitled "Ohne Vater geht es nicht" [Without the Father It Does Not Work], which was distributed to Catholic men in the bishoprics of Münster and Essen during the so-called Lent Education Week in 1961, exhorted fathers to spend less time at work, in bars, and in soccer stadiums. It also advised them to be present at their child's birth to develop an "intimate relationship" with toddlers and to dispense with "nightly cross-examinations" in order not to lose "the child's trust."[59] In May 1961, *Zwischen Dom und Zechen* [Between the Cathedral and the Coal-Mines], a regular supplement to the monthly *Mann in der Zeit,* praised the book *Gute Väter—frohe Kinder* [Good Fathers—Happy Children] as a "nice collection of stories about the world of fathers."[60] At the center of the book was a series of photos from a "course on baby care for men" (*Männer Säuglingspflege-Kurs*) offered regularly by the Associations of Samaritans in Zurich. The book's editor noted that it was important for fathers to learn how to manage a household while not creating a disaster on their "free Saturdays and Sundays ... should their wives be away visiting relatives." Many of the pictures, to be sure, give the impression of being skillfully staged representations of bourgeois decorum rather than icons of gentle fatherhood. Moreover, some of the pictures raise doubts about even progressive Catholic men's willingness to participate in infant care in daily life: in one, for example, two of the four men changing a diaper had put on protective masks (see Figure 7.1).[61]

In the visual aesthetics of the early twenty-first century, this iconography of gentle fatherhood tends to elicit a smile. Nevertheless, that should not keep us from recognizing the great political importance with which family experts imbued the visual realities of the new paternal authority in the late 1950s and early 1960s. Especially in the genre of the *Lichtbildreihe* (photo presentation), a popular pedagogical tool of the time, one can find indicators of just how much authors wished to codify the political message of the new image of the father. In 1964, Rudolf Rüberg put together a photo series designed for adult and young

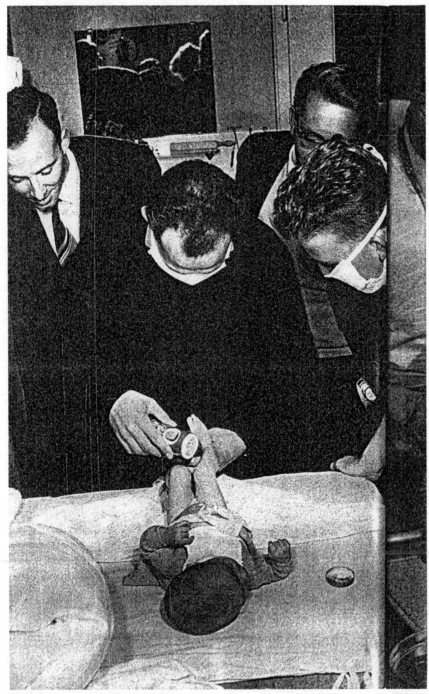

Figure 7.1. From Karl P. Lukaschek, ed., *Gute Väter – frohe Kinder* (n.p. [Münster/ Westf.], n.d. [1961]), 32.

adult education, as well as for use in schools, called *Vater – oder Familienfunk-tionär?* [Father – or Functionary of the Family?]. The Catholic family expert had composed the accompanying explanations—about half a page for each of the forty slides—attempting to influence the interpretation of the series. Like many of his contemporaries, Rüberg assumed that the "question of the father" had become one of the "burning questions" of the moment. Because the image of the patriarchal father had become obsolete, and no "new father image" had come into view, he hoped to make the "contours" of this new image visible.[62]

Rüberg arranged the photographs thematically: The section "The Absent Fathers" was followed by the chapter "The Father—An Outsider in the Family"; after that came "Tiny Cog in the Complex Machine of the World," "No More Real Men?" and "Fear of Responsibility." This visual diagnosis of the crisis culminated in the photo sequence "Lack of Paternal Authority." It began with a picture of soldiers exercising, which Rüberg identified as "Picture 28: Drill in the Barrack Yard" (Fig. 7.2). Twenty years after the apocalypse of a catastrophic militarism and almost ten years after rearmament and the return of a conscript army, this scene of soldierly masculinity was intended to remind viewers that authority must "under no circumstance" be confused with the "right of the strongest or the highest in command," who can force the subordinates "to do anything, even degrading actions." This exhortation was all the more urgent since many people had had "bad experiences with a misused, and thus false, authority."[63]

The focal point of the following photo sequence was an image diametrically opposed to "Drill in the Barrack Yard" labeled "Renaissance of the Father?"

Figure 7.2. Drill in the Backyard, from *Vater – oder Familienfunktionär?* ed. Heinz Budde (Munich, 1964), 44 black and white slides.

Rüberg used it to show ways out of the crisis of paternal authority. "Picture 37: Father with Stroller" marks the turning point of the presentation. Referring to the rhetoric of democratic fatherhood, Rüberg commented on it as follows (Fig. 7.3).[64]

> When one looks closely and long enough, one discovers something new about these fathers, principally the young fathers – a characteristic that could not be better, which he might let show just a bit. Once there was a rule that a father ought to love his children, but not show them. Something seems to be changing here. One can see it most often on Sunday mornings: fathers take their children to a park, to the zoo, or to a playground. Maybe they seem awkward, but they are not ashamed to wipe their children's nose when it's necessary, to comfort them after a fall, or to ride with them on the carousel. Sometimes one can even see them pushing a stroller, or even a big, tall-wheeled "celebrity pram with deluxe lining" – through the parks without any mothers giving them cover ... Something is changing! ... Hence, the relationship of a father to his children is gaining new foundations: love and trust, instead of pure power and fear. These, however, the father's love and the child's trust, are basic requirements for child-rearing. And they are at the core of a new conception of authority.

The 1950s domestication of masculinity developed in tandem with the renaissance of the idea of the "playful father" that had been central to middle-class conceptions of fatherhood between the 1820s and 1880s.[65] In November 1955, the first issue of the journal *Unsere Welt* [Our World], an interconfessional monthly edited by the German Family Association (Deutscher Familienverband), advertised a competition for the best pictures portraying fathers as their children's "great friend and companion in play."[66] The prize-winning photos reveal similar ambivalences as those from the Zurich "course on baby care for men." In most cases, the insignia of middle-class respectability such as the dark suit, white shirt, and dark tie seem as significant as the display of emotional involvement and a gentler kind of masculinity. Interestingly, however, the first prize was awarded for a picture of five youngsters with their father, Helmut Hüber of Stuttgart, who seemed delighted that his children had just defeated him in a pillow fight.[67] Whereas—to the great chagrin of the conservative government—such a large number of children was unusual even for the baby boom years of the 1950s, it was typical that the journal invited its male readers to prove their masculinity in pillow fights with their children rather than in mortal combat.

Democratic Fatherhood in the Liberal Republic

It would be easy to point to the limits of the concept of "democratic fatherhood."[68] Not one of these family experts assumed that fathers could be anything other than married and heterosexual. Nor did they argue that fathers should be more than part-time participants in baby and child care or domestic life. All

Figure 7.3. Father with Stroller, from Rev. Rudolf Rüberg, *Vater – oder Familienfunktionär?* ed. Heinz Budde (Munich, 1964), 44 black and white slides.

agreed that mothers were primarily responsible for child-rearing and the household; even those who advocated mothers' rights to pursue part-time work never questioned the primacy of fathers as breadwinners. Clearly, we should not take at face value the family experts' claim that they were defining forms of paternal authority beyond "patriarchy."

Nevertheless, we must not forget that even conservatives in the 1950s and early 1960s advocated new kinds of paternal authority rather than a return to hierarchical patriarchalism. Even though this new model of a gentler, more loving fatherhood stayed within the framework of patriarchal gender relations, these gender relations were less hierarchical and authoritarian than the Christian conceptions of patriarchy of the interwar years. Catholic and Protestant family experts actively promoted a new kind of paternal authority based on trust and love, as well as a new model of the family in which fathers were expected to play an active role in raising not only their older children, but also their infants and toddlers. The point here is not to claim that Jean Lacroix, Ernst Michel, or other left-wing Catholics of the time who challenged what they considered patriarchal conceptions of the family represented mainstream German or European Catholicism.[69] They did not. Nonetheless, their marginality notwithstanding, these intellectuals, in combination with the increasing laicization of Catholic organizations since the late 1950s, arguably prompted much conceptual and intellectual agitation among mainstream Catholics at the time.[70] To be sure, such attempts to question patriarchy and to envision more egalitarian gender relations were compromised by persisting systems of gendered economic discrimination and the maternalistic presupposition of welfare reforms. Yet we must not overlook the fact that these early advocates of gentle fatherhood articulated demands from about 1950 that a later generation of feminists would build upon in the late 1960s. As Geoff Eley recently noted, critiques of patriarchy from the early 1950s "accumulated languages of rights and capacities that later radicalism could also deploy."[71]

A narrow focus on the attempts of the CDU government and Catholic bishops to restore a patriarchal gender order necessarily excludes the religious and political dynamics behind public debates about paternal authority in the early Federal Republic. Interpreting this debate merely as an expression of concern about changing gender relations is inadequate. Rather, the new model of a "democratic family" must be viewed as an integral part of the rise of democracy as a way of life. Similar shifting perspectives are instructive in this context: society became more tolerant of premarital and extramarital sex, just as attitudes toward working and single mothers relaxed. The dream of a new kind of paternal authority, too, was a part of a vision of egalitarian gender relations, in which both women and men were supposed to be able to combine family and a career.[72]

But public debate about "democratic fatherhood" represented more than that: it became the locus for determining the relationship between authority and democracy in the new republic. The longing for a gentler, more loving kind of fatherhood thus comprises a particularly telling aspect of the West German quest for democracy. Immediately after the war, many observers complained that "democracy" was merely an empty phrase used to cover up the moral failings of the time. But in the 1950s, this guiding concept was filled with life and meaning. The dream of new forms of paternal authority decisively contributed to citizens' ability to leave National Socialism and militarism behind and discard the ideal of masculinity embodied by the heroic working soldier associated with them. Embracing the idea of "democratic fatherhood," West Germans found their way into a democratic polity and learned to feel at home in their "liberal republic."

Notes

* Research for this paper has been made possible by the generous support of the Alexander von Humboldt Foundation, the Fritz Thyssen Foundation and the Social Sciences and the Humanities Research Council.

1. Alois Stiefvater, "Der interessante Vortrag," *Der Männer-Seelsorger* 14 (1964): 204–205.
2. Wilhelm Bitter, ed., *Vorträge über das Vaterproblem in Psychotherapie, Religion und Gesellschaft* : *3. Arbeitstagung der Gemeinschaft "Arzt und Seelsorger"* (Stuttgart, 1954); Paul Wilhelm Wenger, "Vaterlose Gesellschaft," *Rheinischer Merkur*, 7 August 1959, 1–2; Alexander Mitscherlich, "Der unsichtbare Vater: Ein Problem für Psychoanalyse und Soziologie," *Kölner Zeitschrift für Soziologie und Sozialpsychologie* 7 (1955): 188–201; Alexander Mitscherlich, *Auf dem Weg zur vaterlosen Gesellschaft: Ideen zur Sozialpsychologie* (Munich, 1963).
3. Ian Shapiro, *The State of Democratic Theory* (Princeton, NJ, 2003), esp. 87–93; Wolfgang Merkel, "Theorien der Transformation: Die demokratische Konsolidierung postautoritärer Gesellschaften," in *Politische Theorien in der Ära der Transformation*, ed. Klaus von Beyme and Claus Offe (Opladen, 1996), 30–58, esp. 38–39; Charles S. Maier, "Democracy since the French Revolution," in *Democracy: The Unfinished Journey*, ed. John Dunn (Oxford, 1992), 125–154, esp. 148–149; Herfried Münkler and Skadi Krause, "Sozio-moralische Grundlagen der Demokratie," in *Demokratie-Lernen als Aufgabe der politischen Bildung*, ed. Gotthard Breit and Siegfried Schiele (Schwalbach, 2002), 223–240; Marcel Gauchet, "Tocqueville, l'Amérique et nous," *Libre: Politique—anthropologie—philosophie* 7 (1980): 43–120; John Dunn, *Western Political Theory in the Face of the Future*, 2nd ed. (Cambridge, 1993), 1–28.
4. Horst Möller, "Gefährdungen der Demokratie: Aktuelle Probleme in historischer Sicht," *Vierteljahrshefte für Zeitgeschichte* 55, no. 3 (2007): 379–391, here 380–381; Klaus Dicke, "Grußwort," in *Was heißt und zu welchem Ende studiert man Geschichte des 20. Jahrhunderts*, ed. Norbert Frei (Göttingen, 2006), 6–10, here 10. See also Anthony Kauders, "Democratization as Cultural History, or: When is (West) German Democracy Fulfilled?" in *German History* 25 (2007): 240–257.
5. Heinrich Ostermann, SJ, "Wandlungen in der Männerseelsorge," *Der Männer-Seelsorger* 13 (1963): 131–137, here 132.
6. Clemens Vollnhals, *Evangelische Kirche und Entnazifizierung 1945–1949: Die Last der nationalsozialistischen Vergangenheit* (Munich, 1989), esp. 281; Erwin Gatz, "Deutschland," in *Kirche und Katholizismus seit 1945*, vol. 1: *Mittel-, West- und Nordeuropa*, ed. Erwin Gatz (Paderborn, 1998), 53–158, esp. 54, 60. Martin Conway emphasizes that this was by no means a specifically German but a Western European phenomenon; see his "The Rise and Fall of Western Europe's Democratic Age, 1945–1973," *Contemporary European History* 13 (2004): 81–82. According to Callum Brown, the greatest church growth that Britain had experienced since

the mid nineteenth century occurred in the decade following the Second World War; see Callum Brown, *The Death of Christian Britain: Understanding Secularisation 1800–2000* (London, 2001), 170.

7. Michael J. Inacker, *Zwischen Transzendenz, Totalitarismus und Demokratie. Die Entwicklung des kirchlichen Demokratieverständnisses von der Weimarer Republik bis zu den Anfängen der Bundesrepublik 1918–1959* (Neukirchen-Vluyn, 1994), 239–246, quotations 244–245: "In contrast to the situation in 1918," Michael Inacker notes, this self-delusion made it possible "to create new kinds of political worlds, to strive toward new goals, and to go new ways." See in general Martin Greschat, "'Rechristianisierung' and 'Säkularisierung': Anmerkungen aus deutscher protestantischer Sicht," in *Säkularisierung, Dechristianisierung, Rechristianisierung im neuzeitlichen Europa: Bilanz und Perspektiven der Forschung*, ed. Hartmut Lehmann (Göttingen, 1997), 76–85, and Mark E. Ruff, "Integrating Religion into the Historical Mainstream: Recent Literature on Religion in the Federal Republic," *Central European History* 42 (2009): 307–337.

8. Karl Gabriel, "Zwischen Tradition und Modernisierung: Katholizismus und katholisches Milieu in den fünfziger Jahren der Bundesrepublik," in *Kirchliche Zeitgeschichte: Urteilsbildung und Methoden*, ed. Anselm Doering-Mateuffel and Kurt Nowak (Stuttgart, 1996), 248–262, here 252; Christoph Kleßmann, "Kontinuitäten und Veränderungen im protestantischen Milieu," in *Modernisierung im Wiederaufbau: Die Westdeutsche Gesellschaft der 50er Jahre*, ed. Axel Schildt and Arnold Sywottek (Bonn, 1993), 403–417; Martin Greschat, "Zwischen Aufbruch und Beharrung: Die Evangelische Kirche nach dem Zweiten Weltkrieg," in *Die Zeit nach 1945 als Thema kirchlicher Zeitgeschichte*, ed. Victor Conzemius et al. (Göttingen, 1988), 99–126.

9. Institut für Publizistik an der Freien Universität Berlin, ed., *Die deutsche Presse 1954: Zeitungen und Zeitschriften* (Berlin, 1954). Rather than confirming a linear story of "strong" secularization in Western Europe, West Germany in the 1950s can be viewed as a time when Catholics and Protestants participated "in the very struggles to define and set the boundaries between the private and public spheres … between family, civil society, and the state." José Casanova, *Public Religions in the Modern World* (Chicago, 1994), 6.

10. See, for example, Frank Biess, *Homecomings: Returning POWs and the Legacies of Defeat in Postwar Germany* (Princeton, 2006), 98–102, 106–109; for contemporary views, see Hans Hermann Walz, "Die Christenheit in der demokratischen Gesellschaft," *Zeitwende: Die neue Furche* 28, no. 2 (1957), 85–97, quotation 97; Thomas Ellwein, *Klerikalismus in der deutschen Politik*, vol. 1: *Heiße Eisen* (Munich, 1955); Helmut Simon, *Katholisierung des Rechtes? Zum Einfluss katholischen Rechtsdenkens auf die gegenwärtige deutsche Gesetzgebung und Rechtsprechung* (Göttingen, 1962).

11. Casanova, *Public Religions*, 9.

12. For an analysis of the institutional context in which the debates emerged, see Lukas Rölli-Allkemper, *Familie im Wiederaufbau: Katholizismus und bürgerliches Familienideal in der Bundesrepublik Deutschland 1945–1965* (Paderborn, 2000).

13. Bernhard Häring, *Das Gesetz Christi: Moraltheologie, dargestellt für Priester und Laien*, vol. 3: *Das Ja zur allumfassenden Liebesherrschaft Gottes*, 6th rev. and exp. ed., 21.–24. Tsd. (Freiburg, 1961), 647. For the catch phrase "mature layperson" see, for example, Gerd Hirschauer, "Die Kirche in der Welt," in *Christ und Bürger heute und morgen*, ed. Alfred Horné (Stuttgart, 1958), 27ff. Tony Judt emphasizes that this was a pan-European phenomenon in his *Postwar: A History of Europe since 1945* (London 2005), 374.

14. Hans Hermann Walz, "Die Rolle des Laien im Zeugnis der Kirche," *Zeitwende: Die neue Furche* 24, no. 2 (August 1952): 129–138, quotations 129–130, 135, 137.

15. Thus, West German society from 1950 to the mid 1960s can perhaps be understood as a culture in which a challenge to patriarchy (and later to heteronormativity, more generally) was connected in part to the "public presence" of religious discourse. See Juan Marco Vaggione, *Gender and Sexuality beyond Secularism: The Political Mutations of the Religious* (PhD diss., New School, New York, 2006).

16. Volker Berghahn, "Recasting Bourgeois Germany," in *The Miracle Years: A Cultural History of West Germany, 1949–1968*, ed. Hanna Schissler (Princeton, 2001), 326–340, quotation 326; see also Richard J. Bessel and Dirk Schumann, "Introduction: Violence, Normality and the Construction of Postwar Europe," in *Life after Death: Approaches to a Cultural and Social History of Europe During the 1940s and 1950s*, ed. Richard J. Bessel and Dirk Schumann (Cambridge, 2003), 1–13, esp. 13.

17. Dirk van Laak, "Der widerspenstigen Deutschen Zähmung: Zur politischen Kultur einer unpolitischen Gesellschaft," in *50 Jahre Bundesrepublik Deutschland: Daten und Diskussionen,* ed. Eckart Conze and Gabriele Metzler (Stuttgart, 1999), 332; Theodor Heuss, "'Um Deutschlands Zukunft' [18 March 1946]," in *Aufzeichnungen 1945–1947,* ed. Eberhard Pikart (Tübingen, 1966), 207; see in general Raimund Lammersdorf, "'Das Volk ist streng demokratisch': Amerikanische Sorgen über das autoritäre Bewußtsein der Deutschen in der Besatzungszeit und frühen Bundesrepublik," in *Demokratiewunder: Transatlantische Mittler und die kulturelle Öffnung Westdeutschlands 1945–1970,* ed. Arnd Bauerkämper et al. (Göttingen, 2005), 85–103.

18. Karl Markus Michel, "Muster ohne Wert: Westdeutschland 1965," in *Die sprachlose Intelligenz,* ed. Karl Markus Michel (Frankfurt a. M., 1968), 63–124, here 72 (first in *Kursbuch*, no. 4 [February 1966]: 168).

19. Golo Mann, "Deutsche und Juden," in *Deutsche und Juden: Beiträge von Nahum Goldmann, ed.* Nahum Goldmann et al. (Frankfurt a. M., 1967), 49–69, here 69; on Mann's position in intellectual history of the Federal Republic, see Tilmann Lahme, "Nachwort," in Golo Mann, *Briefe 1932–1992,* ed. Tilmann Lahme (Göttingen, 2006), 483–520.

20. Heide Fehrenbach, "Rehabilitating Fatherland: Race and German Remasculinization," *Signs* 24, no. 1 (1998): 107–128; Heide Fehrenbach, *Race after Hitler: Black Occupation Children in Postwar Germany and America* (Princeton, 2005); Robert Moeller, "Heimkehr ins Vaterland: Die Remaskulinisierung Westdeutschlands in den fünfziger Jahren," *Militärgeschichtliche Zeitschrift* 60, no. 2 (2001): 403–436.

21. Karl Christian Lammers, "*Glücksfall Bundesrepublik* : New Germany and the 1960s," *Contemporary European History* 17 (2008): 127–134; Nick Thomas, *Protest Movements in 1960s West Germany* (New York, 2003), esp. 223; Christina von Hodenberg and Detlef Siegfried, "Reform und Revolte: 1968 und die langen sechziger Jahre in der Geschichte der Bundesrepublik," in *Wo "1968" liegt: Reform und Revolte in der Geschichte der Bundesrepublik,* ed. Christina von Hodenberg and Detlef Siegfried (Göttingen, 2006), 7–14, esp. 10; Habbo Knoch, "'Mündige Bürger', oder: Der kurze Frühling einer partizipatorischen Vision. Einführung," in *Bürgersinn mit Weltgefühl: Politische Moral und solidarischer Protest in den sechziger und siebziger Jahren,* ed. Habbo Knoch (Göttingen, 2007), 9–53, esp. 16, 25, as well as Ingrid Gilcher-Holtey, *Die 68er-Bewegung: Deutschland – Westeuropa – USA* (Munich, 2001), 127; and Axel Schildt, *Ankunft im Westen: Ein Essay zur Erfolgsgeschichte der Bundesrepublik* (Frankfurt, 1999), 90–92.

22. Cornelius Adalbert von Heyl, "Autorität," in *Evangelisches Sozialexikon,* 4th ed., ed. Martin Honecker et al., (Stuttgart, 1963), 129–131. In general, see Theodor Eschenburg, *Über Autorität* (Frankfurt a. M., 1965) as well as Jens Kertscher, "Autorität: Kontinuitäten und Diskontinuitäten im Umgang mit einem belasteten Begriff," in *Herausforderungen der Begriffsgeschichte,* ed. Carsten Dutt (Heidelberg, 2003), 133–147. For an indication of how central ideas like "cadaver obedience" and "spirit of subordination" were in dealing with the National Socialist past after the war, see Sean A. Forner, "Für eine demokratische Erneuerung Deutschlands: Kommunikationsprozesse und Deutungsmuster engagierter Demokraten nach 1945," *Geschichte und Gesellschaft* 33 (2007): 228–257, here 247.

23. Heinz-Dietrich Wendland, "Partnerschaft, in evangelischer Sicht," in *Evangelisches Soziallexikon,* 960–961. This entry, as well as those on "Authority" and "Democracy," do not appear in the first edition of the *Evangelical Sozialexikon* (Stuttgart, 1954). In discussing the first edition, Wendland himself criticized it for failing to deal adequately with questions of democracy; Wendland, "Rev. Evangelisches Sozialexikon," *Zeitwende: Die neue Furche* 26 (1955): 563–565. The idea of maturity (*Mündigkeit*) was an important catchword among the (Prot-

estant) laity at the time; see Heinrich Giesen, Heinz-Horst Schrey and Hans Jürgen Schultz, eds., *Der mündige Christ* (Stuttgart, 1956), a book that had sold more than 11.000 copies by 1957.

24. The Aachen-based *Kirchenzeitung* concluded that "the father's love and the child's trust are the fundamental requirements for child-rearing. And this is precisely what has become the defining characteristic of a new concept of authority. "Vater oder Familienfunktionär," *Kirchenzeitung* 20, no. 26 (1965): 16–19, quotation 18–19.

25. Gilcher-Holtey, *Die 68er Bewegung*, 61.

26. Adolf Schüle, "Demokratie als politische Form und als Lebensform," in *Rechtsprobleme in Staat und Kirche: Festschrift für Rudolf Smend zum 70. Geburtstag 15. Jan. 1952*, n. ed. (Göttingen, 1952), 321–344, quotations 326, 329.

27. Ibid., 334–335.

28. The now quite broad body of research on the politics of memory in the 1950s, in my opinion, underestimates the significance of these issues in the public debates about the immediate past of the Federal Republic; see, for example, Robert G. Moeller, *War Stories: The Search for a Usable Past in the Federal Republic of Germany* (Berkeley, 2001), as well as Neil Gregor's stimulating case study "The Illusion of Remembrance: The Karl Diehl Affair and the Memory of Nazism in Nuremberg 1945–1999," *Journal of Modern History* 75 (2003): 590–633. However, compare Peter Reichel's pointed thesis that the "burden of the National Socialist past" was hotly debated as early as the 1950s. In this respect, upon closer examination, the decade lost "everything idyllic and introspective, everything false and restorative." Peter Reichel, *Vergangenheitsbewältigung in Deutschland: Die Auseinandersetzung mit der NS-Diktatur von 1945 bis heute* (Munich, 2001), 139. Emblematic of the debate in Protestant publications is Friedrich Langenfaß, "Dürfen wir die Vergangenheit totschweigen? Der Antisemitismus und seine Früchte," *Zeitwende: Die neue Furche* 29 (1958): 755–762 and Friedrich Langenfaß, "Der Eichmann-Prozeß und Wir," *Zeitwende: Die neue Furche* 32 (1961): 721–725; as well as the special issues "Antisemitismus und Judentum," *Jungenwacht. Ein Blatt evangelischer Jugend* 17, no. 11 (1957) and "Der Nationalsozialismus," *Jungenwacht. Evangelische Schülerzeitschrift* 18, nos. 8–9 (1958); and now also Dirk Moses, *German Intellectuals and the Nazi Past* (Cambridge, 2007).

29. Heinrich Bödeker, "Kein Mut zur Erziehung?" *Kirche und Mann: Monatsschrift für Männerarbeit der Evangelischen Kirche in Deutschland* 12, no. 9 (1959): 3–4, quotation 4.

30. R. Sailer, "Demokratie beginnt in der Familie," *Der Männer-Seelsorger* 2, no. 1 (1952): 23–29, quotation 26. See also Walter Hemsing, "Wenn aus Kindern 'Leute' werden: 'Der Herr Sohn', das 'Fräulein Tochter,'" *Elternhaus, Schule und Gemeinde* 7, no. 9 (1955): 3–4.

31. N. a., "Ehrfurcht vor dem Vater: Mein Sohn sagt 'Otto' zu mir," *Mann in der Zeit: Zeitung für Stadt und Land* 5, no. 11 (1952): 11. The family was only one site among others within this search for new forms of masculinity; see especially Thomas Kühne, "'… aus diesem Krieg werden nicht nur harte Männer heimkehren': Kriegskameradschaft und Männlichkeit im 20. Jahrhundert," in *Männergeschichte—Geschlechtergeschichte: Männlichkeit im Wandel der Moderne*, ed. Thomas Kühne (Frankfurt a. M., 1996), 174–192, and Kaspar Maase, "Entblößte Brust und schwingende Hüfte: Momentaufnahmen von der Jugend der fünfziger Jahre," in Kühne, *Männergeschichte—Geschlechtergeschichte*, 193–217; Kaspar Maase, "Establishing Cultural Democracy: Youth, "Americanization," and the Irresistible Rise of Popular Culture," in Schissler, *The Miracle Years*, 428–450; and Svenja Goltermann, *Die Gesellschaft der Überlebenden: Deutsche Kriegsheimkehrer und ihre Gewalterfahrungen im Zweiten Weltkrieg* (Munich, 2009).

32. Karl Borgmann, "Völker werden aus Kinderstuben: Um die rechte Ordnung in der Familie," *Frau und Mutter: Monatsschrift für die katholische Frau in Familie und Beruf* 35, no. 1 (1952): 4–5. For circulation statistics, see Institut für Publizistik an der Freien Universität Berlin ed, *Die deutsche Presse 1954: Zeitungen und Zeitschriften* (Berlin, 1954), 539.

33. Bernhard Häring, *Ehe in dieser Zeit* (Salzburg, 1960), 102. Häring was granted permission to publish the book by Munich Provincial Councillor of Redemptionists Gerhard Mittermeier on 21 June 1960, and also by Archbishop of Salzburg Zahl 1020/60; see ibid., 4.

34. Ibid., 111.
35. Ibid., 144.
36. Peter Reifenberg, *Situationsethik aus dem Glauben: Leben und Denken Ernst Michels (1889–1964)* (St. Ottilien, 1992); Benno Haunhorst, "Politik aus dem Glauben: Zur politischen Theologie Ernst Michels," in *Sozial- und Linkskatholizismus: Erinnerung, Orientierung, Befreiung*, ed. Heiner Ludwig and Wolfgang Schroeder (Frankfurt a. M., 1990), 101–129. Generally see Thomas Ruster, *Die verlorene Nützlichkeit der Religion: Katholizismus und Moderne in der Weimarer Republik* (Paderborn, 1994) and Wolfgang Schivelbusch, *Intellektuellendämmerung: Zur Lage der Frankfurter Intelligenz in den zwanziger Jahren* (Frankfurt a. M., 1985).
37. Ernst Michel, *Ehe: Eine Anthropologie der Geschlechtsgemeinschaft*, 2nd ed. (Stuttgart, 1950), esp. 49–51. On the pastoral letter of the Catholic bishops' conference, see for example Alfons Fischer, *Pastoral in Deutschland nach 1945*, vol. 2.: *Zielgruppen und Zielfelder der Seelsorge 1945–1962* (Würzburg, 1986), 84–85; on the larger theological context see Norbert Lüdecke, *Eheschließung als Bund: Genese und Exegese der Ehelehre der Konzilskonstitution "Gaudium et spes" in kanonistischer Auswertung (Forschungen zur Kirchenrechtswissenschaft Bd. 7)* (Würzburg, 1989).
38. Reifenberg, *Situationsethik aus dem Glauben*, 164–166; Lüdecke, *Eheschliessung als Bund*, 148–158.
39. Never shy to promote his own work, Michel published his lecture not only in the conference proceedings but also in the leading psychoanalytical journal *Psyche* as well as in the monthly of the German Red Cross, in a condensed version.
40. Ernst Michel, "Das Vaterproblem heute in soziologischer Sicht," in *Vorträge über das Vaterproblem in Psychotherapie, Religion und Gesellschaft*, ed. Wilhelm Bitter (Stuttgart, 1954), 44–74, esp. 52–54 and 56–57, also published in *Psyche* 8 (1954): 161–190 and in condensed version as "Vaterschaft als geschichtlich-soziale Existenzform: Zum Vaterproblem heute," in *Deutsches Rotes Kreuz. Zentralorgan des DRK in der Bundesrepublik Deutschland* 11, no. 2 (1958): 5–8.
41. Ibid., 53.
42. Ibid., 58.
43. Ibid., 66.
44. See the entries on "Personalism" (Jean-François Fourny, 84–85), "Gabriel Marcel" (Thomas Pavel, 604–606), "Jacques Maritain" (Thomas Pavel, 607–609), and "Esprit" (Michel Winock, 699–702) in *The Columbia History of Twentieth-Century French Thought*, ed. Lawrence D. Kritzman (New York, 2006). Whereas Thomas Keller, *Deutsch-Französische Dritte-Weg-Diskurse: Personalistische Intellektuellendebatten der Zwischenkriegszeit* (Munich, 2001) and Christian Roy and John Hellmann, "Le personnalisme et les contacts entre non-conformistes de France et d'Allemagne autour de l'Ordre Nouveau et de Gegner: 1930–1942," in *Entre Locarno et Vichy: les relations culturelles franco-allemandes dans les années 1930*, ed. Hans Manfred Bock et al. (Paris, 1993), 203–215, provide important insights into the role of personalism in Franco-German controversies and conversations in the interwar years, our knowledge of personalism's influence among lay Catholic in postwar West Germany is sketchy at best. In retrospect, Heinrich Böll and Walter Dirks emphasized how much their politics in the late 1940s and early 1950s had been shaped by leading French personalists such as Emmanuel Mounier; see Klaus Große Kracht, "Von der 'geistigen Offensive' zur neuen Unauffälligkeit. Katholische Intellektuelle in Deutschland und Frankreich (1910–1960)," in *Religion und Gesellschaft: Europa im 20. Jahrhundert*, ed. Friedrich Wilhelm Graf und Klaus Große Kracht (Cologne, 2007), 223–246, here 223, 242. In the immediate postwar years, Mounier was a leading proponent of a Franco-German rapprochement, and in 1948 he founded the *Comité français d'échanges avec l'Allemagne nouvelle*; see Alfred Grosser, "Emmanuel Mounier und das Comité français d'échanges avec l'Allemagne nouvelle," *Deutschland – Frankreich: Ludwigsburger Beiträge zum Problem der deutsch-französischen Beziehungen* 1 (1954): 270–280; Christiane Falbisaner, "Emmanuel Mounier et l'Allemagne," *Revue d'Allemagne* 21, no. 2 (1989): 257–279; Carla Albrecht, "Das Comité français d'échanges avec l'Allemagne nouvelle als Wegbereiter des Deutsch-Französischen Jugendwerks," *Lendemains* 27, nos. 107–108 (2002): 177–

189. For a stimulating analysis see generally Jan-Werner Müller, "Die eigentlich katholische Entschärfung? Jacques Maritain und die christdemokratischen Fluchtwege aus dem Zeitalter der Extreme," *Zeitschrift für Ideengeschichte* 2, no. 3 (2008): 40–54.

45. Jean Lacroix, *La force et les faiblesses de la famille*, Collection Esprit, "La Cité Prochaine" (Paris, 1948); German edition: *Hat die Familie versagt? Wege zu einer neuen Sinngebung* (Offenburg 1952), 8 (the book was published in collaboration with the important Franco-German journal *Dokumente: Zeitschrift für übernationale Zusammenarbeit*). Similar arguments can be found in Gabriel Marcel, "Die schöpferische Verpflichtung als Wesen der Vaterschaft," in Gabriel Marcel, *Homo Viator: Philosophie der Hoffnung (Düsseldorf 1949)*, 132–171, here 168–169; Emmanuel Mounier, "Personalism and the Revolution of the Twentieth Century," in *Personalism* (Notre Dame, IN, 1989; first published Paris 1950), 97–123, esp. 106–109 (with an explicit reference to Lacroix's book); and Jacques Maritain, *Christentum und Demokratie* (Augsburg, 1949). For another volume that reflects the great interest in French Catholic conceptions of the family among lay Catholics in postwar Germany see Jean Viollet and Gabriel Marcel, eds., *Vom Wesen und Geheimnis der Familie: 10 Untersuchungen* (Salzburg, 1952). On Jean Lacroix see T. de Morembert, "Art: Jean Lacroix," in *Dictionnaire de Biographie française*, vol. 19, ed. Jules Balteau, Michel Prevost (Paris, 2001), 52–53; Julian Jackson, *France: The Dark Years 1940–1944* (Oxford, 2001), 341–343; Michael Kelly, "Catholicism and the Left in Twentieth-Century France," in *Catholicism, Politics, and Society in Twentieth-Century France*, ed. Kay Chadwick (Liverpool, 2000), 142–174, esp. 161–162, 171; and Goulven Boudic, *Esprit, 1944–1982: Les métamorphoses d'une revue* (Paris, 2005).

46. Lacroix, *Hat die Familie versagt?* 18.

47. Ibid., 37.

48. Ibid., 23.

49. Ibid., 39.

50. Ibid., 41. Internal quotation in Le P. Fr. Coberthrambe, *Le Règne du frère* (Paris, 1936), 160.

51. Jakob David, "Von Würde und Bürde des Vaters in unserer Zeit, pt. II," *Orientierung: Katholische Blätter zur weltanschaulichen Information* 24, no. 10 (1960): 111–114, here 113; Georg Schwerer, *Die Macht des Vaters: Meditationen über Kindschaft, Mündigkeit und Vatertum* (Essen, 1962), 149. See also Bernhard Häring's references to Lacroix, *Ehe in dieser Zeit* (Studia theologiae moralis et pastoralis edita a professoribus academiae alfonsianae in urbe, vol. 7) (Salzburg, 1960), passim as well as Franz M. Kapfhammer, "Leben wir in einer vaterlosen Gesellschaft? Von der Vaterherrschaft zur Vaterliebe," in *Neue Volksbildung: Buch u. Bücherei*, ed. Bundesministerium für Unterricht, 13, no. 4 (1962): 151–156; even in the negative review of the book in the journal *Theologie und Glaube*, Lacroix's conception of democracy as the "'message of brotherliness'" was praised as "very good"; see "Rez. Gustav Ernecke, Jean Lacroix, Hat die Familie versagt?" *Theologie und Glaube* 43 (1953): 145.

52. Lacroix, *Hat die Familie versagt?* 153.

53. Hans Hermann Walz, "Die Christenheit in der demokratischen Gesellschaft," *Zeitwende: Die neue Furche* 28, no. 2 (1957): 85–97, quotations 88, 89, 93, 96. On this and the following, see also Kurt Nowak, "Der lange Weg der deutschen Protestanten in die Demokratie," in *Demokratie in Deutschland: Chancen und Gefährdungen im 19. und 20. Jahrhundert. Fs. Heinrich August Winkler*, ed. Wolther von Kieseritzky and Klaus-Peter Sick (Munich, 1999), 420–434; Albert Stein, "Evangelische Rechtsethik 1945–1963," in *Katholizismus, Rechtsethik und Demokratiediskussion 1945–1963*, ed. Anton Rauscher (Paderborn, 1981), 123–146; Reinhold Lindner, *Grundlegung einer Theologie der Gesellschaft: Dargestellt an der Theologie Paul Tillichs* (Hamburg, 1960); Kurt Sontheimer, "Demokratie," in *Evangelisches Soziallexikon*, 248–252; Inacker, *Zwischen Transzendenz*.

54. "Im Blitzlicht: Demokratie ist eine gute Sache," *Kirche und Mann: Monatsschrift für Männerarbeit der Evangelischen Kirche in Deutschland* 10, no. 9 (1957): 1.

55. Heinz-Horst Schrey, "Glaube jenseits der Tragödie. Die Theologie Reinhold Niebuhrs," *Zeitwende: Die neue Furche* 21, no. 10 (1949/50): 807–815, quotations: 814. In contrast to this, Schrey says that one searches "in vain within continental theology for such a foundation [of

democracy], because Europe's long patriarchal-monarchical habituation makes democracy appear to be not a way of life for modern man but rather a revolutionary matter associated with revolt and bloodshed that disturbs the foundations of social existence" (814).

56. "Beitrag zu Diskussion: Englische Christen über Kirche und Demokratie," *Kirche und Mann: Monatsschrift für Männerarbeit der Evangelischen Kirche* 15, no. 1 (1962): 5; see also Reinhold Freudenstein, "Amerika ist völlig anders: Ein amerikanischer Hitler wäre unmöglich. Erziehung zur Demokratie an oberster Stelle," *Kirche und Mann: Monatsschrift für Männerarbeit der Evangelischen Kirche* 14, no. 2 (1961): 8. Freudenstein (b. 1931), who taught at Manchester College in Indiana after training as a high school teacher, reported that in the US, a political dictatorship was "simply impossible" because the country was a state where "democracy is really lived." This could be seen, for example, in the fact that American parents did not use the word 'obey' but replaced it with 'persuade.' Freudenstein's assertion prompted a prosecuting attorney for juvenile court in Bielefeld to write a polemic on "the breakdown of paternal authority as a force ensuring protection and security," which was especially conspicuous in the US ("Briefe an Kirche und Mann: Der 'Vater' ist nicht mehr gefragt," *Kirche und Mann: Monatsschrift für Männerarbeit der Evangelischen Kirche* 14, no. 3 (1961): 8.

57. In general, see Markus Höffer-Mehlmer, *Elternratgeber: Zur Geschichte eines Genres* (Baltmannsweiler, 2003), 227–235; Miriam Gebhardt, "Frühkindliche Sozialisation und historischer Wandel," *Tel Aviver Jahrbuch für deutsche Geschichte* 32 (2004): 258–273.

58. John Gillis, in particular, has remarked that this "ideal family," derived from a combination of myths, rituals, and images, is much more stable than the "fragmentary and temporary … real family"; John Gillis, *Mythos Familie: Auf der Suche nach einer eigenen Lebensform* (Weinheim, 1997), 11. This rhetoric about fatherhood was more than empty words, as a look at family law reveals. On 29 July 1959 the Federal Constitutional Court declared the so-called *väterlichen Stichentscheid*, a father's right as the final arbiter in the family, unconstitutional, thereby dethroning the family patriarch as a figure supported by civil law; see Till van Rahden, "Demokratie und väterliche Autorität: Das Karlsruher "Stichentscheid"-Urteil in der politischen Kultur der frühen Bundesrepublik," *Zeithistorische Forschungen* 2 (2005): 160–179.

59. Hansmartin Lochner and Robert Svoboda, eds., *Ohne Vater geht es nicht (Bildheft für Erwachsene zur Fastenerziehungswoche 1961)* (n. p. [Hamm, Westfalen], 1961), 4. The brochure had gotten the imprimatur of the Bishop of Paderborn on 13 December 1960; ibid., 15.

60. "Der wiederkehrende Vater," *Zwischen Dom und Zechen: Beilage zum "Mann in der Zeit,"* no. 5 (May 1961).

61. Karl P. Lukaschek, ed., *Gute Väter – frohe Kinder* (s.l. [Münster/Westf.] o.J. [1961]), 32–35, Quotation: 32. Outside of Catholic circles, the growing popularity of the father changing a diaper as an icon of gentle masculinity can be found as early as the mid-1950s. See "Werdende Väter wickeln Puppen," *Constanze* 7, no. 18 (1954), 14–15.

62. Rudolf Rüberg, *Vater oder Familienfunktionär? Lichtbildreihe zum Thema "Ehe und Familie"* (Munich, 1964), 3. Rüberg remarked that the photo series was "especially well-suited for adult education, for men and women, families, parent seminars, and parent-teacher meetings in the church or school. For a youth forum or a group of mature youth, it can serve … as a basis"; ibid., 3.

63. Rüberg, *Vater – oder Familien-Funktionär,* 16.

64. Ibid., 19–20. Appears almost verbatim in Rudolf Rüberg, *Eltern in einer neuen Welt (Zurich, 1964),* 63–64.

65. Stephen M. Frank, *Life with Father: Parenthood and Masculinity in the Nineteenth-Century American North* (Baltimore, 1998); Rebekka Habermas, *Frauen und Männer des Bürgertums: Eine Familiengeschichte (1750–1850)* (Göttingen, 2000); John Tosh, *A Man's Place: Masculinity and the Middle-Class Home in Victorian England* (New Haven, 1999).

66. "Unser Photo-Wettbewerb: Vater als Spielgefährte," *Unsere Welt* 1, no. 1 (1955): 3.

67. "Vater als Spielgefährte," *Unsere Welt* 2, no. 3 (1956): 3. The other pictures appeared in a later issue: "Vater spielt mit!" *Unsere Welt* 2, no. 6 (1956): 4–5.

68. See especially Sonya Michel, "American Women and the Discourse of the Democratic Family in World War II," in *Behind the Lines: Gender and the Two World Wars*, ed. Margaret R. Higonnet et al. (New Haven, 1987), 154–167. For a typical example of the limitations of mainstream pro-emancipation arguments, see Walter Dirks, "Soll er ihr Herr sein? Die Gleichberechtigung der Frau und die Reform des Familienrechts," *Frankfurter Hefte* 7 (1952): 825–837, esp. 835.

69. Walter Dirks, the editor of the influential journal *Frankfurter Hefte*, published a piece on the crisis of marriage in early 1951 that echoed many of the concerns addressed in Michel's book and employed similar language—existentialist, religious, and metaphysical: Dirks, "Was die Ehe bedroht. Eine Liste ihrer kritischen Punkte," *Frankfurter Hefte* 6 (1951): 18–28. In late 1952, however, Dirks revisited these issues in an article that was much more down-to-earth and focused on legal questions; it was also a more fundamental challenge to patriarchal conceptions of marriage and the family: Dirks, "Soll er ihr Herr."

70. Hartmann Tyrell, "Die Familienrhetorik des Zweiten Vatikanums und die gegenwärtige Deinstitutionalisierung von Ehe und Familie," in Franz-Xaver Kaufmann and Arnold Zingerle, eds., *Vaticanum II und Modernisierung: Historische, theologische und soziologische Perspektiven* (Paderborn, 1996), 353–373; Wilhelm Damberg, *Abschied vom Milieu? Katholizismus im Bistum Münster und in den Niederlanden 1945–1980* (Paderborn, 1997); Benjamin Ziemann, *Katholische Kirche und Sozialwissenschaften 1945–1975* (Göttingen, 2007).

71. Geoff Eley, *Forging Democracy: The History of the Left in Europe, 1850–2000* (New York, 2002), 313.

72. See especially Maase, "Establishing Cultural Democracy"; Maria Höhn, *GIs and Fräuleins: The German-American Encounter in 1950s West Germany* (Chapel Hill, 2002), 12; Christine von Oertzen, *Teilzeitarbeit und die Lust am Zuverdienen: Geschlechterpolitik und gesellschaftlicher Wandel in Westdeutschland 1948–1969* (Göttingen, 1999); Carola Sachse, *Der Hausarbeitstag: Gerechtigkeit und Gleichberechtigung in Ost und West 1939–1994* (Göttingen, 2002), esp. 30, as well as Sybille Buske, "Fräulein Mutter vor dem Richterstuhl: Der Wandel der öffentlichen Wahrnehmung und rechtlichen Stellung lediger Mütter in der Bundesrepublik 1948 bis 1970," *Werkstatt Geschichte* 27 (2000): 48–67. Hans-Peter Schwarz brilliantly analyzes the 1950s as a dynamic era in his stimulating "Der Geist der fünfziger Jahre," in *Die Ära Adenauer: Gründerjahre der Republik, 1949–1957*, ed. Hans-Peter Schwarz (Stuttgart, 1981), 375–464.

Part IV

PARENTAL RIGHTS AND STATE DEMANDS

Chapter 8

WHO OWNS CHILDREN?

Parents, Children, and the State in the United States South

Charles A. Israel

Corresponding with co-counsel Sue K. Hicks in the months leading up to the 1925 trial of schoolteacher John T. Scopes on the charges of violating Tennessee's new law prohibiting instruction about evolution, prosecuting attorney William Jennings Bryan expressed his doubts over whether "the question of evolution" was really even "involved" in the trial. Central to the case—Bryan would term it the "real issue"—was "[t]he *right* of the *people* speaking through the legislature, to control the schools which they *create* and *support*."[1] The pretrial maneuvering by the prosecution and their contention that the central issue was the power of parents and legislators, not state superintendents or individual teachers, to set the curriculum, has largely been lost in accounts of the spectacle of the Scopes Monkey Trial. Preserved in history books and popular imagination as a grand encounter in the warfare between science and religion, the spectacle of the trial has too often obscured these real issues at stake in Dayton. Bryan and his opponent, the militantly atheistic Clarence Darrow, must share some of the blame, for despite all of their other legal maneuvering, both relished the national spotlight and opportunity to defend or debunk Christianity in general and, more specifically, a rather literal reading of the Genesis creation narratives.

While our standard accounts of the 1925 Scopes trial present it as a critical battle between science and religion, this essay will suggest a different context for the trial. The anti-evolution movement that succeeded so spectacularly in Tennessee in 1925 (and in several other states around that time) is an important moment in a larger debate over the proper relationship among parents, children, citizens, and the state. The debate surrounding *Scopes* dispels reformers' "unsubstantiated" assumption that "the interests of the state, children, and parents were identical," revealing instead the fractures in this supposed social unity that were always below and often visible on the surface of progressives' rhetoric and policies.[2] Reformers and parents usually agreed—rhetorically at least—that they had the best interests of children in mind; yet they often claimed exclusive power to determine those interests. This question of "who owns children?" stood at the heart of many conflicts in the progressive era; this essay will examine it particularly in the context of evolution and compulsory public education in the American South. If children were not yet legally competent to determine their own best interest, who had the authority to send them to school and set the curriculum? Progressive-era school campaigns at the beginning of the century were premised on the state's interest in an educated citizenry, parents' supposed failure to provide adequate education for children, and the superior ability of professional teachers and school administrators to determine how and what to teach children.

In the wake of the First World War, many Americans began to question the undemocratic tendencies of progressivism and the potential dangers of public education lacking a moral component. With attention to timing and international perspective, the Scopes trial takes on a new identity as more than just an example of southern religious backwardness; instead it is an important moment in a larger anti-statist backlash of the 1920s. The anti-evolution campaign in particular combined a liberal, majority-rule political philosophy with a new call to respect the power of parents to determine what was best for their own children. Parental rights, it would seem, remained a powerful tool with which to leverage power over the school bureaucracy and restore parental power over children.

Creating Public Education in the Post–Civil War South

It may be obvious at first glance, but it is important to keep in mind that at least part of the reason the Scopes trial happened was that there actually were public schools. As Royce Jordan explained in the *New Republic* soon after Tennessee passed its anti-evolution bill in 1925, "one reason the state waited so long before banning evolution is that a large proportion of the inhabitants had never, until comparatively recent times, even heard of the theory."[3] In 1925 there were 50,000 students in Tennessee high schools, compared to only 10,000 in 1900.[4] But this growth can be misleading: as one school superintendent admitted, few county schools taught advanced enough subjects to even encounter evolution; instead, most focused on "entirely elementary" matters like "teaching the children how to distinguish between plant and animal life."[5] Few parents in the state, and indeed throughout the country in 1900, were likely to have been exposed to evolutionary biology in any formal setting; most knew only what they could learn in the popular press or from their ministers, many but certainly not all of whom in the South opposed the theory on the grounds that it conflicted with some understandings of the Biblical creation narratives.[6]

Few southern states had any system of public schools before the Civil War of 1861–1865; those that did typically limited the schools to paupers and orphans in the largest of cities.[7] But Reconstruction governments utilized public funds to educate first freedmen and then both blacks and whites, though typically in segregated institutions. While cognizant of race- and class-based opposition to public education by many white southerners, this essay focuses on other criticisms of the newly established southern public schools, objections grounded in the languages of religion and parental (or, more often, patriarchal) rights to control children. Who would be in charge of the new schools and what would they teach? Southern Methodist Bishop Holland N. McTyeire, a strong supporter of denominational education, explained in 1872 that he was not "hopeful of our public school system ... [It] may supply the need of mere intellectual training, but it omits that higher training" of morality and religion.[8] McTyeire, like many others in his time, recognized at least two distinct forms of education—moral and intellectual—and he warned against separating them: "Illiteracy is a bad thing. A godless education is worse."[9] Assuming that moral training would have to be specifically religious and denominational, few southern Protestants could see any room for the new state schools in a "proper" education of the rising generation. Methodist editor Thomas O. Summers, Sr., reduced the problem to a neat, logical-sounding argument: "the State has no business with religion; but there can be no education without religion, therefore the State has no business with education."[10] Fearing the public schools were to be "godless" institutions, few white southerners of the 1860s and 1870s could see any justification for their existence.

Despite all the ink spilled and pulpit time spent in criticism of the prospects of a "godless" public school system, southern evangelicals by the early 1880s would make their peace with public elementary schooling. Although often criticized as anti-intellectual, most forms of Protestantism in the American South have historically placed a premium on the ability of individual believers to read and understand the Bible for themselves; thus southern religious leaders could not find footing for their opposition to any scheme that proposed to improve the dismal state of popular literacy and therefore potentially improve the religious life of the region.[11] Furthermore, most southern evangelicals agreed with other, less religiously motivated advocates of public schooling that the state demanded an educated citizenry if it were to function effectively.[12] Finally, parents and religious leaders accepted the public schools in the 1880s because they convinced themselves that it was not necessarily a godless education they provided: the public schools would be at least sympathetic to religion, if not instruments for teaching religion directly.[13]

Church leaders envisioned a system whereby religion would neither be excluded from nor included in the public schools forcibly. In Tennessee, evangelical leaders came to accept the public schools through what Methodist editor and former public school superintendent of California Oscar P. Fitzgerald termed the "home rule" compromise. Specifically crafted to answer the question of the role of the Bible in the public school classroom, Fitzgerald's settlement became a model for religion in the public schools in general. In short, he said, the state should not make any legislation to require or ban the use of the Bible in the public schools, instead leaving "each community … to settle the question for itself." Relying on a belief in a Protestant hegemony in most southern states, religious leaders like Fitzgerald assumed most schools would continue to utilize the Bible and teach religious lessons to students. Conscientious Christian parents could still supplement the work of the public schools by teaching religion at home and sending children to Sunday schools to learn denominationally specific beliefs. Furthermore, any schooling beyond the elementary years would occur in the theologically sanitary environment of church colleges, which could more effectively unite the development of the head and heart.[14]

Largely through the efforts of Fitzgerald and his emphasis on local control, the vocal majority of Tennessee parents and religious leaders came to accept the growth of public elementary education in the late nineteenth century. This home rule compromise reached in the 1880s would remain through the end of the century. But the first decades of the twentieth century would destroy the compromise. The campaigns for improved schools, though encouraging local assistance, were often premised on progressive leaders' distrust of the very local communities they enlisted in their service. Most southern religious leaders joined the initial progressive campaigns to improve the public schools, but would grow uneasy about the future of localism and religion in the progressive school program. The progressive coalition was unstable, and the events of the 1910s and 1920s would very publicly split parents and educators, preachers and politicians.

In their campaigns to improve the public schools, the progressive school boosters and their evangelical supporters demonstrated that they shared a modern conception of their society. Whether in academic treatises on political science or philosophy, stump speeches by political candidates, sermons or religious editorials by church leaders, or public addresses in favor of school improvement, the common theme of the progressives and their evangelical collaborators was a belief in an interdependent society.[15] In his first major legislative address as the new governor of Tennessee, Baptist layman Ben Hooper explained his understanding that "the individual citizen of Tennessee is a member of a complex social organization, and, as such, sustains relations to millions of individuals." Hooper, a Republican governor in the typically Democratic South, won the election of 1911 on a promise to enforce alcohol prohibition in the state. Arguing that the state could restrain an individual from drinking "not for the petty purpose of tyrannizing over him, but for the great and righteous purpose of protecting society," Hooper's vision of the interdependent society required the state to increase its activities in the interest of self-preservation, if not for the actual health of its individual citizens.[16] To explain this concept of the interdependent society, southern religious and political leaders repeatedly invoked familial images to help laymen make sense of the new world. Professor George Broadman Eager of the Southern Baptist Theological Seminary began a 1917 essay with a statement that could have been uttered by any of the progressive reformers: "the problem of life used to be the problem of the individual; now it is the problem of the society in its organized form." But he then turned to metaphor, explaining how "one hundred years ago the family was the little world; now the world is fast becoming one vast family and government" must take responsibility for some things previously left to the control of individuals and parents.[17] The expansion of the public schools brought into sharp relief the question of who was responsible for and in charge of the socialization of children. In short, who "owned" minor children and thus could determine how much or what kind of education they would receive?

In 1865, at the same time that a Union-occupied South was just beginning to expand the few publicly funded schools that had existed in the region before the Civil War, the Wisconsin Teachers' Association declared that "children are the property of the state." Such opinions were filtering into the South in the late nineteenth and early twentieth centuries. Speaking to a convention of Baptists, Tennessee state superintendent Seymour Mynders argued that "the State assumes that the child not only belongs to the home, but it is a part of the great family established by the association of all the homes in the land." Progressive public school officials began to posit a concept of "children's rights," especially the right to an education, arguing education was a right that the child "inherits from the state" and thus "the State must protect them in these rights."[18]

Not everyone agreed: many southern legal and religious officials greeted the arguments for children's rights and state patriarchy with great suspicion and even hostility. Writing from Starkville, Mississippi, Judge W. P. Bond strenuously objected to any conception of state patriarchy, arguing instead for the divine right of parents as expressed in "the voice which on Mt. Sinai proclaimed the words, 'Honor thy father and thy mother.'"[19] Other southerners joined in the defense of the family role in education, arguing that "when 'power and discretion' in the matter of the education of children are taken away from the family and lodged with the Government, the rights and duties of the family are seriously invaded, and ... no good can come of it in the long run."[20]

As the historians of domestic law Michael Grossberg and Peter Bardaglio have explained, in the nineteenth century many American courts were moving toward a greater recognition of the individuality of wives and children. Southern courts were beginning to make inroads into the patriarchal family during the late antebellum years, but the experiences of the Civil War and Reconstruction reinforced many southerners' suspicions of enlarged state powers and intervention into domestic relations. Southern education reformers invoked a patriarchal conception of the state in their arguments for compulsory education laws requiring students to attend school a minimum number of days per year.[21] Reformer George Fort Milton argued that children had rights derived as individuals and independent of their parents: "a parent who permits a child to grow up in ignorance is committing an offense not only against the child, but against the State."[22]

Milton's language points us to an important component of the campaigns for improved public schools. More than just a general elitism, reformers' arguments demonstrated a distrust that some, maybe many, parents would to see to the proper education of their children.[23] Most religious leaders in the early twentieth-century South apparently shared in the progressives' concerns about parental failure in the matter of education. Although they might differ on the source of children's "rights"—God or the state—religious leaders and more secularly minded members of the progressive coalition feared that parents were failing in their duties to see that children's minds and hearts were educated.[24]

Concern about parental failure to send their children to the public schools also raised doubts about the religious education of children at home. Worried about "how little Bible reading and Bible teaching is done in the average American home ... even in professedly Christian families" and the potential damage being done to the souls of too many of "the 12,000,000 of children in this country," several southern religious leaders called for the establishment and support of a thorough system of Sunday schools to fill in the gaps. Much as their progressive allies, the advocates of expanded and even mandatory public education, had determined, advocates of religious education worried that "if religious training is left to the homes of the country, thousands of children will grow up without Christian culture." The big southern denominations exerted great efforts around the turn of the century to build up their Sunday schools, both encouraging students to attend and printing reams and reams of books and other materials for use in the schools. The southern Sunday schools would see a steady increase in attendance, but not enough to even keep pace with the expanding school-age population at the beginning of the new century, leaving many church leaders fearful that children were receiving a religious education in neither the home nor the Sunday school.[25]

The Great War, the Demands of Democracy, and the Crisis of Religious Education

The First World War was a galvanizing moment for many American religious, political, and educational leaders. Many American school reformers and academics had been strongly influenced by Germany, and the seemingly sudden emergence of German aggression in the war forced them to reevaluate their admiration of German society and education. The most common understanding among religious leaders during and soon after the war was that the German educational system was ultimately at fault. As southern Baptist editor Albert R. Bond explained in 1918, "German kultur was produced through Prussian militarism, disassociated with the religious sanction for deeds, and became inwrought into the national life through the school system."[26]

Even after the Allies won the war and defeated the Germans, advocates of American religious education warned that the real war was not yet won. Peace would not end the war, explained Methodist educator Stonewall Anderson; in the place of the Western Front "a bloodless war of thought will continue" and thus the task of the church and indeed all of America would be "to resist Germanism" and promote religiously sound education in the United States. American Catholic editors warned of what they described as the "'Prussianization' of education [which] was based on the theory that the child was the creature of the state, to be schooled as the latter saw fit, the theory by which Germany had achieved such an effective autocracy." The traveling evangelist Billy Sunday would be even more direct in his assessment of the Germanic danger to their souls, telling audiences that if they could "turn hell upside down" they would "find 'Made in Germany' stamped on the bottom!" Thus Americans had to choose "whether education shall be Christian or heathen." It was no light decision, for "in that choice [they would] determine the civilization of the future."[27]

At about the same time that the European war was beginning, the Progressive-era campaigns for school improvement were reaching their zenith in the American South. While southern religious leaders had generally supported the campaigns to improve the public schools, by the 1910s they began to fear that the home rule compromise brokered by O. P. Fitzgerald in the 1880s could no longer hold. Centralized school bureaucracies and state certification standards for teachers had left local parents less capable of determining the curriculum and staffing of the public schools. Expanded public school grades were taking children beyond the basic subjects and exposing them to subjects like evolution that could be potentially dangerous to their faith. Evidence was mounting that the campaigns to enlarge the public and Sunday schools were encouraging too many parents to abdicate their responsibilities for buttressing the secular education of the public schools with religious teaching at home.[28] Finally, the keystone to the home rule compromise, the existence of a healthy system of denominational colleges to teach moral and intellectual lessons to the future leaders of society, seemed endangered with such high-profile cases as the 1914 split of Vanderbilt University from its founder, the southern Methodist Church.[29] If parents were failing in their duties, if the public schools were now teaching more students longer, and if the denominational colleges were no longer safe places to complete education, then perhaps southerners would need to start teaching religion more explicitly in the public schools.[30]

The home rule compromise had called for a truce, not the total exclusion of religion from the public schools. Judging the compromise dead, many southerners moved quickly to ensure a more explicit role for religion in public schools. Surprisingly, they did so by continuing to invoke the language of state patriarchy. Building on the image of the state as a parent responsible for its extended family that the progressive reformers had used in their campaigns for compulsory school laws, southern advocates of putting religious education in the public schools explained that it was a duty the patriarchal state owed to itself and its children: "Since our government has taken this parental care of the young, she should see to it that education is thorough and strictly moral."[31] Since the children were not receiving sufficient religious training in the home or the Sunday schools, then the church must reach them where it could—in the public school. "Where there is a Christian home," the Methodist Sunday School Board explained, "the church works with it, if [the home] is not Christian, the church, working through the public school, is perhaps the only hope of the child."[32]

Once again Germany would be invoked by religious advocates interested in "restoring religion and the Bible to their former place of fundamental importance in the educational system of this republic." In 1917, Tennessee Methodist editor Thomas Ivey called for the explicit use of the Bible in public school classrooms, arguing that not to do so would invite destruction similar to "the awful collapse of Germany," which had "virtually dethroned God and substituted for him ungodly Might." While the German "schools [had] made the Bible a thing to be tossed here and there by irreverent critics," Ivey insisted that "the Bible ... must be the supreme book [with] a place now in every common school in the land."[33]

While southern religious leaders were becoming adamant about the need to re-inject religious teaching into the public schools in the form of Bible reading laws, they were also growing concerned about the need to keep irreligion from the schools. Though there had been some scattered evangelical engagement with evolutionary theory in the South since the late nineteenth century, there was really no controversy until after the war. Convulsed by allegations that a professor at one of their denominational colleges was teaching evolution, Baptists in Tennessee set out to find just how far the Darwinian poison had infected American education.[34] The campaign found a national spokesman in William Jennings Bryan, who took the example of German irreligion and militarism, blamed it on a belief in Darwinian evolution and a lack of religious teaching in the public schools, and fought tirelessly against evolutionary education from the 1910s until his death in 1925.

Bryan saw Darwinian evolution behind the philosophy of Nietzsche, the militarism and atheism of the Germans, and the bloody horror of the First World War. Nietzsche, Bryan explained in 1920, had created "a philosophy 'that condemned democracy ... denounced Christianity ... denied the existence of God, overturned all standards of morality, eulogized war ... [and] praised hatred.'"[35] Reading Vernon L. Kellogg's *Headquarters Nights* (1917) convinced Bryan that German army officers' belief in Darwinian evolution had led them to embrace a national version of "survival of the fittest" and thus justify their offensive war. A confirmed pacifist who had so opposed America's entanglement with the European war that he had resigned as Woodrow Wilson's secretary of state in 1915, Bryan feared the implications of evolutionary teaching for world peace. But he grew even more concerned as he traveled the country and heard from many parents and students who had seen their faith challenged and in many cases destroyed by the teachings of Darwin. The "repeated indications of unbelief, especially among college students," puzzled Bryan. He examined the problem further and found in the studies of psychologist James H. Leuba evidence that the more schooling a person had the less likely he or she was to still believe in God and an afterlife. A proper education, Bryan and his many supporters could agree, aimed at conscience and intelligence. But if he had to choose only one or the other, Bryan argued that "I would rather that one should have a good heart than a trained mind." Thus he had to ask: what was gained from teaching children about evolution? Evolutionary teaching could destroy faith, and without faith, how long could the nation endure?[36]

In the campaign against the teaching of evolution, William Jennings Bryan was the most recognizable face, but he was certainly not acting alone. He succeeded, in Tennessee in particular, because he was able to tap into older beliefs about the necessity of religious education, the current desires to inject religion explicitly into the schools, and the lingering discontent among many parents and local school directors over what they perceived as a loss of control over students. Bryan and his religious supporters were not alone; Lynn Dumenil has described the formation of an unlikely coalition in the 1920s—including Catholic bishops, states rights advocates, and even old-line financial conservatives—who revolted in the aftermath of the First World War against what they perceived as an unwarranted growth of federal power over what had quite recently been seen as exclusively familial concerns. While some of these anti-statists' concerns seem overdrawn, there nonetheless was, as Judith Sealander has demonstrated, a long-standing tradition of twentieth-century reformers presenting programs as helping children when they in fact shielded "a more controversial aim—the federally imposed uniformity of law."[37]

What seems surprising is not that Bryan succeeded, but how he and the other anti-evolutionists made their arguments in favor of expelling evolution from the public schools: they turned back the clock on the Progressive-era reformers who had promoted education for the good of the state and passed compulsory attendance laws over the objections of many parents by arguing that the state's interest superseded that of the parent or even the child. Anti-evolutionists would choose parents—in Bryan's formulation the most interested individuals in a child's moral development—as the best tool to lever evolution out of the public schools and, if they could, out of American intellectual life entirely. They sought control of the increasingly patriarchal state with the one weapon best capable of overcoming the abstract claims of state concern for children: actual parents claiming to operate out of a desire to protect actual children.

Mississippi evangelist T. T. Martin, author of the militant anti-evolution book *Hell and the High Schools* (1923), titled one of his more pointed chapters "The Responsibility of Fathers and Mothers for Evolution Being Taught to Their Children." Parents, he stressed, may not have been teaching their children evolution directly, but by failing to exercise control over the public schools, they were in effect teaching their children evolution and condemning them to Hell. He reminded parents that to a large degree "the eternal destiny of" their children was up to them: "it is in your power to save your children from this deadly, soul-destroying teaching" of evolution.[38] In framing his campaign against evolution, William Jennings Bryan realized that "the first question to be decided is: Who shall control our public schools?" He offered several possible answers, dismissing in turn boards of education, scientists, and teachers, suggesting instead that "as the training of children is the chief work of each generation, the parents are interested in the things to be taught the children." Bryan saw little value in a teacher's academic freedom or a scientist's judgment; instead, "the duty of a parent to protect his children is more sacred than the right of teachers to teach what parents do not want taught."[39] Some parents took direct action: writing from Jackson in western Tennessee, Mrs. Fannie Tate Farris instructed her fellow parents to "examine the text books" used in the schools and "ask teachers" what specifically they were teaching the children.[40]

A reassertion of the necessity and right of parents to determine just what their children were learning, which marked a reversal of the progressives' arguments for a paternalistic state that was superior to the interests of individual parents, was actually well supported by legal precedent in the 1920s. Responding to the campaigns of the progressives, nativists, anti-Catholics, and anti-Communists, state legislatures throughout the country were busy enacting and enforcing legislation to control the education of all children. Much of this legislation was influenced by "Americanization" campaigns and a desire to use the schools as an instrument of social control to shape children into citizens. While recognizing the general necessity of public education legislation as a proper exercise of individual states' powers (either police powers or acting in their capacities as *parens patriae*), the United States Supreme Court in the 1920s nonetheless ruled that parents still had an important—in nearly all cases the preeminent—role in determining just what education was appropriate for their own children. When Nebraska passed a law forbidding instruction in any language other than English—a law clearly aimed at the German Lutheran and Catholic parochial schools—the Supreme Court in *Meyer vs. Nebraska* (1923) overturned the law, finding first that parents had a duty to give their children a suitable education and second that "the right to choose the kind of education they should have was a liberty protected by the Fourteenth Amendment."[41] Two years later, in *Pierce vs. Society of Sisters*, the court invalidated an Oregon law that mandated attendance at the state schools and effectively barred access to private schooling. The court did not exempt children from education, but the justices did reassert the rights of parents within reason to determine for themselves just what sort of education was best for their children.[42]

Given these rulings, Mrs. Farris's calls for direct parental action to examine what, if any, evolution education was happening in their schools would seem allowable but perhaps unnecessarily decentralized. While urging parents to take a definite interest in what their children were learning, William Jennings Bryan and his supporters cited the *Pierce* verdict and proposed a much more indirect and top-down plan of action. Reminding the nation that "the State is the creature and servant" of the collection of families it represented, anti-evolutionists called on the state legislatures to recognize the "sacred rights" of "parents and guardians" to determine that their children should not be taught evolution. In reply to his own question of "Who Shall Control" the schools, William Jennings Bryan was unequivocal: "The people are sovereigns and governments derive their just powers from the consent of the governed." Thus parents, "speaking through their legislatures ... would seem to be the natural sources of control of the schools."[43]

In their arguments for barring evolution from the public schools, Bryan and the anti-evolutionists stressed the duty and power of parents to determine the proper education of their children. The Supreme Court had suggested in 1923 and again in 1925 that this was a right parents could exercise even in the contradiction of a majority vote of the people or legislature. Bryan's anti-evolution argument managed to unite these two strains of authority, erasing any possible distinctions by promoting the anti-evolution legislation as the will of a majority of parents *and* citizens. Southern Baptist minister and anti-evolution leader O. L. Hailey made the case explicitly: Christian parents, "who constitute the majority of the citizens of the United States, have a right to object, and do object, to the teaching of anything in the schools which are supported by the state, which is contrary to the doctrines taught in the Bible."[44]

The stress on parental power and rights tied in with the *Scopes* prosecution's strategies and indeed a general backlash against what many Americans, southerners in particular, saw as the excessive powers of newly designated "experts." Prior to the late nineteenth century growth of professionalism and expertise, authority in a field generally belonged to those with the most experience in it. Who could be a better authority on parenting than parents themselves?[45] Thus Bryan and the prosecution lauded the authority and powers of parents while dismissing the proffered testimony of defense experts. Developing their strategy, at least in part because they could not find sufficient scientific experts of their own who would argue against evolution, the prosecution took a three-pronged approach to countering the evolutionists' testimony. First, Bryan rhetorically asked the court if "the parents of this day have not any right to declare that children are not to be taught" something those parents thought dangerous? Secondly, the prosecution, with a heavy appeal to localism and sectional feeling, sought to delegitimize the defense experts as pointy-headed intellectual outsiders, describing them during the trial as "foreign gentlemen" who were attempting "to defeat the purpose of the people of this state" and deriding them in the appellate brief as "a group of self-styled 'intellectuals' who call themselves 'scientists.'" Finally, the prosecution sought to reclaim expertise, at least in biblical interpretation: Bryan proclaimed that "every member of the jury is as good an expert on the Bible as any man" the defense could produce.[46] Thus William Jennings Bryan, who had risen to fame in the Populist movement of the 1890s as "the Great Commoner," sought to reclaim power for the common people and parents of Tennessee from the Progressive-era–anointed experts.[47]

This combination of parental rights and majority rule arguments would prove impossible for the opponents of anti-evolution legislation to overcome in courts either of public opinion or of law. Tennessee scientist and Methodist minister M. M. Black, who frequently wrote and spoke on the harmony of science and religion and opposed the law's assumption that evolution and religion were necessarily in conflict, was forced to concede the power of the majority rule argument. Even though he protested Tennessee's 1925 anti-evolution law as misguided, Black admitted his agreement with "the opinion that a State has the right to forbid any form of teaching or instruction in its schools and colleges which the majority of its citizens regard as hurtful to morals and the Christian religion."[48]

The American Civil Liberties Union (ACLU), which funded the defense of Tennessee teacher John Scopes in hopes of both defeating the law and earning publicity for itself, found few promising judicial avenues, whether in Tennessee or Washington, to invalidate the statute. Constitutionally, the Supreme Court had not yet incorporated the First Amendment protections of the United States Constitution to extend to the actions of states (they would not do so until *Everson vs. Board of Education* [1947]); thus any claims that Tennessee's anti-evolution law was in fact an establishment of religion would have to be lodged against the state, not the federal, constitution. Efforts to criticize the law as unconstitutionally vague or an infringement on the academic freedom of the teacher Scopes seemed more promising but ultimately proved unsuccessful at both the trial and appellate levels.

Even though they found the anti-evolution measure reprehensible and an assault on science, intelligence, and modernity, liberal and progressive advocates, along with many and maybe even most of the supporters of the ACLU, were wary of the judicial strategy pursued by defense counsel Clarence Darrow and Arthur Garfield Hays. Scopes's defense team argued against the law in a variety of ways, but overall they were arguing against the majority actions of the state legislature and asking the court to overturn the apparent will of the majority.[49] The US Supreme Court had frequently utilized the Fourteenth Amendment (especially its "due process of law" clause) in the previous decades to the benefit of corporations, overturning progressive-sponsored legislation aimed at improving the health and safety of workers and others. As one correspondent wrote in the progressive journal *The New Republic,* he was sure there was in fact a majority of teachers and school officials in Tennessee opposed to the anti-evolution law, but "on reflection they would be equally opposed to having that law destroyed by a straining of the Constitution rather than by public opinion, which will inevitably and soon destroy it."[50] The South's history since 1925 suggests such optimism was misplaced: public opinion surveys have charted a growth in the last several decades—not just in the South but throughout the United States—of lay skepticism of scientists' theories of evolution and their place in public school classrooms.[51]

But what if Tennessee parents objected to the anti-evolution measure in 1925? Could they not determine for themselves what was best for their children? Although there might have been a large number of parents who disagreed with the anti-evolution movement, few voiced their opposition publicly. Those who did also adopted the language of parental powers to explain their authority. S. M. Young of Dixon Springs, Tennessee, asked the governor: "Why take tax money from believers in the theory of Evolution, (citizens, parents), and yet maintain on our statute books a law that forbids their children being taught what they wish them to learn?" There is no record of Peay's response, but under the ruling in *Pierce* (1925), and as Bryan and the anti-evolutionists frequently noted, the supposed minority of parents who objected could always decide to educate their children in private schools at their own expense. But they could not overturn the desires of the majority.[52]

Finally, even though the anti-evolutionists appeared to have reinvested parents with the power of determining just what their children were to learn, many southern Protestant leaders still feared that many parents were not up to the task. Describing the "crime wave" in the years following the First World War, Baptist essayist E. K. Cox blamed the disorder on "the failure of the home" to teach children morality. At fault were "parents who ... surrender all their God-given right to train their children to some public school teacher." Religious training in the schools, even schools cleansed of the scourge of Darwinism, might not even be enough to save the country. "A family altar in every home in America would do more for the rising generation than all the laws that Congress can pass in a thousand years. The home must get back on its job before we get out of the woods."[53] Parents had been a useful lever in the anti-evolution fight, but it is clear that religious leaders and even many parents were unsure of the ability or willingness of all parents to continue to provide sufficient religious training or to assert proper moral control over their children. The era following *Scopes* would see religious leaders in the South and indeed throughout the nation taking measures to spread religious teaching. Now they were less likely to endorse teaching in the public schools themselves, but many proposals for "week-day religious education" still made use of the public school infrastructure to reach more children than individual parents or churches ever could.[54]

Current Echoes of Parents' Rhetorical Power

It took several decades before the federal courts directly tackled the central issue of evolution and public education raised in *Scopes*. In *Epperson vs. Arkansas* (1968) the court found Arkansas's law forbidding the teaching of evolution in publicly supported schools to be an unconstitutional establishment of religion by the state. The majority of a state might desire that evolution not be taught, but the court determined that the anti-evolution measure had a religious intent and was therefore unconstitutional.

If majority rule is no longer an effective avenue for anti-evolutionists, what about parental rights to determine what education is appropriate for children? The Supreme Court's exemption of certain Amish children from mandatory high school education in *Wisconsin vs. Yoder* (1972) proved to be a complicated balancing act, recognizing both the state power to set its curriculum but also the "traditional interest of parents with respect to the religious upbringing of their children." Some current anti-evolution activists have invoked this dictum of parental rights in their ongoing campaigns against evolutionary education but have made little headway. In *Yoder* and, not incidentally in that case's citations to *Pierce vs. Society of Sisters* (1925), the court maintained the state's interest in an educated citizenry while stressing that parents retained the ability to choose to provide alternative education, either by sending their children to private schools or educating them at home.[55] American church-state jurisprudence centers most often on the First Amendment to the US Constitution, which contains two key provisions restricting governmental action regarding religion: the "Establishment Clause," which prohibits an official establishment of religion, and the "Free Exercise Clause," which prohibits any legislation abridging a citizen's free exercise of religion.[56] As long as the courts interpret evolution-challenging legislation as an Establishment Clause violation and not as an issue of abridging Free Exercise for parents who claim learning about evolution would harm the religion of their children, parental rights will prove an ineffective constitutional tool in the effort to remove evolution from the public schools.

"In the long sweep of history," Lawrence M. Friedman has recently observed, "parents seem to be losing" in their efforts to wrest control of education (back?) from the state.[57] But the power of parenthood, at least as a rhetorical strategy, remains a powerful tool in the service of anti-evolution political mobilization. In the most recent anti-evolution debates in the United States, much of the talk concerns the scientific specifics of evolution and supposedly scientific critiques now grouped under the heading of "Intelligent Design Theory." But to mobilize supporters, the anti-evolutionists invariably return to the power and duty of parents to look after the best interests of their children and the necessity of the state not excessively hindering that enterprise. T. T. Martin's *Hell and the High Schools* is still in circulation, now posted in full text at a prominent Creationist website. While the website editor's endorsement that Martin's volume "certainly stands the test of time" in some ways rings both hollow and obvious at the same time, Martin's call for parental responsibility has not been lost on the current crop of anti-evolutionists.[58]

When the Cobb County (Georgia) School Board elected to paste disclaimers labeling evolution "a theory, not a fact," to their science textbooks in 2002, the majority of the board members justified their actions as responsive to the concerns of many "parents" and families, over 2,300 of whom had signed a petition to the board *not* to adopt books discussing evolution.[59] According to a 2005 survey by the National Science Teachers' Association, nearly a third of teachers reported significant pressure to "include creationism, intelligent design, or other nonscientific alternatives to evolution in their science classroom." Little of the pressure comes from administrators, however; the teachers reported the pressure was coming from students and parents. When the Pew Forum on Religion and Public Life asked Americans "who should have the primary say on how evolution is taught" a majority of all respondents gave precedence to parents; when the sample is limited to respondents who reject scientific evolution, more than three-fourths would empower parents or elected school boards to determine whether or how science is taught in the public schools.[60] It remains to be seen if these school boards, responding to the pressures of anti-evolutionist parents, can construct a strategy to shift the Supreme Court's interpretation of anti-evolution cases from a question of religious establishment to parental power over their young. At the moment their prospects for success look grim, which is perhaps a victory for quality science education—but the persevering rhetorical power of parenthood should never be underestimated, even in our modern expert culture.

Notes

1. Bryan to Hicks, 28 May 1925, reprinted in William B. Eigelsbach and Jamie Sue Linder, "'If Not the People Who?' Prosecution Correspondence Preparatory to the Scopes Trial," *The Journal of East Tennessee History* 70 (1998), 118 (emphasis in original).

2. Judith Sealander, *The Failed Century of the Child: Governing America's Young in the Twentieth Century* (Cambridge, 2003), 23.

3. Royce Jordan, "Tennessee Goes Fundamentalist," *The New Republic* 29 (April 1925): 258.

4. Edward J. Larson, *Summer for the Gods: The Scopes Trial and America's Continuing Debate over Science and Religion* (New York, 1997), 24.

5. Clipping from Jackson, TN, *Sun* included in letter, Mrs. Fannie Tate Farris to Peay, 31 March 1925. Austin Peay Governor's Papers, GP-40, Box 43, folder 1: Correspondence RE: Anti-evolution bill 1925–26, Tennessee State Library and Archives, Nashville.

6. For the larger history of evolutionary thinking and teaching among southern evangelicals, see Charles A. Israel, *Before Scopes: Evangelicals, Education, and Evolution in Tennessee, 1870–1925* (Athens, 2004), 128–137.

7. Discussing public education in nineteenth-century New York, Benjamin Justice explodes the notion of a "system" of public schools even in the supposedly more educationally progressive North. See Benjamin Justice, *The War that Wasn't: Religious Conflict and Compromise in the Common Schools of New York State, 1865–1900* (Albany, 2005), 17–18.

8. H. N. McTyeire, "A Plea for Denominational Education," *Nashville Christian Advocate* (hereafter *NCA*), 7 December 1872, 6.

9. O. P. Fitzgerald, n.t., *NCA,* 21 May 1881, 8.

10. [Summers], "New Publications," *NCA,* 2 November 1872, 9.

11. See, for example, the criticism by Jackson, Tennessee, city school superintendent J. C. Brooks of school detractors, asking "how any person claiming to be a Christian can in any way oppose the great humanitarian and elevating principle of public education." J. C. Brooks, *First Annual Report of the Superintendent of Schools of the City of Jackson for the Scholastic Year 1879–80* (Jackson, TN, 1880), 7.

12. Tennessee Baptist Convention, *Proceedings* 1887, 24, Minutes of Tennessee Baptist Convention, 1875–1905, Southern Baptist Historical Library and Archive (hereafter SBHLA) microfilm publication 239, reel 1.

13. S. G. Gilbreath, "The Relation of State and Denominational Schools," *Nashville Baptist and Reflector* (hereafter *NBR*), 18 October 1917, 2–3 (quotation). See also O. P. Fitzgerald, "Education," *NCA,* 14 February 1882, 1; A Citizen of North Carolina [Charles Elisha Taylor], *How Far Should a State Undertake to Educate? A Plea for the Voluntary System in the Higher Education* (Raleigh, 1894); and J. W. Storer, "A Unique Opportunity," *NBR,* 5 May 1921, 5.

14. Fitzgerald, "Education," 1 (quotation); and E. E. Hoss, "The Main Object in View," *NCA,* 19 April 1900, 8. Justice explores the tradition of localism in the schools of nineteenth-century New York, finding that the small number of very well publicized battles over the place of religion in the common school classroom in fact obscure the more pervasive power of localism to minimize conflicts about religion and education. See Justice, *The War that Wasn't.*

15. See for example John Dewey, *The Public and Its Problems: An Essay in Political Inquiry* (first published 1927; Chicago, 1946); and James T. Kloppenberg, *Uncertain Victory: Social Democ-*

racy and Progressivism in European and American Thought, 1870–1920 (New York, 1986), 151–153.

16. Hooper, "Legislative Message of January 31, 1911," in *Messages of the Governors of Tennessee,* vol. 9: *1907–1921,* ed. Stephen V. Ash (Nashville, 1990), 204.

17. George Broadman Eager, *Lectures in Ecclesiology* (Louisville, 1917, printed for students), 25; quoted in Keith Harper, *The Quality of Mercy: Southern Baptists and Social Christianity* (Tuscaloosa, 1996), 34.

18. Carl F. Kaestle, *Pillars of the Republic: Common Schools and American Society, 1780–1860* (New York, 1994), 158; Seymour Mynders, "The Relation of the State to the Public Schools," in *Tennessee Baptist Convention Proceedings for 1906* (Clarksville, 1906), 73; R. W. Snell, "Compulsory Education," *Progressive Teacher and Southwestern School Journal* 9 (May 1903): 41; and P. P. Claxton, *Should the General Assembly of Tennessee Enact a Compulsory School Attendance Law?* (n. p., 1907), 6.

19. Judge W. P. Bond, "The Ownership of Children," *NBR,* 17 March 1892, 2.

20. O. P. Fitzgerald, "Public Opinion," *NCA,* 19 March 1887, 13. See also the outspoken Collins D. Elliott, *The Eagle Wing vs. the Mayflower; or, Familyism in Education vs. Stateism; or, Tennessee vs. Massachusetts in Schools* (Columbia, TN, 1886), 4.

21. The fact that the laws punished parents, not children, for noncompliance suggests some limitations on the state's direct relationship to children, but the arguments of the reformers, legislators, and the courts alike suggested that the progressive conception of the interdependent society had carried the political, intellectual, and legal day. Michael Grossberg, *Governing the Hearth: Law and the Family in Nineteenth Century America* (Chapel Hill, 1985), 236–237; and Peter Bardaglio, *Reconstructing the Household: Families, Sex, and the Law in the Nineteenth-Century South* (Chapel Hill, 1985), xii–xiii and 115–175.

22. George Fort Milton, "Compulsory Education and the Southern States," *Sewanee Review* 16 (January 1908): 39–41.

23. On the elitism of the educational reformers, see especially William P. Few, "Education and Citizenship in a Democracy," *South Atlantic Quarterly* 7 (October 1908): 299; and James B. Killebrew, "Report," in *Proceedings of the Seventh and Eighth Annual Sessions of the Tennessee State Teachers Association* (Nashville, 1873), 21.

24. E.E. Folk, "Children's Rights," *NBR,* 13 February 1890, 8. See also George B. Winton, n. t., *NCA,* 16 November 1905, 6; and E. E. Folk, n. t., *NBR,* 8 March 1906, 1.

25. J. M. Phillips, "A Great Work," *NBR,* 14 February 1880, 553. See also T. S. Ray, "Our Debt to Children," *NBR,* 10 May 1900, 2; and Sally G. McMillen, *To Raise up the South: Sunday Schools in Black and White Churches, 1865–1915* (Baton Rouge, 2001), 230.

26. Albert R. Bond, "The Fundamental Factor," *NBR,* 28 March 1918, 9.

27. Stonewall Anderson, "Christian Culture and German Kultur," *NCA,* 2 August 1918, 10–11; Douglas J. Slawson, *The Department of Education Battle, 1918–1932: Public Schools, Catholic Schools, and the Social Order* (Notre Dame, IN, 2005), 23; Christian Education Movement, "Soon There May Be No God but Allah!" advertisement in *NCA,* 18 March 1921, 32; Sunday quoted in George M. Marsden, *Fundamentalism and American Culture: The Shaping of Twentieth-Century Evangelicalism, 1870–1925* (New York, 1980), 142; and Thomas N. Ivey, "Is it Worth the Effort?" *NCA,* 7 January 1921, 6. American critics of German education seem to have mistaken the secularizing desires of some German educational reformers for the realities of an elementary school system still largely in confessional hands at the beginning of the twentieth century: see Marjorie Lamberti, *State, Society, and the Elementary School in Imperial Germany* (New York, 1989).

28. E. E. Hoss, n. t., *NCA,* 15 November 1894, 1.

29. For the Vanderbilt case, see Israel, *Before Scopes,* 59–63; more generally on the fate of denominational schools see James Tunstead Burtchaell, *The Dying of the Light: The Disengagement of Colleges and Universities from Their Christian Churches* (Grand Rapids, 1998).

30. The concern for the decline or lack of religion in education was not an exclusively southern phenomenon, although many advocates of religious education outside of the region were less

likely than southerners to suggest as a remedy the explicit teaching of religion in the public schools. See, for example, George Herbert Betts's 1925 introduction to Philip Henry Lotz, *Current Week-Day Religious Education* (New York, 1925), 19; or the survey by Jerome K. Jackson and Constantine F. Malmberg, *Religious Education and the State* (Garden City, NY, 1928). For the southern approach, which lagged behind the rest of the country because of the continuation of religious teaching in the public schools themselves, see W. E. Hogan, "Week-Day Religious Education," *NCA*, 14 July 1922, 2; and V. R. McDonald, "Why Week-Day Religious Education?" *NCA*, 25 September 1925, 17–18.

31. William S. Johnson, "Our Public School System," *NBR*, 3 May 1894, 2–3.

32. John W. Shackford, "Week-Day Work in Religious Education," *NCA*, 2 March 1923, 24.

33. Thomas N. Ivey, "Education in War Times," *NCA*, 27 July 1917, 4; and Thomas N. Ivey, "One Hundred Per Cent American," *NCA*, 28 March 1919, 7. See also Jackson and Malmberg, *Religious Education and the State*, 1–14.

34. Selsus E. Tull, "The Evolution Issue at Union University," *NBR*, 27 October 1921, 3. For more on the controversy at Union University, see Israel, *Before Scopes*, esp. 139–140.

35. Lawrence W. Levine, *Defender of the Faith, William Jennings Bryan: The Last Decade, 1915–1925* (New York, 1965), 263.

36. William Jennings Bryan and Mary Baird Bryan, *The Memoirs of William Jennings Bryan* (Philadelphia, 1925), 479; James H. Leuba, *The Belief in God and Immortality: A Psychological, Anthropological and Statistical Study* (Boston, 1916); and Levine, *Defender of the Faith*, 279.

37. Lynn Dumenil, "'The Insatiable Maw of Bureaucracy': Antistatism and Education Reform in the 1920s," *Journal of American History* 77, no. 2 (September 1990): 499; and Sealander, *Failed Century of the Child*, 3. For an expanded look at Catholic opposition to NEA plans for a federal Department of Education, one that unfortunately overlooks the complexity of southerners' approach to the issues, see Slawson, *Department of Education Battle*.

38. T. T. Martin, *Hell and the High Schools: Christ or Evolution, Which?* (Kansas City, MO, 1923).

39. William Jennings Bryan, "Who Shall Control?" in Bryan and Bryan, *The Memoirs of William Jennings Bryan*, 526–28.

40. Mrs. Fannie Tate Farris (Jackson, TN), "Safe Text Books for Baptist Schools," *NBR*, 19 October 1922, 6. At roughly the same time, the Methodist paper made the same request of parents and religious leaders: see Thomas Ivey, "Let Us Know Our Schools," *NCA*, 3 October 1919, 7. For a national version of this call for parents to assert their control over the schools, see Henry F. Cope, *Religious Education in the Family* (Chicago, 1915), 212–217.

41. For the opinion of Justice Reynolds on the importance of education and the right of parents to control it, see *Meyer vs. Nebraska* (1923) 262 US 390 at 400. The judgment is summarized in Eva R. Rubin, *The Supreme Court and the American Family* (New York, 1986), 121.

42. *Pierce vs. Society of Sisters* 268 US 510 (1925).

43. Rev. Charles M. Meeks, "A Quadrilateral View of Christian Education," *NCA*, 18 August 1916, 9–10; A. M. Mann, "Partial Review of 'King Knut Redivivus,'" *NCA*, 24 July 1925, 30; and Bryan, "Who Shall Control?" 526. Bryan would cite *Pierce* as justification of the power of states to "forbid the teaching of anything 'manifestly inimical to the public welfare'" and the right and duty of "the parent ... to guard the religious welfare of the child." See "Mr. Bryan's Last Speech," in Bryan and Bryan, *Memoirs of William Jennings Bryan*, 530.

44. Dr. O. L. Hailey, "In Response to Professor Northern," *NBR*, 26 October 1922, 4. See also Hailey's most succinct statement of the problem: "Church or State, Who Shall Define the Education of Our Children? Shall the State Teach Evolution?" *NBR*, 10 August 1922, 4–5. The defense at Dayton would contradict this statement and the implications of Tennessee's anti-evolution law that evolution had to contradict the Bible, arguing both that Christians could also accept evolution without damage to their faith and that the Bible had multiple accounts of human creation. See Larson, *Summer for the Gods*, 107–121; and Edward J. Larson, *Trial and Error: The American Controversy over Creation and Evolution*, 3rd ed. (New York, 2003), 64–66.

45. Till van Rahden suggested this point on parental expertise during the discussions leading to this volume. On the creation and maintenance of a new form of expertise, see especially

Thomas L. Haskell, "Introduction" in *The Authority of Experts,* ed. Thomas L. Haskell (Bloomington, 1984), xii.

46. N. a., *The World's Most Famous Court Trial: State of Tennessee vs. John Thomas* Scopes: *Complete Stenographic Report of the Court Test of the Tennessee Anti-Evolution Act* (1925; rpt. New York, 1971), 175, 163, 172, and 181; appellate brief quoted in Larson, *Summer for the Gods,* 213.

47. Defense attorney Clarence Darrow would famously turn Bryan's notion of expertise to his own advantage, calling Bryan to the stand as an expert on the Bible and then proceeding to elicit from the aging Democratic hero an admission of apparent inconsistencies in biblical history. For the highlights of this testimony, see Jeffrey P. Moran, *The Scopes Trial: A Brief History with Documents* (Boston, 2002), 143–160.

48. M. M. Black, "Christianity and Evolution," *NCA,* 31 July 1925, 8–9. Black's comments seem nearly identical to an argument by Bryan in the *New York Times* two weeks earlier; quoted in Larson, *Summer for the Gods,* 156.

49. The Tennessee Supreme Court did not buy the argument; see Larson, *Trial and Error,* 71.

50. Frederick Bausman, "The Scopes Defense," *The New Republic* (30 September 1925), 157–158. Edward Larson has a larger discussion of this dilemma faced by the ACLU in arguing for the protection of Scopes's rights as a minority in "The *Scopes* Trial and the Evolving Concept of Freedom," *Virginia Law Review* 85 (April 1999): 522–523. Larson argues suggestively that the Scopes Trial in particular forced liberal leaders such as John Dewey to "revise their views on majority rule and minority rights" (520).

51. Larson, *Trial and Error,* 125–213; Pew Forum on Religion and Public Life and the Pew Research Center for the People and the Press, "Public Divided on Origins of Life: Religion a Strength and Weakness for Both Parties," *Pew Reports* (30 August 2005), 7–12; accessed 1 June 2006 at http://pewforum.org/docs/index.php?DocID=115.

52. S. M. Young to Governor Peay, 19 March 1925, Peay Governor's Papers, Box 43, Correspondence RE: Anti-evolution bill 1925–26. For local support of Bryan's argument, see for example the editorial by J. D. Moore, "Evolution Education," *NBR,* 29 March 1923, 2.

53. E. K. Cox, "The Why of the Crime Wave," *NBR,* 22 September 1921, 2.

54. On explicit use of the Bible in the public schools, see W. T. Callaway, "Shall the Bible Be Read in Our Public Schools?" *NBR,* 29 April 1926, 6. In opposition to Callaway, see John D. Freeman, "Teaching the Bible in High School," *NBR,* 18 November 1926, 2. On religious education during the week, see the endorsement by Southern Methodists in Alfred Franklin Smith, "The Week-Day School of Religion," *NCA,* 27 April 1923; and studies of the movement nationally in Lotz, *Current Week-Day Religious Education*; Jackson and Malmberg, *Religious Education and the State*; and Benjamin Winchester, *Religious Education and Democracy* (New York, 1917).

55. *Wisconsin vs. Yoder* (1972) 406 US 205 at 213: "a State's interest in universal education, however highly we rank it, is not totally free from a balancing process when it impinges on fundamental rights and interests, such as those specifically protected by the Free Exercise Clause of the First Amendment, and the traditional interest of parents with respect to the religious upbringing of their children."

56. Until 1940, the US Supreme Court interpreted the First Amendment as limiting the actions of the US Congress but not applying to actions by individual states; thus in 1925 the constitutionality of Tennessee's anti-evolution statute had to be judged at the state level alone. The process of "incorporation" of the federal Bill of Rights through the 14th Amendment to apply to actions within individual states has not been without controversy but has offered a potential for standardizing practices within the states. See Akhil Reed Amar, "The Bill of Rights and the Fourteenth Amendment," *Yale Law Journal* 101 (1992): 1193–1284.

57. Lawrence M. Friedman, *Private Lives: Families, Individuals, and the Law* (Cambridge, MA, 2004), 143.

58. The anti-German hysteria that was so much a part of the original campaigns also remains. The editorial endorsement of Martin's book urges vigilance: "However as each generation passes, the lessons in this book must be passed on—or America too—will be doomed to repeat the

horrific fates of other evolution-believing societies." See "Note from Paul Abramson, Editor," accessed 25 March 2005 at http://www.creationism.org/books/MartinHellSchools/index.htm.

59. References to the concerns of parents pervade the testimony of the board members; see for example *Selman vs. Cobb County* 2005 US Dist. LEXIS 432 at 7–20. The petition by parents, especially the timing of when it was presented to the board, became a contentious issue in the appellate process: the appellate court remanded the case to the trial court to clarify if parental pressure had been brought on the board to adopt the stickers for explicitly religious reasons or if, as the board asserted at trial, it merely aimed to promote critical thinking in science classes. The appellate ruling from the Eleventh Circuit is *Selman vs. Cobb County School District* 2006 US App. LEXIS 13005. The case was settled in December 2006 when the board, hearing the voice of the other parents and taxpayers of the district who overwhelmingly voted against incumbents seeking reelection, agreed to keep the stickers out of the books and pay the plaintiff-parents' court costs. See the editorial coverage in "Ruling Ought to Stick," *Atlanta Journal-Constitution,* 31 May 2006 and "Sign of Sense in Cobb," *Atlanta Journal-Constitution,* 21 December 2006. In *Selman,* as well as in the higher-profile twenty-first–century trial in Dover, Pennsylvania, over a school board policy downplaying instruction on evolution and endorsing instead the scientifically unsupportable Intelligent Design theory that has become the new subterfuge of anti-evolutionists, the plaintiffs in the cases—the people going to court opposing the efforts to weaken instruction in evolution—have had to first prove their standing before the court by showing they are parents of current students. See *Kitzmiller vs. Dover Area School District* (400 F. Supp. 2d 709–10).

60. "Survey Indicates Science Teachers Feel Pressure to Teach Nonscientific Alternatives to Evolution," National Science Teachers Association Pressroom, 24 March 2005. Accessed 25 March 2005 at http://www.nsta.org/pressroom&news_story_ID=50377. Pew Forum, "Public Divided on Origin of Life," 11.

Chapter 9

"Children Betray Their Father and Mother"
Collective Education, Nationalism, and Democracy in the Bohemian Lands, 1900–1948

Tara Zahra

In 1938, Erika Mann, daughter of Thomas Mann, published an exposé of educational methods in Nazi Germany called *School for Barbarians*. In it she linked the evils of the Third Reich to a relentless assault on the family.[1] "The break-up of the family is no by-product of the Nazi dictatorship, but part of the job which the regime had to do if it meant to reach its aim—the conquest of the world," she wrote. "If the world is to go to the Nazis, the German people must first belong to them. And for that to be true, they can't belong to anyone else—neither God, nor their families, nor themselves."[2] In the cold war West after the Second World War, the evil of both the failed Nazi regime and the new Communist regimes in Eastern Europe was often located in the totalitarian claims made on the minds and bodies of children. Particularly in Britain, the United States, and West Germany after the Second World War, policymakers, pedagogues, and psychoanalysts typically rejected collective education and idealized the mother-child bond. They construed the nuclear family, presided over by a stay-at-home mother, as the best hope for rehabilitating Europe's war-damaged youth, an apolitical sanctuary that represented a postwar "return to normality."[3] While popular and scholarly understandings of both Nazism and child-rearing have changed a great deal since the 1950s, Mann's text reflects assumptions that continue to structure histories of mass politics and of childhood. Especially since 1945, the totalitarian potential lurking in mass political movements has often been located in excessive state interventions into an imagined "private" or domestic sphere. Both scholarship and popular memory continue to link state intervention in family life to anti-democratic politics.[4]

Notes from this chapter begin on page 201.

This essay attempts to historicize these assumptions by returning to a setting known as a cradle of mass politics in Central Europe: the Austrian Empire and its successor states. In the late nineteenth century, German and Czech nationalists in the Bohemian Lands constructed a political culture in which children were seen as the "property" of nationalist movements, and in which nationalists' rights to educate children frequently trumped parental rights. Superficially, this history may seem to confirm a broader link between collective education and anti-democratic politics. And yet when nationalists asserted their claims on children in the Bohemian Lands, they often did so in the name of democracy and minority rights. During and after the Second World War, however, experiences and memories of the Nazi occupation helped discredit long-standing traditions of collective education in the Bohemian Lands. This shift resulted in part from the threat Nazism seemed to pose to local (Sudeten German and Czech) nationalist claims on children. Czech and German nationalists in the Bohemian Lands themselves precipitated a shift away from collective education during the Second World War. As they mobilized to protect the nation's children from the competing claims of the Nazi state, nationalists elevated the family to the ideal site of national education. These activists did not, however, depict the family as an "apolitical" sphere that had to be protected from intervention. Rather, they saw the family as the last hope for protecting the nation's overriding political "rights" to children.

The history of nationalist mobilization around children in the Bohemian Lands suggests that changing perceptions and experiences of childhood and child-rearing did not simply reflect underlying social or political structures. Rather, the very concepts that framed politics in twentieth-century Central Europe took shape around particular ideas about the proper relationship of children to both their parents and to imagined political collectives. Nationalist activism around children served not only to construct the boundaries of the nation in the Bohemian Lands, but also to define and transform discursive boundaries between state and society, "public" and "private," "democracy" and "totalitarianism."

The Problem with Parents

In the Bohemian Lands between 1900 and 1945, Czech and German nationalists mobilized against the "Germanization" and "Czechification" of children in the name of national survival. Their claims on children were based on the ascription of authentic national identities to children and families who would not have defined themselves in nationalist terms. In fact, nationalists competed to claim the souls of many working-class and rural children who were neither Czech nor German. These children came from families that were bilingual, flexible about their national loyalties, or altogether indifferent to nationality.[5]

The supranational character of the Austrian state meant that in contrast to nation-states like Germany or France, the initial nationalization of Austrian populations occurred from below, through the activism of mass political movements, rather than through the force of a modernizing state or bureaucracy.[6] At the same time, the imperial state itself created the legal conditions under which nationalist movements flourished. Although the Austrian state refused to recognize nationality as a legal category of identity, beginning in 1880 the census polled Austrian citizens about their so-called "language of everyday use." The more citizens who declared themselves to be German speakers or Czech speakers, the more demands local nationalists could make on the state for local German or Czech schools, civil service appointments, and language rights. The introduction of universal male suffrage in Austria in 1907 further intensified the nationalist battle for numbers, as all male children now represented future voters. In light of these developments, nationalists increasingly represented the denationalization of children in so-called "language frontiers" or mixed-language regions as a direct threat to the expanding democratic rights of nations. This nationalist activism was not, however, directed against the Austrian state, but was rather understood as a strategy for making stronger claims on the imperial state. Czech and German nationalist pedagogical activists sought to educate children to be both loyal Habsburg citizens and self-conscious members of nationalist communities at the same time.

Nationalists first became involved in child welfare in the Bohemian Lands through their campaigns to fill a growing network of German and Czech minority schools. German and Czech nationalists competed to entice working-class and rural parents to enroll their children in these schools by offering generous welfare benefits to their pupils, ranging from free lunches and textbooks to clothing and Christmas gifts. Heinrich Holek, who grew up in a working-class, bilingual Bohemian family, testified in his memoir that his own father decided to send him to a new Czech minority school because of the many benefits being offered to children at the school, writing: "No Czech child should attend a German school! This motto was promoted by the Czechs with great zeal. For my father however this propaganda was less decisive than the fact that the children of poor parents were promised clothing and shoes as Christmas gifts."[7] While Czech and German nationalists alike participated in these campaigns to fill the nation's schools, they simultaneously depicted parents who sent their children to the schools of the national enemy as victims of undemocratic pressures to "sell" their children's souls. A Czech writer in the magazine *Menšinový učitel* thus lamented in 1913: "The Germans began to buy children. And however we may deny it, poverty triumphed among our spiritually plain comrades, and they succeeded."[8]

These nationalist campaigns to increase school enrollments soon inspired more creative schemes to fill classrooms in nationally contested regions. Nationalists began to establish "colonies" of ten to twelve orphans in villages where the local minority school was threatened by declining enrollments. Nationalist orphan colonies and orphanages not only promised to save endangered schools, they were also intended to save orphans from the threat of "Germanization" or "Czechification" in the foster homes and institutions of the national enemy. In a 1913 appeal to build new nationalist orphanages, Czech nationalists insisted, "[e]very day children are lost to us in orphanages, where they are given a piece of bread with one hand and robbed of their mother tongue with the other."[9] The driving force behind these efforts was himself a nationalist orphan. At the turn of the century, Hugo Heller, raised in an orphanage in Prague, was just embarking on what would become a long and impressive career as a nationalist child welfare activist. In 1907, Heller became the leader of the German Provincial Commission for Child Protection and Youth Welfare in Bohemia (Deutsche Landesstelle für Kinderschutz und Jugendfürsorge, DLS), and a parallel Czech organization was established shortly after (Česká zemská komise pro ochranu ditě a péče o mládeže, ČZK). They were followed quickly by German and Czech commissions for child protection in Moravia and Silesia. These nationalist institutions would become the most important and wide-reaching child welfare institutions in the Bohemian Lands.

The nationalist orphan welfare movement reflected nationalists' suspicion of the loyalties and parenting skills of adults on the so-called language frontier. Since the turn of the century, nationalist associations like the Bund der Deutschen had actively campaigned to save orphans for the nation by matching German-speaking orphans with suitably "German" foster parents. Before sending children to their new homes, the DLS issued the following stern instructions to foster parents: "Raise the child to possess an inner, self-sacrificing love of their nation! If you are not in a position to make our child into a loyal, true German comrade, who is proud to be a German, then you are not called upon to raise our foster child."[10] Unfortunately, very few parents lived up to these lofty expectations. Too many German-speaking foster parents failed to raise their charges to be good nationalists, and sometimes they even contributed to the "Czechification" of orphans, German nationalists insisted. The Bund der Deutschen lamented: "Where could we find the degree of understanding which we required, when a strictly national upbringing was a near miracle even among our own erstwhile national comrades?"[11] The nationalist association Südmark shared these concerns. Foster parents, Südmark activists argued, "often fail for the national purpose, or are at the very least insufficient. And it is around this end that all of child-rearing should be oriented." Nationalists came to see collective education in orphanages and orphan colonies as an attractive alternative to placing children with foster parents, who seemed prone to neglect their duties both to the nation and to the children in their care. Members of the Südmark concluded, "Institutions which can take in a greater number of heads and be run in a unified nationalist spirit are necessary, so that *völkisch* concerns are not neglected."[12]

Bolstered by the apparent success of orphan welfare programs, nationalists soon set out to make more ambitious claims on children with living parents. At the first German-Bohemian youth welfare conference in Prague in 1907, Franz Vollgrüber, a delegate to the Bohemian Diet, argued that nationalists should not limit their attention to orphans but rather target "children in general." He proposed that the DLS establish more collective homes for these endangered youth, "and not just for the school year, but also for the holidays. During the summer these children could also be accommodated in the countryside, where they would run around and stay healthy in body and soul."[13] Through the provincial commissions, nationalists in the Bohemian Lands soon assumed responsibilities for children that were typically taken on by the state or private charities in nation-states such as Germany, France, and England. These activists were particularly concerned with improving the quantity and quality of the nation's children by decreasing infant mortality rates and providing child care support for working mothers in the many industrial regions of the Bohemian Lands.

German nationalists sought to combat infant mortality primarily through a network of nationally segregated infant and maternal welfare centers, which dispensed medical supplies and treatment, breast-feeding advice, and basic necessities such as sanitized infant formula, food, and clothing. While working mothers were a source of deep concern, they also afforded nationalists an irresistible opportunity to expand the nation's primary pedagogical influence on children. The DLS insisted that since women were not likely to stop working, "the public has the duty to take youth welfare in its own hands."[14] In 1912 Heller elaborated that nationalist child welfare organizations should share the burden of child-rearing with the working mother, who "should be helped in her difficult situation, to pursue paid employment in order to earn a living, to run a household and to become a mother or simply to be a mother."[15]

At the moment of the Austrian Empire's collapse in 1918, German and Czech nationalists had created an expansive network of semi-public, nationally segregated orphanages, nurseries, kindergartens, summer camps, and medical clinics in nearly every village in the Bohemian Lands. These institutions were based on a profound suspicion of parents' national loyalties—a fear that parents would "denationalize" their own children. "We must exclude from any kind of participation in German education those miserable, impoverished *Sprachgrenze* souls ... those for whom German blood rules in one half of the heart and Czech blood in the other, who take no sides but wherever possible take both ... in short, pitiful people who should be pilloried in a widely visible place," Hugo Heller explained in an interwar manifesto.[16] At the same time, nationalists viewed collective education as essential to their goals of modernizing and democratizing Austrian society. By integrating nationally indifferent workers and peasants into an expanding national community, providing for the welfare of their children, and enlisting as many children as possible in the national struggle, activists hoped to make claims on the supranational Austrian state for expanding political, educational, and social rights.

Minority Rights and Collective Education in Interwar Czechoslovakia

Following the First World War and the dissolution of the Habsburg monarchy, the relationship between nationalists and the state transformed dramatically. In place of the imperial state, which had served as a kind of umpire adjudicating between competing nationalist claims, the new Czechoslovak nation-state ruled in the name of national self-determination. The state itself set out to nationalize children by expanding Czech minority schools and, in Moravia, enforcing laws that required children labeled as Czechs by state officials to attend Czech schools. German nationalists responded in kind by striving to achieve as much autonomy and unity as possible within the framework of the Czechoslovak state. While some German nationalists rejected the legitimacy of the Czechoslovak state altogether, other German political parties, especially Socialist, Christian Socialist, and Agrarian Party members, sought to work within the framework of the Czechoslovak state for gradual reform.

German and Czech nationalists alike insisted that the nation's collective "rights" to educate children were central to the Wilsonian ideals of democracy, minority rights, and national self-determination that structured interwar political culture. They now depicted the battle against the "Germanization" and "Czechification" of children as part of a larger struggle to protect national self-determination and democratic ideals. At a protest on the opening day of the Czechoslovak parliament, German nationalists declared: "To all the protectors and promoters of culture in the whole world! The right to national self-determination demands that every nation, no matter what language they speak, manages and cares for its own cultural riches, and above all its schools."[17] Václav Perek, a well-known Czech nationalist school activist, meanwhile insisted in 1922:

> In reality [the German minorities] don't require the protection of the peace treaties for their development, because they have retained the greater power and greater rights. On the other hand the members of the Czech nationality living [in Germanized regions], the Czech minority, must be brought under state protection if they are not to be destroyed or denationalized.[18]

Moreover, these nationalists continued to view education in collective settings as a critical strategy to protect the nation's children from both denationalization and delinquency. Across Europe, the First World War generated unprecedented levels of anxiety about the dangers of neglected and delinquent youth, and offered political movements and child welfare activists unprecedented opportunities to develop and test new theories and pedagogical methods in summer camps, orphanages, and homes for war-damaged children.[19] In the Austrian Empire, the nationalist DLS and ČZK had taken the leading role in efforts to protect children from deteriorating wartime social conditions. During the social crisis of the First World War, the imperial state had turned explicitly to these nationally segregated institutions to form the basis of a new Imperial Ministry of Social Welfare in 1917/18. Nationalist social workers in the Bohemian Lands thus dramatically expanded their influence and authority over children during the First World War as the imperial state's own trusted agents.[20]

In interwar Czechoslovakia, the DLS and ČZK remained the most important child welfare institutions and retained a close working relationship with the Czechoslovak state. Many DLS activists and social workers, particularly in Moravia, were affiliated with the German Socialist Party, which worked for reform within the framework of the Czechoslovak state after 1926. Nationalist social workers and child welfare activists presided over an impressive network of institutions for collective education in interwar Czechoslovakia. These nationally segregated summer camps, youth groups, nurseries, kindergartens, and counseling centers were supported by activists across the political spectrum as a utopian solution to the perceived crisis of war-damaged youth.

Before the First World War, nationalist social work had focused largely on saving orphans from denationalization and reducing the infant mortality rates of working-class and rural populations. In interwar Czechoslovakia, however, activists in the DLS shifted toward a more universalist pedagogy, looking to the psyche for the causes and solutions to youth delinquency and perceived national degeneration. These strategies were well suited to a world in which German nationalists had less access to state power than they had enjoyed in Habsburg Austria. To secure national "autonomy" and unity nationalist educators now targeted "healthy" children as much as dysfunctional families, middle-class as much as working-class families. Social worker Karl Theimer reflected in 1922: "The war with all its consequences opened up new paths for social welfare. While one was previously content to save single individuals and in particular to offer the needy material support, social welfare is now charged with the task of reaching out to all youth and raising them to the highest possible level of physical, intellectual and moral perfection."[21] According to Hugo Heller, the war had destroyed family life to an extent never seen before, creating an unprecedented "shortage of good mothers and fathers as educators" in industrial regions. He insisted that only after salvageable middle-class children had been rehabilitated could a stronger German nation offer assistance to the neediest children, arguing, "The starting point must lie in the middle classes, only from here outward can the world of misery be unhinged."[22]

The universalist ambitions of the DLS after 1918 demanded new pedagogical methods. The blossoming fields of child psychology and psychoanalytic pedagogy offered the commission's social workers radical new tools with which to expand their claims on children and cultivate national autonomy. The Viennese, mostly Jewish founders of psychoanalytic pedagogy, especially Anna Freud, August Aichhorn, Siegfried Bernfeld, Melanie Klein, and Bruno Bettelheim, would all have been political opponents of German nationalists.[23] And yet, psychoanalytic principles were quite compatible with new and overtly political forms of collective education that flourished across Europe in the wake of the First World War. Bernfeld, a Socialist and Zionist, specifically embraced nationalist views on the utopian potential of orphans to regenerate the nation, using the language of psychoanalysis. He suggested in 1921: "Orphaned youth adapt themselves well into the wider and more meaningful national community. Robbed of their parents, they are more deeply and unconditionally devoted to their nearest relatives. And perhaps the upbringing of orphans should anchor such fleeting emotions to a plan ... elevate the feelings of a lonely boy into a will to build a youth community."[24]

German nationalists in interwar Czechoslovakia eagerly appropriated insights from the fields of psychoanalysis and child psychology for their own cause. The theories of Viennese psychoanalyst August Aichhorn seem to have enjoyed particular resonance among interwar nationalists. In his best-known work, "Wayward Youth," (1925), Aichhorn sought the roots of youth delinquency in the psychoanalytic dramas of early childhood identification. Aichhorn explicitly rejected social influences as the primary cause of youth delinquency. He elaborated: "When I ask the parents of asocial youth how they explain that their child has become delinquent, I regularly get the answer that bad friends, the dangers of the streets, or convenient opportunities are at the source. In some way that is correct, yet thousands of other children live under the same conditions and do not become delinquent. There must certainly be something within the child itself such that the milieu of a child can trigger delinquency."[25]

The practical outgrowth of the movement was an explosion of child-rearing advice in interwar Czechoslovakia, aimed at working-class and middle-class parents alike. The number of "Mother Counseling Centers" managed by the DLS in Bohemia increased from 252 to 534 between 1925 and 1937, and then increased to over 800 by 1938.[26] In 1937 alone 32,438 German women attended courses for new mothers in Czechoslovakia, which were organized by the DLS in 782 different villages. The ČZK, meanwhile, boasted in 1933 that 43 percent of newborn infants passed through their nationalist maternal welfare centers.[27] These centers and courses had originally focused primarily on urging working-class mothers to breast-feed and supplying infants with medical care, in order to combat the high infant mortality rates in industrial regions. Social workers did not abandon these public health goals, but they increasingly devoted themselves to peddling psychological advice in the interwar period, as child mortality rates actually declined significantly with the relative prosperity of the late 1920s.[28] Nationalist social workers now instructed German mothers on topics that extended well beyond breast-feeding and hygiene, including "the influence of the environment on the child, unconscious educational influences, games, toys, picture books, fairy tales, fantasies in the child's life, children's questions, answers, observation of the child at play, children's friendships, handling the lie, punishments, threats, promises, education for self-sufficiency, traits of the child, and speech disorders."[29]

Nationalist child welfare activists simultaneously promoted youth counseling in a rapidly expanding network of child guidance clinics (*Erziehungs-beratungsstelle/dětské poradny*) in order to help children and youth navigate the emotional dangers of growing up. In 1933, the Czechoslovak Ministry for Public Health and Physical Education counted 1,757 child guidance clinics in Czechoslovakia, the majority of which (1,597) were founded and managed by the local branches of the nationalist DLS and ČZK. These clinics, staffed mostly by paid social workers and doctors, provided counseling to 262,470 children by 1933.[30] In that year, the DLS boasted optimistically that these counseling centers would soon offer every German family good advice "when possible behavioral disturbances become noticeable in their children."[31]

Nationalist pedagogues and social workers increasingly found fault with middle-class and working-class parents in almost equal measure. This reflected a shift from pre-1918 nationalist social work, which had focused more on integrating working-class and peasant families into the national community. Aichhorn had elaborated in 1925 that "excessively affectionate relationships with parents or siblings early on can later lead to delinquency."[32] Nationalist social workers in Brno claimed that fragile victims of "too much love" in childhood, typically only children from middle-class families, were prone to develop an excessive fixation on a parent or sibling.[33] Based on this logic, the DLS increasingly focused on the supposed psychological and pedagogical dangers of small families in the 1930s. Because of their isolation from other children, nationalist social workers reasoned, only children were condemned to a lifetime of stunted social relationships and rarely made functional members of the national community. "They fail when they need to submit to others, change directions, when they should order themselves in a community. The upbringing of today's so common only children has therefore become a burning problem, not only from a pedagogical perspective but also from a social point of view," DLS activists warned in 1936.[34] In a radio discussion on "Mother Education and German Child Welfare" in early 1938, experts from the DLS urged parents to have at least three or four children in order to secure the maximum psychological and pedagogical benefits for their offspring: "In a healthy large family the children actually learn from the first day onward to submit themselves to a larger community when necessary, without any grand educational methods ... It never seems all that difficult for them to learn what every upstanding human being must learn sooner or later, especially in today's fated times: to defer to a more important cause, to be able to deny oneself something pleasant and enjoyable for the sake of a duty."[35]

Eugenics and genetics offered interwar social workers another opportunity to look inward for the causes and solutions to social problems. There was, however, considerable disagreement within the DLS about the degree to which children's genes determined their later developmental fate. The psychological turn of the mid 1920s may have shifted attention away from material deprivation and toward psychological dynamics within the family, but it also convinced some social workers that they had actually overestimated the role of heredity in triggering child delinquency. In 1926, the DLS in Bohemia optimistically speculated: "Science has now learned to minimize the concern over heredity to a proper level, and in turn to appreciate the determinant role of the outer environment on humans."[36] Other nationalist social workers agreed that psychological and psychoanalytic theories had largely discredited purely genetic theories of child development. In 1930, one DLS critic of eugenics argued: "All of the difficulties of child-raising can be traced back to negligence and errors in the upbringing of the infant. Isn't it at least in the realm of possibility, that so good as nothing is determined by heredity, and that the entire process of child development is dependent on the type of upbringing?"[37]

In 1933, another DLS nationalist attacked the scientific assumptions behind Nazi forced sterilization laws, defending a commitment to old-fashioned solidarist social programs and warning: "Today one all too often hears attacks against social welfare built on solidarist assistance ... the uneducated lay person is taught that social welfare can be rendered superfluous by surgery. The rejection of influences from the environment on the treatment of diseases has already taken on grotesque forms under the influence of these warped teachers."[38]

While Detlev Peukert and others have linked the economic crisis of the 1930s in Germany to a shift toward exclusionary (and ultimately murderous) social welfare policies, nationalists in the Bohemian Lands were not so eager to distinguish between "educable" and "uneducable" youth and to exclude the "uneducable" from the national community. Competition between German and Czech child welfare organizations to secure the greatest number of children for the nation continued unabated throughout the interwar period, and thereby contributed to a more fundamentally inclusive dynamic than in neighboring nation-states. The terms and strategies for inclusion certainly varied across time, but nationalists were far less concerned with finding a "final solution" to the problem of working-class deviance than with integrating as many children as possible into a unified national community. Nor did child welfare institutions in the Bohemian Lands simplistically replace the tyranny of the father or the authority of primarily female voluntary social workers with the paternal or masculine authority of the state, as is often suggested in histories of the welfare state in Germany and France.[39] In the Bohemian Lands, popular nationalist movements, rather than a growing bureaucratic state, launched the most successful and enduring challenges to parental rights. The national community's claims on children were central to popular understandings and expectations of democracy, minority rights, and social welfare in interwar Czechoslovakia. These links were articulated via expanded pedagogical activism and a nationalized child welfare system that anchored children firmly in the collective, in the name of protecting children from national, hygienic, and emotional dangers at home.

Stay-at-Home Nationalism

If nationalists and child welfare experts shared a certain faith in the power of collective education to repair children's psyche during the interwar period, how did collective education come to be linked with Nazism and totalitarianism in cold war rhetoric? On the eve of the Nazi invasion, German and Czech nationalists shared a political culture centered on protecting nationalist "rights" to educate children and provide for their social needs. The seizure of nationally segregated social and pedagogical institutions by the Nazis state radically disrupted this culture for both Sudeten Germans and Czech nationalists. Nationalists called upon women, as presumed guardians of national culture within the family, to fill in for social welfare and educational institutions discredited by Nazism. Czech and Sudeten German activists radically resituated authentic nationalist education in the family as they mobilized to protect children from the national enemy and the influence of the Nazi state. In doing so they reversed four decades of nationalist pedagogy and social welfare activism that had been based on a profound suspicion of parents' national loyalties.

While the vast majority of Sudeten Germans enthusiastically supported the Nazi dismemberment of the Czechoslovak state in 1938/39, their euphoric expectations of "liberation" centered largely around strengthening nationalist educational and social welfare institutions.[40] Sudeten German Nazis flooded officials in Berlin and Prague with requests for new schools, kindergartens, swimming pools, and nurseries for their children, to compensate for the alleged Czechifying and colonizing policies of the interwar Czechoslovak state. Sudeten German hopes that the Nazis would fulfill all of their nationalist fantasies were soon dashed, however, by the thoughtless Nazi demand that Sudeten German fathers and teachers serve in the army and that Sudeten German women work in war factories. As Nazi priorities shifted from building nurseries to building bombs, informants in the SS repeatedly conveyed Sudeten German complaints that the Nazis were not doing enough to protect German children from Czechification. "In total contrast to the Reich or other linguistically homogenous areas, most national comrades leave their women and children behind among the Czechs with the greatest anxiety," explained one Nazi informant in 1940.[41]

Sudeten Germans soon began to insist that they could serve the national community best by staying at home. Not surprisingly, the stay-at-home nationalism articulated by Sudeten German nationalists required stay-at-home mothers. Conflicts between Nazi officials and local Germans soon began actively to transform fundamental principles of nationalist pedagogy. Konrad Henlein's Sudeten German Party, like the interwar nationalists in the DLS, had actively encouraged collective education in the late 1930s, advising mothers in 1938: "Every child belongs in the community. Even the most tender mother, the most careful education in the parental home, cannot replace an education to become a communal being through the comradery of the *Volksjugend*. Mother should have no exaggerated fears of the dangers which could threaten her child when he is far away from her."[42]

The Nazis initially attempted to harness this local culture to realize their own racial program and war aims. As in Germany, they mobilized children and youth through the Hitler Youth and the BDM (Bund deutscher Mädel). In the Bohemian Lands, however, the Hitler Youth also served another function—that of integrating nationally ambiguous children into the Nazi *Volksgemeinschaft*. These were children who themselves often could not speak German but whose parents nonetheless identified as Nazis. The nationalist campaign to recruit nationally ambiguous children thus continued in new forms under Nazi rule, now in the name of racial "Germanization." In the Hitler Youth in Prerau, for example, 80 percent of the members reportedly spoke Czech, and the leader there was often

forced to give commands in Czech out of necessity. The Hitler Youth in Bat'ha/
Bata was also composed mostly of children of mixed marriages who spoke only
Czech.[43] After the 1942 assassination of Reinhard Heydrich in Prague, a parallel
mandatory youth organization was created for Czech youth, called the Kuratorium for Youth Education. This organization, which became increasingly popular
among Czechs in the final years of the war, explicitly promoted a doctrine labeled
Reich-loyal Czech nationalism by observers. Czech youth were thereby encouraged
to express forms of Czech cultural nationalism—but harnessed firmly to the
Third Reich.

In addition, the Nazi state sought to secure the loyalty of local Sudeten Germans and nationally ambiguous families by expanding schools and child welfare
institutions. Memoirs of Sudeten German expellees confirm that child welfare
programs organized by the Nationalsozialistische Volkswohlfahrt (NSV) bolstered the image of the regime in the early years after the invasion.[44] A German
expellee recalled that in Jihlava/Iglau: "Day care centers were welcomed by the
population of the language islands. They were all new and clean and provided
real relief for women who so often took over the work of their husbands during
the war."[45]

Yet while many women welcomed the new kindergartens and schools for their
children, many also bristled against the "duty" to serve the Nazi war effort in factories. Sudeten German officials and women in the Protectorate now attempted
to depict staying at home as a German national privilege. While the mobilization
of female labor was unpopular in the Altreich as well, in the Bohemian Lands
women claimed that they should be spared from work duty specifically to protect their children from Czechification. Sudeten German officials thus argued in
1942 that "child-rearing requires greater effort from the German woman in the
Protectorate than in the Altreich" and demanded that no German woman be
mobilized for labor until all Czech women were employed.[46] In 1940, Sudeten
German and Deputy Reichsprotektor Karl H. Frank likewise insisted: "In the
Protectorate women cannot be used in the same way as in the Altreich. The special relationships and the position of the German woman in the Protectorate, in
foreign *Raum,* must be taken into account."[47] Much to the chagrin of authorities in Berlin, the labor force participation of German women in the Bohemian
Lands actually declined between 1937 and 1942, with the sharpest drop right
after the outbreak of the war and the onset of Nazi "mobilization," between
1939 and 1942.[48] These conflicts reflected tensions between an understanding of
national community based largely on sacrifice on the battlefield or in the war factory, and a local nationalist culture oriented more around protecting the nation's
preeminent claims on children.

Because the Nazi threat was so much greater to the Czech population, Czech
women adapted a more forceful form of stay-at-home nationalism. Left-wing
communists and feminists and right-wing collaborators both called upon Czech
women to devote themselves fully to the task of protecting the Czech ethnicity
of their children within their own homes during the occupation. In 1939 the

Czech underground magazine *V boj* appealed to women: "With great fanfare, the Germans are opening new German schools where there used to be none. This is your business, women. It is in your hands, whether our children grow up to be Czechs or Germanized, patriots or traitors."[49] That summer the Czech feminist magazine *Ženský obzor* also insisted Czech women were duty-bound to encourage a "healthy nationalism" in their children. "The tepidity of the nation can mostly be blamed on an insufficient understanding of national education in the family. Women too can strive so that our culture is and remains distinctive, pure, and wholly our own," editors urged their readers.[50] The communist resistance echoed these sentiments, identifying education in the home as the only effective antidote to the "poison" of Nazi education and the threat of Germanization. In 1943 the underground communist newspaper *Rudé právo* warned: "Just as in Germany they will turn our children into fanatics, such that they would willingly denounce even their own parents. In every case it is going to depend on the parents themselves to find the Nazi poison in their children, to isolate it and eliminate it."[51] Right-wing Czech conservatives echoed these appeals, accenting traditional family values and racial purity in appeals for national unity.[52]

Czech women responded enthusiastically, whether to protect their children from Germanization or avoid forced labor. The number of Czech women who married and had children skyrocketed during the occupation.[53] "We have to thank the Nazis for a remarkable increase in the birthrate. There have never been so many pregnant women to be seen in Prague or in the countryside," observed one Czech informant in late 1943.[54]

But even as Sudeten German and Czech nationalists and parents depicted Nazi education as a threat, they did not reject collective claims on children, nor did they depict the family as a world apart from politics. Rather, they now depicted education in the home as the last hope to protect the nation's preeminent collective "rights" to children.

The Demise of Collective Education

After the Second World War, rehabilitating war-damaged children became an urgent priority for policymakers, international relief organizations, educators, social workers, and psychologists. "If their numbers had been multiplied by hundreds, child psychologists would still have found the demands on their skill overwhelmed during and after the war," observed journalist Dorothy Macardle in 1951.[55] Moreover, she reported, there was a growing consensus about how best to repair children's war-stunted souls. "Educational psychologists are very generally in accord with Dr. Anna Freud in the conclusion she has expressed repeatedly: that for little children even a mediocre family life is better than the best of communal nurseries."[56]

These arguments were typical of a broader postwar discourse that linked the overt politicization of childhood to anti-democratic politics. In their memories of Nazism, Sudeten German expellees and other West German anti-communists retrospectively contrasted the ostensibly apolitical pedagogical space of the nuclear family to the "invasive" tactics of collective brainwashing allegedly promoted by the Nazis and communists alike. In a typical refrain, German expellee Max Mayer recalled: "It is true that some measures of the party were not always endorsed, but no one dared open resistance. Interference in youth education, in particular, was strongly resented, since children were thereby estranged from their parental homes."[57] These memories downplayed the extent to which Nazi claims on children in the Bohemian Lands had actually built on a local political culture in which children were already seen as the property of the national collective. In their recollections of the Nazi period, Sudeten Germans also attempted to claim victim status by contrasting their democratic nationalist pedagogical and youth movements with the top-down, invasive tactics of the Nazis.[58] In an essay on the incorporation of the Sudeten German youth associations into the Hitler Youth, Eduard Berkert now idealized the final days of Sudeten Germans' "democratic" nationalism in interwar Czechoslovakia, distinguishing it from the conformist militarism that followed under Nazism: "For a short time, the joyous, youthful, independent life in the youth groups was still to a large extent preserved, before voluntarism became service, hiking became marching, diverse ways of thinking became a prescribed world view."[59]

The danger of totalitarianism in the cold war West was soon located in excessive claims on children and interventions into family life. Collective education, once linked with democracy and "minority rights" by nationalists, was now associated with undemocratic practices of "brainwashing" children. Alfred Brauner, a French psychologist, reported a German teacher's observations of children in Nazi Germany to illustrate the effectiveness of Nazi indoctrination. According to Brauner, German children under Nazism "denounced, if required, their father, who remained loyal to his old political party, and their mother, who preferred to believe the priest rather than the Führer. They are the youth who blindly executed all orders, and were prepared for this voluntary submission since their earliest childhood."[60] In these narratives, German parents were typically depicted as helpless victims of the Nazi state's all-powerful claims on their offspring. Macardle thus insisted in 1951: "It was almost impossible for parents to save their children from being impregnated by the Nazi creed ... there were fanatical little devotees of the Führer who blackmailed their parents by threatening to denounce them in the party for lack of zeal."[61]

The trope of the child informant became one of the most powerful symbols of Nazi evil after 1945. Rumors of child informants were already widespread within the Czech resistance during the Nazi occupation. In August of 1944, for example, a Czech informant warned, "At home many cannot speak in front of their children, because children prattle and betray their father and mother."[62] The figure of the child informant served to evoke the omnipotent power of the Nazi police state, a discourse that Klaus Michel Mallman and Gerhard Paul have argued deflected attention from lapses in resistance on the homefront and obscured inefficiencies and weaknesses in Nazi surveillance.[63] Child informants powerfully represented the alleged Nazi destruction of the private sphere, the totalitarian quality of Nazi pedagogy, and the ironic reversals of power in occupied society—a society literally turned upside down.

The postwar critique of collective education and idealization of the "apolitical" family was an integral part of the ideology of reconstruction in West Germany. Focusing on Nazi education as a source of totalitarianism may have helped to "normalize" West Germany, integrating it into a cold war alliance against Communism.[64] These narratives explained the apparent failure of moral reasoning in German society under Nazism in terms of an alleged brainwashing of youth and children, which took place largely against the better judgment and will of their parents.[65] After the war, West German anti-communist propaganda attempted to mobilize citizens to save East German children from the same terrible fate that had befallen German youth under Nazism: being "ripped from the hands of their parents" by the educational and social welfare apparatus of the communist state.[66] Anti-communists reserved harsh criticism for policies that encouraged women to work outside the home and provided state support for child care. In East Germany, women were allegedly required to send their children to state-run nursery schools so as to insure "the undisturbed indoctrination of the child with the Communist world view" from the most tender age, claimed activist Käte Fiedler in 1955.[67] In a 1955 government publication, Hans Köhler likewise reported, "wherever possible mothers have no more opportunities to devote themselves to their children."[68]

If Communist Czechoslovakia retained traditions of collective education, meanwhile, this was only possible in an ethnically cleansed nation-state where the threat of Germanization had been eliminated through the expulsion of the German population. In July of 1944, for example, a Czech informant reported to London: "After the last speech of Dr. Beneš there was disappointment in Bohemia because he wants to keep the loyal Germans here. There are no loyal Germans, they are all alike, and the in best case the children of loyal Germans will grow up to be pan-Germans again. They cannot stay even if they can only attend Czech schools, because the German spirit will be preserved privately. We are doing the same thing ourselves under the Nazi regime, and we are not as sneaky as the Germans would be."[69]

Psychoanalysts and social workers also supported familialist policies after the Second World War, based partly on wartime experiences and experiments with displaced children. It is perhaps no coincidence that the history of psychoanalysts' interwar enthusiasm for collective education (and nationalists' enthusiasm for psychoanalysis) seems to have sunk into obscurity. In the wake of the Second World War, Austrian Jewish émigrés such as Anna Freud, Melanie Klein, and Bruno Bettelheim increasingly focused on the sanctity of the mother-child bond, based in part on research with child survivors of concentration camps and with children separated from their parents by wartime evacuations.[70] While these analysts still located the source of child delinquency in psychological dramas between parents and children, they rarely promoted collective education as a desirable substitute for a flawed parental upbringing.[71] Experiences and memories of the Second World War bolstered the claim that children were best cared for by stay-at-home mothers rather than left to the mercy of the state, political parties, and social activists. Yet parents themselves were under no less scrutiny. They were now both exclusively responsible for their children's woes, and fundamentally irreplaceable by the agents of mass political movements.

This story suggests that popular and scholarly assertions about how Nazism and Communism colonized, invaded, or destroyed the "private" sphere should be greeted with skepticism. These arguments rest on an idealized, liberal conception of the family as an apolitical space that should be protected from intervention. This ideology has historically protected the rights of fathers to rule over women and children with immunity. The idea that Nazism "destroyed the private sphere" does not do justice to the historical experiences of women and children in the family or to the complexity of the relationship between society and state under Nazi rule. It may in fact be a sloppy shorthand for making other, more convincing claims: about the depth of penetration of Nazi ideologies into daily life, for example, or about the limits or barriers to resistance under Nazism.[72]

Moreover, we cannot assume that before the Nazis and Communists came to power, children were anchored firmly in an imagined private sphere. In fact, thanks to decades of nationalist activism, children in the Bohemian Lands were seen as the rightful property of the nation long before the Nazis came to power. Even in Western Europe, working-class children lived public lives in the streets and labor force, were mobilized by religious, socialist, sommunist, nationalist, and fascist movements, and were the targets of political activism and social welfare movements of all kinds. Grasping the progressive intentions of nationalist claims on children can, however, be difficult from an American standpoint, which often defines freedom in terms of the absence of state intervention. Perhaps we can finally move beyond a simple debate over whether progressive or disciplinary tendencies emerged victorious in modern welfare and pedagogical institutions. As nationalists, child welfare activists, psychoanalysts, and postwar politicians debated about where and to whom children "belonged," they simultaneously defined and transformed boundaries between Czech and German, public and private, democracy and dictatorship. These struggles have been central to popular understandings and expectations of family, social welfare, and mass politics in twentieth-century Central Europe.

Notes

1. Erika Mann, *School for Barbarians* (New York, 1938), 28.
2. Mann, *School,* 29.
3. Richard Bessel and Dirk Schumann, "Introduction: Violence, Normality, and the Construction of Postwar Europe," in *Life After Death: Approaches to a Cultural and Social History of*

Europe During the 1940s and 1950s, ed. Richard Bessel and Dirk Schumann (New York, 2003), 2.

4. For a discussion of the uses of the public-private divide in gender history and historiography, see the forum "Women's History in the New Millenium: Rethinking Public and Private," *Journal of Women's History* 15 (spring 2003): 11–69, with articles by Leonore Davidoff, Sandra Graham, Carole Turbin, and Elizabeth Thompson.

5. For more on the nationalist battle for children in the Bohemian Lands, see Tara Zahra, *Kidnapped Souls: National Indifference and the Battle for Children in the Bohemian Lands, 1900–48* (Ithaca, 2008).

6. On nationalization in Austria, see Pieter M. Judson, *Guardians of the Nation: Activists on the Language Frontiers of Rural Austria* (Cambridge, MA, 2006); Jeremy King, *Budweisers into Czechs and Germans: A Local History of Bohemian Politics, 1848–1948* (Princeton, 2002).

7. Heinrich Holek, *Unterwegs: Eine Selbstbiographie mit Bildnis des Verfassers* (Vienna, 1927), 146.

8. J. Loučka, "Stíny menšin," *Menšinový učitel* 4 (December 1913): 42. Emphasis in the original.

9. N.a., "O dětech národu," *Ludmila: Časopis věnovaný ochraně opuštených dětí a sirotků vůbec a zvláště na Ostravsku* 1 (1913): 4.

10. Hugo Heller, "Leitordnung der Zentralstelle für deutsche Waisenpflege und Jugendfürsorge in Böhmen für die Waisenerziehung in Pflegefamilien," *Jahrbuch der deutschen Jugendfürsorge in Böhmen* 2 (1909): 227.

11. N.a., "Dr. Karl Schücker Waisenheim des Bundes der Deutschen in Böhmen," *Jahrbuch der deutschen Jugendfürsorge in Böhmen* 2 (1909): 21.

12. N.a., "Deutschvölkische Waisenhäuser und Kriegswaisenfürsorge," *Mitteilungen des Vereines Südmark* 13 (1918): 156.

13. Jugendfürsorge: Bericht über die erste deutsch-böhmische Jugendfürsorge-Konferenz zu Prag am 23. und 24. Februar 1907. Folder Kinderschutz- Zentralstelle für deutsche Waisenpflege und Jugendfürsorge in Böhmen. Allgemeines Verwaltungsarchiv (AVA), Justizministerium, Carton 425, Österreichisches Staatsarchiv (ÖstA).

14. Wilhelmine Wiechowski, "Mädchenfürsorge," *Jahrbuch der deutschen Jugendfürsorge in Böhmen* 2 (1909): 98.

15. Hugo Heller, *Jugendland: Eine Einführung in die Aufgaben der deutschen Jugendfürsorge in Böhmen* (Prague, 1913), 26.

16. Hugo Heller, *Die Erziehung zu deutschen Wesen* (Prague, 1936), 22.

17. N.a., *Unsere deutsche Schulen und das Vernichtungsgesetz* (Eger, 1920), 14.

18. Václav Perek, *Ochrana menšin národnostních dle mírových smluv a skutečně poměry v naší republice* (Prague, 1922), 17.

19. On the importance of the First World War in the development and popularization of psychoanalysis see especially Paul Lerner, *Hysterical Men: War, Psychiatry, and the Politics of Trauma in Germany, 1890–1930* (Ithaca, 2003); Laurence A. Rickels, *Nazi Psychoanalysis,* 3 vols. (Minneapolis, 2002), vol. 1. On the perceived crisis of the family during and after the First World War, see David Crew, *Germans on Welfare: From Weimar to Hitler* (New York, 1998); Young-Sun Hong, *Welfare, Modernity, and the Weimar State, 1919–1933* (Princeton, 1998); Maureen Healy, *Vienna and the Fall of the Habsburg Empire: Total War and Everyday Life in World War I* (Cambridge, 2004), 211–258. On the "moral panic" over endangered youth inspired by the First World War in Germany, see also Richard Bessel, *Germany after the First World War* (Oxford, 1993) and Elizbeth Harvey, *Youth and the Welfare State in Weimar Germany* (Oxford, 1994).

20. For more on the relationship between nationalist child welfare activists in the Bohemian Lands and the Austrian state during the First World War, see Tara Zahra, "Each Nation Only Cares for Its Own: Empire, Nation, and Child Welfare Activism in the Bohemian Lands, 1900–1918," *American Historical Review* 111 (December 2006): 1378–1402.

21. Karl Theimer, "Praktische Jugendfürsorge," *Jugendfürsorge* 7 (February 1922): 25.

22. Hugo Heller, "Pestalozzi und die moderne Jugendfürsorge," *Jugendfürsorge* 4 (1919): 134–140.

23. Cultural historians such as Carl Schorske and Peter Gay have traditionally described psychoanalysis as either a reaction to or the liberal antithesis of the mass political movements that shook the Austrian Empire in the early twentieth century. Carl Schorske, *Fin de siècle Vienna: Politics and Culture* (New York, 1981), 5–6, 185; Peter Gay, *Freud, Jews, and Other Germans* (New York, 1978), 33.

24. Siegfried Bernfeld, *Kinderheim Baumgarten* (Berlin, 1921), 11.

25. August Aichhorn, *Verwahrloste Jugend: Psychoanalyse in der Fürsorgeerziehung* (Vienna, 1925), 64.

26. N.a., "Deutsche Jugendfürsorge," *Beilage zur Frauenschaftsweisung*, 15 September 1937, Sudetendeutsche Partei (SdP), Carton 22, Národní archiv, Prague (NA); "Was wir alle wissen sollten," *Deutsche Jugendfürsorge Nachtrichtendienst*, 28 April 1938, SdP, Carton 83, NA.

27. "V celé republice nápadný pokles porodnosti," Česká zemská péče o mládež v Brně, č. 6, 1933. Národní jednota severočeská (NJS), Carton 9, Národní Archiv, Prague (NA).

28. Infant mortality rates had dropped to 10.3% in Moravia and 11.6% in Bohemia by 1933, down from over 25% in 1900. On infant mortality in the Habsburg Monarchy see Heinrich Rauchberg, *Der nationale Besitzstand in Böhmen* (Reichenberg, 1905), 586. For an overview of infant mortality rates in Czechoslovakia from 1919 to 1937, see n. ed., *Statistisches Jahrbuch für das Protektorat Böhmen und Mähren* (Prague, 1941), 148.

29. Karl Theimer, "Vermehrte erziehliche Fürsorge für die Kleinkinder," *Jugendfürsorge* 18 (1934): 137.

30. "Dětské poradenství v r. 1933," *Statistická ročenka Republiky československé*, No editor. (Prague, 1936), 194.

31. Heinrich Schubert, "Über die Notwendigkeit einer planmäßigen freien Jugendberatung" *Jugendürsorge* 14 (February 1930): 102–105.

32. Aichhorn, *Verwahrloste Jugend*, 75, 251.

33. "Beratungsstelle für schwererziehbare Kinder," *Jugendfürsorge* 10 (January–February 1926): 55–58.

34. Theodor Heller, "Das abwegige und sittlich defekte Kind," *Jugendfürsorge* 20 (January 1936): 9.

35. Kat Beierl and Uli Simon, "Erziehung in der Familie," *Jugendfürsorge* 22 (June 1938): 272.

36. "Beratungsstelle für schwererziehbare Kinder," *Jugendfürsorge* 10 (January–February 1926): 56.

37. Grete Swoboda, "Seelenkundige Erziehung in frühkindlichem Leben," *Jugendfürsorge* 14 (April–May 1930): 200–203.

38. Theodor Gruschka, "Die Sterilisierung Erbkranker," *Jugendfürsorge* 17 (December 1933): 502.

39. For examples of works on the welfare state that associate the rise of the welfare state with paternalist state intervention see Edward Ross Dickinson, *The Politics of German Child Welfare from the Empire to the Federal Republic* (Cambridge, MA, 1996); Young-Sun Hong, *Welfare, Modernity and the Weimar State, 1919–1933* (Princeton, 1998); Ute Daniel, *The War From Within: German Working-Class Women in the First World War* (Oxford, 1997); Elizabeth Domansky, "Militarization and Reproduction in World War I Germany," in *Society, Culture and the State in Germany, 1871–1930*, ed. Geoff Eley (Ann Arbor, 1996), 427–464; Sonya Michel and Seth Koven, "Womanly Duties: Maternalist Politics and the Origins of Welfare States in France, Germany, Great Britain and the United States, 1880–1920," *American Historical Review* 95 (October 1990): 1076–1108; Sylvia Schafer, *Children in Moral Danger and the Problem of Government in Third Republic France* (Princeton, 1997).

_40. On Sudeten German responses to and participation in the Nazi Gau Sudetenland, see Volker Zimmermann, *Die Sudetendeutschen im NS-Staat: Politik und Stimmung der Bevölkerung im Reichsgau Sudetenland* (Munich, 1999); Ralf Gebel, *Heim ins Reich! Konrad Henlein und der Reichsgau Sudetenland* (Munich, 1999).

41. *Meldungen aus dem Reich: die geheimen Lageberichte des Sicherheitsdienst der SS*, ed. Heinz Boberach (Pawlak, 1984), no. 37, 8 January 1940.
42. Weisung des Frauenamtes OG-18/1938, 18 August 1938, Carton 22, SdP, NA.
43. *Meldungen aus dem Reich*, no. 180, 22 April 1941.
44. Cited in Zimmermann, *Sudetendeutsche im NS Staat*, 77.
45. Ost Doc. 20/66, Iglau und der Iglauer Sprachinsel, 1918–1945, 25. Bundesarchiv Bayreuth.
46. "Leitgedanken zum Fraueneinsatz," 11 July 1942. Carton 868, Úřad říšského protektora (UŘP), NA.
47. Protokoll über die Sitzung von 23 August 1941. Carton 868, UŘP, NA.
48. Ministerium für Wirtschaft und Arbeit, 12 October 1942. Carton 868, UŘP, NA.
49. "Germanisace," *V boj: Edice ilegalního časopisu*, vol. 1: *1939* (Prague, 1992), 333.
50. "Žena má zůstati ženou," *Ženský obzor*, nos. 7–8 (1939): 1–2.
51. "Všem naším instruktorům," *Rudé právo, 1939–45*, January 1943 (Prague, 1971), 380–381.
52. The short-lived Czech Second Republic (October 1938–March 1939) headed by the conservative, Catholic Agrarian Party Leader Rudolf Beran, and the collaborationist regime led by Emil Hácha during the Nazi occupation shared a great deal with Petain's regime in Occupied France. On the Second Republic, see Theodore Procházka, *The Second Republic: The Disintegration of Post-Munich Czechoslovakia* (New York, 1981), 56; Jan Rataj, *O autoritativní národní stát: ideologické proměny české politiky v druhé republice, 1938–1939* (Prague, 1997), 230–234; Melissa Feinberg, "Dumplings and Domesticity: Women, Collaboration and Resistance in the Protectorate of Bohemia and Moravia," in *Gender and War in Twentieth-Century Eastern Europe*, ed. Nancy Wingfield and Maria Bucur (Bloomington, 2006), 95–110.
53. Detlef Brandes, *Die Tschechen unter deutschem Protektorat*, vol. 2 (Munich, 1975), 48; "Fünf Jahre Protektorat Böhmen und Mähren," *Wirtschaft und Statistik* 24 (1944): 17; Albin Eissner, "Die tschechoslowakische Bevölkerung im Zweiten Weltkrieg," *Aussenpolitik* 13 (1962): 334.
54. Zpráva o poměrech ve vlasti, 6 October 1943, sig. 91/6, Fond 37, Vojenské ústřední archív (VÚA).
55. Dorothy Macardle, *Children of Europe: A Study of the Children of Liberated Countries, Their Wartime Experiences, Their Reactions, and Their Needs* (Boston, 1951), 252.
56. Macardle, *Children of Europe*, 270.
57. Ost Doc. 20/50, Max Mayer, Nitschenau, 3 May 1962, 3. Bundesarchiv Bayreuth (BB).
58. See for example Theodor Keil, *Die deutsche Schule in den Sudetenländern* (Munich, 1967).
59. Eduard Burkert, "Die Auflösung der sudetendeutschen Jugendbünde und die Einführung der Hitler-Jugend," in *Deutsche Jugend in Böhmen*, ed. Peter Becher (Munich, 1993), 173.
60. Alfred Brauner, *Ces enfants ont vécu la guerre* (Paris, 1946), 182.
61. Macardle, *Children of Europe*, 35.
62. Zpráva o domově, 14 August 1944; see also Zpráva z domova, 24 January 1944, 91/7, Fond 37, VÚA; Jaroslav P. Blažek, "Národní školy za okupace," *Šest let okupace Prahy* (Prague, 1946), 47.
63. Klaus Michel Mallman and Gerhard Paul, "Omniscient, Omnipotent, Omnipresent? Gestapo, Society, and Resistance," in *Nazism and German Society*, ed. David Crew (New York, 1994); Robert Gellateley, *Backing Hitler: Consent and Coercion in Nazi Germany* (Oxford, 2001).
64. On the importance of the family to postwar reconstruction politics in Western Europe, see Robert Moeller, *Protecting Motherhood: Women and the Family in the Politics of Postwar Germany* (Berkeley, 1993), 69–70; Elizabeth Heineman, *What Difference Does a Husband Make* (Berkeley, 1999); Dagmar Herzog, "Desperately Seeking Normality: Sex and Marriage in the Wake of War," in Bessel and Schumann, *Life after Death*, 161–192; Pat Thane, "Family Life and 'Normality' in Postwar British Culture," in Bessel and Schumann, *Life After Death*, 193–210.
65. On denazification and education in postwar West Germany, see Karl-Heinz Füssl, *Die Umerziehung der Deutschen: Jugend und Schule unter den Siegermächten des Zweiten Weltkriegs 1945–1955* (Paderborn, 1994).

66. Bundesministerium für Gesamtdeutsche Fragen, *Deutsche Kinder in Stalins Hand* (Bonn, 1951), 78. See also Ernst Tillich, "Die psychologische Entwicklung und die psychologische Führung der Menschen hinter dem Eisernen Vorhang," in *Die Jugend der Sowjetzone in Deutschland*, n. ed. (Berlin, 1955).

67. Käte Fiedler, "Der Ideologische Drill der Jugend in der Sowjetzone," in *Die Jugend der Sowjetzone in Deutschland*, n. ed. (Berlin, 1955), 36.

68. Hans Köhler, "Erziehung zur Unfreiheit," in *Jugend zwischen Ost und West: Betrachtungen zur Eingliederung der jugendlichen Sowjetzonenflüchtlinge in das westdeutsche Wirtschafts- und Geistesleben*, ed. Harald v. Koenigswald, (Troisdorf, 1956), 60.

69. Zprávy z domova, 10 July 1944. Sig. 91/7, Fond 37, VÚA.

70. Anna Freud and Dorothy T. Burlingham, *War and Children* (London, 1943), 45. On links between psychoanalysis and familialism in postwar Britain, see Laura Lee Downs, "A 'Very British' Revolution? L'évacuation des enfants urbains vers les campagnes anglaises, 1939–1945," *Vingtième siècle* 89 (January–March 2006): 47–60; Denise Riley, *War in the Nursery: Theories of the Child and the Mother* (London, 1983), 85–110.

71. Macardle, *Children of Europe*, 270. For more on the influence of psychoanalysis in postwar reconstruction efforts in Europe, see Tara Zahra, "Lost Children: Displacement, Family, and Nation in Postwar Europe," *Journal of Modern History* 81 (March 2009): 45–86.

72. See Geoff Eley, "Hitler's Silent Majority? Conformity and Resistance under the Third Reich," *Michigan Quarterly Review* 42 (spring 2003): 389–425.

Chapter 10

ASSERTING THEIR "NATURAL RIGHT"
Parents and Public Schooling in Post-1945 Germany

Dirk Schumann

On 23 June 1953, Roetgen, a village in the Aachen district of North Rhine-West-phalia, was in turmoil. Shortly after eight o'clock, twenty-five 13- and 14-year-old students from the higher boys' class of the eighth grade of the local school marched along main street, carrying placards that read "We are not going to come to school at one o'clock in the afternoon any more" and "We want to come to school at eight o'clock in the morning, starting today!" The march ended at the office of the principal, Mrs. Wynands. She was not amused. Calling the students "a bunch of rascals" and "insolent liars," she confiscated the placards and sent the students away. Having heard rumors that the students might resume their demonstration in the afternoon, the local mayor went to the school shortly after one o'clock, accompanied by the local police chief. They questioned all the students in the classroom and summoned some of them to the police station, where questioning continued. Even more upset than the principal, the mayor attacked the boys' teacher in his report to the president of the district government, defining the main task of an educator in a democracy to be "to strengthen first and foremost the authority of state institutions in every conceivable way."[1]

Why all the commotion? A new school building that was to accommodate all pupils for instruction at the same time (i.e., in the morning) had been under construction for about three years in Roetgen. Its opening, promised for Easter, was delayed considerably for no obvious reason. On Friday, 19 June, students discussed the matter among themselves and decided to organize a demonstration on the coming Tuesday. Their teacher, who heard about their plans and advised them against holding a demonstration (since it would not be effective), later cited the uprising against the Communist regime in East Germany a few days

Notes from this chapter begin on page 222.

earlier, a similar strike action by students in Essen that had been covered in the media, and his discussion of the Peasants War and the Dutch Revolt in class as factors that may have induced his students to protest. At a meeting of the local Schulpflegschaft (Parent-Teacher Association) that was called several days after the incident, parents defended the students, emphasizing that they had used a "democratic form of protest."[2] The *Aachener Nachrichten,* the main regional newspaper, was equally sympathetic and commented with a touch of irony: "One can see that Roetgen's male students have learned something from the practice of democracy. Incidentally, their march took a completely disciplined form. As far as we could ascertain, the children only used the sidewalks for their march to the school. They made all efforts not to disturb the peace in any way."[3] The county school inspector was understanding as well, describing the students' action in her report to the district president as a normal form of public protest in Anglo-Saxon countries and Switzerland and as "possibly" a sign of democratic spirit. But despite these supportive reactions, and despite the fact that none of the students had been charged with anything, parents in the Schulpflegschaft remained upset about the behavior of the local police and asked the district government in a letter to intervene. They were successful: the police chief was rebuked for overstepping his authority; in turn, a Schulpflegschaft delegation reassured the district government of its goodwill and continued support for the school leadership.

In sum, these provincial and presumably staunch Catholics in the Rhineland region of West Germany defended behavior by their children that did not display the deference to authority commonly associated with the 1950s but showed signs of a different, courageous spirit. Parents who might otherwise not have leaned toward a permissive educational style were understanding when their children protested for a worthy cause and voiced their position publicly. Thus, they helped nurture democratic attitudes in their children, even though they may not have explicitly pursued that goal and many of them may have placed great emphasis on upholding their own authority at home.

In this essay I will argue that many West German parents became actively involved in school matters from the 1950s on. These engaged parents were always a minority, but they did not hesitate to challenge school authorities on all levels by participating in newly formed bodies as well as in independent associations of parents and in face-to-face encounters with teachers and officials. In voicing their grievances, they meant to assert their "natural right" as parents as well as their rights as citizens of a new democracy. By challenging state authority, they contributed to undermining the authoritarian legacy of German history, regardless of the specific demands they voiced. As opposed to the pre-1945 period, the role of religion in public schools dominated the discussion about parental participation only in the immediate postwar period. While parents' real power in school affairs always remained minor, with the important exception of the state of Hesse, it increased to some extent, in particular during the 1970s. Following a brief look at parents' participation from the late nineteenth century to the Nazi era, this essay will focus on key developments from the late 1940s through the 1970s.

While the postwar history of parental participation in school affairs in Germany has found very little scholarly attention (as has its history prior to 1945), both the history of the educational system and, more recently, that of the family in the late 1940s and 1950s have been the subject of a number of studies. As Robert Moeller and others have pointed out, the German society that emerged from the devastations of the war was in a deep material and moral crisis that affected gender roles and relations in particular. When the war ended, German men in both East and West no longer seemed capable of fulfilling their established roles as breadwinner and protectors of their wives and children, while women, as Elizabeth Heineman has shown, played the triple role of innocent war victims, energetic "women of the rubble," and promiscuous fraternizers. Apart from allowing Germans to claim universal victimhood (which is of less interest in the context of this essay), this crisis suggested that nuclear families, with their traditional division of labor, be restored as a strategy for overcoming social disorder and reconstructing "normality." This seemed all the more convincing, especially in West Germany, given that the Nazi regime was perceived as having destroyed the family through massive state intervention that targeted children particularly and sought to replace parents as the main educator. Moreover, families also provided emotional shelter amidst cold war angst. Thus the traditional nuclear family, as it was reconstructed in postwar West Germany, had both common Western and specific German aspects.[4]

And yet, as Edward Ross Dickinson has pointed out, this restoration of the family and its concomitant social policy was more than a mere renewal of pre-Nazi traditions. Even conservatives now recognized that the state should provide benefits besides financial support to parents—psychological counseling, for instance—to help them educate their children as active citizens of a new democracy. By the end of the 1950s it also became clear that women were beginning to establish themselves as equals of their male partners, as their increasing rate of employment outside of the home and the end of a husband's right to make the final decision in matters of child-rearing demonstrated.[5] As Ulrich Herbert has argued, the 1950s were initially characterized by an attempt to impose a conservative normalcy on a society that had been through a devastating experience of modernity; however, Herbert notes that at the end of the decade processes of liberalization and democratization set in that would reach their peak in the late 1960s and 1970s.[6] Parents, one should add, came to be engaged as citizens who identified with political parties and as "anxious parents" who found a growing number of reasons to worry about the future of the children, above all the form and quality of their school education.[7] This active and critical participation in school affairs, I will argue here, had already begun by the early 1950s.

Scholars agree that the German school system of the postwar era, with the notable exception of the Soviet zone of occupation, underwent a restoration of key structures, modified by some American success in reforming the curriculum. While French and British occupation authorities did not come with an agenda of fundamental structural change, the American military government sought to thoroughly democratize German education, primarily by replacing the traditional three-tier system with a comprehensive one. However, stubborn resistance by German education ministers and officials who warned of a decline in academic standards and pointed to their credentials as democratically elected representatives of the people stymied this effort at structural reform. The West German school system retained its fairly rigid boundaries between the three tracks of secondary education and continued to be strictly controlled by the administrations of the individual states. West German educators, however, proved more receptive to curriculum reform and adopted a concept of citizenship education in schools that, centered on the new subject of "social studies," could enable young West Germans to overcome the legacy of the Nazi past as well as distance themselves from the Communist East.[8]

As a result, there was a built-in tension in the reconstruction of the family, deemed more important than ever for guaranteeing social stability, and of the school system, which remained firmly in the hands of state administrators, principals, and teachers. With regard to education, questions such as who "owned" children, what was in their best interest, and how future citizens were to be formed were not settled and could only be negotiated between parents and representatives of the school system in formal and informal settings.[9]

Parents' Participation prior to 1945

German parents have had an indirect say in education policy in their capacity as voters, but otherwise have never been vested with much real power in school affairs. All key decisions were (and are) made by state legislatures and ministries and implemented and supervised by state officials. Private schools played only a marginal role, in particular after the revolution of 1918, whereupon all children attended a public elementary school during the first four grades. After that they were separated: the majority stayed in secondary schools that provided basic skills and vocational training, whereas a minority attended a *Gymnasium* to prepare for studies at a university.

Following the Reformation, German states tightened their control of schooling. Epitomizing this development, the Prussian General Civil Code of 1794 unequivocally defined schools as "undertakings of the state" (*Veranstaltungen des Staates*). Prussia granted some influence on local elementary schools to town governments only after 1800 by including several magistrates and aldermen on newly established municipal school boards. Their tasks, however, were largely confined to keeping school buildings in good shape and securing the teachers' salaries. The revolution of 1848/49 gave rise to concepts of a decentralized system of "school communities" in which parents would have been one key player, but its ultimate failure preserved the status quo. It was only in 1906 that a Prussian law somewhat increased citizens'—and indirectly parents'—influence on school affairs by assigning local school boards the new task of strengthening bonds between school and family. In addition to school parties and sports events, "parents' evenings" (*Elternabende*) became one key element in this new field of activity, gaining some traction prior to 1914 even among working-class parents and prefiguring the activities of parents' councils after 1918.[10]

The prewar decade saw another form of parent participation in school affairs that ran counter to state policy and pointed to a major source of conflict about parental rights that would remain important far into the second half of the century. Efforts by the Prussian government to suppress Polish nationalism in the Eastern provinces by banning the use of the Polish language in religious instruction in schools met with fierce resistance. Starting in 1901 with individual parents' refusal to let their children take part in religious instruction held in German, this resistance became a mass movement as Catholic priests got involved and organized protest meetings. In November of 1906, more than half of all Polish pupils being taught in German in the province of Posen (almost 47,000) were kept home. Polish parents were brought to heel only when heavy fines were imposed on them.[11]

Parents' right to determine the religious and confessional character of the school in which their children would be educated—their "confessional parental right" (*konfessionelles Elternrecht*), as experts called it—also was at the heart of controversies in the early Weimar Republic and remained contentious even under the Nazi regime. When revolutionary governments in Prussia and Saxony ended compulsory religious instruction in schools in the fall of 1918, implementing long-standing leftist demands, conservative parents and politicians, Catholics in particular, were alarmed. Although the new Weimar constitution, a compromise between Socialists, Liberals, and Catholics, defined religious instruction again as a regular subject in 1919, Catholics remained wary and blocked legislation that was to turn confessional elementary schools into common schools where Catholics, Protestants, and children of other faiths would have learned side by side, thus preserving the status quo.[12] Almost all Catholic parents in the Ruhr area city of Herne kept their children out of school for one and a half months in June and July 1920 to force the removal of teachers who refused to teach religion (as was their constitutional right). The parents scored only a semi-victory, as the teachers were assigned to special classes with children from non-religious parents in the same school, but they—and the Association of Catholic Parents, a lobby group close to the Catholic Center Party, the organizer of the strike—had shown their power. Similar actions in other cities followed.[13] Parents who belonged to the "Free Thinkers", a comparatively small movement of agnostics closely aligned with the Social Democrats, also resorted to school strikes to have their children taught in classes without any religious instruction.[14] These "culture wars" mobilized parents. The Weimar Republic acknowledged parents' right to educate their children as a "natural right" in its constitution, in contrast to the German monarchies before (but never defined what that meant vis-à-vis the rights of the state). Engaged parents could now claim both this right and their new rights as citizens of a democracy. However, given the deep political cleavages of the Weimar period, these parents remained closely linked to political parties and focused on overarching ideological issues.

Newly established parents' advisory councils suffered both from this political polarization and from a lack of power. German states kept their competencies very limited. School education remained firmly in the hands of state administrations, as moderates feared too much influence by either conservative Catholics or radical leftists, and teachers were opposed to undue interference by non-experts. In Prussia, parents' councils were to foster and deepen the relationship between family and school—a task very similar to that of the school boards prior to 1918—but they were neither allowed to organize beyond the level of individual schools nor to hold meetings without the approval of principal and teachers, nor were their decisions binding on principal and teachers. As they were elected on the basis of a system of proportional representation—a concept that secured minority rights and was therefore dear to Social Democrats as well as to Catholics—party politics was unavoidably brought into the councils.[15] Hamstrung by the polarization between left and right and by their lack of real power, parents' councils of the 1920s and early 1930s failed to become meaningful institutions. This made it easy for the Nazi regime to effectively shut them down after 1933 by replacing elected councils with advisory bodies chaired by principals, who also appointed their members.[16] Parents were not completely silenced: protests by staunch Catholics flared up when the regime abolished confessional schools at the end of the 1930s. However, their objections did not meet with success.[17]

New Beginnings: The Debate over Parents' Rights in West Germany after 1945

The two German states that emerged after 1945 reestablished parents' formal participation in the school system. As West and East German governments continued the German tradition of keeping school education under strict state control, in neither case did parents gain decisive influence, except in the West German state of Hesse. The ideological premises on which the new bodies were built, however, diverged enormously and resulted in substantial differences in real parental power in school matters, rendering it rather marginal in East Germany.

While the first East German constitution of 1949 acknowledged a "natural right" of parents to educate their children, this right was bound by precisely defined goals, including the rearing of "state-conscious personalities" (*staatsbewusste Persönlichkeiten*) in the emerging socialist community. Parents' councils on the class and the school level were established from 1951 on, but their clearly defined goal was to help mobilize parents' support for the measures of the school administration.[18] In contrast, the West German constitution of 1949, the Basic Law, defined educational policy as a responsibility of the individual states and left the basic tension between state and parental rights unresolved. While it again acknowledged parents' right to educate their children as their "natural right" and their most important duty in Article 6, it stipulated in Article 7 that the state acted as supervisor of the educational system, repeating verbatim a clause in the Weimar constitution.[19] As had been the case after 1918, public debate about parental rights in educational matters initially centered on confessional issues. In states with Catholic majorities, in particular Bavaria and North Rhine-Westphalia, governments led by the CDU, a successor party to the former Catholic Center Party, reestablished the Catholic and Protestant local schools that had been turned into religiously neutral institutions under the Nazi regime.[20] Some voices in the North Rhine-Westphalian CDU even called for handing control of the school system over to a new State Chamber of Education (Landesbildungskammer) in which, in addition to parents, teachers and the Catholic Church would have had decisive influence. The concept met with fierce resistance, in particular from the oppositional SPD and the center-left teachers' union GEW, and was then abandoned.[21] Again the debate over parental rights seemed to have fallen prey to the polarization between conservative Christians and modernists.

Bonn was not Weimar, however. As had already become clear in the early 1950s, to the surprise of conservative lawmakers and the leadership of the Catholic Church, parents were not overly enthusiastic about the reconfessionalization of the public school systems. A poll commissioned by the archdiocese of Cologne in October 1952 found that while only 26 percent of all West German parents called for confessional elementary schools, 65 percent preferred nonconfessional ones. Even among Catholics who regularly went to church, only a relative majority—47 percent—wanted their children taught in explicitly Catholic schools. Thus it was not surprising that in confessionally mixed regions—and there were now quite a few, due to the many expellees and refugees from the East—few parents made use of their right to demand their own confessional schools. On the contrary, demands that many small elementary schools in rural areas be replaced with larger and more sophisticated ones in central locations, which then would automatically shed their confessional character, gained ground among parents from the late 1950s on and even led to a successful plebiscite in the otherwise conservative Bavaria in the mid 1960s.[22] Hence, the leadership of the Catholic Church as well as their followers in the CDU (and its Bavarian partner, the CSU) had in fact attempted to instrumentalize parents' rights when undertaking the reestablishment of the confessional school system in the early 1950s. Increased contacts with members of the other confession and closer links between rural areas and the cities, however, modernized parents' attitudes and substantially curtailed church influence. As of the early 1960s, parental rights were no longer understood primarily as confessional rights.

They were also strengthened in general by the concept of "natural law," which exerted profound influence on West German legal thinking in the 1950s.[23] This concept, holding that certain individual rights were inalienable and had to form the basis for any man-made law, was convincing and helpful in denouncing laws of the Nazi regime as travesties of genuine laws, in bringing Nazi perpetrators to justice, and in distancing the fledgling West German democracy from the Nazi past as well as from the totalitarian Soviet bloc. It was less convincing in matters of gender and family, as it allowed diverging interpretations. Conservative Catholics preferred a polarized interpretation of gender roles and family hierarchies, which gave a boost to the reconstituted patriarchalism of the 1950s.[24] As children's rights, however, also could be seen as "natural," a conflict between their natural rights and that of the parents was conceivable and possibly to be determined by the state.[25] Neither lawmakers nor courts were able to draw a clear boundary between the rights of the state and that of the parents, but legal experts agreed that parents' rights were basic rights and on an equal footing with those of the state in educational matters.[26] Because the status of parents' constitutional rights was bolstered by the "natural law" theory, school authorities and teachers found themselves rather on the defensive when conflicts with parents arose, for example about pupils' activities after school.[27]

Another factor strengthening parents' position toward the schools was that teachers now were more willing than their predecessors twenty-five years earlier to see school as a place where children were not only taught specific subjects but were also educated in a broad sense, in particular as future citizens of a democratic state. As neither parents nor school were able to bring this about alone, both had to cooperate closely.[28]

State governments reestablished parents' councils after 1945, either as joint *Schulpflegschaften* or as bodies representing parents alone. In contrast to the Weimar Republic, parents directly elected their representatives as individual candidates for only one class. In the case of Lower Saxony, for example, this body consisted of a chairperson, a deputy chair, and at least three more members. Class representatives then elected from their midst representatives for the whole school.[29] This made a politicization along Weimar lines rather unlikely. Until the early 1970s, with the exception of the city-states Hamburg and Bremen as well as Hesse, school laws did not set up parents' councils on a local or regional level. State governments were also reluctant to vest parents' councils with real power and largely confined them to giving advice and support in matters not directly related to teaching, such as the material conditions at their school and after-class activities.[30] In Hesse, however, where a grand coalition between a reformist CDU and the SPD took the crucial decisions in the second half of the 1940s, educational policy broke more radically with the past than in the other West German states. As part of this reformist course, parents' involvement in school affairs was enshrined in the state constitution and spelled out in a 1958 law that established parents' councils in addition to the class and school on the regional and state level and provided the state council with veto power on important issues of school policy, such as curriculum guidelines and the introduction of comprehensive high schools.[31]

All in all, conditions for parents to wield some power in school matters were better after 1945 in West Germany than they had ever been before in German history. No radical restructuring of the educational system took place, but the constitutional guarantee of parents' "natural right" and the absence of political polarization in the newly established parents' councils, as well as Hesse's far reaching regulations, strengthened parents' position vis-à-vis the state.

An Active Minority: Parents' Participation in the 1950s

How did parents use their rights in the 1950s? Parents' councils got off to a mixed start. Teachers often perceived the new institutions as sources of unwanted interference in their work and tried to discourage them from becoming too active. Parents were not always sufficiently informed about the councils. Some saw no need for a council as long as "their" school operated without serious problems, or deemed it not worth their while to participate in an institution that had little real power. This was especially true of parents in the countryside. As late as 1964, the Catholic priest of a Franconian village complained that interest in the council was waning because the district school administration was paring back the council's right to determine the start of the summer and fall break, an important issue to the local farmers who needed their children to help them with the harvest. If this trend were to continue, the priest warned, "Our modest exercise in democracy will be stifled by administrative fiat."[32]

Administrative action—or its absence—did, however, cause many councils to become active in the 1950s and early 1960s. One key issue was dissatisfaction with the material conditions under which schools operated—most often an unhealthy environment or the lack of space, as we saw in the case of Roetgen. Other issues that caused councils to send sharply worded protest notes to the authorities and sometimes even to threaten to keep children at home until their position prevailed (what they called a "strike") included the appointment of a new principal whom parents did not regard as qualified, classes that were too large, an insufficient number of teachers, and safety problems on the way to and from school. These were common, not isolated incidents; the protests did not always achieve their goals but they at least forced the school authorities to take notice and react.[33] While the parents who organized these protests may have sympathized with parties on both sides of the center, their actions probably weakened rather than strengthened authoritarian views their children might have held.

The same tentative conclusion suggests itself with respect to another major issue in school affairs in the 1950s that caused parents to get involved, both through organizations and individually: corporal punishment. Following the defeat of the Nazi regime, most new state governments had resumed the line their predecessors, inspired by reform pedagogy, had taken during the Weimar Republic: they wanted corporal punishment to be administered by teachers only as a means of last resort and to be limited to the rare cases of a student's brutal or extremely insolent behavior. Only two states, Hesse and West Berlin, went a step further and banned the practice completely. Both positions, the reformist and the radical, met with stubborn opposition from teachers, who regarded wielding the cane or slapping pupils in the face as their customary right. More often than not, they found understanding judges if they were brought to trial and had not inflicted serious injury on the pupil in question.

Parents in general were more in favor of corporal punishment than against it. Of all parents polled in Hamburg in 1949, 52 percent wanted to keep the practice in the classroom, 43 percent were against it, and only 18 percent rejected it at home as well. In 1965, according to an Allensbach poll, only 16 percent of those questioned in West Germany were still unequivocally against corporal punishment, while almost 50 percent saw it as a means of last resort and a third as a normal educational practice.[34] The majority was clear but its margin not overwhelming. Even in generally conservative Bavaria, consent was not universal: when parents were asked to vote on the issue (with signed ballots) by the minister of education in 1947, 60 percent of all Bavarian parents wanted to allow corporal punishment in the classroom, whereas in (largely Protestant) Upper and Middle Franconia, particularly in Nuremberg and other cities, a majority were opposed to it.[35]

It seems that support of the practice was more pronounced in rural than in urban areas, and it therefore came as no surprise that its ban by the Hessian government led parents' councils in the countryside to petition the minister to reconsider. Not only were they not allowed to transfer their parental power to punish to the teacher, the council of Stockdorf wrote, they were also not allowed to heed the Bible, in which God said that he who loved his son would punish him. The parents of Schaafheim saw their personal freedom infringed by the minister's decree.[36] However, parents who opposed granting teachers the right to corporal punishment or who felt that they had meted it out inappropriately did not hesitate to make their voices heard. In North Rhine-Westphalia alone, sixty-seven teachers were brought to trial for such offenses in the 1950s.[37] Mothers confronted teachers who had wielded the cane or slapped their children in the school and filed suit against them. In a case in 1953, parents sent protests about an abusive teacher to the local school inspector, who reprimanded the teacher—but to no avail. The press was then informed and, led by the national tabloid BILD, put so much pressure on school authorities that the teacher was punished by a heavy fine and transferred to another school, where it appears he behaved himself.[38]

There is no question that protests and actions such as these did not fundamentally alter the conservative character of education in the 1950s and early 1960s. They did, however, demonstrate that authority could be legitimately criticized and held accountable, and thus they contributed to the gradual liberalization of education that had its breakthrough in the late 1960s. While in 1951 only 28 percent of parents saw "self-reliance and exerting one's free will" as educational goals, 45 percent did so in 1969. Over the same period, the appreciation of "obedience and subservience" dropped from 25 percent to 19 percent.[39]

The Appeal and the Limits of "Democratization" in the 1960s and 1970s

Parents' participation in school matters became a prominent issue in public debates and legislation in the late 1960s and continued to trigger conflicts with political overtones throughout the 1970s. While parents' formal power in the school system did not increase substantially, their participation in parents' councils and their involvement through independent parent associations and as individuals became well-established features of West German democracy.

In the early 1960s, West German experts grew alarmed by an emerging "educational catastrophe" (*Bildungskatastrophe*): a lack of properly qualified young people, with potentially devastating consequences for West Germany's ability to meet the challenges of modern industrial society. Experts pointed in particular to neglected talent reserves among blue-collar workers and girls, not least in the countryside. Subsequently state governments, regardless of party affiliation, oversaw a massive expansion of public education from the mid 1960s on.[40] Preserving West Germany's scientific and technological competency was not the only rationale for the growth, however. Academic experts and politicians of all stripes now also agreed that a good education was the precondition for exerting one's rights as citizen in a democracy. Young people were not only to be enabled to master complex jobs but also to voice their own opinions, criticize social and political conditions, and make suggestions about how to change them. The term "emancipation" epitomized this line of reasoning, specifically among reformers on the left.[41] Prominent sociologist and liberal political thinker Ralf Dahrendorf succinctly summed up the social and the political connotations of the new concept of public education by noting that "Bildung ist Bürgerrecht"—obtaining a good education was every citizen's right.[42]

As this new approach triggered an unfailing public interest in education from the mid 1960s on, the traditional concept of school as an institution where administrators controlled the system unchecked and teachers had free rein in the classroom came under attack. A number of court rulings expanded the realm of decisions by school administrations that could become subject to legal challenges. A key decision was a ruling by the Federal Constitutional Court in 1972 that allowed measures such as suspension and expulsion to be reviewed in court. It also meant that students were now regarded as junior citizens with basic constitutional rights that could only be curtailed on the basis of well-defined legal procedures. The new approach taken by the courts forced a new body of complex legal rules upon schools and their administrations and made teachers more aware of the power parents (and students themselves) were able to wield.[43]

A second factor that gave a boost to parents' involvement in school matters was the political mobilization of the later 1960s and one of its key outcomes, the formation of a coalition between the leftist Social Democrats and the center-left Liberal Democrats in 1969 under Chancellor Willy Brandt. Pledging in his inaugural address that his government would "dare to be more democratic," he pointedly summarized what many on the political left thought to be a necessary next step in West Germany's evolution into a real democracy. Parliaments should not be the only site of democratic decision-making. Unless institutions in society such as companies and schools were to adopt similar forms of participation and co-determination by citizens, democracy itself would fail to take firm root and ultimately descend to a mere form devoid of substance.[44] Conservatives countered that a comprehensive democratization of society could give rise to new totalitarian utopias, cause an overall radicalization, and thus maybe ultimately destroy the basic compromises on which democracy was founded. Therefore, they argued, democratic decision-making needed to remain confined to political institutions.[45] At the same time, however, parents' participation in school matters, especially in the state of Hesse, seemed a convenient instrument to thwart leftist school reforms.

Not surprisingly, the question of how the concept of "democratization" should be applied to schools triggered a lively discussion in the early 1970s. That students, parents, and also teachers should be granted more influence on school matters elicited general approval, but its range and its potential consequences were controversial issues, not least when it came to parents. Legal scholar and educationist Lutz Dietze, one of the most pronounced advocates of a greatly expanded institutionalized influence of parents, marshaled arguments from organizational sociology, pedagogy, and the theory of democracy to bolster his case. Schools would become more efficient if parents, students, and teachers were able to voice their opinions on problems and concepts in institutionalized bodies, he argued. Students learned better when directly involved in the organization of instruction; school education moreover had an obligation to help them develop their own personality, which also would enable them to become citizens of a democracy. For this to happen, participation in decision-making about school matters was essential. Denying a conflict of interest between parents and their children, Dietze contended that parental rights were to be defined as the right and duty to protect their children's right to develop their own personality. Therefore, parents' participation in school matters was central, in particular in the case of the students in lower grades. Given their importance, parental rights had no clear boundaries, affecting every aspect of school life. Dietze admitted that at present it was mainly middle-class parents who were actively involved in school affairs. If public schools were to change and to become training grounds for democracy, however, lower-class parents in particular had to get involved. For this to happen, Dietze demanded that they be brought into close contact with the schools and be well informed about school life and their rights.[46]

Other advocates of an expansion of institutionalized parental participation warned that this would not be an easy task. One key argument centered on the heterogeneity of parents' interests. Altogether, these interests reflected the heterogeneity of society at large and resembled those of consumers, which also were difficult to organize. This indicated that expanding the influence of parents' councils would not necessarily raise involvement in them. Rather, involvement would increase primarily in the event of drastic social changes or as a result of parents' groups aligning with political parties—which would be easier for parents' voluntary associations than for institutionalized participatory bodies.[47]

Proponents of increased participation of parents pointed to another problem that was even more difficult to overcome. In order to enable students to master the challenges of modern industrial society, school instruction had to become more science-oriented.[48] Its prerequisite was a more scientific teacher training. As pedagogy turned from a form of training based on practical expertise and skills into a scientific discipline itself, however, the language of curricula and classroom instruction became more abstract, presenting parents who had not attended a *Gymnasium* or studied at a university with new obstacles to getting involved. Ensuring the functionality of an increasingly science-oriented institution while granting important influence over it to the parents of its students seemed a difficult task. The growing size and complexity of schools, in conjunction with their distance from home, compounded the problem.[49]

In a ruling of December 1972, the so-called Förderstufenurteil, the West German Constitutional Court, provided a guideline for settling conflicts between parental and state rights in matters of school education. The Hessian government had extended common schooling in all public schools to grades 5 and 6; during these two years, students should be closely observed and given individual support to help their parents choose the appropriate track of secondary schooling. Previously (and as in the other West German states), in many school districts pupils went their separate ways as early as the fifth grade. Conservative middle-class parents regarded the new extension of common schooling as a measure that put their children at a disadvantage and took legal action. The Constitutional Court refused to place state rights and parental rights in a hierarchical order. State and parents, the court declared, had a "joint educational task" and therefore had to cooperate "in a meaningful way." This authoritatively (up to the present day) defined the relationship between the rights of both sides. However, the court left no doubt that the state had the right, according to Article 7, 1 of the Basic Law, to determine not only the organization of the school system but also the goals of classroom instruction and its curricula. Hence, Hesse was free to introduce a *Förderstufe* in all school districts. However, as parents had the right, according to Article 7, 4 of the Basic Law, to send their children to a school of their choice, the court held that their rights were infringed if the state did not allow their children to attend a school without a *Förderstufe*, possibly in a district outside of Hesse, or a private school.[50]

The ruling left open the question of how the "meaningful cooperation" between state and parents in school matters should be organized in detail and thus did not prohibit Hesse or any other West German *Land* from granting parents substantially more rights in school affairs. But it made it not very likely. In the following years, all the states (except Bavaria and North Rhine-Westphalia) that did not yet have parental advisory councils on the local and regional levels revised their legislation to set them up. The city-state of Hamburg, governed by Social Democrats, went a small step further by creating a new body, the *Schulkonferenz*, that was to elect the principal and the deputy principal for a tenure of ten years and in which representatives of teachers, parents, and students were each granted a third of the seats.[51] However, in 1973 when the West German *Bildungskommission*, an advisory body of education experts, submitted far-reaching proposals for decentralizing the school system, granting teachers together with parents and students the right to manage individual schools and reducing state control to mere judicial oversight, state governments rejected them out of hand.[52]

Several factors now blocked a further extension of parents' formal rights in school matters. Path-dependency and "conservatism due to complexity," as German sociologist Niklas Luhmann put it,[53] proved major obstacles, particularly as pragmatism replaced reform enthusiasm in the political climate following the first oil crisis of 1973. State school administrations, large hierarchical apparatuses under the control of state ministries, were not eager to share power and feared the bureaucratic turmoil that would result from a decentralization of the system.[54] While arguments such as these appealed chiefly to conservatives, leftist reformers also grew receptive as they became increasingly concerned that conservative parents would use their participatory powers to block changes in the curriculum and the structure of the school system.

Hesse, where parents enjoyed wide-ranging participatory rights, not least through the *Landeselternbeirat* on the state level, exemplified the reformers' conundrum. In late 1968, Hesse's concept of wide-ranging parental participation still seemed to be a model for other reform-oriented states. As Hildegard Hamm-Brücher, a leading educational reformer in the center-left Free Democratic Party and at the time state secretary in the Hessian Ministry of Education, stated in a letter to the deputy chairman of her party in the state of Lower Saxony, overall parents' participation had been a success. On the state level, the *Landeselternbeirat* had made important contributions to rendering ministerial decrees more accessible to ordinary citizens and thus to gaining the support of parents for the planned measures. Parental participation could jeopardize reform legislation, however, Hamm-Brücher noted, as shown by the *Landeselternbeirat's* veto on the introduction of a mandatory *Förderstufe* and comprehensive high schools.[55] Overruling such a veto was not impossible, but this could only happen after failed negotiations with the *Landeselternbeirat* and required a cabinet decision or parliamentary legislation; it thus incurred political costs that might be dangerously high.

This became painfully obvious when a draft proposal of new guidelines for teaching social studies in Hessian schools was published in 1972. Its explicit focus on social conflict and "emancipation" triggered massive resistance among conservatives. Supported by the Hessian Parents' Association, an unabashedly conservative lobby group, the *Landeselternbeirat* voiced its resistance against the government proposal. Heated public discussions abated somewhat after Education Minister von Friedeburg, an advocate of drastic reforms, stepped down and the recommendations of a newly established expert committee took the radical edge off the guidelines.[56] But the issue lingered and, along with the question of *Förderstufe* and comprehensive high schools, remained a bone of contention that helped solidify conservative control of the *Landeselternbeirat* far into the 1980s.

This one-sidedness and its concomitant instrumentalization for political ends reached a peak when, under a chairman who was also a leading member of the Hessian Parents' Association and with the support of the main conservative opposition party, the CDU, the *Landeselternbeirat* attempted in 1976 to gain de facto veto power in all matters of educational policy. New arbitration bodies comprising members of the *Landeselternbeirat* and the parliament were to make a decision if the minister and the parents' council were unable to reach an agreement on decrees and bills. The minister saw this as a breach of the constitution and adamantly refused to consider such a proposal.[57] However, when the *Landeselternbeirat* went to court to overturn a new state law that stipulated comprehensive high schools as the only form of high schools, it again scored a success, as the Hessian State Court decided in 1981, along the same lines as its West German counterpart in 1972, that parents must have the right to choose between different forms of high schools for their children.[58]

Parents' Pragmatism in the 1970s

As these debates show, political tensions in matters of educational policy could run high even in a period when the heated general discussions about reforms to make West Germany a more democratic country had largely died down. Retaining the opportunity to send their children to a fairly selective traditional high school remained a key political issue for conservative middle-class parents.[59] On the whole, however, conflicts about school education reform were now less acrimonious and less directly influenced by political parties than in the Weimar Republic. Together with continuing concerns about the material conditions of schools and sufficient qualified personnel, they helped maintain parents' involvement in school affairs at the school and local level.

When a small group of radical young teachers awarded good grades to children from working-class families regardless of their performance and used very explicit language in sex education classes at a newly established comprehensive school in a lower middle-class neighborhood in Frankfurt, a majority of teachers and parents protested vigorously, the latter also threatening to keep their children at home if the teachers were not recalled. The turmoil even caught the attention of the press nationwide and forced the minister to close down the school for a while before he finally gave in to the demands of the protesters.[60]

The parents' advisory council of one of the first full-fledged comprehensive high schools in Hesse, located in its capital Wiesbaden, generally aimed to soften the radicalism that teachers and the principal sometimes brought to this reform experiment, yet it also supported certain students' demands. Parents' representatives firmly objected to allowing students to address their teachers on a first-name basis, insisting on emphasizing the teachers' responsibility for maintaining discipline when rules and regulations for the school were drafted. They also objected when students declared an unlimited strike and left the school premises to demonstrate in front of the ministry, demanding a sufficient number of teachers, compensation for the costs of commuting and books, and introduction of comprehensive high schools all over Hesse. Time and again throughout the 1970s, however, lack of teachers and canceled classes triggered similar complaints by parents and their councils.

Another topic of great importance to these Wiesbaden parents was securing the presence of a sufficient number of school psychologists, given the complexitiy of social relationships in a comprehensive school. When the local school administration announced plans to remove the one school psychologist in the school to a central location in Wiesbaden where he could also serve other schools, the parents' council, emphatically claiming parental rights, launched a passionate complaint.[61] Meanwhile, even in these reform-oriented schools parents were rather conservative in terms of the content and style of instruction, and they did not hesitate to make their views known. They were no less engaged when they found conditions in their schools wanting and explicitly referred to their rights. The combination of shrinking state budgets and ongoing reforms of the school system, in Hesse and elsewhere, served as an incentive for continuous parental involvement in a "normal" democratic fashion.

Several empirical studies conducted during the 1970s in various parts of West Germany indicated that parents were interested in close cooperation with the schools of their children. This cooperation was defined in a clearly focused way, with no significant differences between the different tracks of secondary education. What parents wanted most was a school that imparted to students the knowledge and skills necessary to obtain a qualified job and possibly climb up the social ladder. While parents regarded their relationship with the school and the teachers generally as good, they wanted to be better informed about job prospects for their children and saw the introduction of new teaching methods and subjects as problems preventing them from giving their children more support at home. In contrast with this concern, expansion of the institutionalized influence of parents on school matters appeared less important. Parents saw existing forms of participation as sufficient but not as used as widely as possible. At the same time, only between 10 and 30 percent were willing to be actively engaged in parents' councils.[62] Members of parents' councils themselves, though they wanted closer contact with the parents they represented, were not eager to interfere with classroom instruction but strove to improve the material conditions of their school.[63]

Fears that parents would abuse increased participatory rights to push political agendas or unduly interfere with the teachers' work seemed unfounded at the end of the 1970s. Pragmatism prevailed. The downside was a separation of labor that now assigned the task of conveying knowledge to the school, whereas imparting norms and values was clearly the parents' domain.[64] While school was no longer an authoritarian institution that disregarded students' as well as parents' rights, it had become a bureaucratic institution that served the circumscribed function of allocating chances in a complex job market. Parents' participation in school matters had become the norm for the citizens of West German, even though it failed to generate much enthusiasm. Experts pointed to the pedagogical chances that a closer cooperation between parents and teachers would provide but were not sure how to achieve it.[65] It took an increasing awareness of social disintegration and school violence in the 1990s to trigger a new debate about the function of public education and parents' role in it.

Notes

1. See the reports, minutes, and letters in Hauptstaatsarchiv (HStA) Düsseldorf, Reg. Aachen, BR 1038/940, fol. 218–247, the quote 219, Amtsverwaltung Roetgen to Regierungspräsident, 24 June 1953 (translation by the author).

2. Ibid., fol. 233, Schulpflegschaft Roetgen to Regierungspräsident, 29 June 1953 (translation by the author).

3. *Aachener Nachrichten,* edition for Eifel region, 2 July 1953 (translation by the author).

4. Robert G. Moeller, *Protecting Motherhood: Women and the Family in the Politics of Postwar West Germany* (Berkeley, 1993); Robert G. Moeller, "Reconstructing the Family in Reconstructing Germany: Women and Social Policy in the Federal Republic, 1949–1955," in *West Germany under Construction: Politics, Society, and Culture in the Adenauer Era,* ed. Robert G. Moeller (Ann Arbor, 1997), 109–133. Cf. Pat Thane, "Family Life and 'Normality' in Postwar British Culture," in *Life After Death: Approaches to a Cultural and Social History of Europe during the 1940s and 1950s,* ed. Richard Bessel and Dirk Schumann (New York, 2003), 193–210; Elaine Tyler May, *Homeward Bound: American Families in the Cold War Era,* rev. and updated ed. (New York, 1999).

5. Edward Ross Dickinson, *The Politics of German Child Welfare from the Empire to the Federal Republic* (Cambridge, MA, 1996), 244–285; Christine von Oertzen, *The Pleasure of a Surplus Income: Part-Time Work, Gender Politics, and Social Change in West Germany, 1955–1969,* trans. Pamela Selwyn (New York, 2007); Till van Rahden, "Demokratie und väterliche Autorität: Das Karlsruher 'Stichentscheid': Urteil in der politischen Kultur der frühen Bundesrepublik," *Zeithistorische Forschungen* 2, no. 2 (2005): 160–179, and his contribution to this volume.

6. Ulrich Herbert, "Liberalisierung als Lernprozeß: Die Bundesrepublik in der deutschen Geschichte—eine Skizze," in *Wandlungsprozesse in Westdeutschland: Belastung, Integration, Liberalisierung 1945–1980,* ed. Ulrich Herbert (Göttingen, 2002), 7–49.

7. Peter N. Stearns, *Anxious Parents: A History of Modern Childrearing in America* (New York, 2003).

8. Beate Rosenzweig, *Erziehung zur Demokratie? Amerikanische Besatzungs- und Schulpolitik in Deutschland und Japan* (Stuttgart, 1998); James F. Tent, *Mission on the Rhine: Reeducation and Denazification in American-Occupied Germany* (Chicago, 1982).

9. This is the key point also made by Charles A. Israel and Tara Zahra in their contributions to this volume.

10. Karl Josef Kreuzer, "Das Verhältnis von Elternhaus und Schule: unter besonderer Berücksichtigung einer Mitwirkung der Eltern in der Schule: eine historische Strukturanalyse" (PhD diss., University of Essen, 1977), 21–55, 109–156, 184–189, 207–225.

11. Marjorie Lamberti, *State, Society, and the Elementary School in Imperial Germany* (New York, 1989), 139–147.

12. Marjorie Lamberti, *The Politics of Education: Teachers and School Reform in Weimar Germany* (New York, 2002), 45, 60–64.

13. Luise Wagner-Winterhager, *Schule und Eltern in der Weimarer Republik: Untersuchungen zur Wirksamkeit der Elternbeiräte in Preußen und der Elternräte in Hamburg, 1918–1922* (Weinheim, 1979), 219–31.

14. Examples from the Ruhr area in Wagner-Winterhager, *Schule*, 200–214.

15. Wagner-Winterhager, *Schule*, 110–126, 245–265; Lamberti, *Politics*, 69–74.

16. Dieter Mohrhart, *Elternmitwirkung in der Bundesrepublik Deutschland: ein Beitrag zur politisch-historischen und pädagogischen Diskussion* (Frankfurt a. M., 1979), 28.

17. See, e.g., the correspondence in HStA Düsseldorf, BR 1004/1193.

18. Lutz R. Reuter, "Partizipation im Schulwesen," in *Handbuch der deutschen Bildungsgeschichte, vol VI: 1945 bis zur Gegenwart. Zweiter Teilband, Deutsche Demokratische Republik und neue Bundesländer*, ed. Christopher Führ and Carl-Ludwig Furck (Munich, 1998), 228–233; Friedrich W. Busch, "Deutsche Demokratische Republik," in *Elternhaus und Schule: Kooperation ohne Erfolg?* ed. Klaus Schleicher (Düsseldorf, 1972), 56–79; Eberhard Mannschatz, *Einführung in die sozialistische Familienerziehung* (East Berlin, 1971).

19. Reuter, "Partizipation," 36–37.

20. Dorothee Buchhaas, *Gesetzgebung im Wiederaufbau: Schulgesetz in Nordrhein-Westfalen und Betriebsverfassungsgesetz. Eine vergleichende Untersuchung zum Einfluss von Parteien, Kirchen und Verbänden in Land und Bund 1945–1952* (Düsseldorf, 1985).

21. Buchhaas, *Gesetzgebung*, 122–124; Maria Meyer-Sevenich, *Elternrecht und Kindesrecht* (Frankfurt, 1954), 94f..

22. Buchhaas, *Gesetzgebung*, 301; Winfried Müller, Ingo Schröder, and Markus Mößlang, "'Vor uns liegt ein Bildungszeitalter': Umbau und Expansion—das bayerische Bildungssystem 1950 bis 1975," in *Bayern im Bund, vol. 1: Die Erschließung des Landes 1949–1973*, ed. Thomas Schlemmer and Hans Woller (Munich, 2001), 273–355, here 277–290.

23. Hermann Weinkauff, "Der Naturrechtsgedanke in der Rechtsprechung des Bundesgerichtshofes," *Neue Juristische Wochenschrift* 13 (1960): 1689–1696.

24. Gisela Baumgarte, *Das Elternrecht im Bonner Grundgesetz* (Cologne, 1966).

25. Klaus Liske, *Elternrecht und staatliches Schulerziehungsrecht* (Münster, 1966).

26. Liske, *Elternrecht*, 97; Hans Heckel, *Schulrechtskunde: Ein Handbuch für Lehrer, Eltern und Schulverwaltung—Ein Studienbuch für die Lehrerbildung* (Neuwied, 1957), 257–258.

27. Mentioned by Baumgarte, *Elternrecht*, 103.

28. Heckel, *Schulrechtskunde*, 257, 304–305, 321–322.

29. Rüdiger Meyenberg, *Elternmitbestimmung in Niedersachsen* (Neuwied, 1980), 32–40.

30. See the overview of regulations in individual states in Liske, *Elternrecht*, 82–93. For subsequent changes and the broadening of the scope of responsibilities, especially in Berlin and the Saarland, see Mohrhart, *Elternmitwirkung*, 45–48.

31. Christoph Führ, "Schulpolitik in Hessen 1945–1994," in *Hessen: Gesellschaft und Politik*, ed. Bernd Heidenreich (Stuttgart, 1995), 157–177; Dieter J. Klein, *Elternmitbestimmung in Hessen* (Neuwied, 1980). As in the other states, parents directly elected their representatives only at the class level.

32. Bayerisches Hauptstaatsarchiv (BayHStA) MK 61243, Pastor Krug to Ministry of Education, 14 October 1964 (my translation), see also the reports and correspondence in BayHStA MK 61242 and 61243; HStA Düsseldorf, BR 1038/940, fol. 80–150; Hessisches Hauptstaatsarchiv Wiesbaden (HHStAW) Abt. 504 Nr. 3362, working group of parents' councils in Wetzlar to education minister, 10 October 1949.

33. Examples in HStA Düsseldorf, NW 244-92; HHStAW Abt. 504 Nr. 851; HHStAW Abt. 504 Nr. 978a; HHStAW Abt. 504 Nr. 978b; HStA Düsseldorf, BR 1038/941.

34. "Schulreform? Ja! Aber wie?," *Hamburger Allgemeine*, 28 January 1949; Horst Petri and Matthias Lauterbach, *Gewalt in der Erziehung: Plädoyer zur Abschaffung der Prügelstrafe. Analysen und Argumente* (Frankfurt, 1975), 124. Similar figures for 1951 Darmstadt in Gerhard Baumert, *Jugend der Nachkriegszeit: Lebensverhältnisse und Reaktionsweisen* (Darmstadt, 1952), 87–88.

35. BayHStA MK 61940, report of 12 June 1947.

36. HHStA Wiesbaden Abt. 504 Nr. 3384a, parents' council Stockdorf to Minister, 6 January 1950; parents' council Schaafheim to Minister, 9 June 1950.

37. Peter Leifert, "Das Züchtigungsrecht des Lehrers (zugleich eine kriminologische Untersuchung" (Diss. Jur., University of Münster, 1960).

38. HStA Düsseldorf, Gerichte Rep. 231 Nr. 354 and 390; HStA Düsseldorf NW 20-108, fol. 76–77, 111–118. More on this issue in Dirk Schumann, "Legislation and Liberalisation: The Debate about Corporal Punishment in Schools in Postwar West Germany, 1945–1975," *German History* 25 (2007): 192–218.

39. Mohrhart, *Elternmitwirkung,* 121–125. The German terms are "Selbständigkeit und freier Wille" and "Gehorsam und Unterordnung."

40. Carl-Ludwig Furck, "Allgemeinbildende Schulen: 1. Entwicklungstendenzen und Rahmenbedingungen," in Führ and Furck, *Handbuch,* 245–260, here 250–251.

41. Moritz Scheibe, "Auf der Suche nach der demokratischen Gesellschaft," in Herbert, *Wandlungsprozesse,* 245–277. A good example is Heinrich Roth, *Autoritär oder demokratisch erziehen?* (Munich, 1965).

42. Ralf Dahrendorf, *Bildung ist Bürgerrecht: Plädoyer für eine aktive Bildungspolitik* (Hamburg, 1965).

43. Summarized by Torsten Gass-Bolm, "Das Ende der Schulzucht," in Herbert, *Wandlungsprozesse,* 436–466, here 447–451, 462–464. Cf. Hans Heckel, *Schulrechtskunde,* 284. For a similar development in the US see David B. Tyack and Larry Cuban, *Tinkering Toward Utopia: A Century of Public School Reform* (Cambridge, MA, 1995), 18–19.

44. Gabriele Metzler, "Der lange Weg zur sozialliberalen Politik: Politische Semantik und demokratischer Aufbruch," in *Bürgersinn mit Weltgefühl: Politische Moral und solidarischer Protest in den sechziger und siebziger Jahren,* ed. Habbo Knoch (Göttingen, 2006), 157–180, in particular 169–176.

45. Scheibe, "Auf der Suche," 267–275.

46. Lutz Dietze, *Zur Mitbestimmung in der Schule: Welche verfassungsrechtlichen Anforderungen sind unter dem Aspekt der Mitbestimmung von Schülern, Lehrern und Eltern an eine demokratische Regelung des Schulwesens zu stellen? Gutachten im Auftrag des Gesamtelternbeirats der Stadt Mannheim* (Mainz, 1970). See also Lutz Dietze, "Chancen und Grenzen des Elternrechts," in *Elternmitsprache und Elternbildung,* ed. Klaus Schleicher (Düsseldorf, 1973), 120–143.

47. Andreas Fischer, "Funktionen von Elternvertretungen und Elternverbänden in der Verbandsdemokratie," in Schleicher, *Elternmitsprache,* 144–181, here 152–153.

48. Theodor Wilhelm, *Theorie der Schule: Hauptschule und Gymnasium im Zeitalter der Wissenschaften* (Stuttgart, 1969).

49. Mohrhart, *Elternmitwirkung,* 55–59.

50. Bundesverfassungsgericht (BVerfG) 34, 165, ruling of 6 December 1972. Cf. Mohrhart, *Elternmitwirkung,* 41.

51. Mohrhart, *Elternmitwirkung,* 37–39, 46f.; cf. Heckel, *Schulrechtskunde,* 93f. See Karl Neumann, "Elternmitwirkung aus der Sicht der Gesetzgebung der Bundesländer," in *Kooperation Elternhaus—Schule: Analysen und Alternativen auf dem Weg zur Schulgemeinde,* ed. Rudolf W. Keck (Bad Heilbrunn, 1979), 92–100, for an overview of state regulations and key fields of activity.

52. Mohrhart, *Elternmitwirkung,* 35–37; cf. Reuter, "Partizipation," 262; Furck, "Allgemeinbildende Schulen," 252–253.

53. Niklas Luhmann, "Komplexität und Demokratie," in *Politische Planung,* ed. Niklas Luhmann (Opladen, 1971), 35–45.

54. Herbert, "Liberalisierung," 14; Mohrhart, *Elternmitwirkung,* 39–40.

55. HHStA Wiesbaden Abt. 504 Nr. 4189, letter of 8 December 1968.

56. Führ, "Schulpolitik," 167–168.

57. See the coverage of the controversy in the press and an official statement by the ministry in HHStAW Abt. 504 Nr. 4193.

58. Staatsgerichtshof Hessen P.St. 880, ruling of 30 December 1981. See also Führ, "Schulpolitik," 168.

59. Klein, *Elternmitbestimmung,* 43. Sex education was another field in which conservative parents fought in and outside of the *Landeselternbeirat* to interpret parental rights very broadly. Cf. the exchange with the representatives of lay Catholics of the Limburg diocese in HHStAW Abt. 504 Nr. 4193.

60. HHStAW Abt. 504 Nr. 7451a and b; see in particular the insightful reports in *Frankfurter Rundschau* 78, 2 April 1973, 20 and *Süddeutsche Zeitung* 81, 6 April 1973, 10.

61. See the numerous minutes and memos in HHStAW Abt. 814/1 Nr. 64. Cf. HHStAW Abt. 504 Nr. 8695 for a case of parental "self-help" to find teachers for their school.

62. Hans-Dieter Göldner, *Elternmeinung, Elternwille und ihr Einfluss auf die Schule: Ergebnisse einer schriftlichen Befragung von Eltern in Bayern* (Munich, 1978); Institut für Lehrerfortbildung Mainz, ed., *Kooperation zwischen Schule und Eltern in der Hauptschule: Ergebnisse einer empirischen Untersuchung* (Mainz, 1981).

63. Fischer, *Funktionen,* 156–163; Mohrhart, *Elternmitwirkung,* 70–76.

64. Pointed out by Institut, *Kooperation,* 11–19. Cf. also Heckel, *Schulrechtskunde,* in particular 309 and 339.

65. Mohrhart, *Elternmitwirkung,* 77–78; cf. Keck, *Kooperation.*

Chapter 11

"SPECIAL RELATIONSHIPS"
The State, Social Workers, and Abused Children in the United States, 1950–1990

Lynne Curry

In February 1989 the United States Supreme Court issued an opinion in a case involving an abused child, a sad and disturbing story that had begun more than five years earlier in central Wisconsin. In *DeShaney v. Winnebago County Department of Social Services,* Chief Justice William H. Rehnquist, writing for a six-to-three majority, ruled that children do not enjoy a constitutional right to be protected from their parents' violence. When he was four years old, Joshua DeShaney had been severely beaten by his father and legal custodian, Randy DeShaney, leaving the little boy permanently brain damaged and partially paralyzed. Joshua and his mother (who had divorced Randy when Joshua was a toddler) sued the state of Wisconsin, claiming that over a period of over eighteen months, state social service workers had failed to protect the child by removing him from his father's violent home despite having knowledge that he was in danger. While the nation's high court acknowledged that the facts in the case were "undeniably tragic," the chief justice went on to assert that under the federal constitution, individual rights are protected from infringement due to actions taken by the state.[1] Since Joshua's beatings came not at the hands of the social workers themselves, but rather those of his father, a private actor, the state of Wisconsin could not be held liable for violating the boy's civil rights. Counsel for Joshua had argued that a "special relationship" existed between the child and Wisconsin through the boy's extensive involvement with the state's child protection services. Under the law, a "special relationship" imposed an affirmative duty on the part of states to take actions safeguarding citizens' national rights.[2] But the high court disagreed. While Wisconsin was free to amend its own child protection statutes

---

to require state action, the federal constitution afforded no protection to children victimized by their parents' violence.

The court's ruling shocked and angered many Americans. Protecting the nation's most vulnerable citizens seemed an urgent duty worthy of the highest priority. Newspaper editorials, professional journals, law reviews, and the public at large expressed dismay that both Wisconsin's child welfare apparatus and the nation's high court had failed outrageously in their obligations to Joshua. "Shame on you," one angry citizen wrote to the justices. "Shame on all of us for putting up with you." Another letter writer called the *DeShaney* opinion nothing less than "the most misguided and dangerous pronouncement of the court since *Dred Scott*" (a notorious 1857 decision that many scholars believe contributed to the outbreak of the American Civil War four years later).[3] While child abusers could be duly punished under the criminal law (Randy DeShaney served two years in prison under Wisconsin's felony child abuse statutes), many Americans wondered whether more could be done to prevent such tragedies from occurring in the first place.

The grim details of Joshua's case, as well as the public outcry over the court's opinion, reflected a wider societal unease about the role of the state in child welfare that pervaded the late twentieth-century US. Since the 1960s, a "rediscovery" of child abuse (following several decades of relative public inattention to the issue) had resulted in a flurry of new federal and state statutes requiring professionals working with children, such as teachers, day care providers, and doctors, to report their suspicions of abuse to child welfare authorities. Consequently the problem of child abuse, regardless of whether or not it was actually on the increase, nevertheless became much more visible—and thus more alarming—to the public. According to the National Center on Child Abuse and Neglect (a federal agency created in 1974), Joshua's injuries at the hands of adults in his home occurred during a period in which reported cases of child abuse doubled, reaching two million by 1986 and 2.25 million in 1987, the years when *DeShaney v. Winnebago County* was wending its way through the legal system. One child abuse expert estimated that in the 1980s more than one thousand children died each year in the United States as a result of physical maltreatment by their own parents.[4] Even in the small Midwestern city of Oshkosh, Wisconsin, Joshua was one of three severely abused children whose cases made local headlines in the spring of 1984; one involved a three-year-old girl who died as a result of the beatings she had received from her mother's boyfriend.[5]

The public responded to these terrible revelations with demands for new and more effective state and national child protective systems that empowered authorities to take action on behalf of endangered children. Significantly, the growth of child protection systems took place outside of the established realm of law enforcement.[6] In the 1980s Wisconsin, like most states, gave the power to determine whether children should be removed from their parents' homes to social workers rather than to police officers or other law enforcement agents. All reports of suspected child abuse, both voluntary and mandatory (those required by law of teachers or medical personnel, for example), were routed to the child protective case worker assigned to the family involved, who in turn made decisions about what, if any, actions should be taken.

But the rapid growth of these myriad policies and programs soon came into direct conflict with long-standing social values surrounding the sanctity of the private family and, for many Americans, signified the unwelcome intrusion of an ever-expanding welfare state.[7] These values were supported by a long legal tradition that vested parents—particularly fathers—with rights to their children, including the right to use their children's labor, transfer their guardianship to others, and employ physical punishment to discipline and control them. For centuries children had occupied a legal status closer to that of chattel, or personal property, than that of full-fledged citizens endowed with rights of their own. Courts had regarded state interference in the hierarchical relationship between parents and children as a threat to the larger social order. Such views still resonated in the late twentieth century.

Americans' ambivalence about the state's role in children's welfare was reflected in the "family preservation" model that had come to dominate the child protection field in the 1980s. Family preservation stressed the provision of a broad range of state-sponsored social welfare services to shore up the private family, thereby reducing the need to remove children from their parents' homes and place them in the foster care system, a bureaucratic labyrinth that critics regarded as hopelessly overburdened and indeed even harmful to the children who found themselves placed in its care. Under the family preservation paradigm, domestic violence resulted from families' lack of sufficient resources for providing a proper environment in which individual members could function adequately; economic and other stresses exacerbated tensions and thus the potential for violence in the home. Specially trained social workers, therefore, were to serve as intermediaries between private households considered to be "at risk" for family violence and the states' social welfare bureaucracies, which had been growing substantially since the 1950s.

While state child protection laws placed an enormous amount of responsibility for children's safety on social workers, the family preservation model required them to invest an extraordinary amount of time and attention toward the goal of keeping the troubled family intact, a job that necessitated a high degree of cooperation and trust from the families they supervised. The effectiveness of child protection services, therefore, relied on the case worker's professional judgment about when to switch roles—from one that was basically therapeutic and cooperative, working with the family to help them access social services and assuage their difficulties, to one that was fundamentally authoritative and punitive, judging parents to be unfit and removing children from their custody, temporarily or perhaps permanently. Only in the 1990s did the field of social work begin to address systematically the dilemma of child protective workers' dual roles as therapist and legal authority, in no small measure because of the national notoriety *DeShaney v. Winnebago County Department of Social Services* brought to the problem.

Joshua Enters the State Child Protection System

At the time of Joshua's last beating in March 1984, the DeShaney household was well known to the child protective workers in the Winnebago County Department of Social Services (DSS). Joshua was born in the state of Montana in 1979. His parents divorced, and Joshua's mother surrendered legal custody of the fourteen-month-old child to his father, Randy DeShaney. Randy took the boy to live in the small central Wisconsin town of Neenah, in the area where he had been raised and still maintained family ties. The child first came to the attention of DSS workers in January 1982. An attorney representing Randy's second wife, who was suing for divorce, reported that his client had expressed fears for Joshua's safety after she moved out of the couple's home. A child protective worker from DSS made a brief investigation but, finding no cause for further action, closed the case.

One year later, emergency room personnel at a Neenah hospital notified DSS of their suspicions that three-year-old Joshua, who had been brought in for stitches to a wound on his forehead, was a victim of domestic abuse. Staff members were unconvinced by the explanation of the head injury offered by Randy's new girlfriend, Marie, who had brought Joshua to the hospital; they also found it unusual that she objected to their removing the boy's clothing during their examination. Preparing the child to be x-rayed, they discovered numerous severe bruises of differing ages to the child's legs and buttocks. The staff contacted DSS and a child protective worker, Ann Kemmeter, took the case. The state took temporary custody of Joshua and he was admitted to the hospital's pediatric unit for further tests and observation. A "child protective team" consisting of social workers, police detectives, hospital staff, and the Winnebago County corporation counsel was assembled to investigate the family's situation. The team concluded that there was not enough evidence that Joshua was being abused to apply to the juvenile court for an order to remove the boy from his father's home, and he was discharged from the hospital into Randy's custody.

But there were conditions to Joshua's release. Randy DeShaney entered into a "voluntary social service" agreement with DSS. (Since Randy was not legally charged with abusing his son, his agreement with DSS was considered to be voluntary and its terms were not binding. In a court-ordered mandate, by contrast, all provisions would have the force of law.) The terms of the agreement DSS made with Randy DeShaney were as follows: Joshua would be enrolled in a local Head Start class, a federally-funded educational enrichment program for preschool children from low-income families. The child protective worker, Ann Kemmeter, also believed that Randy held inappropriate expectations for his young child's behavior, and therefore the department directed him to participate in activities designed to increase his understanding of child development and enhance his parenting skills. DSS personnel also informed Randy that they believed it best that Marie move out of the house; several members of the child protective team, in fact, suspected that it was Marie who was actually the abuser. (It should be noted that Marie was never criminally charged with child abuse in Joshua's case.) Ann Kemmeter reported in her case notes that she was optimistic she could work cooperatively with the DeShaneys to resolve the family's problems. On 14 February 1983 the Winnebago County juvenile court closed the child protective case on Joshua DeShaney.

On a follow-up visit to the DeShaney home ten days after Joshua's release from the hospital, Kemmeter noted in her files that Randy was not present in the home, but Marie was. Marie told Kemmeter that Randy and Joshua would be spending two weeks visiting Randy's father in another town, and Kemmeter arranged to visit again upon their return. The entry in her official report ends with the following notations:

> Goal—PROTECTION
> Primary Objective—RESOLUTION OF ABUSE, NEGLECT, OR EXPLOITATION
> Service Area—INDIVIDUAL AND FAMILY ADJUSTMENT
> Role—COUNSELING
> I will continue to provide counseling services to Randy to improve his knowledge of child development and parenting skills.
> Service Area—EDUCATION
> Role—ADVOCATE
> I will advocate either a pre-school of Headstart [sic] Program, in which Joshua could participate to improve his intellectual and social skills.
> Service Area—EMPLOYMENT RELATED
> I will advocate for full-time employment for Randy in having him explore possible job opportunities. He is presently exploring the possibility of employment in Florida, although nothing has materialized to date.
> Service Area—HEALTH RELATED
> I will advocate sound health care practices for Joshua and monitor to be sure that he gets in for his bi-monthly exams with Dr. Gehringer [a Neenah pediatrician who had examined Joshua in the hospital].[8]

Note here that Ann Kemmeter's stated goal was "protection" and her stated objective "resolution of abuse, neglect, or exploitation." Yet she identified her own role as that of "COUNSELING" and "ADVOCATE"—not as an authority or law enforcement figure. Her job title within DSS was "child protective worker," but under the voluntary agreement between DSS and Randy DeShaney she would take on a helping, rather than an authoritative, role. She planned to work with Randy to "improve his knowledge of child development and parenting skills," as well as to assist him in finding a full-time job. Joshua would attend Head Start to "improve his intellectual and social skills," and Kemmeter herself—again in the role of "advocate"—would ensure that the child received regular pediatric checkups. DSS would provide services on a "voluntary" basis. While Wisconsin law gave her authority to determine whether it was safe for Joshua to remain in Randy's home, Kemmeter's notes make it clear that she envisioned her role in the

DeShaney case as being therapeutic rather than authoritative. As she later told a local newspaper, the social worker was keenly aware of the fact that, just as Randy had entered into the social service agreement voluntarily, he could also choose to withdraw, severing contacts between Joshua and DSS. She believed it was in the child's best interest to keep the door to the DeShaney home open to her supervision and planned to make monthly visits to check on the family's progress.

Kemmeter's notes provide a clear illustration of the family preservation model in action. As the family's case worker, Ann Kemmeter's role was to inform, advise, and counsel Randy DeShaney, enabling him to better fulfill his responsibilities to his young son. This required her to maintain an open and at least cordial relationship with the DeShaney household, remaining sensitive to the family's interpersonal dynamics and aware of any changes in its economic and social situation. If the state of Wisconsin provided a "safety net" of social services to troubled families like the DeShaneys, Kemmeter herself was the designated "lifeline" connecting the state to the private household.

But the web of interconnections between public and private realms were further complicated by the social worker's parallel role as the state's eyes and ears in determining whether Joshua remained safe in his father's home. Under Wisconsin's child protection statutes (originally enacted in 1955, subsequently modified in 1977 and known as the Children's Code), Ann Kemmeter was authorized—indeed, required—to investigate household members, interrogate them, and keep them under the state's surveillance. This law enforcement role necessitated a different sort of relationship between the state and the DeShaneys, one in which the DSS worker would assume authority and initiate action to protect the child should the situation call for it. Kemmeter herself acknowledged as much in a memorandum she had written to the juvenile court when Joshua was in the hospital. While recommending that the temporary custody the state had assumed be dismissed, Kemmeter had added that she "will refer it back into Court should there be any further injuries to this child of an unexplained origin."[9] Thus, under the family preservation model, Kemmeter's position vis-à-vis the DeShaneys was a profoundly ambiguous one. Although her function as counselor and advocate on the family's behalf required her to gain their trust and cooperation, her simultaneous responsibility as Joshua's protector demanded that she abruptly change direction and assume the role of law enforcer if so required. Whether Kemmeter could have known that it was time to make such a shift in roles became a central dispute in the civil law suit that eventually came before the US Supreme Court.

While in the harsh light of history Ann Kemmeter's apparently sanguine attitude concerning Joshua's situation seems tragically misguided, she was not inexperienced in the field of child protection. Kemmeter was working in her hometown, a small town in Wisconsin's Fox River Valley, the place where she had grown up and felt comfortable. She worked for the Winnebago County DSS while she pursued her professional training at the University of Wisconsin-Madison, receiving a BA in social work in 1971 and an MS in the same field the following year. Two years later, in 1974, Kemmeter became the supervisor of the Child Protective

Services Unit for Winnebago County. She had served in that capacity for ten years when she took on the responsibility of healing the DeShaneys. One of her supervisors at DSS would later tell a local newspaper that Kemmeter was "one of our very best employees."[10] Perhaps Kemmeter's many years of professional experience in child protection work and her intimate familiarity with the small Neenah community led her to feel confident that the voluntary social service agreement Randy entered into with DSS would be an effective means of securing Joshua's safety.

The Emergence of Child Protection Professionals

The profession of social work itself had emerged in the early twentieth-century United States during an age characterized by wide-ranging social reform movements, the period historians have labeled the Progressive era. Within this context of reform activism, social workers were to be the foot soldiers of the emerging welfare state. Removed from the higher echelons of politics and policy-making, social workers attended to the day-to-day demands of the new welfare apparatuses under construction at the local, state, and to a lesser extent, national levels. "Casework" consisted of these new professionals working directly with the poor to ensure that social services reached them. Case workers had frequent contact with their clients in their own homes, and therefore they saw in a more direct and intimate way the myriad problems and needs of the poor. They were also much more likely than other state authorities to note bruises, cuts, and burns on the bodies of women and children in the home, and thus they were particularly well positioned to advocate on behalf of victims of domestic abuse.[11]

With the deepening of the Great Depression during the 1930s, however, the problem of family violence became largely overshadowed in the public arena by the pressing concerns of destitute families in need of immediate economic relief. When the issue of child abuse eventually resurfaced in the early 1960s, it did so primarily within a medical, rather than a social welfare, context. Scholars point to the publication of a seminal article in the *Journal of the American Medical Association* in 1962 as a watershed in the reawakening of the nation's attention to domestic violence. The five physicians who authored "The Battered Child Syndrome" created this label and applied it to identifiable patterns of childhood injuries, such as distinctive types of bone fractures, that medical personnel could now detect using x-rays, and later, CAT scans. (A CAT, or computerized axial tomography, scan, is an x-ray procedure that, with the aid of a computer, provides three-dimensional views of the body.) During the 1950s, pediatrics had firmly established itself as a prominent specialty in American medicine. Pediatricians, most of whom were in private practice rather than public service, replaced social reformers as national spokespeople for children's well-being.[12]

Pediatricians in the emerging field of child abuse prevention were soon joined by their colleagues in psychiatry. Like pediatrics, psychiatry shared a growing influence and authority in American life in the 1950s. Thus, efforts to prevent family violence increasingly entailed investigations into the psyches of adult abusers.[13] Departing from their origins in the social reform movements of the Progressive era, social workers now allied themselves with the ascendant medical/psychological model of child welfare. They were in direct daily contact with social services clientele, and they had been professionally trained to investigate and analyze myriad details about their clients' lives, including the behavior of individuals and the family dynamics at work within the household. Thus, as historian Daniel Walkowitz has asserted, the role of family therapist was not too far a professional stretch for case workers in the social services. In 1960 the Child Welfare League of America published the first set of professional standards for child protective workers, which became the generally accepted norms of the field.[14]

A contemporary publication by the American Humane Association, *Child Abuse Legislation in the 1970s,* provides a succinct summary of the social work profession's therapeutic approach to remedying domestic violence. The authors characterize states' reliance on criminal prosecution as "a natural consequence [of] the desire to exact retribution" on the assailants of children. More preferable, they asserted, was social planning for the entire family. Child protective workers were

> especially qualified to 'reach out' to families where children are neglected or abused … The 'helping-through-social-services' philosophy is stretched to include the parents. This is based on the recognition that destructive parental behavior is symptomatic of deeper emotional problems. Rarely is child abuse the product of wanton, willful or deliberate acts of cruelty. It results from emotional immaturity and from lack of capacity for coping with the pressures and tensions of modern living.[15]

The key to addressing domestic violence, then, was for the child protective worker to adopt the role of family counselor and therapist rather than serving solely as an authoritative enforcer of the child protection laws. Ann Kemmeter's professional training in the 1970s reflected this paradigm.

The Family Preservation Model of Child Abuse Prevention

Another crucial consequence of the "pediatric awakening" to the issue of child abuse in the 1960s was the widespread public concern, and indeed alarm, that it engendered. Influential pediatricians suggested in both professional and popular media that child abuse was a prevalent problem that went largely undetected due to lack of training in spotting the tell-tale physical and psychological symptoms on the part of doctors, nurses, social workers, teachers, day care providers, and others who dealt with children on a daily basis. The public became outraged by frequent and sensational stories of brutalized children that now began to appear in the mass media. In response to public pressure, states in rapid succession passed mandatory reporting laws making it a crime for specified professionals to fail to report suspected cases of abuse. By 1967, just five years after the publication of "The Battered Child Syndrome," forty-four states had such laws on their books.[16] The first federal law came with the passage by Congress of the Child Abuse and Treatment Act (CAPTA) of 1974, which provided over eighty-five million dollars in funding to states to develop programs for detecting and preventing child abuse and neglect and limited authority to experiment with treatments. Introduced by Senator Walter Mondale of Minnesota and passed easily through both houses of Congress, CAPTA also established a national data collection system requiring states to report certain data regarding child abuse and neglect, and required states to enact statutes providing for the protective custody of abused children in accordance with new federal standards. (It was during this time that the Wisconsin system that became involved with the DeShaney household was established. According to the process established in that state, a child protective case worker filed a petition for removing a child from an abusive home with the juvenile court, thereby allowing the state to take temporary custody of the child without a formal termination of parental rights.[17]) In 1980 Congress followed up with the Adoption Assistance and Child Welfare Act, which, among other provisions, mandated that child welfare agencies make "reasonable efforts" to preserve family units before removing children from homes where child abuse was suspected (it was left to the individual states to determine the definition of "reasonable") and required social workers to document their efforts toward this end in their written case plans. Ann Kemmeter's case notes describing her interactions with the DeShaney family and her plan for their rehabilitation reflect these federal reporting requirements.[18]

But of course children being abused in their own homes need a safe place to live. An initial consequence of the flurry of child abuse legislation and programs of the 1960s and 1970s was an increase in the number of children placed in the foster care system, which had evolved in all fifty states as an alternative to the institutionalization of children from abusive or neglectful homes. The number of children living in foster homes rose to 500,000 by 1977. States soon found, however, that foster care systems were accompanied by their own myriad problems. According to social welfare researchers Lela B. Costin, Howard Jacob Karger, and David Stoesz, state foster care systems were often poorly organized and haphazardly administered, prompting critics to doubt whether they could even be regarded as genuine "systems" at all. Horror stories began to emerge in the media of children becoming virtually "lost" in foster care bureaucracies, seeming to vanish from the oversight of overworked—or just plain careless—child protection workers. Further, emerging psychological evidence pointed to the trauma that children—even abused children—experienced when they were separated from their siblings and parents. Foster children often lived in a kind of limbo, critics asserted, moving from family to family with devastating emotional and psychological consequences, including the inability to form normal relationships with others and the perpetuation of patterns of abuse and neglect they had experienced themselves as children.[19]

In addition, both legal and social traditions in the United States made it difficult to permanently remove children from their parents' homes so that they could be eligible for adoption by another family. Critiques of foster care came from both ends of the political spectrum. Conservatives decried the growth of the welfare state as a dangerous intrusion into the legal rights of parents. Among liberals, by contrast, a backlash emerged against Senator Daniel Patrick Moynihan's influential social policy report, issued more than a decade earlier under President Lyndon Johnson's administration, which had posited a "culture of poverty" in which the children of the poor never learned to become economically self-sufficient and thus perpetuated welfare dependency across generations. Sociologists Peter and Brigitte Berger, for example, published an influential book, *The War Over the Family*, a strong condemnation of state social service workers' alleged undermining of poor families through the practice of removing children from their parents' homes. The authors criticized the growth in the size and authority of the welfare state as a dangerous usurpation of the traditional rights accorded to the private family.[20]

In addition, racial tensions, violence in urban ghettoes, and the emergence of Black Power had significantly altered the trajectory of the civil rights movement by the 1970s. This shift brought forward a radical critique of the widespread institutional bias within social service bureaucracies that stigmatized poor African American families (many of which were female-headed) as deviant or unworthy simply because they did not reflect the middle-class, and largely white, ideal of a nuclear family. Racist white social workers, the new critics charged, ignored African American traditions of employing extended kin networks in raising children and labeled all female-headed households as inherently "dysfunctional" regardless of how well adjusted they actually may have been. Black nationalists as well as African American social workers denounced the practice employed in many states of removing black children from their homes and placing them with white foster families, labeling it nothing less than "cultural genocide." By 1983, after a decade of attacks from both ends of the political spectrum, the number of children in the foster care system had been cut in half.[21]

Of no little importance in the growing critique of the foster care system was the fact that it was proving to be an expensive enterprise for states. Notably, the public's outrage at child abusers was not accompanied by an equally enthusiastic opening of its pocketbooks to adequately staff and maintain quality alternative living arrangements for their young victims. In 1980, Ronald Reagan was elected to the presidency on a campaign to "get big government off our backs" and to lower taxpayers' contributions to social welfare. In 1981, Congress cut family welfare services (Title XX of the Adoption Assistance and Child Welfare Act) by 21 percent, despite a significant increase in reported cases of child abuse and neglect. Political conservatives began arguing that federal interventions in family social services represented an intrusion on the rights of states to conduct their own programs in accordance with the needs of their own constituents. Religious conservatives, on the other hand, expressed suspicion of anti-domestic violence activities that had emerged from the feminist movement of the 1970s, arguing that such programs undermined traditional patriarchal authority in the home and encouraged the breakup of nuclear families. Feminist activists stressed women's lack of economic independence from men as a crucial factor that entrapped women and their children in violent situations. They also pressed for the prosecution of violent husbands and fathers as criminals.[22] "Discovering" domestic violence, as it turned out, had been the easy part. Finding politically satisfactory, socially effective, long-term solutions for abused children would prove to be much harder.

The answer, or so it seemed at the time, was the adoption of the family preservation model, which had become the standard for state child protection services by the time Joshua DeShaney first came to the attention of the Winnebago County DSS. The journey Joshua's case took through the Winnebago County DSS in 1983 and 1984 was typical of the child protective system erected in all fifty states by that time. As a case worker, Ann Kemmeter operated within a professional paradigm that stressed her relationship with the DeShaney family as a therapist and counselor. At the same time, however, the state of Wisconsin placed responsibility for Joshua's safety in her hands, requiring her to abruptly shift her role to that of a law enforcement official. It was a change that the case worker who took on the responsibility of shoring up the DeShaney household failed to make, with dire consequences for the child.

Joshua's Tragedy

On 25 July 1983, seven months after Joshua's release from the hospital, Ann Kemmeter placed a social service review in the DeShaney file. The report noted that she had made a total of four visits to the home; three additional appointments had been canceled by the family, who had moved to Oshkosh, Wisconsin, fifteen miles south of Neenah. Significantly, Kemmeter continued her social service arrangement with Randy rather than handing over the case to a DSS worker in Oshkosh, even though it would now require her to drive thirty miles round-trip for the monthly home visits. The DeShaneys' relocation to another city also placed the child protective worker farther away from Joshua, whose safety she continued to be responsible for under Wisconsin law. Furthermore, although the voluntary agreement had been with Randy alone, Marie was still very much in the picture.

That summer Kemmeter also noted in the file her concern that Joshua continued to have "accidents." Two months after his release from the hospital in Neenah, she had received a call from the staff notifying her that the boy had returned to the emergency room, where he received stitches to another laceration on his forehead. Marie later told police that the cut was the result of Joshua crawling under his bed and hitting his head on the metal bed frame. On a home visit several weeks later, Kemmeter noted a bump on Joshua's forehead that was explained (in the notes it is unclear by whom) as the result of a fall off a tricycle.

Although she concluded that "there is enough of the accident-prone syndrome present for me to continue to want to follow this family for a while," Kemmeter was not particularly alarmed.[23] Whether or not the child protective worker could have realized it based on the facts she had at hand, in reality the DeShaney home was a dangerous place for the little boy, and indeed the violence appeared to be escalating.

The DeShaneys moved to Oshkosh in June 1983, and over the following months police responded to domestic violence complaints at their home six times. Joshua made another trip to the emergency room, this time at Mercy Hospital in Oshkosh, for a corneal abrasion. In October, Kemmeter noted in the case file another injury she observed during a home visit, a swelling she described as a "large goose bump" on Joshua's left forehead. At the following month's visit, on 9 November, she observed what she thought were cigarette burns on the boy's neck and chin. Nor was the violence in the DeShaney home restricted to Joshua's injuries. The Oshkosh police went to the home twice on 11 November and then again the following day to investigate what was apparently a sustained physical fight between Randy and Marie, leaving Marie with a very badly bruised eye. (Several weeks later, Randy again beat Marie, requiring her to receive stitches in her lip.) On 30 November Joshua appeared again at the emergency room at Mercy Hospital, this time for yet another laceration on his forehead, and the attendees who examined him also noted blood in his left nostril, a red and swollen left ear, and injuries to both shoulders. When they confronted Randy, he explained that Joshua had fallen in the bathroom and hit his head on the toilet. A police officer later said that, upon being called to the home by neighbors during one dispute between Randy and Marie, he had spoken with Joshua himself and had become concerned for the child's safety. As appropriate under Wisconsin law, the officer did not investigate the child's safety himself but instead relayed his concerns to DSS.

Ann Kemmeter's social service review for January 1984 reflected for the first time her growing doubts about the true nature of Joshua's "accidents." A year after her first encounter with the DeShaneys, Joshua's numerous injuries (three involving trips to the emergency room) and several police reports of domestic violence between the adults in the home now made the social worker willing to consider the possibility that the boy's frequent injuries were being caused by one or possibly two perpetrators. But despite her uncertainty, Kemmeter still hesitated to assume the role of law enforcer. "I am not certain who the abuser of Joshua would be," she speculated in her case notes. "However, I cannot help but hypothesize that the probability of Randy becoming upset with Marie—using physical violence, and Marie not knowing what to do with her frustrations, and anger, possibly taking them out on Joshua."[24] Kemmeter attached to her review the police reports on the domestic violence incidents between Randy and Marie that had taken place the previous November.

Despite the police reports, however, her case notes indicate that she found it difficult to relinquish the role of therapist, speculating about the family's emotional dynamics and analyzing the ways in which the state's social services could best address their needs. "We will make continued attempts to improve the parenting skills within this family unit," she wrote, "and to lower their expectations of Joshua's behavior and general motor development skills."[25] Although she was becoming suspicious about the true nature of Joshua's injuries, Kemmeter had not altered her original view that the real threat to the boy's safety was Marie, not his father. She believed she had developed a good working relationship with Randy DeShaney, and was confident that she had built a solid foundation of trust with the family. A close reading of her case notes suggests that Kemmeter may have had difficulty reconciling the Randy DeShaney she frequently described as an agreeable and cooperative client, interested in improving his parenting skills and finding help for Joshua's behavior problems, with the mounting indications that he may in fact have been a dangerous perpetrator of domestic violence.

When Kemmeter arrived for her scheduled home visit later that January, she was informed that Joshua was in bed with the flu and the adults did not want him disturbed. She did not insist on seeing him (an action Wisconsin law empowered child protective workers to do), nor did she reschedule her visit for later that month. Arriving in February, Kemmeter found no one at home. If the social worker believed the DeShaneys were deliberately avoiding contact with her, she did not indicate as much in her notes. Marie would later tell the Oshkosh police that she had begun resenting Kemmeter because Joshua's behavior became worse after the social worker's visits. When the case worker left the house, according to Marie, Joshua "wanted to go with her" and became upset and unruly. A few weeks later on 3 March, Marie was treated at the Mercy Hospital emergency room for a split lip and a broken nose, the result of another fight with Randy.

Kemmeter made another attempt to visit the DeShaney home on 7 March 1984. While she had noted her concerns that Joshua was a possible victim of child abuse in her January review, she had not actually seen the boy since 9 November, a full four months earlier. Kemmeter appears to have changed her strategy for dealing with the DeShaneys because, unlike her previous calls, this time Kemmeter arrived at their home unannounced. Later, she dictated into her notes her own recollection of what had taken place during that March visit:

> It was Rusty's second birthday and Marie and Randy were in the kitchen decorating his birthday cake. [Rusty was Marie's child by her former husband.] I wrote Happy Birthday Rusty on the cake and Randy finished decorating. Both Marie and Randy seemed to be at ease and told me there were fewer fights and they were getting along much better ... [Marie told Kemmeter that her stitches were due to "nose surgery for some type of blockage." If the social worker was suspicious of the explanation, she did not indicate so in her notes.] Rusty and Joshua were taking a nap. Joshua had woken up. Marie went back to his bedroom quieting him down and then came back to the kitchen where we all were. I don't know why but I did not ask to see Joshua. All appeared to be okay and [there was] a relaxed atmosphere in the household. They did mention that Joshua had fainted several days earlier in the bathroom for no apparent reason.[26]

Despite the disturbing revelation about Joshua's fainting, and Marie's facial injuries, Kemmeter's report describes a tranquil scene in the DeShaney household. She joined in the domestic ritual of decorating Rusty's cake. She noted that Randy was cleaning fish for dinner, and even added the detail that he was carefully removing the bones so the children would not choke on them. The DeShaneys said they were expecting friends later that evening who were coming to help celebrate Rusty's birthday. By her account, Kemmeter stayed about forty-five minutes and then drove the fifteen miles back to Neenah. Apparently still regarding her relationship with the DeShaneys as a voluntary social service agreement, Kemmeter did not invoke her legal authority as a child protective worker and insist upon seeing Joshua that evening, although she had been told he had fainted and had not in fact actually seen him in months. She did not advise them to seek medical treatment for the child.

The following evening, 8 March, Kemmeter received a telephone call from a nurse at Mercy Hospital. The nurse informed her that Joshua had been brought to the emergency room, this time with a severe head injury. Kemmeter asked if a DSS worker in Oshkosh could take the call, but was told that she had been requested specifically, although it is not clear from the record who had made the request. The social worker drove the fifteen miles from Neenah that evening. Arriving at Mercy she was met by the nurse, the hospital's chaplain, and Marie. They told her that Randy was with Joshua, who was undergoing a CAT scan. Kemmeter asked Marie what had happened to the boy, and was told that Joshua had fallen down the basement stairs in their home. He had been brought into the emergency room unconscious by Randy and Marie. Kemmeter spoke separately with the nurse and hospital chaplain, who revealed that Randy had been quite violent when the DeShaneys arrived, "pounding on the doors and walls." They worried that he would strike one of the hospital staff. Randy then returned from Joshua's CAT scan; he was, in Kemmeter's words, "crying, shaking, and speaking very loudly," a reaction she attributed to stress and grief. The social worker took Randy to a small lounge area, and at her request he was given an injection of a sedative by a nurse. After seeing to the distressed Randy's needs, she then called the Oshkosh police.[27]

At that point Kemmeter went to see Joshua, whom she found in an appalling condition. An array of tubes covered his face, and the child was breathing through a hand respirator being operated by a nurse. Both eyes had been taped shut. Through the tubes and tape Kemmeter could make out severe bruising on both of Joshua's cheeks and along the base of his throat. The nurse told her that the CAT scan had revealed hemorrhaging in the boy's brain, and he was being prepared for emergency neurosurgery to relieve pressure from the swelling. Tests had revealed blood in Joshua's urine, and physicians were trying to determine whether there were broken bones or internal injuries in addition to the apparently severe head injury. They told Kemmeter that Joshua's chances of surviving the neurosurgery that night were only about 25 percent.

Dr. Marc Letellier, a neurosurgeon, spoke to Kemmeter after the surgery. He revealed that the extent of swelling in Joshua's brain (the CAT scan showed the hemorrhage nearly covered the entire right hemisphere) had required the removal of a large section of the skull. The child had been moved to the intensive care unit, and Letellier informed her that "it could be weeks before Joshua would wake up if he did at all."[28] He also informed her that he had also noticed a number of older bruises on Joshua's shaved head. Upon removing the section of the skull, he saw several deposits of bilirubin within the boy's brain, a substance left behind when blood had been reabsorbed into the brain tissue. This, along with the bruises on the scalp, indicated to the neurosurgeon that numerous such seepages had occurred on previous occasions. Significantly, the surgeon did not find any external points of impact—the kinds of cuts or abrasions that one would expect to find had the child fallen down the stairs, as Randy and Marie insisted he had done. Letellier told Kemmeter that the bleeding in Joshua's brain was the result of "violent shaking or continuous hard hitting of the head as by an open hand."[29] (In the 1990s, the general public would come to know this condition in abused children by the label "shaken baby syndrome." Violent shaking of a baby or small child may cause the brain to reverberate within the skull. Blood vessels are torn from the brain, and the subsequent hemorrhaging results in brain damage or even death.) Letellier gave only a guarded prognosis for the boy's recovery. In fact, after years of rehabilitation services and additional surgeries, Joshua would remain severely brain damaged and partially paralyzed, recovering only minimally from the injuries he had received, apparently over an extended period.

Faced with the enormity of a lifetime of expensive medical care for the boy, his mother filed suit in federal court against Ann Kemmeter and the DSS. Both the district and federal appeals courts, however, found that Joshua had failed to establish a constitutional claim to child protective services from the state of Wisconsin, rulings affirmed by the US Supreme Court in February 1989. While Chief Justice Rehnquist was harsh in his assessment of the state's social service apparatus, charging that "state functionaries had stood by and done nothing when suspicious circumstances dictated a more active role for them," his opinion urged that "it is well to remember that the harm [to Joshua] was inflicted, not by the State of Wisconsin, but by Joshua's father." The Chief Justice even imagined a scenario in which, had social workers "moved too soon to take custody of the son away from the father, they would likely have been met with charges of improperly intruding into the parent-child relationship," charges that, ironically, would be based in the same constitutional protections Joshua's counsel had claimed for the boy's civil rights.[30] Protecting children required active state child welfare systems, but such systems must be bounded by the rights afforded to the private family.

Conclusion

Only recently have historians of the United States begun to investigate the complex interactions between private and public realms as child protection laws, policies, and institutions developed over the course of the twentieth century, especially in that century's second half. The emerging scholarship demonstrates the ambiguous and ever-changing approaches that policy—and lawmakers, persuaded by shifting political winds and public opinion—have taken toward best remedying the persistent and profoundly disturbing problem of child abuse. A close examination of the DeShaney case reveals the weaknesses inherent in the family preservation model that came to dominate the field of child protection in the 1970s, and vividly illustrates the tragic consequences for children who, like Joshua, found themselves trapped in violent homes.

The American public abhors child abuse. But genuine concern for the plight of abused children has always been filtered through the prism of other values that are held dear, including the importance of families as the fundamental building blocks of society, citizens' rights to be protected from unwarranted government intrusion into their private lives, and an effective but limited—and inexpensive—welfare state. In the twenty-first century, the "special relationship" that exists among the state, social workers, and abused children continues to evolve.

Notes

1. *DeShaney v. Winnebago County Department of Social Services*, 489 U.S. 189 (1989). Material presented in this chapter is included in Lynne Curry, *The DeShaney Case: Child Abuse, Family Rights, and the Dilemma of State Intervention* (Lawrence, KS, 2007) and has been used with the permission of the press.

2. The "special relationship" theory holds that states may be considered liable for failing to protect individuals from harm by private actors when the state places the individual in harm's way with no way to defend himself. For example, previous courts had determined states were responsible when prison guards knowingly placed an inmate in a position to be attacked by another prisoner (*Spence v. Staras*, 507 F.2d 554, 1974), and when police officers making an arrest left minor children stranded in a car unaccompanied by an adult (*White v. Rochford*, 592 F. 2d 381, 1979). The Supreme Court found no such relationship between Joshua DeShaney and Wisconsin's child protection system.

3. Harry A. Blackmun Collection, Library of Congress, Manuscripts Division. Box 514, folder 3. Washington, D.C. Blackmun (1908–1999) served as Associate Justice of the United States Supreme Court from 1970 to 1994.

4. Lela B. Costin, Howard Jacob Karger, and David Stoesz, *The Politics of Child Abuse in America* (New York, 1996), 116–117. It should be noted that these figures represent the number of cases *reported* in these years, not the number *substantiated*, which for a variety of reasons is likely to be lower. There is substantial disagreement among various child welfare professionals, however, regarding the degree, explanation, and significance of child abuse overreporting. See, for example: Douglas J. Besharov and Lisa A. Laumann, "Child Abuse Reporting," *Society* 33, no. 4 (1996): 40–47; Elizabeth D. Hutchison, "Mandatory Reporting Laws: Child Protective Case Finding Gone Awry?" *Social Work* 38, no. 1 (1993): 56–63; Seth Kalichman, *Mandated Reporting of Suspected Child Abuse: Ethics, Law, and Policy*, 2nd ed. (Washington, D.C., 1999). One complicating factor is the fact that national statistics were not systematically collected until 1974.

5. *Appleton* [Wisconsin] *Post-Crescent*, 1 June 1984. Microfilm, Wisconsin Historical Society, Madison, Wisconsin.

6. Following the *DeShaney* opinion, a number of legal scholars offered critiques of state child protection systems in which children receive less police protection than adults do. See, for

example, Laura Oren, "The State's Failure to Protect Children and Substantive Due Process: DeShaney in Context," *North Carolina Law Review* 68 (April 1990): 659–731; Martha Minow, "Words and the Door to the Land of Change: Law, Language and Family Violence," *Vanderbilt Law Review* 43 (November 1990): 1665–1699; Barbara Bennett Woodhouse, "'Who Owns the Child?': *Meyer* and *Pierce* and the Child as Property," *William and Mary Law Review* 33 (summer 1992): 995–1122; and Catherine A. Crosby-Currie and N. Dickon Reppucci, "The Missing Child in Child Protection: The Constitutional Context of Child Maltreatment from *Meyer* to *DeShaney,*" *Law and Policy* 21 (April 1999): 129–159.

7. Elizabeth Pleck, *Domestic Tyranny: The Making of American Social Policy Against Family Violence from Colonial Times to the Present* (Urbana, 2004). See also Barbara J. Nelson, *Making an Issue of Child Abuse: Political Agenda Setting for Social Problems* (Chicago, 1984).

8. Plaintiffs' Reply Brief in Opposition to Defendants' Motion for Summary Judgment at 114–115. *DeShaney v. Winnebago County Department of Social Services,* US District Court, Eastern District of Wisconsin (1986, unpublished). National Archives and Records Administration, Great Lakes Region Headquarters, Chicago, Illinois.

9. Petition for Writ of Certiorari at 16. *DeShaney v. Winnebago County Department of Social Services,* Case No. 37-154, Supreme Court of the United States.

10. Petition for Writ of Certiorari at 169–173; *Appleton Post-Crescent,* 24 February 1989. Microfilm, Wisconsin Historical Society, Madison, Wisconsin.

11. Historian Daniel J. Walkowitz has identified one of the earliest uses of the term "social work" in an address by Mary E. Richmond of the Russell Sage Foundation at the 1897 National Conference of Charities and Corrections, an organization that in 1917 quite symbolically changed its own name to the National Association of Social Work. In the United States, the profession of social work began as, and has remained, a heavily female-dominated occupation. According to federal census figures, women comprised 55.7 percent of social workers in 1910 and by 1930 made up 79 percent of the profession. The 1950s saw a slight decline in women's majority, down to 57 percent by 1960, but by 1970, around the time when Ann Kemmeter was entering the field, women's proportion had climbed back to 62.9 percent. As in most occupations, female social workers historically have received lower salaries than their male counterparts. See Walkowitz, *Working with Class: Social Workers and the Politics of Middle Class Identity* (Chapel Hill, 1999). For other historical perspectives on the social work profession, see Michael Katz, *In the Shadow of the Poorhouse: A Social History of Welfare in America* (New York, 1986) and Linda Gordon, *Pitied But Not Entitled: Single Mothers and the History of Welfare, 1890–1935* (New York, 1994).

12. C. Henry Kempe, Frederic N. Silverman, Brandt F. Steele, William Droegemuller, and Henry K. Silver, "The Battered Child Syndrome," *Journal of the American Medical Association* 81 (1962): 17–24.

13. Historian Linda Gordon's path-breaking research in the case histories of the Massachusetts Society for the Prevention of Cruelty to Children, for example, reveals several interesting historical constants among child abusers that lend credence to present-day notions of a "cycle of violence" between generations. Many child abusers were themselves abused as children, an experience engendering deep-seated feelings of powerlessness and self-loathing in victims. Adult assailants who terrorize those who are smaller and weaker nevertheless continue to see themselves as victims, often attributing outsized motives and disproportionate power to the children whom they assault. Gordon's historical evidence also supports psychological observations that abusive parents often carry inappropriate expectations of their children's physical, cognitive, and emotional maturity. But, as Gordon points out, swinging the pendulum too far to the side of individual psychological explanations distracts from larger structural variables that also contribute to family violence. The stress of losing a job or a child's demanding and expensive illness, for example, can trigger an adult's sense of victimization and powerlessness, and in that distressed state he or she may be more likely to abuse a child. See Gordon, *Heroes of Their Own Lives: The Politics and History of Family Violence* (New York, 1988).

14. Walkowitz, *Working with Class,* 202–208.

15. Vincent DeFrancis and Carroll L.Frucht, *Child Abuse Legislation in the 1970s,* rev. ed. (Denver, 1974), 3–5. The American Humane Association was founded in 1886 to address the problems of cruelty to animals as well as to children. DeFrancis, an attorney who had served as director of the New York Society for the Prevention of Cruelty to Children, became head of the AHA's Children's Division in 1954. Historian Elizabeth Pleck describes DeFrancis as one who "single-handedly invigorated the child protection movement with the force of his ideas." *Domestic Tyranny,* 165–166.
16. Costin, Karger, and Stoesz, *Politics of Child Abuse,* 116.
17. Wisconsin Legislative Fiscal Bureau, Child Welfare Services in Wisconsin, *Informational Paper 50* (January 2005), 1–5.
18. Costin, Karger, and Stoesz, *Politics of Child Abuse,* 122–126.
19. Ibid., 122.
20. Brigitte Berger and Peter L. Berger, *The War Over the Family* (Garden City, NY, 1983).
21. Dorothy E. Roberts, "Is There Justice in Children's Rights? The Critique of Federal Family Preservation Policy," *University of Pennsylvania Journal of Constitutional Law* 2 (December 1999): 112–140.
22. Pleck, *Domestic Tyranny,* 182–200. The seminal feminist analysis of domestic violence is Susan Brownmiller's *Against Our Will: Men, Women and Rape* (New York, 1975).
23. Plaintiffs' Reply Brief at 116.
24. Ibid. at 120.
25. Ibid.
26. Ibid. at 130–131.
27. Ibid. at 122.
28. Ibid. at 125–126.
29. Ibid. at 125.
30. *DeShaney v. Winnebago County* at 263.

SELECT BIBLIOGRAPHY

Addams, Jane. *Newer Ideals of Peace*. New York, 1915.

Allen, Ann Taylor. *Feminism and Motherhood in Germany, 1800–1914*. New Brunswick, 1991.

———. "The Kindergarten in Germany and the United States, 1840–1914: A Comparative Perspective," *History of Education* 35, no. 2 (1995): 173–188.

Apple, Rima D. *Perfect Motherhood: Science and Childrearing in America*. New Brunswick, 2006.

Arbeitsgruppe "Lehrer und Krieg," ed. *Leherer helfen siegen: Kriegspädagogik im Kaiserreich*. Berlin, 1987.

Bardaglio, Peter. *Reconstructing the Household: Families, Sex, and the Law in the Nineteenth-Century South*. Chapel Hill, 1985.

Beatty, Barbara. *Preschool Education in America: The Culture of Young Children from the Colonial Era to the Present*. New Haven, 1995.

Bellingham, Bruce, and Mary Pugh Mathis. "Race, Citizenship and the Bio-Politics of the Maternalist Welfare State: 'Traditional' Midwifery in the American South under the Sheppard-Towner Act, 1921–29." *Social Politics* 1, no. 2 (1994): 157–189.

Berg, Christa. "Rat Geben: Ein Dilemma pädagogischer Praxis und Wirkungsgeschichte." *Zeitschrift für Pädagogik* 37, no. 5 (1991): 709–734.

Biess, Frank. *Homecomings: Returning POWs and the Legacies of Defeat in Postwar Germany*. Princeton, 2006.

Bucur, Maria, and Nancy M. Wingfield, eds. *Gender and War in Twentieth-Century Eastern Europe*. Bloomington, IN, 2006.

Budde, Gunilla-Friederike. *Auf dem Weg ins Bürgerleben: Kindheit und Erziehung in deutschen und englischen Bürgerfamilien 1840–1914*. Göttingen, 1994.

Buhle, Mari Jo. *Feminism and Its Discontents: A Century of Struggle with Psychoanalysis*. Cambridge, 1998.

Busch, Friedrich W. "Deutsche Demokratische Republik," in *Elternhaus und Schule: Kooperation ohne Erfolg?* ed. Klaus Schleicher, 56–79. Düsseldorf, 1972.

Canning, Kathleen. "The Concepts of Class and Citizenship in German History," in *Gender History in Practice: Historical Perspectives on Bodies, Class, and Citizenship*, ed. Kathleen Canning, 193–211. Ithaca, 2006.

Clark, Anna. *The Struggle for the Breeches: Gender and the Making of the British Working Class*. Berkeley, 1995.

Conway, Martin. "The Rise and Fall of Western Europe's Democratic Age, 1945–1973." *Contemporary European History* 13, no. 1 (2004): 67–88.

Curry, Lynne. *The DeShaney Case: Child Abuse, Family Privacy, and the Dilemma of State Intervention*. Lawrence, KS, 2007.

Czerny, Adalbert. *Der Arzt als Erzieher des Kindes*. Leipzig, 1908; rpt. 1942.

Dawley, Alan. *Changing the World: American Progressives in War and Revolution*. Princeton, 2003.

Dickinson, Edward Ross. *The Politics of German Child Welfare from the Empire to the Federal Republic*. Cambridge, MA, 1996.

Early, Frances H. *A World Without War: How U.S. Feminists and Pacifists Resisted World War I.* Syracuse, 1997.

Eisenach, Eldon J. *The Lost Promise of Progressivism.* Lawrence, 1994.

Engel, Max. *Leipzigs Volksschulen im Zeichen des Weltkrieges: Auf Grund von Einzelberichten und unter Mitarbeit von Lehrern und Direktoren.* Leipzig, 1915.

Fehrenbach, Heide. *Race after Hitler: Black Occupation Children in Postwar Germany and America.* Princeton, 2005.

Feldstein, Ruth. *Motherhood in Black and White: Race and Sex in American Liberalism, 1930–1965.* Ithaca, 2000.

Flitner, Wilhelm. *Der Krieg und die Jugend.* New Haven, 1927.

Führ, Christoph, and Carl-Ludwig Furck, ed. *Handbuch der deutschen Bildungsgeschichte, vol VI: 1945 bis zur Gegenwart. Zweiter Teilband, Deutsche Demokratische Republik und Neue Bundesländer.* Munich, 1998.

Gass-Bolm, Torsten. "Das Ende der Schulzucht," in *Wandlungsprozesse in Westdeutschland: Belastung, Integration, Liberalisierung 1945–1980,* ed. Ulrich Herbert, 436–466. Göttingen, 2002.

Goltermann, Svenja. *Die Gesellschaft der Überlebenden: Deutsche Kriegsheimkehrer und ihre Gewalterfahrungen im Zweiten Weltkrieg.* Munich, 2009.

Gordon, Linda. *Heroes of Their Own Lives: The Politics and History of Family Violence.* New York, 1988.

Grant, Julia. "A 'Real Boy' and not a Sissy: Gender, Childhood, and Masculinity, 1890–1940." *Journal of Social History* 37, no. 4 (2004): 829–851.

Grossberg, Michael. *Governing the Hearth: Law and the Family in Nineteenth Century America.* Chapel Hill, 1985.

Habermas, Rebekka. "Parent-Child Relationships in the Nineteenth-Century," *German History* 16 (1998): 43–55.

Healy, Maureen. *Vienna and the Fall of the Habsburg Empire: Total War and Everyday Life in World War I.* Cambridge, 2004.

Herbert, Ulrich, ed. *Wandlungsprozesse in Westdeutschland: Belastung, Integration, Liberalisierung 1945–1980,* Göttingen, 2002.

Herbert, Ulrich. "Liberalisierung als Lernprozeß: Die Bundesrepublik in der deutschen Geschichte—eine Skizze," in *Wandlungsprozesse in Westdeutschland: Belastung, Integration, Liberalisierung 1945–1980,* ed. Ulrich Herbert, 7–49. Göttingen, 2002.

Herman, Sondra R. *Eleven against War: Studies in American Internationalist Thought, 1898–1921.* Stanford, 1969.

Höhn, Maria. *GIs and Fräuleins: The German-American Encounter in 1950s West Germany.* Chapel Hill, 2002.

Hulbert, Ann. *Raising America: Experts, Parents, and a Century of Advice about Children.* New York, 2003.

Israel, Charles. *Before Scopes: Evangelicals, Education, and Evolution in Tennessee, 1875–1925.* Athens, GA, 2004.

Jacobs, Margaret D. "Maternal Colonialism: White Women and Indigenous Child Removal in the American West and Australia, 1880–1940." *The Western Historical Quarterly* 36, no. 4 (2005): 453–476.

Jones, Kathleen W. *Taming the Troublesome Child: American Families, Child Guidance, and the Limits of Psychiatric Authority.* Cambridge, MA, 1999.

Judson, Pieter M. *Guardians of the Nation: Activists on the Language Frontiers of Rural Austria.* Cambridge, MA, 2006.

Karstädt, Otto, ed. *Kinderaug' und Kinderaufsatz im Weltkrieg.* Osterwieck, 1916.

Kerber, Linda K. "The Meanings of Citizenship." *Journal of American History* 84, no. 3 (1997): 833–854.

Kertzer, David, and Marzio Barbagli, eds. *Family Life in the Long Nineteenth Century, 1789–1913. vol. 2: The History of the European Family.* New Haven, 2002.

King, Jeremy. *Budweisers into Czechs and Germans: A Local History of Bohemian Politics, 1848–1948.* Princeton, 2002.

Kline, Wendy. *Building a Better Race: Gender, Sexuality and Eugenics from the Turn-of-the-Century to the Baby Boom.* Berkeley, 2001.

Koven, Seth, and Sonya Michel, eds. *Mothers of a New World: Maternalist Politics and the Origins of Welfare States.* New York, 1993.

Ladd-Taylor, Molly. *Mother-Work: Women, Child Welfare and the State, 1890–1930.* Champaign, 1994.

Lamberti, Marjorie. *State, Society, and the Elementary School in Imperial Germany.* New York, 1989.

———. *The Politics of Education: Teachers and School Reform in Weimar Germany.* New York, 2002.

Larson, Edward J. *Trial and Error: The American Controversy over Creation and Evolution.* 3rd ed. New York, 2003.

Lees, Andrew. *Cities, Sin, and Social Reform in Imperial Germany.* Ann Arbor, 2002.

Lemmermann, Heinz. *Kriegserziehung im Kaiserreich: Studien zur politischen Funktion von Schule und Schulmusik 1890–1918.* Bremen, 1984.

Lindenmeyer, Kriste. *"A Right to Childhood": The U.S. Children's Bureau and Child Welfare, 1912–1946.* Urbana, 1997.

Maase, Kaspar. "Entblößte Brust und schwingende Hüfte: Momentaufnahmen von der Jugend der fünfziger Jahre," in *Männergeschichte—Geschlechtergeschichte: Männlichkeit im Wandel der Moderne,* ed. Thomas Kühne, 193–217. Frankfurt a. M., 1996.

Marshall, T. H. *"Citizenship and Social Class" and Other Essays.* Cambridge, 1950.

Matthias, Adolf. *Wie erziehen wir unsern Sohn Benjamin?* Munich 1896; rpt. 1911.

May, Elaine Tyler. *Homeward Bound: American Families in the Cold War Era.* New York, 1988.

McDougall, Alan. *Youth Politics in East Germany: The Free German Youth Movement 1946–1968.* Oxford, 2004.

Mettler, Suzanne. *Dividing Citizens: Gender and Federalism in New Deal Public Policy.* Ithaca, 1998.

Meyerowitz, Joanne, ed. *Not June Cleaver: Women and Gender in Postwar America.* Philadelphia, 1994.

Michel, Sonya. *Children's Interests/Mothers' Rights: The Shaping of America's Child Care Policy.* New Haven, 1999.

Mihaly, Jo [Piete Kuhr]. *Da gibt's ein Wiedersehen! Kriegstagebuch eines Mädchens, 1914–1918.* Freiburg, 1982. Translated as *There We'll Meet Again: A Young German Girl's Diary of the First World War.* Gloucester, 1998.

Mintz, Steven. *Huck's Raft: A History of American Childhood.* Cambridge, MA, 2004.

Moeller, Robert. *Protecting Motherhood: Women and the Family in the Politics of Postwar Germany.* Berkeley, 1993.

Mohrhart, Dieter. *Elternmitwirkung in der Bundesrepublik Deutschland: ein Beitrag zur politisch-historischen und pädagogischen Diskussion.* Frankfurt a. M., 1979.

O'Leary, Cecilia Elizabeth. *To Die For: The Paradox of American Patriotism.* Princeton, 1999.

Patterson, David S. "An Interpretation of the American Peace Movement, 1898–1914," in *Peace Movements in America,* ed. Charles Chatfield, 20–38. New York, 1973.

Pleck, Elizabeth. *Domestic Tyranny: The Making of American Social Policy Against Family Violence from Colonial Times to the Present*. Urbana, 2004.

Rahden, Till van. "Demokratie und väterliche Autorität. Das Karlsruher 'Stichentscheid'-Urteil in der politischen Kultur der frühen Bundesrepublik." *Zeithistorische Forschungen* 2, no. 2 (2005): 160–179.

Ravitch, Diane. *The Troubled Crusade: American Education 1945–1980*. New York, 1983.

Reuter, Lutz R. "Partizipation im Schulwesen," in *Handbuch der deutschen Bildungsgeschichte, vol. VI: 1945 bis zur Gegenwart. Zweiter Teilband, Deutsche Demokratische Republik und Neue Bundesländer*, ed. Christoph Führ and Carl-Ludwig Furck, 228–233. Munich, 1998.

Rockman, Seth. *Welfare Reform in Early America*. Boston, 2003.

Rodgers, Daniel T. *Atlantic Crossings: Social Politics in a Progressive Age*. Cambridge, MA, 1998.

Rogin, Michael Paul. "Kiss Me Deadly: Communism, Motherhood, and Cold War Movies." *Representations* 6 (spring 1984): 1–36.

Rölli-Allkemper, Lukas. *Familie im Wiederaufbau: Katholizismus und bürgerliches Familienideal in der Bundesrepublik Deutschland 1945–1965*. Paderborn, 2000.

Saul, Klaus. "Jugend im Schatten des Krieges: Dokumentation," *Militärgeschichtliche Mitteilung* 34 (1983): 91–184.

Scheibe, Wolfgang. *Die reformpädagogische Bewegung (1900–1932): Eine einführende Darstellung*. 8th ed. Weinheim, 1982.

Schissler, Hanna, ed. *The Miracle Years: A Cultural History of West Germany, 1949–1968*. Princeton, 2001.

Schreiber, Adele, ed. *Das Buch vom Kinde,* 2 vols. Leipzig, 1907.

Schumann, Dirk. "Legislation and Liberalisation: The Debate about Corporal Punishment in Schools in Postwar West Germany, 1945–1975." *German History* 25 (2007): 192–218.

Schwarz, Hans-Peter. "Der Geist der fünfziger Jahre," in *Die Ära Adenauer: Gründerjahre der Republik, 1949–1957,* ed. Hans-Peter Schwarz, 375–464. Stuttgart, 1981.

Sealander, Judith. *The Failed Century of the Child: Governing America's Young in the Twentieth Century*. Cambridge, 2003.

Shapiro, Michael Steven. *Child's Garden: The Kindergarten Movement from Froebel to Dewey*. University Park, PA, 1983.

Skocpol, Theda. *Protecting Soldiers and Mothers: The Political Origins of Social Policy in the United States*. Cambridge, 1992.

Spree, Reinhard. "Shaping the Child's Personality: Medical Advice on Child-Rearing from the Late Eighteenth to the Early Twentieth Century in Germany." *Social History of Medicine* 5 (1992): 331–332.

Stargardt, Nicholas. *Witnesses of War: Children's Lives Under the Nazis*. London, 2005.

Stearns, Peter N. *Anxious Parents: A History of Modern Childrearing in America*. New York, 2003.

Stern, William. *Jugendliches Seelenleben und Krieg*. Leipzig, 1915.

Stoler, Ann Laura. *Race and the Education of Desire*. Durham, NC, 1995.

Terry, Jennifer. "'Momism' and the Making of Treasonous Homosexuals," in *"Bad" Mother: The Politics of Blame in Twentieth-Century America,* ed. Molly Ladd-Taylor and Lauri Umansky, 169–190. New York, 1998.

Tyack, David B. *The One Best System: A History of American Urban Education*. Cambridge, MA, 1974.

Walkowitz, Daniel J. *Working with Class: Social Workers and the Politics of Middle Class Identity*. Chapel Hill, 1999.

Weber-Kellermann, Ingeborg. *Die Deutsche Familie*. Frankfurt a. M., 1974.

Weiss, Jessica. *To Have and to Hold: Marriage, the Baby Boom and Social Change*. Chicago, 2000.

Woodhouse, Barbara Bennett. *The Status of Children: A Story of Emerging Rights, Cross-Currents: Family Law in England and the United States*. New York, 2000.

Zahra, Tara. *Kidnapped Souls: National Indifference and the Battle for Children in the Bohemian Lands, 1900–48*. Ithaca, 2008.

———. "Lost Children: Displacement, Family, and Nation in Postwar Europe." *Journal of Modern History* 81, no. 1 (2009): 45–86.

Zelizer, Viviana. *Pricing the Priceless Child: The Changing Social Value of Children*. Princeton, 1994.

Zieger, Robert H. *America's Great War: World War I and the American Experience*. Lanham, 2000.

CONTRIBUTORS

Ellen L. Berg is Affiliate Assistant Professor at the University of Maryland. She received her PhD in US history from the University of California at Berkeley for her dissertation, "Citizens in the Republic of Childhood: Immigrants and the American Kindergarten, 1880–1920," which she has revised for publication. She has held postdoctoral fellowships at the Rothermere American Institute, University of Oxford; the Library of Congress; and the Smithsonian Institution's National Museum of American History.

Katharine S. Bullard is Assistant Professor in the School of History, Political and International Studies at Fairleigh Dickinson University, where she teaches US and world history. She is currently working on a book manuscript tentatively entitled *Civilizing the Child: Race, Colonialism and National Belonging.*

Lynne Curry is Professor of History at Eastern Illinois University. Her publications include *The DeShaney Case: Child Abuse, Family Privacy, and the Dilemma of State Intervention* (University Press of Kansas, 2007); *The Human Body on Trial: A Handbook with Cases, Laws, and Documents* (ABC-CLIO, 2002); and *Modern Mothers in the Heartland: Gender, Health, and Progress in Illinois, 1900–1930* (The Ohio State University Press, 1999). She is also the co-editor, with Christopher R. Waldrep, of a four-volume set of edited and annotated primary documents in US constitutional history, *The Constitution and the Nation* (Peter Lang, 2003).

Andrew Donson is Assistant Professor of History at the University of Massachusetts at Amherst. He is author of *Youth in the Fatherless Land: War Pedagogy, Nationalism, and Authority in Germany, 1914–1918* (Harvard University Press, 2010), which won the Fraenkel Prize in Contemporary History. He is currently writing a cultural history of the 1918/19 German revolution and preparing projects on communist spies in the 1920s and 1930s and autobiographies of early Nazi Party members.

Charles A. Israel is Associate Professor and Chair of the Department of History at Auburn University, where he teaches courses in American cultural and intellectual history, including the history and religion of the American South. He is the author of *Before Scopes: Evangelicalism, Education, and Evolution in Tennessee, 1870–1925* (University of Georgia Press, 2004) and was a contributor to the sesquicentennial history of Sewanee: the University of the South. Dr. Israel's research has been supported by the Spencer Foundation, the Southern Baptist Historical Library and Archives, and the Center for the Study of Religion and American Culture, where he was a fellow in the Young Scholars in American Religion program. He is currently researching religion, race, gender, and social reform in the early twentieth-century South.

Carolyn Kay received her PhD from Yale in 1994 and is a professor at Trent University (Canada), where she teaches modern German history. Her publications include the book *Art and the German Bourgeoisie: Alfred Lichtwark and Modern Painting in Hamburg, 1886–1914* (University of Toronto Press, 2002). She is currently completing a research project on child-rearing ideals in Imperial Germany.

Sonya Michel, Director of United States Studies at the Woodrow Wilson International Center for Scholars, is an expert on US social policy in contemporary, historical, and comparative perspective. Her publications include *Civil Society and Gender Justice: Historical and Comparative Perspectives,* co-edited with Karen Hagemann and Gunilla Budde (Berghahn Books, 2009); *Child Care at the Crossroads: Gender and Welfare State Restructuring,* co-edited with Rianne Mahon (Routledge, 2002); and *Children's Interests/Mothers' Rights: The Shaping of America's Child Care Policy* (Yale University Press, 1999). She was also a founding co-editor of the journal *Social Politics: International Studies in Gender, State and Society,* published by Oxford University Press. Michel is currently completing a study entitled "Old-Age Insecurity: Inequality and Inequity in America's Retirement Provision," to be published by Princeton University Press.

Rebecca Jo Plant is currently an associate professor at the University of California, San Diego. Her work focuses on gender relations and the rise of the psychological professions in the twentieth-century US. She recently published her first book, *Mom: The Transformation of Motherhood in Modern America,* with the University of Chicago Press. The book is a revised version of her dissertation, which won the Organization of American Historians' Lerner-Scott Prize for the best doctoral dissertation in US women's history in 2003.

Till van Rahden holds the Canada Research Chair in German and European Studies, and is Associate Professor of German Studies at the Université de Montréal. Recent publications include two monographs, *Jews and Other Germans: Civil Society, Religious Diversity and Urban Politics in Breslau, 1860–1925* (Madison: The University of Wisconsin Press, 2008) and *La civilité et ses ambivalences : Les Juifs dans la société civile en Europe centrale 1800–1933* (Québec: Les Presses de l'Université Laval, 2010), and he co-edited *Demokratie im Schatten der Gewalt: Geschichten des Privaten im deutschen Nachkrieg 1945–2005* (Göttingen: Wallstein-Verlag, 2009). While he continues to work in the field of Jewish history, his research interests are currently focused on a book entitled *Bringing*

Democracy to Daddy: Changing Conceptions of Paternal Authority in West Germany, 1945–1979.

Dirk Schumann is Professor of History at Georg-August University, Göttingen. His most recent books are *Political Violence in the Weimar Republic, 1918–1933: Fight for the Streets and Fear of Civil War* (New York, 2009) and *Between Mass Death and Individual Loss: The Place of the Dead in Twentieth-Century Germany* (New York, 2008, co-edited with Alon Confino and Paul Betts). He is currently conducting research for a book on education and discipline in Germany and the US since 1945.

Eszter Varsa is a Ph.D. Candidate in Comparative Gender Studies at Central European University, Budapest, Hungary. Her dissertation, "Gender, 'Race'/Ethnicity, Class and the Institution of Child Protection in Hungary, 1949–1956," examines national policy-making and institutional practice on child protection and the lived experience of children, with specific focus on Romani children, in state care. Her main areas of research are state socialism and welfare history, in particular child welfare history, and the history of social work from an intersectional perspective. Most recent publication: "Child Protection, Residential Care and the 'Gypsy-Question' in Early State Socialist Hungary," in *Social Care under State Socialism (1945–1989)*, ed. Sabine Hering, 149–159. Opladen and Farmington Hills, 2009.

Tara Zahra is Assistant Professor of History at the University of Chicago. She is the author of *Kidnapped Souls: National Indifference and the Battle for Children in the Bohemian Lands, 1900–1948* (Cornell University Press, 2008). She is currently writing a history of displacement, international humanitarianism, and the family in twentieth-century Europe, which will be published by Harvard University Press.

INDEX

Lightning Source UK Ltd.
Milton Keynes UK
UKOW03f0741041213

222329UK00002B/49/P